❦ ❦ ❦

482 Tried-and-True Recipes In a Handy Single Source

OKAY, we *were* a bit skeptical back in 1999 when we produced a *Taste of Home Annual Recipes* volume featuring every single recipe from 1995. Would folks really want a book with timeless recipes first published some 4 years earlier? The answer from our loyal readers was a resounding "Yes!"

And that's not all—these everyday cooks wanted *even more* tried-and-true dishes. We were happy to oblige and created this all-new edition featuring every single recipe from 1994!

Here's why this *1995 Taste of Home Annual Recipes* book will hold a special place of honor on your bookshelf:

1. Its 300 pages are organized into 16 convenient chapters for easy reference. Between its covers, you have at hand every single *Taste of Home* recipe we published in 1994.

2. Finding all of the 482 recipes is a snap with this book's *two different indexes*. One lists every dish by food category, major ingredient and/or cooking method. The other provides an alphabetical listing of each and every recipe.

3. The full-color pictures in this classic collection are *bigger* than ever, so you can plainly see what many of these dishes look like before you begin preparing them.

4. We've used large print for easy reading while cooking. And each recipe is presented "all-on-a-page"—you never have to turn pages back and forth while cooking.

5. This volume is printed on the highest quality coated paper that lets you wipe away spatters easily.

6. The book lies open and *stays open* as you cook. Its durable hard cover will give you *years* of use.

But the real proof of this volume's value is in the tasting. Here's a small sample of what you'll find inside:

The Skinny on Beef. You can lean on Cheesy Spinach-Stuffed Meat Loaf, Pot Roast with Vegetables and Updated Beef Stroganoff (recipes on pages 74 and 75) even when watching your waistline.

Popcorn's a Perennial Favorite. Add spark to your days with Caramel Corn, Parmesan-Garlic Popcorn, Candied Popcorn and more (see pages 14 and 15).

The Beauty of Bread Machines. You'll have more time for loafing with convenient Onion Dill Bread, Oatmeal Bread and Buttermilk Wheat Bread (page 104).

Choice Chocolate. Turn to page 114 for chocolate confections such as Sandy's Chocolate Cake, Soda Cracker Chocolate Candy, Double Chocolate Chip Cookies and Packable Chocolate Chip Cake.

Mouth-Watering Menus. Beginning on page 188, you'll find 30 complete menus for every day and for special occasions.

With 482 down-home dishes to choose from in this taste treasury, you and your family can enjoy delicious dining for years to come!

❦ ❦ ❦

☕ ☕ ☕

1995 Taste of Home Annual Recipes

Editors: Heidi Reuter Lloyd, Julie Schnittka
Art Director: Claudia Wardius
Food Editor: Janaan Cunningham
Associate Editor: Kristine Krueger
Food Photography Artist:
Stephanie Marchese

Taste of Home®

Executive Editor: Kathy Pohl
Food Editor: Janaan Cunningham
Associate Food Editors: Coleen Martin,
Diane Werner
Senior Recipe Editor: Sue A. Jurack
Test Kitchen Director: Karen Johnson
Senior Editor: Bob Ottum
Managing Editor: Ann Kaiser
Assistant Managing Editor: Faithann Stoner
Associate Editors: Kristine Krueger, Sharon Selz
Test Kitchen Home Economists: Sue Draheim,
Julie Herzfeldt, Pat Schmeling,
Wendy Stenman, Karen Wright
Test Kitchen Assistants: Sue Hampton,
Kris Lehman
Editorial Assistants: Barb Czysz,
Mary Ann Koebernik
Design Director: Jim Sibilski
Art Director: Vicky Marie Moseley
Food Photography: Dan Roberts
Food Photography Artist: Stephanie Marchese
Photo Studio Manager: Anne Schimmel
Production: Ellen Lloyd, Claudia Wardius
Publisher: Roy Reiman

Taste of Home Books
©2000 Reiman Publications, LLC
5400 S. 60th St., Greendale WI 53129

International Standard Book Number:
0-89821-296-0
International Standard Serial Number:
1094-3463

PICTURED AT RIGHT. Clockwise from upper left:
Fudge Brownies (p. 116), Spinach Chicken Salad
(p. 226), Hawaiian Dessert (p. 223), Norwegian
Parsley Potatoes (p. 222), Mexican Turkey Roll-
Ups (p. 82), Fruit 'n' Nut Cherry Pie (p. 239), As-
paragus with Sesame Butter (p. 222) and Baked
Ham with Cumberland Sauce (p. 222).

☕ ☕ ☕

Taste of Home 1995 Annual Recipes

PICTURED ON FRONT COVER. Clockwise from top: Wilted Lettuce (p. 200), Peach Shortcake (p. 140), Teriyaki Shish Kabobs (p. 64) and Kathy's Herbed Corn (p. 59).

PICTURED ON BACK COVER. Top to bottom: Layered Lemon Dessert (p. 143), Creamy Chocolate Cupcakes (p. 128) and Cherry Pie (p. 137).

FOR ADDITIONAL COPIES of this book, write *Taste of Home* Books, P.O. Box 908, Greendale WI 53129.
To order by credit card, call toll-free 1-800/344-2560 or visit our Web site at www.reimanpub.com.

Snacks & Beverages

Curb hunger in a hurry with these snacks, appetizers and beverages.

— 🍴 🍴 🍴 —

M-M-M-MUNCHIES! Clockwise from upper left: Quick Guacamole and Stromboli (p. 10); Snack Crackers and Tomato Cheese Melt (p. 13); Fruit on a Stick (p. 18); Italian Stuffed Mushrooms (p. 19).

RELY ON the snack appeal of Mini Hamburgers, Tater-Dipped Veggies and Homemade Orange Refresher (shown above, clockwise from upper right) when midday munchies strike.

Mini Hamburgers

(Pictured above)

I guarantee these will be the first snack cleared from your table! —Judy Lewis, Sterling Heights, Michigan

- 1/2 cup chopped onion
- 1 tablespoon butter *or* margarine
- 1 pound lean ground beef *or* ground round
- 1 egg, beaten
- 1/4 teaspoon seasoned salt
- 1/4 teaspoon ground sage
- 1/4 teaspoon salt
- 1/8 teaspoon pepper
- 40 mini rolls, split
- 8 ounces process American cheese slices, cut into 1-1/2-inch squares, optional
- 40 dill pickle slices, optional

In a skillet, saute onion in butter. Transfer to a bowl; add meat, egg and seasonings. Spread over bottom halves of the rolls; replace tops. Place on baking sheets; cover with foil. Bake at 350° for 20 minutes. If desired, place a cheese square and pickle on each hamburger; replace tops and foil and return to the oven for 5 minutes. **Yield:** 40 appetizers.

— 🍷 🍷 🍷 —

Homemade Orange Refresher

(Pictured at left)

Family and friends will thank you for serving this cool, tangy orange drink on warm evenings. —Iola Egle
McCook, Nebraska

      1 can (6 ounces) frozen orange juice
        concentrate, thawed
    1/3 cup sugar
    1/3 cup nonfat dry milk powder
      2 teaspoons vanilla extract
    3/4 cup cold water
     10 to 12 ice cubes
Orange slices and mint, optional
Sugar and orange juice, optional

Combine the first five ingredients in a blender container and process at high speed. Add ice cubes, a few at a time, blending until slushy. Garnish with orange slices and mint if desired. Serve immediately. **Yield:** 4 servings. **Editor's Note:** For a fancy glass edge, invert glass and dip into orange juice and then sugar; let dry 1 hour before filling glass.

— 🍷 🍷 🍷 —

Tater-Dipped Veggies

(Pictured at left)

With this great recipe, you get the crispiness of deep-fried vegetables without the mess and fuss.
—Earleen Lillegard, Prescott, Arizona

      1 cup instant potato flakes
    1/3 cup grated Parmesan cheese
    1/2 teaspoon celery salt
    1/4 teaspoon garlic powder
    1/4 cup butter *or* margarine, melted and
        cooled
      2 eggs
      4 to 5 cups raw bite-size vegetables
        (mushrooms, peppers, broccoli,
        cauliflower, zucchini *and/or* parboiled
        carrots)
Prepared ranch salad dressing *or* dip, optional

In a small bowl, combine potato flakes, Parmesan cheese, celery salt, garlic powder and butter. In another bowl, beat eggs. Dip vegetables, one at a time, into egg, then into potato mixture; coat

well. Place on an ungreased baking sheet. Bake at 400° for 20-25 minutes. Serve with dressing or dip if desired. **Yield:** 6-8 servings.

— 🍷 🍷 🍷 —

Puffed Wheat Balls

(Pictured below)

Whenever my Grandma Hunt comes over, she makes her famous Puffed Wheat Balls by the dozen. Her 82 grandchildren and 168 great-grandchildren love them.
—Lucile Proctor, Panguitch, Utah

     12 cups puffed wheat cereal
      2 cups packed brown sugar
      1 cup corn syrup
      2 tablespoons butter *or* margarine
      1 cup evaporated milk
    1/3 cup sugar

Place cereal in a large bowl; set aside. In a heavy saucepan, bring brown sugar and corn syrup to a boil. Add butter. Combine evaporated milk and sugar; add to boiling mixture and continue cooking until a soft ball forms when liquid is dropped into cold water (240° on a candy thermometer). Pour over cereal and stir to coat. Shape into 2-in. balls. **Yield:** 2-1/2-3 dozen.

No-Fuss Snack Spread

Make an easy no-cook cracker spread by grinding leftover roast with a dash of Worcestershire sauce, a bit of mayonnaise and salt and pepper.

Edible "Play Dough"

Believe it or not, I encourage our kids to play with their food! When they were younger, they'd roll out this dough and use cookies cutters to cut out shapes. Then they ate their works of art as a nutritious snack.
—*Kathy Scott, Hemingford, Nebraska*

1 cup powdered dry milk
1 cup creamy peanut butter
1 cup honey

In a bowl, combine all ingredients. Chill. Shape into faces, letters, shapes, etc. or cut out with cookie cutters. If mixture is too sticky, roll in additional powdered milk. Decorate with raisins or candy if desired. **Yield:** 2-1/2 cups.

— ☕ ☕ ☕ —

Horseradish Cheese Spread

I got this recipe from a friend, Pam Bloom, many years ago. Although it makes a big batch, this zippy cheese spread will quickly disappear. —*Connie Simon, Reed City, Michigan*

2 pounds process American cheese, cubed
1/2 cup prepared horseradish
1/3 cup mayonnaise
1 teaspoon hot pepper sauce
1/4 teaspoon garlic salt
1/4 teaspoon Worcestershire sauce
Crackers *or* raw vegetables

Melt cheese in the top of a double boiler over simmering water until smooth. Add remaining ingredients and stir until smooth. Spoon into containers and refrigerate. Serve with crackers or raw vegetables. **Yield:** 4 cups.

— ☕ ☕ ☕ —

Seafood Dip

I got this recipe from my sister-in-law, who's an excellent cook. She makes this dip every Christmas Eve for our annual "appetizer meal". This hot dip is welcome at our winter gatherings. —*Marilyn Dick, Centralia, Missouri*

1 cup (6 ounces) flaked imitation crabmeat
1/2 cup shredded cheddar cheese

1/4 cup cream cheese, softened
1/4 cup mayonnaise
1/4 cup sour cream
1/4 cup grated Parmesan cheese
1/4 cup sliced green onions
1 teaspoon lemon juice
1/4 teaspoon Worcestershire sauce
1/8 teaspoon garlic powder
1/4 cup bread crumbs
Crackers *or* raw vegetables

In a bowl, mix the first 10 ingredients until smooth. Spread in a 9-in. pie plate. Sprinkle with the bread crumbs. Cover and bake at 350° for 20 minutes or until bubbly. Uncover and bake 5 minutes more. Serve with assorted crackers or raw vegetables. **Yield:** 6-8 servings.

— ☕ ☕ ☕ —

Quick Guacamole

(Pictured at right and on page 6)

This delicious dip is extremely easy to make and always hits the spot when we have a craving for something to munch on. For a quick recipe, it really has authentic guacamole taste. —*Linda Fox, Soldotna, Alaska*

1 ripe avocado
1/2 cup small curd cottage cheese
1/3 cup hot picante sauce *or* salsa
1/2 teaspoon minced seeded jalapeno pepper,* optional
Tortilla chips *or* raw vegetables

In a bowl, mash the avocado. Stir in cottage cheese and picante sauce. Add jalapeno if desired. Serve with chips or vegetables. **Yield:** about 1-1/2 cups. ***Editor's Note:** When cutting or seeding hot peppers, use rubber or plastic gloves to protect your hands. Avoid touching your face.

— ☕ ☕ ☕ —

Stromboli

(Pictured at right and on page 6)

I've made this many times for parties, and it gets great reviews. It's nice because you can add ingredients and spices to suit your taste. This recipe is so good! —*Leigh Lauer, Hummelstown, Pennsylvania*

2 loaves (1 pound *each*) frozen bread dough, thawed
1/4 pound sliced ham
1/4 pound sliced pepperoni
1/4 cup chopped onion
1/4 cup chopped green pepper

DELICIOUS DUO of savory snacks, Quick Guacamole and Stromboli (shown above, top to bottom) are super for serving your family or guests.

    1 jar (14 ounces) pizza sauce, *divided*
1/4 pound sliced mozzarella cheese
1/4 pound sliced bologna
1/4 pound sliced hard salami
1/4 pound sliced Swiss cheese
    1 teaspoon dried basil
    1 teaspoon dried oregano
1/4 teaspoon garlic powder
1/4 teaspoon pepper
    2 tablespoons butter *or* margarine, melted

Let the dough rise in a warm place until doubled. Punch down. Roll loaves together into one 15-in. x 12-in. rectangle. Layer ham and pepperoni on half of the dough (lengthwise). Sprinkle with the onion and green pepper. Top with 1/4 cup of pizza sauce. Layer the mozzarella, bologna, salami and Swiss cheese over sauce. Sprinkle with basil, oregano, garlic powder and pepper. Spread another 1/4 cup of pizza sauce on top. Fold plain half of dough over filling and seal edges well. Place on a greased 15-in. x 10-in. x 1-in. baking pan. Bake at 375° for 30-35 minutes or until golden brown. Brush with melted butter. Heat the remaining pizza sauce and serve with sliced stromboli. **Yield:** 8-10 servings.

Chewy Snack Squares

These chewy bars are a nice change of pace from the usual marshmallow cereal bars. Adding peanuts and coconut makes a tasty, interesting snack.
—*Cheryl Miller, Fort Collins, Colorado*

  5 cups cornflakes
  4 cups crisp rice cereal
  1 cup salted peanuts
  1 cup flaked coconut
  1 cup light corn syrup
  1 cup sugar
  1/2 cup butter *or* margarine
  1/2 cup half-and-half cream

In a large bowl, combine cereals, peanuts and coconut; set aside. In a saucepan, combine corn syrup, sugar, butter and cream; cook and stir over medium heat until the mixture reaches soft-ball stage (240°), about 25-30 minutes. Pour over cereal mixture and toss to coat evenly. Pat into a greased 15-in. x 10-in. x 1-in. baking pan. Cool before cutting. **Yield:** 2-1/2 to 3 dozen.

———— ☕ ☕ ☕ ————

Cheesy Onion Roll-Ups

These roll-ups are very fast to fix. You can make them ahead and keep them wrapped in the refrigerator until you're ready to serve.
—*Barbara Keith Faucett, Missouri*

  1 cup (8 ounces) sour cream
  1 package (8 ounces) cream cheese,
    softened
  1/2 cup finely shredded cheddar cheese
  3/4 cup sliced green onions
  1 tablespoon lime juice
  1 tablespoon minced seeded jalapeno
    pepper*
  1 package (10 ounces) flour tortillas (6
    inches)
Picante sauce

Combine the first six ingredients in a bowl; mix well. Spread on one side of tortillas and roll up tightly. Wrap and refrigerate for at least 1 hour. Slice into 1-in. pieces. Serve with picante sauce. **Yield:** about 5 dozen. ***Editor's Note:** When cutting or seeding hot peppers, use rubber or plastic gloves to protect your hands. Avoid touching your face.

Iced Tea Trick

To clear up a cloudy pitcher of iced tea, try stirring in a little hot water. Then you can add a few more ice cubes to chill it.

Crab and Spinach Quiche

When I hosted a Christmas cookie exchange several years ago, I served this quiche as an appetizer. You can also cut it into wedges to serve as a main dish for breakfast or brunch.
—*Arliene Hillinger Rancho Palos Verdes, California*

  5 eggs
1-1/2 cups milk
  1/4 teaspoon salt
  1/8 teaspoon pepper
  1/8 teaspoon ground nutmeg
  1 cup (4 ounces) shredded Swiss cheese
1-1/2 cups grated Parmesan cheese
  3 tablespoons all-purpose flour
  6 to 8 ounces canned *or* frozen crabmeat,
    thawed, drained and flaked
  1 package (10 ounces) frozen chopped
    spinach, thawed and well drained
Pastry for double-crust pie (9 inches)

In a large bowl, lightly beat eggs. Add milk, salt, pepper and nutmeg; set aside. Combine cheeses and flour; add to egg mixture with the crab and spinach. Mix well. Pour into two pastry-lined 9-in. pie plates or quiche pans. Bake at 350° for 50 minutes or until a knife inserted near center comes out clean. Cut into narrow pieces. Serve warm. **Yield:** 32-36 servings.

———— ☕ ☕ ☕ ————

Sweet Graham Snacks

This sweet snack mix is a nice change of pace from the more salty varieties. I've shared the recipe many times. —*Artimece Schmidt, Farmington, New Mexico*

  10 to 12 graham crackers, broken into
    quarters
  1 cup butter *or* margarine
  1/2 cup sugar
  1/3 cup ground nuts

Line a 15-in. x 10-in. x 1-in. baking pan with graham crackers. In a saucepan, bring butter and sugar to a boil; boil for 2 minutes. Remove from the heat; stir in nuts. Spoon over the graham crackers. Bake at 325° for 10 minutes. Immediately remove from pan onto foil. Cool. Break apart. **Yield:** 3-4 dozen.

———— ☕ ☕ ☕ ————

Pimiento Cheese Spread

I like to keep this simply delicious spread in the refrigerator so my family can spread some on crackers or bread anytime they need a little snack.
—*Tammy Moore-Worthington, Artesia, New Mexico*

2 cups (8 ounces) shredded cheddar cheese
3 tablespoons mayonnaise *or* salad dressing
1 can (4 ounces) chopped green chilies
1 jar (2 ounces) diced pimientos, undrained
1/8 teaspoon garlic powder
1/8 teaspoon cayenne pepper
Crackers *or* bread

Combine the first six ingredients. Cover and chill. Spread on crackers or bread. **Yield:** 2 cups.

Quick Turkey Nachos

My husband is one of the biggest snackers around. I keep the ingredients on hand so I can whip up a batch of these nachos "pronto". —Kathy Faulk
East Hartford, Connecticut

1 pound ground turkey
1 envelope taco seasoning mix
3/4 cup water
Tortilla chips
1/2 cup sour cream
1/2 cup salsa
1/2 cup shredded Monterey Jack cheese
1/2 cup shredded cheddar cheese
Shredded lettuce, chopped tomatoes *and/or* green onions, optional

In a skillet, brown the turkey; drain. Add taco seasoning and water; simmer for 15 minutes. Place the tortilla chips on a greased baking sheet. Layer with turkey, sour cream and salsa. Sprinkle with the cheeses. Microwave or broil for a few minutes or until cheese melts. Top with lettuce, tomatoes and/or onions if desired. **Yield:** 6-8 servings. **Editor's Note:** Ground beef can be substituted for the turkey.

Tomato Cheese Melt

(Pictured at right and on page 7)

I love this as a late-night snack, but it also goes great with a bowl of soup at lunch. Cayenne pepper gives a bit of zip. —Suzanne Winters, Middletown, Delaware

1 onion bagel *or* English muffin, split
1/4 cup shredded cheddar cheese
1/8 teaspoon cayenne pepper
2 tomato slices
1 tablespoon shredded Parmesan cheese

On each bagel or muffin half, sprinkle half of the cheddar cheese and cayenne pepper. Top with a tomato slice. Sprinkle half of the Parmesan cheese over each tomato. Broil 6 in. from the heat for 4-5 minutes or until cheese is bubbly. **Yield:** 2 servings.

Snack Crackers

(Pictured below and on page 7)

Our 13-year-old daughter, Dana, loves to make this crunchy and flavorful snack for us. Her four older brothers finish off a batch in no time. —Sue Manel
Milladore, Wisconsin

3/4 cup vegetable oil
1-1/2 teaspoons dill weed
1 envelope dry ranch salad dressing mix
2 packages (10 ounces *each*) oyster crackers

Combine oil, dill and salad dressing mix. Place the crackers in a large bowl; pour dressing mixture over and toss gently. Allow to stand at least 1 hour before serving. **Yield:** 12 cups.

"LOVE THOSE SNACKS!" is what your family will say when you offer Snack Crackers and Tomato Cheese Melt (shown above, top to bottom).

Cooks Get Popping with A Perennial Favorite!

NO MATTER what time of year, a big bowl brimming with light and airy popcorn is perfect for munching while watching television, reading a book, playing a board game or just chatting with family members and friends.

But don't rely on microwave popcorn or even plain homemade popped kernels. These sweet, spicy, savory and cheesy versions provide a nice change of pace and will really get your evenings popping!

Caramel Corn
(Pictured below)

For years I've taken this snack to our church retreat. I take it in two containers—one for each night—so it doesn't all disappear the first night. Other church members tell us that if we can't attend, we should just send the caramel corn! —Nancy Breen
Canastota, New York

TASTY TRIO of Candied Popcorn, Parmesan-Garlic Popcorn and Caramel Corn (shown above, clockwise from upper right) is worth a late-night try.

12 quarts plain popped popcorn
1 pound peanuts
2 cups butter *or* margarine
2 pounds brown sugar
1/2 cup dark corn syrup
1/2 cup molasses

Place popcorn in two large bowls. Mix 1/2 pound nuts into each bowl. In a 5-qt. saucepan, combine remaining ingredients. Bring to a boil over medium heat; boil and stir for 5 minutes. Pour half of syrup over each bowl of popcorn and stir to coat. Turn coated popcorn into a large roasting pan. Bake at 250° for 1 hour. Remove from the oven and break apart while warm. Cool. Store in airtight containers. **Yield:** 12 quarts.

Parmesan-Garlic Popcorn

(Pictured at left)

This is my husband's favorite late-night snack. He gobbles the entire bowlful while watching television! It's amazing how a simple blend of seasonings can enliven plain kernels. —Sharon Skildum
Maple Grove, Minnesota

2-1/2 quarts popped popcorn, buttered
1/4 cup grated Parmesan cheese
1 teaspoon garlic powder
1 teaspoon dried parsley flakes
1/2 teaspoon dill weed

Place popcorn in a large bowl. In a small bowl, combine Parmesan cheese, garlic powder, parsley and dill; sprinkle over popcorn and toss lightly. Serve immediately. **Yield:** 2-1/2 quarts.

Candied Popcorn

(Pictured at left)

I got this family-favorite recipe in the 1950s. It makes a big chewy batch that you can't stop eating until it's gone. The unique candy coating keeps people guessing. —Victoria Walzer, Lakeport, California

6 quarts plain popped popcorn
3/4 cup light corn syrup
1/4 cup butter *or* margarine
2 tablespoons water
4 cups (1 pound) confectioners' sugar
1 cup miniature marshmallows

Place popcorn in a large roasting pan. In a 3-qt. saucepan, combine remaining ingredients; cook and stir over low heat just until mixture comes to a boil. Pour over popcorn and toss to coat. Cool. Store in an airtight container. **Yield:** 6 quarts.

Cheese Popcorn

This great snack reminds me of my high school days. My sisters and girlfriends and I would stay up late, listen to music, talk and munch this crunchy treat. —Denise Baumert, Jameson, Missouri

4 quarts plain popped popcorn
1/4 cup butter *or* margarine, melted
1/2 teaspoon garlic salt
1/2 teaspoon onion salt
2 cups (8 ounces) shredded cheddar cheese

Place popcorn in two 13-in. x 9-in. x 2-in. baking pans. Drizzle with melted butter. Combine garlic salt and onion salt; sprinkle over popcorn. Top with cheese. Bake at 300° for 5-10 minutes. Serve immediately. **Yield:** 4 quarts.

Sweet and Spicy Popcorn

This crisp snack has a fun, different flavor and appeals to all palates. I took some to my neighbor's house one evening when we were visiting and it didn't last long. —Flo Burtnett, Gage, Oklahoma

1 tablespoon sugar
1 teaspoon chili powder
1/2 teaspoon ground cinnamon
1/4 teaspoon salt
Dash cayenne pepper
6 cups plain popped popcorn

Place sugar, chili powder, cinnamon, salt and cayenne pepper in a large resealable plastic bag or other 2-qt. airtight container; mix well. Add popcorn. Spray popcorn with nonstick cooking spray. Close bag and shake. Repeat one or two times until popcorn is coated. **Yield:** 6 cups.

Kernel Clues

Popcorn that keeps its natural moisture yields larger popped kernels. So it's best to store unpopped popcorn in an airtight container in the refrigerator or freezer.

1/2 cup unpopped kernels yields about 4 cups of popped popcorn.

To help salt and other flavorings stick to air-popped popcorn, lightly spritz the popped kernels with nonstick cooking spray before seasoning.

family. They also make a nice breakfast treat with a thermos of hot coffee if you're on your way early in the morning. —*Nancy Reichert, Thomasville, Georgia*

1 pound mild pork sausage
4 cups buttermilk biscuit mix
2 cups (8 ounces) shredded cheddar cheese
1 cup water

In a skillet, cook and crumble sausage; drain. In a large bowl, combine biscuit mix and cheese. Add the sausage and stir until well blended. Stir in water just until mixed. Shape into 1-1/2-in. balls. Place on greased baking sheets. Bake at 375° for about 15 minutes or until golden. Baked bites may be frozen; reheat at 375° for 6-8 minutes. **Yield:** 4 dozen.

— 🍵 🍵 🍵 —

Cheddar Herb Snacks

These quick herbed rolls really hit the spot when you're looking for a hearty snack. You can also serve this as a side dish alongside soup or a meaty entree. Kids love the cheesy topping. —*Peggy Burdick, Burlington, Michigan*

6 to 8 hot dog buns
1 cup (4 ounces) shredded cheddar cheese
1/2 cup butter *or* margarine, softened
2 tablespoons minced fresh parsley
2 tablespoons minced chives
2 tablespoons chopped pimientos
1 tablespoon chopped green onion

Slice hot dog buns lengthwise. Mix remaining ingredients together; spread over the buns. Place on a baking sheet. Bake at 400° for 6-8 minutes or until cheese is melted. Cut each bun into 1-in. pieces. **Yield:** 12-16 servings.

— 🍵 🍵 🍵 —

Cajun Party Mix

(Pictured above)

This savory snack mix—featuring cereals, pretzels and nuts—packs a little punch, thanks to the cayenne pepper and hot pepper sauce. Once they get started eating this crisp treat, your family will find it hard to stop! —*Miriam Hershberger, Holmesville, Ohio*

2-1/2 cups Corn Chex cereal
2 cups Rice Chex cereal
2 cups Crispix cereal
1 cup mini pretzels
1 cup mixed nuts
1/2 cup butter *or* margarine, melted
1 tablespoon dried parsley flakes
1 teaspoon celery salt
1 teaspoon garlic powder
1/4 to 1/2 teaspoon cayenne pepper
1/4 teaspoon hot pepper sauce

Combine the cereals, pretzels and nuts. Pour into an ungreased 15-in. x 10-in. x 1-in. baking pan. Mix remaining ingredients; pour over the cereal mixture and stir to coat. Bake at 250° for 40-60 minutes, stirring every 15 minutes. Store in airtight containers. **Yield:** 8 cups.

— 🍵 🍵 🍵 —

Cappuccino Shake

(Pictured at right)

I created this quick and easy shake for my mom, who's been diabetic for more than 30 years. She was tickled pink with the great flavor! —*Paula Pelis, Rocky Point, New York*

✓ Uses less fat, sugar or salt. Includes Nutritional Analysis and Diabetic Exchanges.

1 cup skim milk
1-1/2 teaspoons instant coffee granules
Sugar substitute equivalent to 4 teaspoons sugar
2 drops brandy extract *or* rum extract
Dash ground cinnamon

Sausage Cheese Bites

These savory little bites are such a tasty snack to serve for a get-together or as an evening surprise for the

In a blender, combine milk, coffee granules, sugar substitute and extract. Blend until coffee is dissolved. Serve with a dash of cinnamon. For a hot drink, pour into a mug and heat in a microwave. **Yield:** 1 serving. **Nutritional Analysis:** One serving equals 90 calories, 130 mg sodium, 4 mg cholesterol, 13 gm carbohydrate, 9 gm protein, trace fat. **Diabetic Exchanges:** 1 milk.

— 🍽 🍽 🍽 —

Shrimp Spread

(Pictured below)

This colorful and tasty appetizer is always a crowd-pleaser whenever I take it to potlucks and picnics. People will never know you've used lighter ingredients.
—Norene Wright, Manilla, Indiana

✓ Uses less fat, sugar or salt. Includes Nutritional Analysis and Diabetic Exchanges.

- 1 package (8 ounces) **light cream cheese,** softened
- 1/2 cup **nonfat sour cream**
- 1/4 cup **fat-free mayonnaise**
- 1 cup **seafood cocktail sauce**
- 2 cups (8 ounces) **shredded reduced-fat mozzarella cheese**
- 2 cans (4-1/4 ounces *each*) **shrimp, rinsed and drained**
- 3 **green onions, sliced**
- 3/4 cup **finely chopped tomato**

In a small mixing bowl, beat the cream cheese, sour cream and mayonnaise until smooth. Spread on a 12-in. round serving platter. Cover with seafood sauce. Sprinkle with cheese, shrimp, onions and tomato. Cover and chill. Serve with crackers. **Yield:** 10 servings. **Nutritional Analysis:** One serving equals 165 calories, 606 mg sodium, 66 mg cholesterol, 11 gm carbohydrate, 15 gm protein, 6 gm fat. **Diabetic Exchanges:** 1 meat, 1 fat.

Simple Snack

For a yummy treat to share at Halloween or Thanksgiving gatherings, add an equal amount of salted peanuts to a bag of candy corn. Kids just can't quit eating it!

LOW-FAT SNACKS like Cappuccino Shake and Shrimp Spread (shown above) are good for you and great tasting, too!

Tuna Dill Spread

*We like to slather crackers with this tasty tuna spread.
It can be made in a jiffy.* —Geraldine Grisdale
Mt. Pleasant, Michigan

  1 can (6-1/8 ounces) tuna, drained and
  flaked
  1 package (3 ounces) cream cheese,
  softened
  1/3 cup finely chopped seeded cucumber
  2 tablespoons lemon juice
  1 to 2 tablespoons minced fresh dill
  1/2 teaspoon salt
  1/4 teaspoon pepper
Crackers *or* bread

In a bowl, combine the first seven ingredients;
mix well. Spread on crackers or use as a sandwich
filling. **Yield:** 1-1/4 cups.

——— 🍷 🍷 🍷 ———

Fruit on a Stick

(Pictured below and on page 7)

*In the summer, my family likes to snack on an assort-
ment of the season's freshest fruits. To make this nutritious snack a little more fun, I serve fruit "kabobs"
with a sweet and creamy dip.* —Faye Hintz
Springfield, Missouri

  1 package (8 ounces) cream cheese,
  softened
  1 jar (7 ounces) marshmallow creme
  3 to 4 tablespoons milk
Halved strawberries
Melon and kiwifruit, cut into bite-size pieces

Mix cream cheese, marshmallow creme and milk
until smooth. Thread fruit on wooden skewers.
Serve with dip. **Yield:** 1-1/2 cups dip.

——— 🍷 🍷 🍷 ———

Triple Cheese Spread

*Even folks not on restricted diets will love this cheesy
and creamy spread. The shredded carrots add nice col-
or and crunch, while the combination of cheeses
gives great flavor. Serve it with crackers or vegetable
dippers.* —Debbi Smith, Crossett, Arkansas

✓ Uses less fat, sugar or salt. Includes Nutritional Analysis
and Diabetic Exchanges.

  1 cup fat-free cottage cheese
  1/2 cup shredded reduced-fat Swiss cheese
  1/4 cup grated Parmesan cheese
  2 tablespoons skim milk
  1/8 teaspoon dill weed
  1/8 teaspoon pepper
  1/4 cup shredded carrots
  1/4 cup unsalted sunflower seeds, optional

In a blender or food processor, combine cheeses, milk, dill and pepper. Process until smooth. Stir in carrots. Cover and chill. Just before serving, stir in the sunflower seeds if desired. Serve with crackers. **Yield:** 1-3/4 cups. **Nutritional Analysis:** One 2-tablespoon serving (prepared without sunflower seeds) equals 30 calories, 116 mg sodium, 6 mg cholesterol, 1 gm carbohydrate, 5 gm protein, 2 gm fat. **Diabetic Exchanges:** 1/2 meat.

Broccoli Dip

With its zesty cheese and broccoli flavor, I always choose this nicely seasoned dip for parties.
—*Bertha Johnson, Indianapolis, Indiana*

- 1 small onion, chopped
- 3/4 cup finely chopped celery
- 1 tablespoon butter *or* margarine
- 1 package (10 ounces) frozen chopped broccoli, cooked and drained
- 1 carton (8 ounces) garlic process cheese spread
- 1 can (10-3/4 ounces) condensed cream of mushroom soup, undiluted

Dash *each* hot pepper sauce, cayenne pepper, paprika and Worcestershire sauce
Corn chips *or* raw vegetables

In a saucepan, saute onion and celery in butter until tender. Chop broccoli in small pieces. Add to onion mixture with cheese spread, soup and seasonings. Cook and stir over low heat until cheese is melted. Serve warm with corn chips or vegetables. **Yield:** 12-16 servings (4 cups).

Italian Stuffed Mushrooms

(Pictured above right and on page 6)

Every year during the holidays, I use this delicious recipe that I got from my brother. These appealing appetizers get hearty flavor from the ham, bacon and cheese. They look lovely and really curb the hunger of guests waiting for a meal. —*Virginia Slater*
West Sunbury, Pennsylvania

- 4 bacon strips, diced
- 24 to 30 large fresh mushrooms
- 1/4 pound ground fully cooked ham
- 2 tablespoons minced fresh parsley
- 1/4 cup grated Parmesan cheese
- 1 cup onion and garlic salad croutons, crushed
- 1 cup (4 ounces) shredded mozzarella cheese

- 1 medium tomato, finely chopped
- 1-1/2 teaspoons minced fresh oregano *or* 1/2 teaspoon dried oregano

In a skillet, cook the bacon until crisp. Meanwhile, remove mushroom stems from caps; set caps aside. Mince half the stems and discard the rest. Add minced stems to bacon and drippings, saute for 2-3 minutes. Remove from the heat and stir in remaining ingredients. Firmly stuff into mushroom caps. Place in a greased jelly roll pan. Bake at 425° for 12-15 minutes or until the mushrooms are tender. **Yield:** 2-1/2 to 3 dozen.

Elderberry Blossom Tea

Back in the 1960s, I bought an old cookbook at an auction. Inside were several old recipes handwritten on plain paper, including recipes for home remedies like this tea.
—*Genevieve Corley*
Amesbury, Massachusetts

- 1 to 2 tablespoons dried elderberry blossoms *or* 2 to 3 tablespoons fresh elderberry blossoms
- 1 cup boiling water

Sugar to taste
Thin lemon slice

In a tea cup or mug, steep elderberry blossoms in boiling water for 5-10 minutes; strain. Add sugar and lemon. **Yield:** 1 serving.

Garden-Fresh Salads

Chock-full of lettuce, fruits, vegetables and more, salads complete any meal.

—— 🛒 🛒 🛒 ——

COLORFUL COMBINATIONS. Clockwise from upper left: Grilled Chicken Salad (p. 28); Ambrosia Waldorf Salad (p. 23); Marinated Mushroom Salad (p. 29); Mustard Potato Salad, Classic Macaroni Salad and Old-Fashioned Egg Salad (p. 31); Salmon Pasta Salad (p. 26).

a large bowl, combine potatoes, carrots and parsley; pour the sauce over and stir gently to coat. Season to taste with additional salt. Spoon into a serving dish; garnish with crumbled bacon. Serve warm. **Yield:** 14-16 servings.

Tomatoes Supreme

After I retired, I persuaded my wife to let me do most of the food preparation. This refreshing salad is simple to put together, but the results are fantastic.
— Wendell Obermeier, Charles City, Iowa

- 8 thick tomato slices
- 1 teaspoon salt
- 1/2 teaspoon pepper
- 2 teaspoons sugar
- 8 thin sweet onion slices
- 1/2 cup vinegar
- 8 green pepper rings

Chopped fresh parsley

Place tomato slices on paper towel to drain excess moisture; place on serving plate. Combine salt, pepper and sugar; lightly sprinkle half over tomatoes. Top each tomato with an onion slice. Sprinkle 1 tablespoon of vinegar over each onion. Sprinkle remaining salt mixture over onions. Cover and refrigerate at least 30 minutes before serving. Garnish with green pepper rings and parsley. **Yield:** 8 servings.

Deluxe German Potato Salad

(Pictured above)

I make this salad for all occasions—it goes well with any kind of meat. I often take this salad to potlucks, and there's never any left over. The celery, carrots and ground mustard are a special touch not usually found in traditional German potato salad. —Betty Perkins Hot Springs, Arkansas

- 1/2 pound sliced bacon
- 1 cup thinly sliced celery
- 1 cup chopped onion
- 1 cup sugar
- 2 tablespoons all-purpose flour
- 1 cup vinegar
- 1/2 cup water
- 1 teaspoon salt
- 3/4 teaspoon ground mustard
- 5 pounds unpeeled red new potatoes, cooked and sliced
- 2 carrots, shredded
- 2 tablespoons chopped fresh parsley

Additional salt to taste

In a skillet, cook bacon until crisp. Drain, reserving 1/4 cup drippings. Crumble bacon and set aside. Saute the celery and onion in drippings until tender. Combine sugar and flour; add to skillet with vinegar, water, salt and mustard. Cook, stirring constantly, until mixture thickens and bubbles. In

Zesty Spinach Salad

The Leafy Greens Council promotes good-for-you spinach with savory salad recipes like this one, which includes crisp radishes and bacon along with a tangy, quick-to-mix dressing.

- 1/3 cup vegetable oil
- 3 tablespoons cider vinegar
- 1/2 teaspoon onion salt
- 1/2 teaspoon sugar
- 1/2 teaspoon ground mustard
- 1/8 teaspoon paprika

Dash cayenne pepper
- 1 bag (10 ounces) fresh spinach, torn
- 6 to 8 radishes, sliced
- 2 hard-cooked eggs, sliced
- 1 small onion, thinly sliced
- 2 bacon strips, cooked and crumbled

In a small bowl or jar with a tight-fitting lid, combine the first seven ingredients; mix well. Chill. Just before serving, lightly toss spinach, radishes, eggs, onion and bacon in a large salad bowl. Mix the dressing again; pour over salad and toss. **Yield:** 6 servings.

— ☕ ☕ ☕ —

Easy Layered Salad

Because I enjoy spending a fair amount of time in the kitchen, our kids have also learned to like cooking. All four kids make this salad together and take pride in serving it to the family. —*Marsha Ransom*
South Haven, Michigan

    1 head lettuce, torn into bite-size pieces
    1 cup diced green pepper
1/4 cup sliced green onions
    1 package (10 ounces) frozen peas, thawed
    2 cups salad dressing *or* mayonnaise
    2 to 4 cups (8 to 16 ounces) shredded
       cheddar cheese

In a 13-in. x 9-in. x 2-in. pan, layer lettuce, green pepper, onions and peas; do not toss. Spread salad dressing over all; sprinkle with cheese. Cover and refrigerate overnight. **Yield:** 8-10 servings.

Ambrosia Waldorf Salad

(Pictured below and on page 21)

A light, lovely pink salad, this recipe puts a different spin on traditional Waldorf salad. It is super served with roast turkey or baked ham. People always go back for seconds. My family didn't think they liked cranberries until they tried this sweet crunchy salad.
—*Janet Smith, Smithton, Missouri*

    2 cups fresh *or* frozen cranberry halves
1/2 cup sugar
    3 cups miniature marshmallows
    2 cups diced unpeeled apples
    1 cup seedless green grape halves
3/4 cup chopped pecans
    1 can (20 ounces) pineapple tidbits, drained
    1 cup whipping cream, whipped
Shredded *or* flaked coconut

Combine cranberries and sugar. In a large bowl, combine the marshmallows, apples, grapes, pecans and pineapple. Add cranberries and mix well. Fold in whipped cream. Cover and chill. Sprinkle with coconut before serving. **Yield:** 12-14 servings.

Turkey Mandarin Salad

(Pictured below)

A refreshing, interesting combination of turkey, pasta and fruit with a lightly sweet dressing makes this a family favorite. I found the recipe in an old church cookbook years ago. —Bernice Smith
Sturgeon Lake, Minnesota

    2 cups cubed cooked turkey
    1 tablespoon finely chopped onion
  1/2 teaspoon salt
    1 cup seedless red grape halves
    1 cup diced celery
    1 can (15 ounces) mandarin oranges, drained
    1 cup cooked macaroni
  3/4 cup mayonnaise
  3/4 cup whipping cream, whipped
  1/3 cup slivered almonds
Toasted almonds, optional

In a large bowl, combine turkey, onion and salt; mix well. Add grapes, celery, oranges and macaroni; toss lightly to mix. Cover and refrigerate. Just before serving, combine mayonnaise and whipped cream; fold into salad along with almonds. Top with toasted almonds if desired. **Yield:** 6-8 servings.

Tropical Salad Bar

A zippy lime vinaigrette perfectly blends the sunny flavors in this Leafy Greens Council recipe featuring fresh greens with pineapple, oranges and banana.

  1/3 cup vinegar
  1/4 cup lime juice
  3/4 cup sugar
    1 teaspoon salt
    1 teaspoon ground mustard
    1 teaspoon celery seed
    1 teaspoon paprika
    1 cup vegetable oil
  1/2 teaspoon grated onion
    4 cups torn leaf lettuce
    1 cup torn curly endive
    1 cup torn escarole
    1 fresh pineapple, trimmed and cut into pieces
    3 large oranges, peeled and sectioned
    1 large firm banana, sliced
Flaked coconut

In a small saucepan, bring vinegar and lime juice to a boil. In a medium bowl, combine the sugar, salt, mustard, celery seed and paprika. Add lime juice mixture and stir until sugar dissolves. Whisk in oil and onion until dressing is well mixed and slightly thickened; transfer to a jar or serving dish. Chill. Just before serving, place greens in a large bowl. Arrange fruit on a plate or in a shallow bowl and sprinkle with coconut. Pass greens, fruit and dressing separately or place on a buffet. **Yield:** 6-8 servings.

Coleslaw in a Bag

You only need to dirty a few dishes when creating this taste-tempting portable coleslaw. I've been relying on this recipe for years. —Alice Baker
Woodstock, Illinois

    2 large carrots, shredded
    1 small head cabbage, shredded
    1 medium green pepper, chopped
    1 small onion, chopped
DRESSING:
    1 cup (8 ounces) sour cream
  1/2 cup mayonnaise *or* salad dressing
    2 tablespoons vinegar
    2 tablespoons sugar
    2 teaspoons celery seed
  1/2 to 1 teaspoon lemon juice
  1/4 to 1/2 teaspoon grated lemon peel
  1/2 teaspoon salt
  1/4 teaspoon pepper

In a large plastic bag, toss the carrots, cabbage, green pepper and onion. In a bowl, combine all dressing ingredients. Pour into bag; toss. Chill until serving. **Yield:** 15-20 servings.

❦ ❦ ❦

Missouri Peach and Applesauce Salad

Fresh peaches combine with applesauce in this creamy-textured, refreshing side dish.
—_Bernice Morris, Marshfield, Missouri_

- 1 cup lemon-lime soda
- 1 package (3 ounces) peach gelatin
- 1 cup applesauce
- 1 cup whipping cream
- 1 tablespoon sugar
- 1/8 teaspoon ground nutmeg
- 1/8 teaspoon vanilla extract
- 1 cup chopped peeled ripe peaches

Red grapes and mint leaves, optional

In a saucepan, bring soda to a boil. Remove from the heat; stir in gelatin until dissolved. Add applesauce. Chill until mixture mounds slightly when dropped from a spoon. In a mixing bowl, whip cream with sugar, nutmeg and vanilla until stiff. Fold into gelatin mixture along with the peaches. Transfer to a 1-1/2-qt. glass bowl. Chill until firm. Garnish with grapes and mint if desired. **Yield:** 8-12 servings.

❦ ❦ ❦

Old-Fashioned Wilted Lettuce

I remember my grandmother making this wonderful "wilted" salad with leaf lettuce from her garden and serving it with a creamy dressing. —_Rose Shawyer, Otterbein, Indiana_

- 2 eggs
- 1/2 cup milk
- 1/4 cup cider vinegar
- 1/2 teaspoon salt
- 1/4 teaspoon pepper
- 8 bacon strips, cut into 1-inch pieces
- 1 head iceberg _or_ bunch leaf lettuce, torn
- 1 large onion, sliced into rings

In a small bowl, beat eggs, milk, vinegar, salt and pepper until smooth; set aside. In a skillet, cook bacon until crisp. Remove bacon to paper towels to drain, reserving drippings; reduce heat under skillet to medium. Whisk egg mixture into drippings; cook and stir until thickened, about 3-4 minutes. Place lettuce, onion and bacon in a large salad bowl. Pour dressing over and toss well. Serve immediately. **Yield:** 6-8 servings.

❦ ❦ ❦

'I Wish I Had That Recipe...'

OLD-FASHIONED and flavorful, a delightful salad prompted this request from Mrs. Harry Cook of Mt. Auburn, Illinois:

"When our club had a monthly meeting at The Raspberry Room in Elwin, Illinois, I ordered a sweet potato salad that was absolutely delicious! I sure wish I could have that recipe."

We passed on Mrs. Cook's comments to restaurant owner Jeanette Ball.

"Sweet Potato Apple Salad is our version of an old family recipe," relates Jeanette. "Very popular with our chicken dishes, it's colorful, sweet and fruity. I like to cook fresh sweet potatoes when preparing this salad, but you can use canned if you need to save time."

Vintage recipes suit patrons' palates and The Raspberry Room's setting in an antique mall. "Natural barn siding and old barn windows were used to remodel this former motel into a complex of shops and the restaurant," notes Jeanette. "This background is perfect for our antique tables and chairs, mix-and-match service plates."

Jeanette's partner, Virginia Biyeau, bakes 10 to 15 desserts a day for the tearoom in addition to the homemade biscuits and muffins.

The Raspberry Room, open 10 a.m. to 3 p.m. Tuesday through Saturday, is on Route 51 and its telephone number is 1-217/865-2916.

Sweet Potato Apple Salad

- 4 cups cubed cooked sweet potatoes
- 1 can (20 ounces) pineapple chunks, drained
- 1 package (10-1/2 ounces) miniature marshmallows
- 4 red delicious apples, chopped
- 1/2 cup flaked coconut
- 1/2 cup walnuts, chopped
- 1 carton (12 ounces) frozen whipped topping, thawed
- 3/4 cup mayonnaise _or_ salad dressing

In a large bowl, gently toss first six ingredients. Combine whipped topping and mayonnaise; fold into fruit mixture. Cover and chill at least 1 hour. **Yield:** 32 servings.

❦ ❦ ❦

Salmon Pasta Salad

(Pictured above and on page 20)

This recipe was one of my husband's favorite ways to enjoy salmon. I've had it so long I don't even remember where it came from originally. This salad is a nice light meal for a hot summer day, and it lets the salmon flavor come through. —Mary Dennis, Bryan, Ohio

    1 package (8 ounces) spiral pasta, cooked
       and drained
    2 cups fully cooked salmon chunks *or* 1 can
       (14-3/4 ounces) pink salmon, drained,
       bones and skin removed
1-1/2 cups quartered cherry tomatoes
    1 medium cucumber, quartered and
       sliced
    1 small red onion, sliced
  1/2 cup vegetable oil
  1/3 cup fresh lemon *or* lime juice
1-1/2 teaspoons dill weed
    1 garlic clove, minced
  3/4 teaspoon salt
  1/4 teaspoon pepper
Leaf lettuce

In a large bowl, toss the pasta, salmon, tomatoes, cucumber and onion. For dressing, combine the oil, lemon or lime juice, dill, garlic, salt and pepper; mix well. Pour over pasta. Cover and chill. Serve over lettuce. **Yield:** 6-8 servings.

Strawberry Onion Salad

The color and sweetness fresh berries add to this lovely salad make it perfect for company. When strawberries are out of season, use fresh orange sections. —Ruth Benning, Hamburg, New York

  1 bunch romaine, torn
  1 pint fresh strawberries, sliced
  1 small red onion, thinly sliced
  1 cup salad dressing *or* mayonnaise
1/3 cup sugar
1/4 cup milk
  2 tablespoons cider vinegar
  1 tablespoon poppy seeds

In a large salad bowl, toss the romaine, strawberries and onion. Combine all remaining ingredients in a small bowl or jar with tight-fitting lid; mix well. Pour over salad and toss lightly. Serve immediately. **Yield:** 6-8 servings.

Raisin Cheese Slaw

Crisp cabbage and raisins comprise this salad from the California Raisin Marketing Board.

1/3 cup salad dressing *or* mayonnaise
  2 teaspoons lemon juice
  1 teaspoon sugar

1/2 teaspoon salt
1/2 teaspoon prepared mustard
1/4 teaspoon onion powder *or* dried minced
    onion
  2 cups finely shredded cabbage
  1 cup finely shredded carrot
1/2 cup shredded cheddar cheese
1/2 cup raisins

In a small bowl, combine salad dressing, lemon juice, sugar, salt, mustard and onion powder. In a large bowl, combine cabbage, carrot, cheese and raisins. Fold in dressing. Cover and refrigerate for at least 1 hour. **Yield:** 8 servings.

— 🍷 🍷 🍷 —

Dilly Potato Salad

Each spring and fall, I make large amounts of this potato salad for festivals at our church. Everyone says it goes well with the meats the other men barbecue.
—*Howard Haug, Hewitt, Texas*

  6 large red potatoes, cooked, peeled and
    diced
  4 celery ribs, diced
  3 medium dill pickles, finely chopped
  1 jar (4 ounces) diced pimientos, drained
  3 hard-cooked eggs, diced
  1 green pepper, chopped
1/4 cup mayonnaise
  1 teaspoon prepared mustard
  1 teaspoon salt
Paprika
  6 green pepper strips (1/4 inch wide)

In a large bowl, combine the potatoes, celery, pickles, pimientos, eggs and chopped green pepper. In a small bowl, combine mayonnaise, mustard and salt; add to the potato mixture and mix well. Spoon into a serving bowl. Sprinkle with paprika. Arrange green pepper strips in the center in the shape of wheel spokes. Chill. **Yield:** 8 servings.

— 🍷 🍷 🍷 —

Southern Sweet Potato Salad

(Pictured at right)

I do some catering, so I'm always looking for good new recipes. I love to take this deliciously different potato salad to potlucks and cookouts. Even folks who are reluctant to try it at first come back for more!
—*Marlyn Woods, Lakeland, Florida*

  2 pounds sweet potatoes, peeled and cut
    into 1/2-inch cubes
  2 tablespoons lemon juice

  1 cup mayonnaise
  2 tablespoons orange juice
  1 tablespoon honey
  1 teaspoon grated orange peel
1/2 teaspoon ground ginger
1/4 teaspoon salt
1/8 teaspoon ground nutmeg
  1 cup sliced celery
1/3 cup chopped dates
1/2 cup chopped pecans
Lettuce leaves
  1 can (11 ounces) mandarin oranges,
    drained

In a medium saucepan, cook sweet potatoes in boiling salted water just until tender, about 5-8 minutes (do not overcook). Drain; toss with the lemon juice. In a large bowl, combine mayonnaise, orange juice, honey, orange peel, ginger, salt and nutmeg. Add the warm potatoes, celery and dates. Toss to coat well. Cover and chill. Before serving, gently stir in the pecans. Spoon salad onto a lettuce-lined platter. Arrange oranges around salad. **Yield:** 6-8 servings.

Super Salad Dressing

To save yourself time the day of your picnic or potluck, mix your potato salad dressing the night before and store in the refrigerator. The next day, prepare the rest of the salad as directed in the recipe and add the dressing.

Grilled Chicken Salad

(Pictured below and on page 20)

A few years back, I found this easy, light salad recipe and made it for a picnic for my boyfriend and myself. Now that guy is my husband, and we still enjoy going on picnics and dining on this satisfying salad.
—Juli Stewart, Coppell, Texas

     6 boneless skinless chicken breast halves
     2 tablespoons fresh lemon juice
     1 pound macaroni, ziti *or* corkscrew pasta, cooked and drained
     1 medium sweet red pepper, chopped
2-1/2 cups sliced celery
     1 medium red onion, chopped
  1/4 cup minced fresh dill *or* 5 teaspoons dill weed
     3 tablespoons white wine vinegar
     2 tablespoons mayonnaise
     2 tablespoons Dijon mustard
  1/2 teaspoon salt
  1/4 teaspoon pepper
  2/3 cup olive *or* vegetable oil
Leaf lettuce

Grill the chicken breasts over medium-hot heat for 15-18 minutes, turning once, or until tender and juices run clear. Remove from the grill and place in a single layer on a platter; sprinkle with lemon juice and set aside. In a large bowl, toss pasta, red pepper, celery, onion and dill. Remove chicken from platter; pour juices into a bowl. Slice chicken crosswise into thin strips; add to pasta mixture. To the juices, add vinegar, mayonnaise, mustard, salt and pepper; whisk well. Add oil very slowly in a stream until dressing is thickened. Pour over salad and toss. Serve in a lettuce-lined bowl or on individual lettuce-lined plates. **Yield:** 6 servings.

Cranberry Pecan Salad

We harvest close to 500,000 pounds of pecans on our land here in West Texas. So, of course, I use pecans in many recipes. This tasty, colorful salad is great for holiday gatherings. —Janice Rogers, Gardendale, Texas

     3 packages (3 ounces *each*) orange gelatin
     3 cups boiling water
2-1/2 cups fresh *or* frozen cranberries, chopped
1-1/2 cups finely chopped celery
     2 navel oranges, peeled and diced
     1 can (8 ounces) crushed pineapple, undrained
     2 tablespoons grated orange peel
     1 cup sugar
     2 tablespoons lemon juice
Dash salt
  3/4 cup chopped pecans

In a bowl, dissolve gelatin in boiling water. Stir in cranberries, celery, oranges, pineapple with liquid, orange peel, sugar, lemon juice and salt. Chill until partially set. Stir in pecans. Pour into an 8-cup mold coated with nonstick cooking spray. Chill until firm. **Yield:** 12-16 servings.

Slick Gelatin Mold Tips

To get gelatin cleanly out of a mold, first run a thin, warm knife around the edge. Then wet a kitchen towel with warm water, squeeze almost dry and wrap around the mold for a few minutes. The gelatin will slide right out. Also, wet the serving dish before turning the gelatin out onto it. You'll be able to slide the gelatin to the center of the plate.

Layered gelatin salads featuring different colors are eye-catching additions to a meal. But making such a salad takes time because each layer needs to set before the next one can be added.

Zucchini Orange Salad

The ingredients in this recipe may surprise you, but not as much as the delightful flavor and refreshing crunch the blend produces! —Clarice Schweitzer
Sun City, Arizona

    2 medium zucchini, thinly sliced
    1 medium onion, thinly sliced
    1 cup chopped celery
    1 can (16 ounces) green beans*, drained
    1 can (16 ounces) wax beans*, drained
    1 can (15 ounces) mandarin oranges,
        drained
    1 can (8 ounces) sliced water chestnuts,
        drained
1-1/2 cups sugar
    1 cup vinegar
    1 tablespoon water
    1 teaspoon salt

In a large bowl, toss zucchini, onion and celery. Cover with boiling water; let stand for 1 hour. Drain. Add beans, oranges and water chestnuts. Combine remaining ingredients in a saucepan. Bring to a boil; boil for 1 minute. Pour over salad; cover and refrigerate 24 hours before serving. **Yield:** 16-20 servings. ***Editor's Note:** Home-canned or fresh green and wax beans can be substituted for purchased canned beans. Use 2 cups of each, and if using fresh beans, cook until crisp-tender before adding to salad.

—— 🝞 🝞 🝞 ——

Marinated Mushroom Salad

(Pictured above right and on page 21)

Packed with mushrooms and loads of crunchy colorful ingredients, this salad is perfect at picnics and parties. It keeps well in the refrigerator, so you can easily make it ahead of time. —Sandra Johnson
Tioga, Pennsylvania

2-1/2 quarts water
    3 tablespoons lemon juice
    3 pounds small fresh mushrooms
    2 carrots, sliced
    2 celery ribs, sliced
1/2 medium green pepper, chopped
    1 small onion, chopped
    1 tablespoon minced fresh parsley
1/2 cup sliced stuffed olives
    1 can (2-1/4 ounces) sliced ripe olives,
        drained
DRESSING:
1/2 cup prepared Italian salad dressing
1/2 cup red *or* white wine vinegar
    1 garlic clove, minced

1/2 teaspoon dried oregano
1/2 teaspoon salt

In a large saucepan, bring water and lemon juice to a boil. Add mushrooms and cook for 3 minutes, stirring occasionally. Drain; cool. Place mushrooms in a large bowl with carrots, celery, green pepper, onion, parsley and olives. Combine all dressing ingredients in a small bowl or a jar with tight-fitting lid; shake or mix well. Pour over salad. Cover and refrigerate overnight. **Yield:** 6-8 servings.

—— 🝞 🝞 🝞 ——

Cucumber Salad

I like to cook and entertain for friends. This cool, crunchy cucumber salad seems to go with whatever main dish I prepare. —Philip Stent, Houston, Texas

    1 cup (8 ounces) sour cream
1/4 cup chopped onion
    2 tablespoons lemon juice
    2 tablespoons cider vinegar
Salt and pepper to taste
    3 large cucumbers, peeled and thinly sliced

In a bowl, combine sour cream, onion, lemon juice, vinegar, salt and pepper. Add cucumbers and mix well. Chill for at least 1 hour. **Yield:** 6-8 servings.

Hard-Cooked Eggs Make Easy Salads

HARD-COOKED EGGS are the basis for some delicious dishes from the American Egg Board, which shares a classic recipe for Old-Fashioned Egg Salad. Serve it as a side dish or use it as a sandwich filling. Or toss in some other ingredients for two tasty twists.

Starting with the basic egg salad recipe, you can add diced cooked potatoes and a zesty mustard sauce to create tasty Mustard Potato Salad. Try varying the taste each time you make it by using different flavored mustards, which are readily found in most grocery stores.

A second variation pairs pasta with eggs for Classic Macaroni Salad, brightened by green pepper and pimientos.

Hard-cooked eggs are also worth their "stuff" in Yogurt Deviled Eggs. In this recipe developed by the Egg Board, yogurt lowers fat as it fills in smoothly for the traditional mayonnaise. This cool and creamy finger food can also be served as a snack.

Photo courtesy of the American Egg Board

EGGS-ACTLY HOW YOU LIKE IT! Traditionalists may choose Old-Fashioned Egg Salad, but Mustard Potato Salad and Classic Macaroni Salad (shown above, clockwise from top) offer hearty options.

Hard-Cooked How-tos

• For perfect hard-cooked eggs, place eggs in a single layer in a saucepan and add enough water to come at least 1 inch above eggs. Cover and quickly bring just to a boil. Turn off heat.

Let eggs stand, covered, in hot water 15 minutes for large eggs (about 18 minutes for extra-large eggs and about 12 minutes for medium eggs).

• To prevent a dark surface on the yolks, immediately run cold water over the eggs or place them in ice water until completely cooled.

• Peel eggs right after cooling for immediate use or refrigerate in the shell for use within 1 week.

• Using the freshest eggs possible will help keep the yolk centered within the white, but very fresh eggs are more difficult to peel after hard-cooking. The best compromise for attractive hard-cooked eggs with centered yolks that are relatively easy to peel seems to be cooking eggs that have been refrigerated for about a week to 10 days.

Old-Fashioned Egg Salad

(Pictured at left and on page 20)

```
1/4 cup mayonnaise
  2 teaspoons lemon juice
  1 teaspoon dried minced onion
1/4 teaspoon salt
1/4 teaspoon pepper
  6 hard-cooked eggs, chopped
1/2 cup finely chopped celery
```
Lettuce leaves *or* bread

In a bowl, combine mayonnaise, lemon juice, onion, salt and pepper. Stir in eggs and celery. Cover and chill. For each serving, spoon about 1/2 cup onto a lettuce leaf or spread on bread. **Yield:** 3-4 servings.

Mustard Potato Salad

(Pictured at left and on page 20)

```
  2 cups diced peeled potatoes (about 1
    pound)
  1 recipe Old-Fashioned Egg Salad (on this
    page)
1/4 cup mayonnaise
  1 teaspoon prepared mustard
1/2 teaspoon dried minced onion
1/4 teaspoon salt
```
Lettuce leaves
Sliced radishes, optional

In a saucepan, cover potatoes with water and cook until tender but firm. Drain and cool. In a bowl, combine egg salad, mayonnaise, mustard, onion and salt. Stir in cooled potatoes. Cover and chill. Serve on lettuce leaves; garnish with radishes if desired. **Yield:** 6-8 servings.

Classic Macaroni Salad

(Pictured at far left and on page 20)

```
  1 recipe Old-Fashioned Egg Salad (on this
    page)
  1 box (7 ounces) elbow macaroni, cooked
    and drained
1/2 cup chopped green pepper
1/4 cup mayonnaise
  1 jar (2 ounces) chopped pimientos, drained
```
Lettuce leaves
Paprika, optional

In a bowl, combine egg salad, macaroni, green pepper, mayonnaise and pimientos. Cover and chill. For each serving, spoon about 3/4 cup onto a lettuce leaf. Sprinkle with paprika if desired. **Yield:** 8 servings.

Yogurt Deviled Eggs

```
  6 hard-cooked eggs
1/4 cup plain yogurt
  1 teaspoon dried minced onion
  1 teaspoon dried parsley flakes
  1 teaspoon lemon juice
3/4 teaspoon prepared mustard
1/4 teaspoon salt
1/4 teaspoon Worcestershire sauce
1/8 teaspoon pepper
```
Paprika, optional

Cut eggs in half lengthwise. Remove yolks and set whites aside. In a small bowl, mash yolks; blend in the next eight ingredients. Refill whites, using about 1 tablespoon yolk mixture for each. Sprinkle paprika on top of eggs if desired. **Yield:** 1 dozen.

Upright Deviled Eggs

Here's a great way to keep deviled eggs from tipping over on the serving platter as you travel to a potluck: Cook a bag of green spinach noodles; drain and cool. Spread the noodles on the platter and "nest" the eggs on the noodles. It looks lovely, and all the eggs remain upright.

Tropical Chicken Salad

(Pictured below)

Over the years my husband and I have moved to different areas, and I've collected recipes from all over the United States. This flavorful salad recipe comes from New York. I've served it for luncheons for many years, and it's one of my husband's very favorites.
—Linda Wheatley, Garland, Texas

- 2 cups cubed cooked chicken
- 1 cup chopped celery
- 1 cup mayonnaise
- 1/2 to 1 teaspoon curry powder
- 1 can (20 ounces) chunk pineapple, drained
- 2 large firm bananas, sliced
- 1 can (11 ounces) mandarin oranges, drained
- 1/2 cup flaked coconut
- Salad greens, optional
- 3/4 cup salted peanuts *or* cashew halves

Place chicken and celery in a large bowl. Combine mayonnaise and curry powder; add to chicken mixture and mix well. Cover and chill for at least 30 minutes. Before serving, add the pineapple, bananas, oranges and coconut; toss gently. Serve on salad greens if desired. Sprinkle with nuts. **Yield:** 4-6 servings.

Creamy Sweet Potato Salad

The North Carolina Sweet Potato Commission encourages you to give this novel combination a try. Refreshing and colorful, it's a real taste treat.

- 2 cups mayonnaise
- 1/3 cup buttermilk
- 2 tablespoons lemon juice
- 1 tablespoon Dijon mustard
- 1 teaspoon sugar
- 3 pounds sweet potatoes, cooked, peeled and cubed
- 1 cup peas
- 1/2 cup chopped green *or* sweet red pepper
- 1/2 cup sliced green onions
- 1 bunch fresh spinach
- 3 bacon strips, cooked and crumbled

In a bowl, blend mayonnaise, buttermilk, lemon juice, mustard and sugar until smooth. In a large bowl, combine sweet potatoes, peas, pepper and onions. Pour dressing over all; toss to blend. Chill 2 hours or overnight. To serve, spoon salad into a large bowl lined with spinach; top with bacon. **Yield:** 12-16 servings.

Crunchy Sauerkraut Salad

Apple and dill combine with sauerkraut for a tangy crisp salad. —Debbie Jones, California, Maryland

- 1 can (27 ounces) sauerkraut, rinsed and drained
- 1 unpeeled apple, chopped
- 1 small onion, chopped
- 3/4 cup finely chopped dill pickle
- 1/2 cup vegetable oil
- 3 tablespoons lemon juice
- 2 tablespoons sugar
- 1/2 teaspoon dried parsley flakes
- 1/2 teaspoon dried basil
- 1/2 teaspoon dill weed
- 1/4 teaspoon pepper

In a bowl, combine all ingredients. Cover and chill for at least 1 hour. **Yield:** 10-12 servings.

Low-Fat Potato Salad

If you love potato salad but need to watch your diet, this low-fat version is for you. Everyone loves this crunchy, refreshing salad. —Paula Pelis
Rocky Point, New York

✓ Uses less fat, sugar or salt. Includes Nutritional Analysis and Diabetic Exchanges.

1-1/2 pounds small salad potatoes
  3/4 cup plain nonfat yogurt
    3 tablespoons cider *or* white wine vinegar
    1 tablespoon minced fresh dill
    1 tablespoon minced fresh parsley
    2 teaspoons minced fresh tarragon
  1/2 medium onion, chopped
    1 celery rib, chopped
    1 small carrot, coarsely shredded

Cook potatoes until tender but firm; cool and slice. In a large bowl, combine remaining ingredients. Add potatoes and stir until well coated. Chill for several hours. **Yield:** 8 servings. **Nutritional Analysis:** One serving equals 95 calories, 26 mg sodium, trace cholesterol, 17 gm carbohydrate, 3 gm protein, trace fat. **Diabetic Exchanges:** 1 starch, 1/2 vegetable.

Peeling Salad Potatoes

Before boiling red potatoes for potato salad, use a paring knife to pierce the skin in a circular pattern around each potato. Once boiled, the potatoes are much easier to peel.

Frozen Cranberry Banana Salad

(Pictured above)

A luscious combination of sweet and tangy, crunchy and creamy, this pretty salad makes a great side dish or dessert. Its light pink color and delicate banana flavor make it perfect for a bridal shower or ladies' luncheon. —Phylis Hoffmann, Conway, Arkansas

    1 can (20 ounces) pineapple tidbits
    5 medium firm bananas, halved lengthwise and sliced
    1 can (16 ounces) whole-berry cranberry sauce
  1/2 cup sugar
    1 carton (12 ounces) frozen whipped topping, thawed
  1/2 cup chopped walnuts

Drain pineapple juice into a medium bowl; set pineapple aside. Add bananas to the juice. In a large bowl, combine cranberry sauce and sugar. Remove bananas, discarding juice, and add to cranberry mixture. Stir in pineapple, whipped topping and nuts. Pour into a 13-in. x 9-in. x 2-in. dish. Freeze until solid. Remove from the freezer 15 minutes before cutting. **Yield:** 12-16 servings.

Soups & Sandwiches

Make a mouth-watering midday meal by serving a savory simmering soup and hearty sandwich.

CLASSIC COMBINATIONS. Clockwise from upper left: Mushroom and Potato Chowder (p. 43), Scrum-Delicious Burgers (p. 40), Buffalo Chili Con Carne (p. 36), Peasant Soup (p. 44) and Turkey Wild Rice Soup (p. 37).

Buffalo Chili Con Carne

(Pictured above and on page 35)

This classic recipe of the American frontier is so meaty you can almost eat it with a fork. The zippy combination of ingredients complements the buffalo.
—*Donna Smith, Victor, New York*

☑ Uses less fat, sugar or salt. Includes Nutritional Analysis and Diabetic Exchanges.

- 1 pound cubed *or* coarsely ground buffalo meat
- 2 tablespoons vegetable oil
- 1 to 2 cups diced onion
- 1 to 2 cups diced green pepper
- 2 cans (14-1/2 ounces *each*) diced tomatoes, undrained
- 1-1/2 to 2 cups tomato juice
- 1 can (16 ounces) red kidney beans, rinsed and drained
- 1 can (15 ounces) pinto beans, rinsed and drained
- 1 can (4 ounces) chopped green chilies
- 2 teaspoons chili powder
- 1 teaspoon salt, optional
- 1/2 teaspoon pepper

In a large kettle or Dutch oven, brown meat in oil; drain. Add onion and green pepper; saute for 5 minutes. Stir in remaining ingredients and bring to a boil. Reduce heat; cover and simmer 1-1/2 to 2 hours or until the meat is tender. **Yield:** 6 servings (1-1/2 quarts). **Nutritional Analysis:** One serving (prepared without added salt) equals 326 calories, 674 mg sodium, 27 mg cholesterol, 39 gm carbohydrate, 23 gm protein, 3 gm fat. **Diabetic Exchanges:** 2 lean meat, 2 starch, 1 vegetable.

— 🍵 🍵 🍵 —

Bologna Salad Sandwiches

This spread makes a filling sandwich perfect for a big appetite. I also keep some in the refrigerator for late-night snacks. —*Joyce Walker, Ridgeway, Virginia*

- 1-1/2 pounds bologna *or* ham, ground
- 1 to 1-1/4 cups mayonnaise
- 3/4 cup sweet pickle relish, well drained
- 3 tablespoons chopped onion
- 1 tablespoon Worcestershire sauce
- 30 slices bread
- 15 slices process American cheese

Lettuce leaves, optional

In a bowl, mix the bologna, mayonnaise, relish, onion and Worcestershire sauce. Use about 1/3 cup of the salad for each sandwich, and top with a slice of cheese and lettuce if desired. **Yield:** 15 sandwiches. **Editor's Note:** All of the sandwiches don't have to be made at once. The salad will keep for 4-5 days stored in a covered container in the refrigerator.

— 🍵 🍵 🍵 —

Barley Peasant Soup

In this recipe from the National Barley Foods Council, the good-tasting grain simmers in a broth brightened with a cornucopia of vegetables. Try it for a savory supper or lunch.

- 1 pound beef stew meat, cut into 1/2- to 3/4-inch cubes
- 1 tablespoon olive *or* vegetable oil
- 2 cups chopped onion
- 1 cup sliced celery
- 2 garlic cloves, minced
- 5 cups water
- 5 cups beef broth
- 2 cups sliced carrots
- 1-1/2 cups pearl barley
- 1 can (16 ounces) kidney beans, rinsed and drained
- 1 can (15 ounces) garbanzo beans *or* chickpeas, rinsed and drained
- 4 cups sliced zucchini
- 3 cups diced plum tomatoes

2 cups chopped cabbage
1/4 cup snipped fresh parsley
1 teaspoon dried thyme
1-1/2 teaspoons Italian seasoning
Salt and pepper to taste
Grated Parmesan cheese, optional

In a large saucepan or Dutch oven, brown meat in oil. Add onion, celery and garlic. Cook until beef is no longer pink. Add water and broth; bring to a boil. Add carrots and barley. Reduce heat; cover and simmer for 45-60 minutes or until barley is tender. Add beans, zucchini, tomatoes, cabbage, parsley and seasonings; simmer 15-20 minutes or until vegetables are tender. Top individual bowls with Parmesan cheese if desired. **Yield:** 16-20 servings (5 quarts).

Hearty Beef Sandwiches

Perfect for the ballpark, these beefy rolls from the Cattlemen's Beef Association will label you a "good sport" whenever you serve them. Zesty cream cheese-horseradish filling cheers on the flavorful roast beef.

2 teaspoons lemon juice
1 small apple, finely chopped
1 package (3 ounces) cream cheese, softened
1 tablespoon milk
1 tablespoon prepared horseradish
1/3 cup chopped walnuts
6 kaiser rolls, split
6 lettuce leaves
1 pound thinly sliced fully cooked roast beef
2 tablespoons sliced green onions

Sprinkle lemon juice over apple. In a small bowl, combine cream cheese, milk and horseradish; add apple and walnuts and mix well. Spread onto cut side of roll tops. On each roll bottom, place the lettuce, roast beef and green onions; replace tops. **Yield:** 6 servings.

Turkey Wild Rice Soup

(Pictured at right and on page 34)

An area turkey grower shared this recipe with me. A rich and smooth soup, it makes great use of two Minnesota resources—turkey and wild rice. Be prepared to serve seconds!
—Terri Holmgren
Swanville, Minnesota

1 medium onion, chopped
2 celery ribs, diced
2 carrots, diced

1/2 cup butter *or* margarine
1/2 cup all-purpose flour
4 cups chicken *or* turkey broth
2 cups cooked wild rice
2 cups half-and-half cream
2 cups diced cooked turkey
1 teaspoon dried parsley flakes
1/2 teaspoon salt
1/4 teaspoon pepper

In a large kettle or Dutch oven, saute onion, celery and carrots in butter until onion is transparent. Reduce heat. Blend in flour and cook until bubbly. Gradually add chicken broth, stirring constantly. Bring to a boil; boil for 1 minute. Reduce heat; add wild rice, cream, turkey, parsley, salt and pepper; simmer for 20 minutes. **Yield:** 10-12 servings (about 3 quarts).

Handling Leftover Turkey

Remove leftover turkey meat from the bones within 2 hours of roasting and refrigerate. Keep in the coldest part of the refrigerator. Leftovers may be used up to 4 days after storing. Cooked turkey will keep up to 4 months in the freezer in heavy foil or freezer bags.

'I Wish I Had That Recipe...'

"WHENEVER I visit Scott's Prime Rib in East Hazel Crest, Illinois, I can't pass up their hearty, delicious Sweet-and-Sour Beef Cabbage Soup," says Mae Lavan of Chicago, Illinois.

Mae—a longtime patron of this suburban eatery—asked owner Marilyn Hackett to share the savory soup recipe...and she did!

The popular soup was created by head chef Frazier Thomas. "It's been a favorite with customers for years," Marilyn confirms. "Since so many people rave over it and request the recipe, we've made copies available for guests."

You'll find Scott's Prime Rib at 175th and Center St., East Hazel Crest IL 60429 (near the intersection of Interstates 80 and 294). Phone 1-708/798-5741.

Sweet-and-Sour Beef Cabbage Soup

    2 quarts water
    3/4 cup diced cooked roast beef
    1 cup chopped onion
    1 cup chopped tomato
    1/2 cup shredded cabbage
    1/2 cup sliced celery
    1/3 cup chopped carrot
    1 cup sugar
    1/2 cup cider vinegar
    1/4 cup burgundy, optional
    2 tablespoons browning sauce
    2 tablespoons Worcestershire sauce
    2 teaspoons tomato sauce
    6 beef bouillon cubes
    1/2 teaspoon garlic powder
    1/4 teaspoon dried thyme
Salt and pepper to taste
    2 tablespoons all-purpose flour
    2 tablespoons vegetable oil

In a Dutch oven, combine all ingredients except flour and oil. Bring to a boil over medium heat. Reduce heat; simmer, uncovered, until vegetables are tender. Combine flour and oil until well blended; stir into the soup. Simmer until slightly thickened. Serve hot. **Yield:** 8-10 servings (2-3/4 quarts).

Chicken Salad Sandwiches

Crisp cukes give a refreshing twist to the traditional in this recipe. I like to set out the filling with a tray of assorted breads and pita pockets to let family or friends fix their own sandwiches. —Anna Mowan Spencerville, Indiana

    2 cups diced cooked chicken
    1 celery rib, diced
    2 hard-cooked eggs, chopped
    1 small cucumber, diced
    1/3 cup salad dressing or mayonnaise
    1/4 teaspoon salt
    1/8 teaspoon ground mustard
    1/8 teaspoon white pepper
Bread or pita bread

In a bowl, combine the first eight ingredients. Serve on bread or in pita bread. **Yield:** 4-6 servings.

Corn Chowder

Fresh corn gives wonderful appeal to this recipe I got from my sister. This full-bodied soup is also satisfying on a chilly fall or winter day, using frozen or canned corn. —Muriel Lerdal, Humboldt, Iowa

    3/4 cup chopped onion
    2 tablespoons butter or margarine
    1 cup diced cooked peeled potatoes
    1 cup diced fully cooked ham
    2 cups fresh, frozen or canned sweet corn
    1 cup cream-style corn
    1 can (10-3/4 ounces) condensed cream of
      mushroom soup, undiluted
2-1/2 cups milk
Salt and pepper to taste
    1 tablespoon chopped fresh parsley

In a heavy saucepan, cook the onion in butter until tender. Add all remaining ingredients; bring to a boil. Reduce heat; simmer, uncovered, for 20-30 minutes. **Yield:** 6-8 servings (2 quarts).

"Humpty-Dumpty" Sandwiches

Instead of relying on ordinary egg salad, I like to spark up brown-bag lunches with this hearty sandwich. Every bite is filled with eggs, cheese and flavor. —Cheryl Miller, Fort Collins, Colorado

    1 hard-cooked egg, chopped
    1 celery rib, chopped
    1/3 cup small curd cottage cheese
    1/4 cup shredded cheddar cheese
    1 to 1-1/2 teaspoons spicy brown mustard

1/4 teaspoon salt
1/8 teaspoon pepper
   4 slices whole wheat bread
Lettuce leaves

In a bowl, combine the first seven ingredients. Spread on 2 slices of bread. Top with lettuce and remaining bread. **Yield:** 2 servings.

——— ▆ ▆ ▆ ———

Top-Dog Hot Dogs

This is one of the first recipes I let our sons prepare completely by themselves. They love the pizza-like flavor these hot dogs get from chili sauce and cheese.
   —*Kathy Burggraaf, Plainfield Township, Michigan*

   8 hot dogs
   8 hot dog buns, sliced
   1 jar (10 ounces) hot dog relish *or* chili
      sauce
   1 small green pepper, chopped
   1 small onion, chopped
   1 small tomato, chopped and seeded
Shredded mozzarella cheese

Cook hot dogs according to package directions. Place in buns; top with relish or chili sauce, green pepper, onion and tomato. Sprinkle with mozzarella cheese. **Yield:** 8 servings.

——— ▆ ▆ ▆ ———

Fresh Tomato Soup

When tomatoes are in season, my family knows they can expect to see this soup on the dinner table. It tastes better than any store-bought soup.   —*Edna Hoffman*
Hebron, Indiana

   1/2 cup chopped onion
   1/4 cup butter *or* margarine
   1/4 cup all-purpose flour
   2 cups water
   6 medium tomatoes, peeled and diced
   1 tablespoon minced fresh parsley
1-1/2 teaspoons salt
   1 teaspoon sugar
   1 teaspoon minced fresh thyme *or* 1/2
      teaspoon dried thyme
   1 bay leaf
   1/4 teaspoon pepper
Thin lemon slices, optional

In a large saucepan, cook onion in butter until tender. Stir in flour to form a smooth paste. Gradually add water, stirring constantly until thickened. Add the tomatoes, parsley, salt, sugar, thyme, bay leaf and pepper; bring to a boil. Reduce heat;

cover and simmer for 20-30 minutes or until tomatoes are tender. Remove bay leaf. Garnish with lemon if desired. **Yield:** 4 servings (5 cups).

Baked Potato Soup
(Pictured above)

This recipe was given to me by a dear friend with whom I taught school. She came to Texas from Michigan, and I from Oklahoma. Her entire family has become very special to me. I think of them whenever I make this rich savory soup, which is a great way to use up leftover baked potatoes.
   —*Loretha Bringle*
Garland, Texas

   2/3 cup butter *or* margarine
   2/3 cup all-purpose flour
   7 cups milk
   4 large baking potatoes, baked, cooled,
      peeled and cubed (about 4 cups)
   4 green onions, sliced
   12 bacon strips, cooked and crumbled
1-1/4 cups shredded cheddar cheese
   1 cup (8 ounces) sour cream
   3/4 teaspoon salt
   1/2 teaspoon pepper

In a large soup kettle or Dutch oven, melt the butter. Stir in flour; heat and stir until smooth. Gradually add milk, stirring constantly until thickened. Add potatoes and onions. Bring to a boil, stirring constantly. Reduce heat; simmer for 10 minutes. Add remaining ingredients; stir until cheese is melted. Serve immediately. **Yield:** 8-10 servings (2-1/2 quarts).

Scrum-Delicious Burgers

(Pictured above and on page 35)

I'm not sure where this recipe originated, but it's one of my family's summertime favorites. I usually serve these juicy burgers when we have company. The guests rave about the flavorful cheesy topping. It's fun to serve a burger that's a little more special.
—Wendy Sommers, West Chicago, Illinois

   3 tablespoons finely chopped onion
1/2 teaspoon garlic salt
1/2 teaspoon pepper
1-1/2 pounds ground beef
   1 cup (4 ounces) shredded cheddar cheese
1/3 cup canned sliced mushrooms
   6 bacon strips, cooked and crumbled
1/4 cup mayonnaise
   6 hamburger buns, split
Lettuce leaves and tomato slices, optional

In a medium bowl, combine onion, garlic salt and pepper. Add beef and mix well. Shape into six patties, 3/4 in. thick. In a small bowl, combine the cheese, mushrooms, bacon and mayonnaise; refrigerate. Grill burgers over medium-hot heat for 10-12 minutes, turning once. During the last 3 minutes, spoon 1/4 cup of the cheese mixture onto each burger. Serve on buns with lettuce and tomato if desired. **Yield:** 6 servings.

"Forgotten" Minestrone

I'm a free-lance writer, and I can compose articles while this full-flavored soup simmers. I sprinkle servings with Parmesan cheese and serve with garlic bread. —Marsha Ransom, South Haven, Michigan

☑ Uses less fat, sugar or salt. Includes Nutritional Analysis and Diabetic Exchanges.

   1 pound lean beef stew meat
6 cups water
   1 can (28 ounces) diced tomatoes, undrained
   1 low-sodium beef bouillon cube
   1 medium onion, chopped
2 tablespoons minced dried parsley
2-1/2 teaspoons salt, optional
1-1/2 teaspoons ground thyme
   1/2 teaspoon pepper
   1 medium zucchini, thinly sliced
   2 cups finely chopped cabbage
   1 can (15 ounces) garbanzo beans *or* chickpeas, rinsed and drained
   1 cup uncooked small elbow *or* shell macaroni
   1/4 cup grated Parmesan cheese, optional

In a slow cooker, combine the first nine ingredients. Cover and cook on low for 7-9 hours or until the meat is tender. Add zucchini, cabbage, beans and macaroni; cook on high, covered, 30-45 minutes more or until the vegetables are tender. Sprinkle individual servings with Parmesan cheese if desired. **Yield:** 8 servings. **Nutritional Analysis:** One serving (without added salt and Parmesan cheese) equals 138 calories, 261 mg sodium, 33 mg cholesterol, 7 gm carbohydrate, 11 gm protein, 6 gm fat. **Diabetic Exchanges:** 1-1/2 vegetable, 1-1/2 meat.

— 🍲 🍲 🍲 —

Hamburger Vegetable Soup

When my family's in the mood for soup, this is the recipe I reach for. They love the unique combination.
—Diana Frizzle, Knowlton, Quebec

1 pound ground beef
1 cup chopped onion
3 cups beef broth
1 can (28 ounces) diced tomatoes, undrained
1 cup sliced carrots
1 cup sliced celery
1 cup cubed peeled potatoes
2 bay leaves
1 teaspoon salt

In a large saucepan or Dutch oven, brown ground beef; drain. Add onion and cook until tender. Add remaining ingredients; bring to a boil. Reduce heat; cover and simmer until vegetables are tender, about 45-60 minutes. Remove bay leaves. **Yield:** 8-10 servings (2-1/2 quarts).

— 🍲 🍲 🍲 —

Open-Faced Tuna Sandwiches

A pantry standby, tuna takes on a new dimension in this appealing open-faced sandwich from the U.S. Tuna Foundation. Chopped apple and walnuts give nice crunch to the tuna mixture under bubbly melted cheese.

1 can (6-1/8 ounces) tuna, drained and flaked
1 cup chopped unpeeled apple
3 tablespoons finely chopped onion
1/4 cup finely chopped walnuts
1/4 cup salad dressing *or* mayonnaise
2 teaspoons lemon juice
1/4 teaspoon salt
1/8 teaspoon pepper
4 slices bread, toasted
4 slices Monterey Jack *or* Muenster cheese

In a bowl, combine tuna, apple, onion, walnuts, salad dressing, lemon juice, salt and pepper.

Spread on bread; top with a cheese slice. Broil 4 in. from the heat for 5 minutes or until the cheese is melted. **Yield:** 4 servings.

— 🍲 🍲 🍲 —

Potato Cheese Soup

(Pictured below)

My father was Swiss, so cheese has been a basic food in our family as long as I can remember. With its big cheese taste, you'll want to prepare this soup often. A steaming bowl plus a salad and slice of bread makes a wonderful light meal.
—Carol Smith
New Berlin, Wisconsin

3 medium potatoes (about 1 pound), peeled and quartered
1 small onion, finely chopped
1 cup water
1 teaspoon salt
3 cups milk
3 tablespoons butter *or* margarine, melted
2 tablespoons all-purpose flour
2 tablespoons minced fresh parsley
1/8 teaspoon white pepper
1 cup (4 ounces) shredded Swiss cheese

In a saucepan, bring potatoes, onion, water and salt to a boil. Reduce heat; cover and simmer until potatoes are tender. Do not drain; mash slightly. Stir in milk. In a small bowl, blend butter, flour, parsley and pepper; stir into the potato mixture. Cook and stir over medium heat until thickened and bubbly. Remove from the heat; add cheese and stir until almost melted. **Yield:** 6 servings (1-1/2 quarts).

Vegetable Bean Soup

(Pictured below)

This soup is packed with nutritious vegetables and beans and has a unique robust flavor. It's no wonder this is a family favorite. —*Laura Letobar Livonia, Michigan*

✓ Uses less fat, sugar or salt. Includes Nutritional Analysis and Diabetic Exchanges.

- 2 cups chopped onion
- 1 cup chopped carrots
- 1 cup chopped celery
- 6 cups water
- 3 low-sodium beef bouillon cubes
- 2 cans (14-1/2 ounces *each*) no-salt-added tomatoes, undrained
- 1 can (15 ounces) black beans, rinsed and drained
- 1 cup quick-cooking barley
- 1 teaspoon garlic powder
- 3/4 teaspoon pepper
- 1 package (10 ounces) frozen chopped spinach, thawed

In a large saucepan or Dutch oven coated with nonstick cooking spray, saute onion, carrots and celery over medium heat until onion is soft, about 8 minutes. Stir in water, bouillon, tomatoes, beans, barley, garlic powder and pepper; bring to a boil. Reduce heat; cover and simmer for 10 minutes. Add spinach; cover and simmer for 10-15 minutes or until the vegetables are tender. **Yield:** 14 servings. **Nutritional Analysis:** One serving equals 113 calories, 126 mg sodium, 0 cholesterol, 23 gm carbohydrate, 6 gm protein, 1 gm fat. **Diabetic Exchanges:** 1 starch, 1 vegetable.

———— 🥄 🥄 🥄 ————

Pork Poor Boy

A wealth of flavor stacks up in this National Pork Producers Council idea, featuring thin-sliced pork loin roast with a garden medley of fresh spinach, sprouts, cucumber and other toppings. Use leftover roast or fix one especially for these super sandwiches!

- 1 boneless pork loin roast (1 pound)
- 1/2 teaspoon pepper
- 1 loaf (1 pound) French *or* Italian bread
- 4 ounces fresh spinach
- 1 medium tomato, sliced
- 1 medium cucumber, thinly sliced
- 1 ripe avocado, sliced
- 1 medium green pepper, cut into strips
- 1/2 pound alfalfa sprouts
- 1/4 cup bottled Italian salad dressing

Rub roast with pepper; place in a shallow roasting pan. Bake, uncovered, at 325° for 45-60 minutes or until meat is no longer pink. Let stand 10 minutes; slice thin. Slice bread lengthwise. On bottom half of bread, layer spinach, meat, tomato, cucumber, avocado, green pepper and alfalfa sprouts. Drizzle with dressing. Replace top of bread; slice and serve immediately. **Yield:** 4 servings. **Editor's Note:** Leftover cooked pork may be substituted for roast.

———— 🥄 🥄 🥄 ————

Chicken Soup with Spaetzle

Here's a new and interesting twist to traditional chicken soup. Everyone who samples it can't resist the delicious soup paired with homemade spaetzle. —*Elaine Lange, Grand Rapids, Michigan*

- 1 broiler-fryer chicken (2 to 3 pounds), cut into pieces
- 2 tablespoons vegetable oil
- 2 quarts chicken broth
- 2 bay leaves
- 1/2 teaspoon dried thyme
- 1/4 teaspoon pepper
- 1 cup sliced carrots
- 1 cup sliced celery

   3/4 cup chopped onion
     1 garlic clove, minced
   1/3 cup medium barley
     2 cups sliced fresh mushrooms
SPAETZLE:
1-1/4 cups all-purpose flour
   1/8 teaspoon baking powder
   1/8 teaspoon salt
     1 egg, lightly beaten
   1/4 cup water
   1/4 cup milk

In a large kettle or Dutch oven, brown chicken pieces in oil. Add the broth, bay leaves, thyme and pepper. Simmer until chicken is tender. Cool broth and skim off fat. Skin and bone chicken and cut into bite-size pieces; return to broth along with carrots, celery, onion, garlic and barley. Bring to a boil. Reduce heat; cover and simmer for 35 minutes. Add mushrooms and simmer 8-10 minutes longer. Remove bay leaves. Combine first three spaetzle ingredients in a small bowl. Stir in egg, water and milk; blend well. Drop batter by 1/2 teaspoonfuls into simmering soup. Cook for 10 minutes. **Yield:** 8-10 servings (2-1/2 quarts).

"ABC" Sandwiches

With one bite, you'll no longer wonder why this tasty sandwich is my favorite. I just love the combination of apple, bacon and cheddar—that's how this recipe got its name.   —Marilyn Dick, Centralia, Missouri

     2 cups (8 ounces) shredded cheddar cheese
     1 medium apple, finely chopped
   3/4 cup salad dressing *or* mayonnaise
   1/2 cup finely chopped walnuts
   12 slices bread, toasted and buttered
   12 bacon strips, cooked
     6 hard-cooked eggs, sliced
     6 tomato slices, optional

In a bowl, combine cheese, apple, salad dressing and walnuts. Spread on 6 slices of bread; place 2 slices of bacon on each. Cover with egg slices. Top with tomatoes if desired and remaining slices of bread. **Yield:** 6 servings.

Cleaning Mushrooms

To clean mushrooms, quickly rinse in a colander with cool water or wipe gently with a damp cloth. Do not soak—mushrooms are porous and will absorb water. Before using, cut a thin slice off the bottom of the stem.

Mushroom and Potato Chowder

(Pictured above and on page 34)

My daughter shared this delightful recipe with me. Its rich broth, big mushroom taste and medley of vegetables make this chowder a little different from ordinary mushroom soup.
                      —Romaine Wetzel
               Lancaster, Pennsylvania

   1/2 cup chopped onion
   1/4 cup butter *or* margarine
     2 tablespoons all-purpose flour
     1 teaspoon salt
   1/2 teaspoon pepper
     3 cups water
     1 pound fresh mushrooms, sliced
     1 cup chopped celery
     1 cup diced peeled potatoes
   1/2 cup chopped carrots
     1 cup half-and-half cream
   1/4 cup grated Parmesan cheese

In a large kettle, saute onion in butter until tender. Add flour, salt and pepper; stir to make a smooth paste. Gradually add water, stirring constantly. Bring to a boil; cook and stir for 1 minute. Add the mushrooms, celery, potatoes and carrots. Reduce heat; cover and simmer for 30 minutes or until vegetables are tender. Add cream and Parmesan cheese; heat through. **Yield:** 4-6 servings.

Peasant Soup

(Pictured above and on page 34)

This hearty vegetable broth soup really satisfies, and it's inexpensive as well. —*Bertha McClung Summersville, West Virginia*

✓ Uses less fat, sugar or salt. Includes Nutritional Analysis and Diabetic Exchanges.

- **1 pound dry great northern beans**
- **3 carrots, sliced**
- **3 celery ribs, sliced**
- **2 medium onions, chopped**
- **2 garlic cloves, minced**
- **2 bay leaves**
- **1 can (14-1/2 ounces) diced tomatoes, undrained**
- **1 teaspoon dried basil**
- **1/2 teaspoon pepper**
- **2 tablespoons olive *or* vegetable oil**

Place the beans in a Dutch oven and cover with water; bring to a boil. Boil for 2 minutes. Remove from the heat; cover and let stand for 1 hour. Drain and rinse beans; return to Dutch oven. Add 6 cups water, carrots, celery, onions, garlic, bay leaves, tomatoes, basil and pepper; bring to a boil. Reduce heat; cover and simmer for 1-1/2 hours or until the beans are tender. Discard the bay leaves. Add oil and heat through. **Yield:** 12 servings (3 quarts). **Nutritional Analysis:** One 1-cup serving equals 176 calories, 73 mg sodium, 0 cholesterol, 30 gm carbohydrate, 8 gm protein, 3 gm fat. **Diabetic Exchanges:** 1 vegetable, 1 starch, 1/2 lean meat, 1/2 fat.

—— 🏆 🏆 🏆 ——

Lunch-Box "Handwiches"

These unique sandwich pockets are filled with ingredients most kids like. I sometimes double the batch and keep some handy in the freezer for a fast lunch. —*Callie Myers, Rockport, Texas*

- **1 loaf (1 pound) frozen bread dough, thawed**
- **2-1/2 cups finely chopped fully cooked ham**
- **1 cup (4 ounces) shredded Swiss cheese**
- **1 egg yolk**
- **1 tablespoon water**

Allow dough to rise according to package directions. Punch down; divide into 10 equal pieces. Roll each piece into a 5-in. circle. Place about 1/4 cup ham and 2 tablespoons cheese on each circle; press filling to flatten. Mix egg yolk and water; brush on edges of circles. Fold into semicircles and pinch edges to seal. Brush tops with egg yolk mixture. Place on a greased baking sheet. Bake at 375° for 15-20 minutes or until golden brown. Serve warm or cold. If desired, cool and freeze. **Yield:** 10 sandwiches.

Schoolhouse Chili

When I was a school cook, the students loved my chili because they thought it didn't have beans in it. They didn't know I'd puree the beans, tomatoes, onions and green pepper to create a tasty, vitamin-packed chili!
—Mary Selner, Green Bay, Wisconsin

```
1/2  cup chopped onion
1/4  cup chopped green pepper
  1  can (16 ounces) mild chili beans with
     sauce
  1  can (14-1/2 ounces) diced tomatoes,
     undrained
  1  pound ground beef
  1  to 2 teaspoons chili powder
1-1/2 teaspoons salt
  1  teaspoon ground cumin
1/2  teaspoon pepper
Cooked spaghetti, optional
```

Puree onion, green pepper, beans and tomatoes in a blender or food processor until smooth. In a large saucepan or Dutch oven, brown the beef; drain. Add seasonings and the pureed vegetables. Simmer for 1 hour. Add cooked spaghetti before serving if desired. **Yield:** 4-6 servings (1-1/2 quarts).

Reuben Soup

This soup is often served in the staff cafeteria at the high school where I work. It's been a special favorite for years. *—Mary Lindell, Sanford, Michigan*

```
1/2  cup chopped onion
1/2  cup sliced celery
  2  tablespoons butter or margarine
  1  cup chicken broth
  1  cup beef broth
1/2  teaspoon baking soda
  2  tablespoons cornstarch
  2  tablespoons water
3/4  cup sauerkraut, rinsed and drained
  2  cups half-and-half cream
  2  cups chopped cooked corned beef
  1  cup (4 ounces) shredded Swiss cheese
Salt and pepper to taste
Rye croutons, optional
```

In a large saucepan, saute onion and celery in butter until tender. Add broth and baking soda. Combine cornstarch and water; add to pan. Bring to a boil; boil for 2 minutes, stirring occasionally. Reduce heat. Add sauerkraut, cream and corned beef; simmer and stir for 15 minutes. Add cheese; heat until melted. Add salt and pepper. Garnish with croutons if desired. **Yield:** about 6 servings (1-1/2 quarts).

'I Wish I Had That Recipe...'

THEY may be located a thousand miles apart, but the 4B's Restaurants in Missoula, Montana and Grants, New Mexico have something in common: Old-Fashioned Cream of Tomato Soup.

So say two readers who have visited both restaurants. "They serve the best tomato soup at the 4B's Restaurant in Missoula, and I would so much like to have the recipe," relates Ada Allen of Charlo, Montana.

We also heard from Anita Poggemiller of Burlington, Iowa. "Driving my mother back home after she'd spent the winter months in Arizona, we stopped for lunch at the 4B's Restaurant in Grants, New Mexico.

"I ordered the Old-Fashioned Cream of Tomato Soup, and it was the best I had ever tasted! I asked if I could have the recipe to take home to Iowa with me. To my surprise, they handed me a pre-printed recipe card!"

Bill Hainline Sr. opened the first 4B's in Missoula in 1947. The name is a tribute to his family—Bill (now deceased), wife Buddy and children Barbara and Bill Jr.

"The tomato soup is an original recipe of my father's that's been a favorite on our menu since the early days," reveals Bill Jr., who now runs the company with his son, Jeff.

"We're always flattered when we receive requests for our tomato soup recipe, and we're proud to share it with others," he says.

Old-Fashioned Cream of Tomato Soup

```
  1  can (28 ounces) diced tomatoes,
     undrained
  1  cup chicken broth
1/4  cup butter or margarine
  2  tablespoons sugar
  1  tablespoon chopped onion
1/8  teaspoon baking soda
  2  cups whipping cream
```

In a saucepan, combine the first six ingredients. Cover and simmer for 1 hour. Heat cream in the top of a double boiler over simmering water; add to the tomato mixture just before serving. **Yield:** 8 servings (about 1-1/2 quarts).

Side Dishes

***Turn to this chapter for
a host of dishes to serve alongside
any of your main meals.***

—— 🍴 🍴 🍴 ——

PERFECT PARTNERS. Clockwise from upper left: Sugared Asparagus (p. 56), Oven Parmesan Chips (p. 58), Paradise Cran-Applesauce (p. 56), Campfire Potatoes (p. 50) and Hungarian Noodle Side Dish (p. 49).

Grilled Mushrooms

(Pictured below)

Mushrooms cooked over hot coals always taste good, but this easy recipe makes the mushrooms taste fantastic. As the mother of two children, I love to cook entire meals on the grill. It's fun spending time outdoors with the kids.
—Melanie Knoll
Marshalltown, Iowa

1/2 pound whole fresh mushrooms (medium size work best)
1/4 cup butter *or* margarine, melted
1/2 teaspoon dill weed
1/2 teaspoon garlic salt

Thread mushrooms on skewers. Combine butter, dill and garlic salt; brush over mushrooms. Grill over hot heat for 10-15 minutes, basting and turning every 5 minutes. **Yield:** 4 servings.

Mushroom Tips

To keep mushrooms fresh, store in their original packaging in the refrigerator or spread in a single layer on a flat dish and cover with a dampened paper towel. Moisten the towel every day. Mushrooms need air circulation, so don't store them in the crisper drawer. Handle mushrooms as little as possible and be careful not to stack items on top of them—they bruise easily.

Lima Bean Casserole

When my daughter was growing up, I could get her to eat lima beans in this casserole with lots of cheese. She's an adult now and still thinks cheese helps almost every vegetable recipe!
—Tickle Ragland
Hodgenville, Kentucky

2 cups frozen baby lima beans
1 can (10-3/4 ounces) condensed cream of mushroom soup, undiluted
1/2 cup chopped celery
1/2 cup milk
1 cup (4 ounces) shredded cheddar cheese
1/4 cup seasoned bread crumbs

In a bowl, combine lima beans, soup, celery and milk. Pour into a greased 11-in. x 7-in. x 2-in. baking dish. Sprinkle with the cheese and bread crumbs. Cover and bake at 350° for 25 minutes. Uncover; bake 10 minutes longer or until the bread crumbs are lightly browned. **Yield:** 6-8 servings.

Fresh Vegetable Stew

Sunny, colorful and brimming with garden flavor, this easy stovetop dish from the United Fresh Fruit and Vegetable Association stirs in two types of squash along with other favorite veggies.

✓ Uses less fat, sugar or salt. Includes Nutritional Analysis and Diabetic Exchanges.

1 large onion, sliced
3 garlic cloves, minced
1 tablespoon olive *or* vegtetable oil
1 pound yellow squash, cut into 1/2-inch cubes
1 pound pattypan squash, cut into 1/2-inch cubes
2 medium tomatoes, peeled and chopped
3/4 pound fresh green beans, cut into 1-inch pieces
1-1/4 cups fresh sweet corn
1 teaspoon salt, optional
1/4 teaspoon pepper

In a large skillet, saute onion and garlic in oil until tender. Add squash, tomatoes and beans. Reduce heat; cover and simmer for 15 minutes or until squash is tender. Add corn, salt if desired and pepper. Cook for 3 minutes or until corn is tender. **Yield:** 12 servings. **Nutritional Analysis:** One 2/3-cup serving (prepared without added salt) equals 59 calories, 8 mg sodium, 0 cholesterol, 11 gm carbohydrate, 2 gm protein, 2 gm fat. **Diabetic Exchanges:** 1-1/2 vegetable.

—— 🥄 🥄 🥄 ——

Hungarian Noodle Side Dish

(Pictured at right and on page 46)

I first served this creamy, rich casserole at our ladies meeting at church. Everyone liked it and many of the ladies wanted the recipe. The original recipe was from a friend, but I changed it a bit to suit our tastes.
—Betty Sugg, Akron, New York

3 chicken bouillon cubes
1/4 cup boiling water
1 can (10-3/4 ounces) condensed cream of mushroom soup, undiluted
1/2 cup chopped onion
2 tablespoons Worcestershire sauce
2 tablespoons poppy seeds
1/8 to 1/4 teaspoon garlic powder
1/8 to 1/4 teaspoon hot pepper sauce
2 cups (16 ounces) cottage cheese
2 cups (16 ounces) sour cream
1 package (16 ounces) medium noodles, cooked and drained
1/4 cup shredded Parmesan cheese
Paprika

In a large bowl, dissolve bouillon in water. Add the next six ingredients; mix well. Stir in the cottage cheese, sour cream and noodles; mix well. Pour into a greased 2-1/2-qt. baking dish. Sprinkle with the Parmesan cheese and paprika. Cover and bake at 350° for 45 minutes or until heated through. **Yield:**

8-10 servings. **Editor's Note:** Casserole may be prepared ahead, covered and refrigerated overnight. Remove from the refrigerator 30 minutes before baking.

Corn Pudding Supreme

This traditional, slightly sweet side dish is big on corn taste. When I'm hungry for a good corn recipe, I bake this golden pudding.   —Martha Fehl
Brookville, Indiana

1 package (8 ounces) cream cheese, softened
2 eggs, beaten
1/3 cup sugar
1 package (8-1/2 ounces) corn bread/muffin mix
1 can (16-1/2 ounces) cream-style corn
2-1/3 cups fresh, frozen *or* canned sweet corn
1 cup milk
2 tablespoons butter *or* margarine, melted
1 teaspoon salt
1/2 teaspoon ground nutmeg

In a mixing bowl, blend cream cheese, eggs and sugar. Add the remaining ingredients and mix well. Transfer to a greased 13-in. x 9-in. x 2-in. baking dish. Bake, uncovered, at 350° for 45-50 minutes or until set. **Yield:** 12-16 servings.

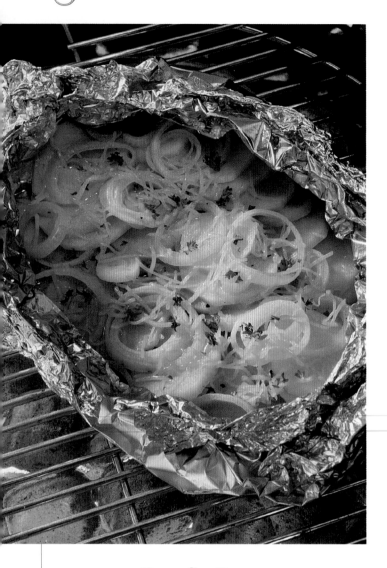

tightly. Grill, covered, over medium heat for 35-40 minutes or until the potatoes are tender. **Yield:** 4-6 servings.

— 🍸 🍸 🍸 —

Polish Sausage Patties

I like to prepare these patties when I'm serving a special breakfast for family or friends. They're quite easy to make, and everyone enjoys the down-home flavor in every bite. —Loretta Ruda, Kennesaw, Georgia

    5 pounds pork butt *or* steak, trimmed
    5 teaspoons dried marjoram
    5 teaspoons salt
    1 teaspoon garlic powder
    1/4 teaspoon pepper
    2 cups water

In a food processor, process pork until coarsely ground (or have your butcher grind the meat); place in a large bowl. Add marjoram, salt, garlic powder and pepper; mix well. Add water and mix well. Shape into 20 patties, 4 in. each. Fry in a skillet over medium heat for 20-25 minutes or until thoroughly cooked. **Yield:** 20 servings. **Editor's Note:** Patties can be frozen. Sausage can also be stuffed into casings to make links.

— 🍸 🍸 🍸 —

Scalloped Potatoes

This creamy, stick-to-your-ribs potato casserole is a perfect accompaniment to an enticing beef roast or baked ham. It's an easy recipe to double when feeding a crowd or a hungry family like mine! —Wendell Obermeier, Charles City, Iowa

      8 medium potatoes, peeled and diced
      1 tablespoon all-purpose flour
    1-1/2 teaspoons salt
      1/4 to 1/2 teaspoon pepper
      1 medium onion, finely chopped
      1 can (10-3/4 ounces) condensed cream of
        mushroom soup, undiluted
      1 cup milk *or* half-and-half cream
      1/2 cup dry bread crumbs
      3 tablespoons butter *or* margarine, melted

In a greased 2-qt. baking dish, layer a third of the potatoes. Combine flour, salt and pepper; sprinkle a third over potatoes. Top with a third of the onion. Combine soup and milk; pour a third over onion. Repeat layers twice. Combine bread crumbs and butter; sprinkle over top. Cover and bake at 350° for 1 hour. Uncover and bake 30 minutes more. **Yield:** 8 servings.

Campfire Potatoes

(Pictured above and on page 46)

We like grilling because it's a no-fuss way to make a meal. This pleasing potato recipe is one we use often! The onion, cheddar cheese and Worcestershire sauce combine to make a super side dish for any grilled meat. Plus, cooking in the foil makes cleanup a breeze. —JoAnn Dettbarn, Brainerd, Minnesota

    5 medium potatoes, peeled and thinly sliced
    1 medium onion, sliced
    6 tablespoons butter *or* margarine
    1/3 cup shredded cheddar cheese
    2 tablespoons minced fresh parsley
    1 tablespoon Worcestershire sauce
Salt and pepper to taste
    1/3 cup chicken broth

Place the potatoes and onion on a large piece of heavy-duty foil (about 20 in. x 20 in.); dot with butter. Combine the cheese, parsley, Worcestershire sauce, salt and pepper; sprinkle over potatoes. Fold foil up around potatoes and add broth. Seal the foil

Butternut Squash Bake

(Pictured below)

If I ask our two girls what to fix for a special meal, this dish is always requested. I discovered this slightly sweet and crunchy-topped casserole at a church dinner more than 10 years ago. Now I take it to potluck dinners and come home with an empty dish!
—*Julie Jahn, Decatur, Indiana*

- 1/3 cup butter *or* margarine, softened
- 3/4 cup sugar
- 2 eggs
- 1 can (5 ounces) evaporated milk
- 1 teaspoon vanilla extract
- 2 cups mashed cooked butternut squash

TOPPING:
- 1/2 cup crisp rice cereal
- 1/4 cup packed brown sugar
- 1/4 cup chopped pecans
- 2 tablespoons butter *or* margarine, melted

In a mixing bowl, cream butter and sugar. Beat in eggs, milk and vanilla. Stir in squash (mixture will be thin). Pour into a greased 11-in. x 7-in. x 2-in. baking dish. Bake, uncovered, at 350° for 45 minutes or until almost set. Combine topping ingredients; sprinkle over casserole. Return to the oven for 5-10 minutes or until bubbly. **Yield:** 6-8 servings.

— 🏺 🏺 🏺 —

Surprise Stuffing

When my grandchildren refused to eat yellow summer squash, I came up with this recipe, a tasty side dish for any meat. It's a lightly sweet, hearty stuffing that's a hit with kids and adults.
—*Frances Tanner*
Milledgeville, Georgia

- 2 cups chopped yellow summer squash
- 1 medium onion, chopped
- 1/4 cup butter *or* margarine
- 4 cups crumbled corn bread
- 1 can (10-3/4 ounces) condensed cream of chicken soup, undiluted
- 3 eggs, beaten
- 1/4 teaspoon salt

Dash pepper

In a large skillet, saute the squash and onion in butter until tender. Remove from the heat; stir in remaining ingredients. Transfer to a greased 1-qt. baking dish. Bake, uncovered, at 350° for 40 minutes. **Yield:** 6 servings.

Sweet Potato Success

RICH COLOR, pleasing texture and great taste have given sweet potatoes their delicious reputation on dinner tables year-round.

— 🏺 🏺 🏺 —

Sweet Potatoes with Apples

(Pictured below)

The tart apple slices taste so good baked on top of the mild sweet potatoes. —Jean Winfree
Merrill, Wisconsin

- 3 to 3-1/2 pounds sweet potatoes
- 2 tart apples, peeled, cored and cut into 1/4-inch rings
- 1/2 cup orange juice
- 1/4 cup packed brown sugar
- 1/4 teaspoon ground ginger
- 1/4 teaspoon ground cinnamon
- 2 tablespoons butter *or* margarine

In a large saucepan, cover sweet potatoes with water; bring to a boil. Reduce heat; cover and simmer for 30 minutes or until just tender. Drain and cool slightly. Peel and cut into 1/4-in. slices. Alternate layers of potatoes and apples in a greased 13-in. x 9-in. x 2-in. baking dish. Pour orange juice over. Mix brown sugar, ginger and cinnamon; sprinkle over potatoes and apples. Dot with butter. Bake, uncovered, at 350° for 35-45 minutes or until apples are tender. **Yield:** 8 servings.

Candied Sweet Potato Bake

This tasty casserole from the North Carolina Sweet Potato Commission has a sweet streusel-like topping.

- 3 medium sweet potatoes, cooked, peeled and sliced
- 2 large unpeeled apples, thinly sliced
- 1/3 cup golden raisins
- 1/4 cup chopped toasted almonds
- 2 tablespoons butter *or* margarine, melted
- 1/3 cup packed brown sugar
- 1/2 cup quick-cooking oats
- 2 teaspoons grated lemon peel

In a large bowl, combine sweet potatoes, apples, raisins and almonds. Spoon into a 1-1/2-qt. baking dish. In a small bowl, combine butter, brown sugar, oats and lemon peel; sprinkle over sweet potato mixture. Bake, uncovered, at 350° for 35 minutes or until apples are tender. **Yield:** 6 servings.

— 🏺 🏺 🏺 —

Stuffed Sweet Potatoes

In this recipe from the North Carolina Sweet Potato Commission, pineapple lends a sweet accent to twice-baked favorites.

- 6 medium sweet potatoes
- 1 can (8 ounces) crushed pineapple, drained
- 1/2 cup orange juice
- 3 tablespoons butter *or* margarine, melted
- 3/4 teaspoon salt

Pierce sweet potatoes with a fork. Bake at 400° for 55-65 minutes or until tender. Cool slightly. Remove pulp from potatoes, keeping the skins intact. In a bowl, combine the pulp with pineapple, orange juice, butter and salt. Refill potato shells and place in a greased 13-in. x 9-in. x 2-in. baking dish. Bake at 400° for 20 minutes or until heated through. **Yield:** 6 servings.

Serving Sweet Potatoes

Top cooked sweet potatoes with sour cream or yogurt and freshly ground black pepper.

Swirl hot mashed sweet potatoes with browned mushrooms for a change.

Mash together the scooped-out pulp of two baked russet potatoes and two baked sweet potatoes, then restuff into the shells.

Pasta with Asparagus

(Pictured above)

Many terrific recipes change hands at the monthly get-togethers of my bridge group. That's where I discovered this zippy, tempting dish. The garlic, asparagus, Parmesan cheese and red pepper flakes create an irresistible taste combination. —Jean Fisher
Redlands, California

5 garlic cloves, minced
1 teaspoon crushed red pepper flakes
2 to 3 dashes hot pepper sauce
1/4 cup olive *or* vegetable oil
1 tablespoon butter *or* margarine
1 pound fresh asparagus, cut into 1-1/2-inch
   pieces
Salt to taste
1/4 teaspoon pepper
1/4 cup shredded Parmesan cheese
1/2 pound mostaccioli *or* elbow macaroni,
   cooked and drained

In a skillet, cook garlic, red pepper flakes and hot pepper sauce in oil and butter for 2-3 minutes. Add asparagus, salt and pepper; saute until asparagus is crisp-tender, about 8-10 minutes. Add Parmesan cheese; mix well. Pour over hot pasta and toss to coat. Serve immediately. **Yield:** 4-6 servings.

Freezer Sweet Corn

Whenever I serve this corn, people can't believe that it's frozen, not fresh. It's always crisp!
—Judi Oudekerk, St. Michael, Minnesota

4 quarts fresh-cut sweet corn (18 to 20
   ears)
1 quart hot water
2/3 cup sugar
1/2 cup butter *or* margarine
2 teaspoons salt

Combine all ingredients in a large kettle; simmer for 5-7 minutes, stirring occasionally. Pour into large shallow containers to cool; stir occasionally. Spoon into freezer bags or containers; freeze. **Yield:** 3 quarts.

Cheese Potato Puff

(Pictured above)

I got this comforting potato recipe from my mother-in-law. It's wonderful because I can put it together in no time and it contains basic ingredients that everyone loves, like milk and cheddar cheese.
—Beverly Templeton, Garner, Iowa

 12 medium potatoes, peeled (about 5
   pounds)
  1 teaspoon salt, *divided*
 3/4 cup butter *or* margarine
  2 cups (8 ounces) shredded cheddar cheese
  1 cup milk
  2 eggs, beaten
Fresh *or* dried chives, optional

Place potatoes in a large kettle; cover with water. Add 1/2 teaspoon salt; cook until tender. Drain; mash potatoes until smooth. In a saucepan, cook and stir butter, cheese, milk and remaining salt until smooth. Stir into potatoes; fold in eggs. Pour into a greased 3-qt. baking dish. Bake, uncovered, at 350° for 40 minutes or until puffy and golden brown. Sprinkle with chives if desired. **Yield:** 8-10 servings.

Creamy Dilled Carrots

I'm not sure where my love of cooking comes from, but I speculate it's because I like to eat! This recipe from a treasured cookbook is a wonderfully different way to serve carrots. They go with most any meal and add nice color to the table.   —Howard Koch, Lima, Ohio

  4 cups thinly sliced carrots
 3/4 cup water
  1 tablespoon butter *or* margarine
 1/2 teaspoon salt
 1/4 teaspoon sugar
Pinch white pepper
  1 tablespoon all-purpose flour
 1/2 cup half-and-half cream
  2 teaspoons dried dill *or* 2 tablespoons
   fresh dill

In a saucepan, combine the carrots, water, butter, salt, sugar and pepper. Cover and simmer until carrots are crisp-tender, about 10 minutes. Drain liquid into a small saucepan; set the carrots aside and keep warm. Bring liquid to a boil. In a small bowl, combine flour and cream until smooth; slowly add to liquid, stirring constantly. Simmer for 10 minutes, stirring occasionally. Pour over the carrots; stir in dill. Cover and let stand for 15 minutes before serving. **Yield:** 6-8 servings.

— 🍴 🍴 🍴 —

Summer Squash Saute

Lucky for me, my family loves squash of all kinds, which is a real plus when the garden is in full bloom. This fresh-tasting dish is sparked with flavors of bacon and Parmesan cheese. —Jane Chartrand
Shelbyville, Tennessee

- 1 large red onion, sliced
- 2 tablespoons vegetable oil
- 2 cups halved small sunburst *or* pattypan squash
- 2 small yellow squash, cut into 1/2-inch slices
- 1 medium sweet red pepper, julienned
- 1 medium green pepper, julienned
- 2 teaspoons minced fresh basil *or* 1/2 teaspoon dried basil
- 2 tablespoons red wine vinegar
- 4 bacon strips, cooked and crumbled
- 1/4 cup grated Parmesan cheese

In a large skillet, saute onion in oil until tender. Stir in the squash, peppers and basil. Cover and cook until vegetables are crisp-tender. Remove from the heat; stir in vinegar and bacon. Sprinkle with Parmesan cheese. **Yield:** 8-10 servings.

— 🍴 🍴 🍴 —

Parsley Rice Casserole

Who says rice has to be plain? Everyone will rave about the subtle flavors in this easy-to-assemble casserole. Fresh parsley and cheddar cheese lend to its terrific color, while celery salt makes it taste great.
—Mary Alice Stefanick, Westlake, Ohio

- 2 eggs, beaten
- 2 cups milk
- 2 cups cooked rice
- 1 cup chopped fresh parsley
- 1/2 cup butter *or* margarine, melted
- 1 tablespoon finely chopped onion
- 1 teaspoon celery salt
- 1/2 teaspoon salt
- 3/4 cup shredded cheddar cheese

In a bowl, combine eggs, milk and rice. Stir in parsley, butter, onion, celery salt and salt. Pour into a greased 2-qt. baking dish; sprinkle with cheese. Set dish in a 13-in. x 9-in. x 2-in. pan; add 1 in. of hot water to pan. Bake at 350° for 50-60 minutes or until a knife inserted in the center comes out clean. **Yield:** 4-6 servings.

Sweet Broiled Grapefruit

(Pictured below)

I was never a fan of grapefruit until I had it broiled at a Florida restaurant—it was so tangy and delicious! I finally got the recipe and now make it often for my husband Ron and our children and grandchildren.
—Terry Bray, Haines City, Florida

- 1 large grapefruit, sliced in half
- 2 tablespoons butter *or* margarine, softened
- 2 tablespoons sugar
- 1/2 teaspoon ground cinnamon

Maraschino cherry for garnish, optional

Cut membrane out of the center of each grapefruit half. Cut around each section so it will be easy to spoon out when eating. Place 1 tablespoon butter in the center of each half. Combine sugar and cinnamon; sprinkle over each. Broil until butter is melted and sugar is bubbly. Garnish with a cherry if desired. Serve immediately. **Yield:** 2 servings.

Super Citrus Secrets

When choosing citrus in the store, look for fruit that's firm, with no soft spots. Avoid bumpy, bruised or wrinkled peels.

Citrus will keep at room temperature for 1 to 2 weeks. For longer storage, refrigerate in a plastic bag or crisper.

Dilly Mashed Potatoes

In this recipe, dill adds a little spark to ordinary mashed potatoes. Plus, the green flecks of this delightful herb make for a pretty presentation.
—Annie Tompkins, Deltona, Florida

6 medium potatoes, peeled and cubed
1/2 cup milk
1 cup (8 ounces) sour cream
2 tablespoons minced fresh dill *or* 2 teaspoons dill weed
1 tablespoon dried minced onion
3/4 teaspoon seasoned salt

In a saucepan, cover potatoes with water; cook until very tender. Drain; mash with milk. Stir in remaining ingredients. **Yield:** 6-8 servings.

——— 🍴 🍴 🍴 ———

Sugared Asparagus

(Pictured below and on page 46)

When my husband and I moved from Oklahoma to the Rio Grande Valley in Texas years ago, I gained an appreciation for a variety of fresh vegetables. This tasty recipe is a simple way to dress up one of our favorites—asparagus!
—Billie Moss
El Sobrante, California

3 tablespoons butter *or* margarine
2 tablespoons brown sugar
2 pounds fresh asparagus, cut into 2-inch pieces (about 4 cups)
1 cup chicken broth

In a skillet over medium-high, heat butter and brown sugar until sugar is dissolved. Add asparagus; saute for 2 minutes. Stir in chicken broth; bring to a boil. Reduce heat; cover and simmer for 8-10 minutes or until asparagus is crisp-tender. Remove asparagus to a serving dish and keep warm. Cook sauce, uncovered, until reduced by half. Pour over asparagus and serve immediately. **Yield:** 4-6 servings.

——— 🍴 🍴 🍴 ———

Fried Squash Blossoms

Savvy gardeners know that flowers from plants in the squash family make flavorful fare. Remove only the male blossoms—those with thin, trim stems—if you'd also like to harvest some squash. You'll find these to be a treat that's tender on the inside and crisp on the outside.
—Lynn Buxkemper, Slaton, Texas

1/2 cup all-purpose flour
1/2 teaspoon baking powder
1/4 teaspoon garlic salt
1/4 teaspoon ground cumin
1 egg
1/2 cup milk
1 tablespoon vegetable oil
Additional oil for frying
12 large freshly picked squash blossoms

In a medium bowl, combine flour, baking powder, garlic salt and cumin. In another bowl, beat egg, milk and oil; add to dry ingredients and stir until smooth. In a skillet, heat 2 in. of oil to 375°. Dip blossoms into batter and fry in oil a few at a time until crisp. Drain on paper towels. Keep warm until serving. **Yield:** 4 servings.

——— 🍴 🍴 🍴 ———

Paradise Cran-Applesauce

(Pictured above right and on page 47)

Appealing apple slices peek through a tangy ruby-red cranberry sauce in this simple but extraordinary side dish. Whether I use this recipe for a holiday dinner or to spark up a Sunday supper, it wouldn't be a feast without a beautiful bowl of this delicious applesauce!
—Sallie McQuay, Sayre, Pennsylvania

4 cups fresh *or* frozen cranberries
1/4 cup water

8 cups sliced peeled cooking apples
2 cups sugar

In a covered saucepan, simmer cranberries and water for 20-25 minutes or until tender. Press through a sieve or food mill; return to the saucepan. Add apples; cover and simmer for 35-40 minutes or until apples are tender but retain their shape. Add sugar. Simmer for 5 minutes, stirring occasionally. **Yield:** 8-10 servings.

— 📏 📏 📏 —

Corn Medley

This garden-fresh medley showcases corn in a colorful blend with tomato, green pepper and onion. This is one of my favorite recipes when corn's in season. Cumin sparks this delicious side dish.
—Ruth Andrewson, Peck, Idaho

✓ Uses less fat, sugar or salt. Includes Nutritional Analysis and Diabetic Exchanges.

2 cups fresh-cut sweet corn (3 to 4 ears)
2 tablespoons butter *or* margarine
1/4 cup chopped onion
1/4 cup chopped green pepper
1/2 teaspoon salt, optional
1/4 teaspoon ground cumin
1 large tomato, chopped and seeded
Sugar substitute equivalent to 2 tablespoons sugar

Combine the first six ingredients in a medium saucepan; cook and stir over medium heat until butter is melted. Cover and cook over low heat for 10 minutes. Stir in tomato and sugar substitute; cook, covered, 5 minutes longer. **Yield:** 5 servings. **Nutritional Analysis:** One 2/3-cup serving (prepared with reduced-fat margarine and without added salt) equals 93 calories, 65 mg sodium, 0 cholesterol, 16 gm carbohydrate, 2 gm protein, 4 gm fat. **Diabetic Exchanges:** 1 starch, 1/2 fat.

Better Baked Beans

To your favorite recipe, stir in some chopped green pepper and onion, pineapple tidbits or chunks and a bit of ketchup and mustard.

For a sweeter variety, add some pitted dark sweet cherries. Thin the sauce with the cherry juice, toss the cherries in with the beans and bake as usual.

Dilled Carrots

Most people don't think of pairing dill and carrots. But my family agrees that dill adds a nice tang to this slightly sweet vegetable. An herb that is easy to grow, dill also looks lovely in the garden.
— *Verona Koehlmoos, Pilger, Nebraska*

    2 to 3 cups sliced carrots
    1/4 cup diced green pepper
    2 tablespoons minced fresh dill
    1 tablespoon honey
    1 tablespoon butter *or* margarine
    2 teaspoons lemon juice
    1/2 teaspoon salt
    1/4 teaspoon ground ginger

In a saucepan, cook carrots in a small amount of water until crisp-tender; drain. Add remaining ingredients. Cook over low heat for 1-2 minutes or until hot. **Yield:** 3-4 servings.

—————— 🍶 🍶 🍶 ——————

Indian Rice

My wife says I'm an expert at stretching our food budget…I can get several meals from one chicken! Golden raisins and curry powder give this economical rice dish a tasty twist, while slivered almonds add a nice crunch. — *Ralph Wheat, Bedford, Texas*

    2 tablespoons butter *or* margarine
    1/4 cup thinly sliced onion
    3 tablespoons slivered almonds
Dash curry powder, optional
    1/4 cup golden raisins
    2 cups hot cooked long grain rice

In a saucepan, melt butter; add onion, almonds and curry powder if desired. Cook until golden brown. Stir in raisins; heat until the raisins plump, about 5 minutes. Remove from the heat; stir in rice. Serve immediately. **Yield:** 4 servings.

—————— 🍶 🍶 🍶 ——————

Oven Parmesan Chips

(Pictured above and on page 47)

My husband and I avoid fried foods, but potatoes are part of our menu almost every day. These delectable sliced potatoes get nice and crispy and give our meals a likable lift. — *Mary Lou Kelly*
Scottdale, Pennsylvania

    4 medium unpeeled baking potatoes
    1/4 cup butter *or* margarine, melted
    1 tablespoon finely minced onion
    1/2 teaspoon salt
    1/8 teaspoon pepper
Dash paprika
    2 tablespoons grated Parmesan cheese

Cut potatoes into 1/4-in. slices; place on a greased baking sheet in a single layer. Mix butter, onion, salt, pepper and paprika; brush on one side of potatoes, then turn and brush other side. Bake at 425° for 15-20 minutes or until potatoes are tender and golden. Sprinkle with Parmesan cheese; serve immediately. **Yield:** 4-6 servings.

Green Beans with Hazelnut-Lemon Butter

Oregon is famous for terrific produce (we grow 40 acres of beans on our farm!) and hazelnuts. This recipe combines those two resources for a delectable side dish. — *Earlene Ertelt, Woodburn, Oregon*

    1 pound fresh green beans, cut
    1/4 cup butter *or* margarine
    1/2 cup toasted chopped hazelnuts*
    1 tablespoon lemon juice
    1 teaspoon minced fresh parsley

1/2 teaspoon dried basil
1/2 teaspoon salt

In a saucepan, cover beans with water; cover and cook until crisp-tender, about 15 minutes. Meanwhile, in a small saucepan over medium-high heat, brown the butter. Add the hazelnuts, lemon juice, parsley, basil and salt; heat through. Drain beans; add the butter mixture and toss to coat. Serve immediately. **Yield:** 4 servings. ***Editor's Note:** Almonds may be substituted for the hazelnuts.

— 🍷 🍷 🍷 —

Kathy's Herbed Corn

(Pictured below and on front cover)

My husband and I agreed that the original recipe for this corn needed a little jazzing up, so I added the thyme and cayenne pepper to suit our tastes. Now fresh summer corn makes a regular appearance on our grill.
—Kathy vonKorff, North College Hill, Ohio

1/2 cup butter *or* margarine, softened
2 tablespoons minced fresh parsley
2 tablespoons minced fresh chives
1 teaspoon dried thyme
1/2 teaspoon salt
1/4 teaspoon cayenne pepper
8 ears sweet corn, husked

In a small bowl, combine the first six ingredients. Spread 1 tablespoon over each ear of corn. Wrap corn individually in heavy-duty foil. Grill, covered, over medium heat for 10-15 minutes, turning frequently, or until corn is tender. **Yield:** 8 servings.

— 🍷 🍷 🍷 —

Broccoli and Swiss Bake

Instead of pairing broccoli with cheddar cheese, I decided to use Swiss. This creamy side dish is especially comforting on cool evenings.
—Philip Stent
Houston, Texas

8 cups broccoli florets
1/4 cup butter *or* margarine
2 tablespoons all-purpose flour
1 small onion, finely chopped
1-1/4 cups milk
4 cups (16 ounces) shredded Swiss cheese
2 eggs, beaten

In a saucepan, cook broccoli until crisp-tender; drain and set aside. In another saucepan, melt butter; add flour. Cook and stir until thickened and bubbly. Stir in onion. Gradually add milk; bring to a boil and cook for 1 minute. Remove from the heat; stir in cheese, eggs and broccoli. Pour into a greased 2-qt. baking dish. Bake, uncovered, at 325° for 30 minutes. **Yield:** 6-8 servings.

Main Dishes

From beef, chicken and turkey to pork, fish and game, these oven entrees, stir-fries, slow-cooker specialties and grilled favorites will please every palate.

— 🏺 🏺 🏺 —

THE MAIN EVENTS. Clockwise from upper left: Dilly Barbecued Turkey (p. 69), Glazed Chicken with Lemon Relish (p. 82), Grilled Venison and Vegetables (p. 81), Slow-Cooked Pepper Steak (p. 80), Zesty Grilled Ham (p. 65) and Asparagus Cheese Strata (p. 87).

Saucy Chicken and Asparagus

(Pictured below)

You won't believe how delicious yet how easy this dish is. We tasted it for the first time when our son's godparents made it for us. Even my grandmother likes to serve this creamy dish for luncheons with friends!
—Vicki Schlechter, Davis, California

1-1/2 pounds fresh asparagus spears, halved
    4 boneless skinless chicken breast halves
    2 tablespoons vegetable oil
  1/2 teaspoon salt
  1/4 teaspoon pepper
    1 can (10-3/4 ounces) condensed cream of
      chicken soup, undiluted
  1/2 cup mayonnaise
    1 teaspoon lemon juice
  1/2 teaspoon curry powder
    1 cup (4 ounces) shredded cheddar cheese

If desired, partially cook asparagus; drain. Place the asparagus in a greased 9-in. square baking dish. In a skillet over medium heat, brown the chicken in oil on both sides. Season with salt and pepper. Arrange chicken over asparagus. In a bowl, mix soup, mayonnaise, lemon juice and curry powder; pour over chicken. Cover and bake at 375° for 40 minutes or until the chicken is tender and juices run clear. Sprinkle with cheese. Let stand for 5 minutes before serving. **Yield:** 4 servings.

Inside-Out Ravioli

With 10 children, I know the challenge of finding a recipe everyone will eat. But the whole family loves this spinach pasta.
—Ethel Allbritton
Poplar Bluff, Missouri

    1 pound ground beef
    1 medium onion, chopped
    1 teaspoon salt
  1/8 teaspoon pepper
  1/8 teaspoon garlic powder
    1 jar (14 ounces) spaghetti sauce
    1 can (8 ounces) tomato sauce
    1 can (6 ounces) tomato paste
    1 can (4 ounces) mushrooms, drained
    1 package (10 ounces) frozen chopped
      spinach, thawed and well drained
    1 package (16 ounces) corkscrew noodles,
      cooked and drained
    2 eggs, beaten
  1/2 cup soft bread crumbs
    2 cups (8 ounces) shredded cheddar cheese
1-1/2 cups (6 ounces) shredded mozzarella
      cheese

In a large skillet, cook beef with onion, salt, pepper and garlic powder until the onion is tender; drain. Stir in spaghetti sauce, tomato sauce, tomato paste and mushrooms; simmer 10 minutes. Combine the spinach, noodles, eggs, bread crumbs and cheddar cheese; place half in a greased 13-in. x 9-in. x 2-in. baking dish. Top with half of the meat sauce. Repeat layers. Cover and bake at 350° for 40-45 minutes or until hot and bubbly. Sprinkle with mozzarella cheese; let stand for 10 minutes before serving. **Yield:** 8-10 servings.

🍴 🍴 🍴

Curried Lamb and Barley

Fresh and deliciously different, this main dish from the National Barley Foods Council can be made ahead and then baked before serving. Crisp cucumber and hints of lemon, mint and garlic in the sauce complement this recipe's appealing blend.

    1 pound ground lamb
    1 large onion, chopped
    1 cup pearl barley
  1/2 cup sliced celery
    1 tablespoon vegetable oil
    3 cups chicken broth
    1 to 2 tablespoons curry powder
CUCUMBER SALSA:
1-1/2 cups coarsely chopped seeded cucumber
  1/2 cup plain yogurt
  1/4 cup snipped fresh parsley

1 tablespoon chopped green onion
1 tablespoon snipped fresh mint
2 teaspoons lemon juice
2 teaspoons olive *or* vegetable oil
1 garlic clove, minced

In a skillet, saute lamb, onion, barley and celery in oil until lamb is browned and barley is golden. Add broth and curry powder; bring to a boil. Pour into a 2-qt. baking dish. Bake, uncovered, at 350° for 1-1/4 to 1-1/2 hours or until barley is tender. In a small bowl, combine the salsa ingredients. Cover and refrigerate for 1 hour. Serve with the lamb. **Yield:** 4-6 servings.

Roast Prime Rib

When I first prepared this roast for a family reunion, "scrumptious" was the word used most to describe it. This roast is an easy yet elegant entree that turns out moist and tender every time. —Wendell Obermeier Charles City, Iowa

1 tablespoon ground mustard
1-1/2 teaspoons salt
1/2 teaspoon paprika
1/4 teaspoon ground allspice
1/4 teaspoon pepper
1 prime rib roast (4 to 5 pounds), rolled and tied
1 small onion, cut into thin slivers
2 garlic cloves, cut into slivers
Fresh parsley sprigs

In a small bowl, combine mustard, salt, paprika, allspice and pepper; set aside. Using a sharp knife, cut long deep slits in the top of the roast, approximately 1 in. apart. Stuff each slit with onion, garlic, parsley and a small amount of the spice mixture. Rub remaining spice mixture on the outside of the roast. Place on a rack in a deep roasting pan. Bake, uncovered, at 325° for 2 to 2-1/2 hours or until a meat thermometer reads 160°. **Yield:** 8-10 servings.

Herbed Pork and Apples

(Pictured above right)

Whenever I make this dish for friends and family, I'm reminded of the wonderful scent of the Maine orchards where we picked our own apples every fall until we moved to Missouri a few years ago. The aroma of the pork and apples certainly takes the chill out of crisp autumn air. My family devours every delicious bite. —Louise Keithley, Columbia, Missouri

1 teaspoon *each* dried sage, thyme, rosemary and marjoram, crushed
1 teaspoon salt
1 teaspoon pepper
1 pork loin roast with bone (about 6 pounds)
4 medium tart apples, cut into 1-inch chunks
1 large red onion, cut into 1-inch chunks
3 tablespoons brown sugar
1 cup apple juice
2/3 cup maple syrup

Combine herbs, salt and pepper; rub over roast. Cover and refrigerate for several hours or overnight. Bake, uncovered, at 325° for 1-1/2 hours. Drain fat. Mix apples and onion with brown sugar; spoon around roast. Continue to roast 1 hour or until a meat thermometer reads 160°-170°. Transfer the roast, apples and onion to a serving platter and keep warm. Skim excess fat from meat juices; pour into a heavy skillet (or leave in the roasting pan if it can be heated on stovetop). Add apple juice and syrup. Cook and stir over medium-high heat until liquid has been reduced by half, about 1 cup. Slice roast and serve with gravy. **Yield:** about 12 servings.

Teriyaki Shish Kabobs
(Pictured above and on front cover)

My father worked for an airline in the 1960s, when I was a teenager, and my family lived on the island of Guam in the South Pacific. A friend of Mother's there gave her this wonderful recipe. We ate this delicious warm-weather dish often, and now I prepare it for my family. —Suzanne Pelegrin, Ocala, Florida

- 1/2 cup ketchup
- 1/2 cup sugar
- 1/2 cup soy sauce
- 1 teaspoon garlic powder
- 1 teaspoon ground ginger
- 2 pounds boneless beef sirloin steak (1-1/2 inches thick), cut into 1-1/2-inch cubes
- 1/2 fresh pineapple, trimmed and cut into 1-inch chunks
- 2 to 3 small zucchini, cut into 1-inch chunks
- 1/2 pound whole fresh mushrooms (medium size work best)
- 1/2 pound boiling onions, peeled
- 1 large green *or* sweet red pepper, cut into 1-inch pieces

Combine the first five ingredients; toss with beef. Cover and refrigerate overnight. Drain beef, reserving marinade. Thread meat, pineapple and vegetables alternately on long skewers. Grill over hot heat for 15-20 minutes, turning often, or until meat reaches desired doneness and vegetables are tender. Simmer the marinade in a small saucepan over low heat for 15 minutes. Remove meat and vegetables from skewers; serve with marinade. **Yield:** 6-8 servings.

Heavenly Crab Cakes

Every bite of these specially seasoned crab cakes is a piece of paradise. Whenever I crave seafood, this is the dish I prepare. —Laura Letobar, Livonia, Michigan

✓ Uses less fat, sugar or salt. Includes Nutritional Analysis and Diabetic Exchanges.

- 1 pound imitation crabmeat, flaked
- 1 cup Italian bread crumbs, *divided*
- Egg substitute equivalent to 1 egg
- 2 tablespoons fat-free mayonnaise
- 2 tablespoons Dijon mustard
- 1 tablespoon dill weed
- 1 tablespoon lime juice
- 1 teaspoon lemon juice
- 1 teaspoon Worcestershire sauce

Combine crabmeat, 1/2 cup of the bread crumbs, egg substitute, mayonnaise, mustard, dill, lime and lemon juices and Worcestershire sauce. Shape into eight patties. Place remaining bread crumbs in a shallow bowl; dip each patty into crumbs to cover. Refrigerate for 30 minutes. In a large skillet coated with nonstick cooking spray, cook patties over medium heat until browned on both sides. **Yield:** 8 servings. **Nutritional Analysis:** One serving equals 133 calories, 725 mg sodium, 12 mg cholesterol, 18 gm carbohydrate, 11 gm protein, 2 gm fat. **Diabetic Exchanges:** 1 lean meat, 1 starch.

Scalloped Potatoes and Pork Chops

I truly enjoy trying new recipes and baking hearty casseroles like this one for my family. This dish is easy to prepare, and baking the chops with the potatoes gives the whole meal great flavor.
—*Susan Chavez, Vancouver, Washington*

    5 cups thinly sliced peeled potatoes
    1 cup chopped onion
Salt and pepper to taste
    1 can (10-3/4 ounces) condensed cream of
       mushroom soup, undiluted
 1/2 cup sour cream
    6 pork loin chops (1 inch thick)
Chopped fresh parsley

In a greased 13-in. x 9-in. x 2-in. baking dish, layer half of the potatoes and onion; sprinkle with salt and pepper. Repeat layers. Combine the soup and sour cream; pour over potato mixture. Cover and bake at 375° for 30 minutes. Meanwhile, in a skillet, brown pork chops on both sides. Place chops over potatoes. Cover and return to the oven for 45 minutes or until chops are tender, uncovering during the last 15 minutes of baking. Sprinkle with parsley. **Yield:** 6 servings.

———— 🥄 🥄 🥄 ————

Zesty Grilled Ham

(Pictured on page 60)

This is my children's first choice of ham dishes. The mixture of sweet and tangy flavors is mouth-watering on a grilled piece of ham. Even the small ones eat adult-sized portions! —*Mary Ann Lien, Tyler, Texas*

    1 cup packed brown sugar
 1/3 cup prepared horseradish
 1/4 cup lemon juice
    1 fully cooked ham steak (1 to 1-1/2 pounds
       and 1 inch thick)

In a small saucepan, bring brown sugar, horseradish and lemon juice to a boil. Brush over both sides of ham. Grill over medium-hot heat, turning once, until heated through and well glazed, about 20-25 minutes. **Yield:** 4 servings.

———— 🥄 🥄 🥄 ————

Spaghetti Squash Casserole

(Pictured at right)

Spaghetti squash, like zucchini, can take over a garden. This is an excellent way to put that abundance to good use. I got the original recipe at a cooking class, and I've made it many times since. —*Myna Dyck Boissevain, Manitoba*

    1 small spaghetti squash (1-1/2 to 2 pounds)
 1/2 cup water
    1 pound ground beef
 1/2 cup chopped onion
 1/2 cup chopped sweet red pepper
    1 garlic clove, minced
    1 can (14-1/2 ounces) diced tomatoes,
       undrained
 1/2 teaspoon dried oregano
 1/4 teaspoon salt
 1/8 teaspoon pepper
    1 cup (4 ounces) shredded mozzarella *or*
       cheddar cheese
    1 tablespoon chopped fresh parsley

Cut squash in half lengthwise; scoop out seeds. Place with cut side down in a baking dish; add water. Cover and bake at 375° for 20-30 minutes or until it is easily pierced with a fork. When cool enough to handle, scoop out squash, separating the strands with a fork; set aside. In a skillet over medium heat, cook beef, onion, red pepper and garlic until meat is no longer pink and vegetables are tender; drain. Add tomatoes, oregano, salt, pepper and squash. Cook and stir for 2 minutes or until most of the liquid is absorbed. Transfer to an ungreased 1-1/2-qt. baking dish. Bake, uncovered, at 350° for 25 minutes. Sprinkle with the cheese and parsley; let stand a few minutes. **Yield:** 6-8 servings.

Tuna Mushroom Casserole

(Pictured below)

I love to serve this dressed-up version of a tuna casserole. The green beans add nice texture, color and flavor. The first time I made this dish, my uncle asked for seconds even though tuna casseroles are not usually his favorite. —Jone Furlong, Santa Rosa, California

      1/2 cup water
        1 teaspoon chicken bouillon granules
        1 package (10 ounces) frozen green beans
        1 cup chopped onion
        1 cup sliced fresh mushrooms
      1/4 cup chopped celery
        1 garlic clove, minced
      1/2 teaspoon dill weed
      1/2 teaspoon salt
      1/8 teaspoon pepper
        4 teaspoons cornstarch
   1-1/2 cups milk
      1/2 cup shredded Swiss cheese
      1/4 cup mayonnaise
   2-1/2 cups medium noodles, cooked and
             drained
        1 can (12-1/4 ounces) tuna, drained and
             flaked
      1/3 cup dry bread crumbs
        1 tablespoon butter *or* margarine

In a large saucepan, bring water and bouillon to a boil, stirring to dissolve. Add the next eight ingredients; bring to a boil. Reduce heat; cover and simmer 5 minutes or until vegetables are tender. Dissolve cornstarch in milk; add to vegetable mixture, stirring constantly. Bring to a boil; boil 2 minutes or until thickened. Remove from the heat; stir in cheese and mayonnaise until cheese is melted. Fold in noodles and tuna. Pour into a greased 2-1/2-qt. baking dish. Brown bread crumbs in butter; sprinkle on top of casserole. Bake, uncovered, at 350° for 25-30 minutes or until heated through. **Yield:** 4-6 servings.

Potluck Special

I often take this hearty meal-in-a-dish to potluck suppers. It's delicious for sauerkraut lovers and easy to double for a larger crowd. —Reta Christensen, New Denmark, New Brunswick

        1 pound ground beef
        1 medium onion, chopped
        1 can (28 ounces) diced tomatoes,
             undrained
        1 can (16 ounces) sauerkraut, rinsed and
             drained
   1-1/2 cups cooked rice
        1 medium green pepper, chopped

In a skillet, brown the ground beef and onion; drain. Add remaining ingredients; transfer to a 2-qt. baking dish. Cover and bake at 350° for 1 hour. **Yield:** 6-8 servings.

Sage Pot Roast

Sage really adds enhances the flavor of beef in this pot roast. —Naomi Giddis, Grawn, Michigan

✓ Uses less fat, sugar or salt. Includes Nutritional Analysis and Diabetic Exchanges.

        1 lean boneless beef chuck roast (about 5
             pounds)
        1 tablespoon vegetable oil
        1 to 2 teaspoons rubbed dried sage
      1/2 teaspoon salt, optional
      1/4 teaspoon pepper
        1 cup beef broth
        6 medium red potatoes (about 2 pounds),
             cut in half
        3 to 4 carrots, cut into 2-inch pieces
        2 medium onions, quartered
        5 teaspoons cornstarch
      1/4 cup water

In a Dutch oven, brown roast on both sides in oil. Season with sage, salt and pepper. Add beef broth. Cover and bake at 325° for 2-1/2 hours. Add potatoes, carrots and onions. Cover and bake 1 hour longer or until the meat is tender and vegetables are cooked. Remove roast and vegetables to a serving platter and keep warm. Combine cornstarch and water; stir into pan juices. Cook until thickened and bubbly. Serve with the roast. **Yield:** 20 servings. **Nutritional Analysis:** One serving (prepared with low-sodium beef broth and without added salt) equals 342 calories, 77 mg sodium, 78 mg cholesterol, 11 gm carbohydrate, 23 gm protein, 23 gm fat. **Diabetic Exchanges:** 3 meat, 2-1/2 fat, 1/2 vegetable.

Turkey Stir-Fry

(Pictured at right)

Here's a tasty way to prepare turkey anytime of year. My family loves the tender turkey strips, colorful vegetables and crunchy cashews. You don't have to fix the whole bird to enjoy the wonderful taste of turkey.
—Julianne Johnson, Grove City, Minnesota

✓ Uses less fat, sugar or salt. Includes Nutritional Analysis and Diabetic Exchanges.

1-1/2 pounds uncooked boneless turkey, cut into strips
1 tablespoon vegetable oil
1 small onion, chopped
1 carrot, julienned
1/2 medium green pepper, sliced
2 cups fresh mushrooms, sliced
1 cup chicken broth
3 tablespoons cornstarch
3 tablespoons soy sauce
1/2 teaspoon ground ginger
2 cups pea pods, trimmed
Cooked rice, optional
1/3 cup cashews, optional

In a large skillet or wok, stir-fry turkey in oil over medium-high heat until no longer pink, about 5-6 minutes. Remove turkey and keep warm. Stir-fry the onion, carrot, green pepper and mushrooms until crisp-tender, about 5 minutes. In a small bowl, combine chicken broth, cornstarch, soy sauce and ginger. Add to the skillet; cook and stir until thickened and bubbly. Return turkey to skillet with pea pods; cook and stir until heated through. If desired, serve over rice and top with cashews. **Yield:** 6 servings. **Nutritional Analysis:** One serving (prepared with low-sodium chicken broth and light soy sauce, and served without rice or cash-

ews) equals 277 calories, 546 mg sodium, 74 mg cholesterol, 17 gm carbohydrate, 28 gm protein, 11 gm fat. **Diabetic Exchanges:** 3-1/2 lean meat, 1 vegetable, 1 fat, 1/2 starch.

Thyme-Lime Chicken

This recipe cleverly combines thyme and lime juice in a fresh-tasting basting sauce. You can also grill the chicken when weather permits. —Marge Clark West Lebanon, Indiana

2 tablespoons butter _or_ margarine
2 tablespoons olive _or_ vegetable oil
2 tablespoons fresh lime juice
1 tablespoon minced fresh thyme _or_ 1 teaspoon dried thyme
1 teaspoon grated lime peel
1 garlic clove, minced
1/2 teaspoon salt
1/4 teaspoon pepper
4 chicken breast halves
4 chicken thighs

In a small saucepan over low heat, melt butter in oil; add lime juice, thyme, lime peel, garlic, salt and pepper. Place chicken on a greased broiler pan. Brush with sauce. Broil, basting frequently, 6-7 in. from the heat for 15-20 minutes on each side or until the chicken juices run clear. **Yield:** 4-6 servings.

In a large bowl, combine milk and oats; let stand for 5 minutes. Stir in egg, oil and molasses. Combine dry ingredients; stir into oat mixture just until moistened. Beat egg whites until soft peaks form; fold gently into batter. Set aside. Heat butter in a skillet until foamy. Add apples, lemon juice and peel; cook, uncovered, for 8-10 minutes, stirring occasionally. Meanwhile, cook oatcakes: Pour batter by 1/4 cupfuls onto a hot greased griddle. Cook until bubbles form; turn and cook until browned on other side. For apples, combine sugar, cornstarch and nutmeg; add to apple mixture and cook 2 minutes longer or until tender. Serve warm over oatcakes. **Yield:** 6-8 servings.

A Little Lemon Juice

Need just a small amount of lemon juice? Pierce a fresh lemon with a toothpick and squeeze out the amount of juice needed. Put the toothpick back in the hole and store the lemon in the refrigerator.

Apple-Topped Oatcakes

(Pictured above)

During the week we have quick breakfasts...but on Saturday I like to make something special. This is one of our favorite recipes because the oatcakes and apple topping are a tasty, wholesome combination. They also can be made ahead so a hungry family doesn't have to wait long. —Lois Hofmeyer, Aurora, Illinois

1-1/2 cups hot milk
   3/4 cup old-fashioned oats
     1 egg, beaten
     2 tablespoons vegetable oil
     2 tablespoons molasses
     1 cup all-purpose flour
1-1/2 teaspoons baking powder
   3/4 teaspoon ground cinnamon
   1/4 teaspoon ground ginger
   1/4 teaspoon baking soda
   1/4 teaspoon salt
     3 egg whites
LEMON APPLES:
     2 tablespoons butter *or* margarine
     5 medium tart apples, peeled and sliced
     1 tablespoon lemon juice
     1 teaspoon grated lemon peel
   1/2 cup sugar
     1 tablespoon cornstarch
   1/8 teaspoon ground nutmeg

Shipwreck

I'm not sure of the origin of this recipe's name. But we ate this inexpensive meal frequently while I was growing up. —Cary Letsche, Bradenton, Florida

1/2 pound sliced bacon
  1 pound ground beef
  1 large onion, chopped
  1 cup ketchup
1/2 cup packed brown sugar
  1 can (32 ounces) pork and beans

In a skillet, cook bacon until crisp. Remove to paper towels to drain; crumble and set aside. Drain drippings from skillet. Brown the beef; drain. Add onion and cook until tender, about 5 minutes. Combine ketchup and brown sugar; stir into beef mixture. Stir in pork and beans and all but 2 tablespoons of the bacon. Transfer to an 8-in. square baking dish. Top with the remaining bacon. Bake, uncovered, at 350° for 1 hour. **Yield:** 6-8 servings.

Barbecued Trout

This delicious recipe came from a friend here in Mountain Home. The sauce really gives the fish a wonderful flavor.
—Vivian Wolfram
Mountain Home, Arkansas

  6 pan-dressed trout
2/3 cup soy sauce
1/2 cup ketchup

2 tablespoons lemon juice
2 tablespoons vegetable oil
1 teaspoon crushed dried rosemary
Lemon wedges, optional

Place the trout in a single layer in a plastic bag or glass baking dish. Combine the soy sauce, ketchup, lemon juice, oil and rosemary; pour into bag or dish. Cover (or close bag) and refrigerate for 1 hour, turning once. Remove fish and reserve marinade. Place fish in a single layer in a well-greased hinged wire grill basket. Grill, covered, over medium coals for 8-10 minutes or until fish is browned on the bottom. Turn and baste with reserved marinade; grill 5-7 minutes longer or until fish flakes easily with a fork. Serve with lemon if desired. **Yield:** 6 servings.

Dilly Barbecued Turkey

(Pictured on page 60)

This is one of my brother-in-law's special cookout recipes. The onions, garlic and herbs in the marinade make a tasty, tender turkey, and the tempting aroma prompts the family to gather around the grill.
—Sue Walker, Greentown, Indiana

✓ Uses less fat, sugar or salt. Includes Nutritional Analysis and Diabetic Exchanges.

1 turkey breast half with bone (2-1/2 pounds)
1 cup plain yogurt
1/4 cup lemon juice
3 tablespoons vegetable oil
1/4 cup minced fresh parsley
1/4 cup chopped green onions
2 garlic cloves, minced
2 tablespoons fresh minced dill *or* 2 teaspoons dill weed
1/2 teaspoon dried rosemary, crushed
1/2 teaspoon salt, optional
1/4 teaspoon pepper

Place turkey breast in a glass baking dish. In a small bowl, combine all remaining ingredients. Spread the marinade over the turkey. Cover and refrigerate for 6-8 hours or overnight. Remove turkey and discard marinade. Grill turkey, covered, over medium-hot heat for 1 to 1-1/4 hours or until juices run clear and a meat thermometer reads 170°. **Yield:** 6 servings. **Nutritional Analysis:** One serving (prepared with nonfat yogurt and without added salt) equals 266 calories, 103 mg sodium, 74 mg cholesterol, 5 gm carbohydrate, 28 gm protein, 15 gm fat. **Diabetic Exchanges:** 3-1/2 lean meat, 2 fat.

Spanish Rice and Chicken

(Pictured below)

My mother has always been an avid cook, and my sister, two brothers and I were raised on this casserole. When I poll our family to see what meal I should make, this fresh-tasting, well-seasoned chicken casserole comes out on the top of the list. I know you'll enjoy it as much as we do.
—Cindy Clark
Mechanicsburg, Pennsylvania

1 broiler/fryer chicken (2-1/2 to 3 pounds), cut up
1 teaspoon garlic salt
1 teaspoon celery salt
1 teaspoon paprika
1 cup uncooked rice
3/4 cup chopped onion
3/4 cup chopped green pepper
1/4 cup minced fresh parsley
1-1/2 cups chicken broth
1 cup chopped tomatoes
1-1/2 teaspoons salt
1-1/2 teaspoons chili powder

Place chicken in a greased 13-in. x 9-in. x 2-in. baking pan. Combine garlic salt, celery salt and paprika; sprinkle over chicken. Bake, uncovered, at 425° for 20 minutes. Remove chicken from pan. Combine rice, onion, green pepper and parsley; spoon into the pan. In a saucepan, bring broth, tomatoes, salt and chili powder to a boil. Pour over rice mixture; mix well. Place chicken pieces on top. Cover and bake for 45 minutes or until chicken and rice are tender. **Yield:** 4-6 servings.

Cordon Bleu Casserole

(Pictured below)

Whenever I'm invited to attend a potluck, people usually ask me to bring this tempting casserole. The turkey, ham and cheese are delectable combined with the crunchy topping.
—Joyce Paul
Moose Jaw, Saskatchewan

4 cups cubed cooked turkey
3 cups cubed fully cooked ham
1 cup (4 ounces) shredded cheddar cheese
1 cup chopped onion
1/4 cup butter *or* margarine
1/3 cup all-purpose flour
2 cups half-and-half cream
1 teaspoon dill weed
1/8 teaspoon ground mustard
1/8 teaspoon ground nutmeg
TOPPING:
1 cup dry bread crumbs
2 tablespoons butter *or* margarine, melted
1/4 teaspoon dill weed
1/4 cup shredded cheddar cheese
1/4 cup chopped walnuts

In a large bowl, combine turkey, ham and cheese; set aside. In a saucepan, saute onion in butter until tender. Add flour; stir to form a paste. Gradually add cream, stirring constantly. Bring to a boil; boil 1 minute or until thick. Add dill, mustard and nutmeg; mix well. Remove from the heat and pour over meat mixture. Spoon into a greased 13-in. x 9-in. x 2-in. baking dish. Toss bread crumbs, butter and dill; stir in cheese and walnuts. Sprinkle over the casserole. Bake, uncovered, at 350° for 30 minutes or until heated through. **Yield:** 8-10 servings.

— 🍷 🍷 🍷 —

Spaghetti Chop

This is a delicious dish perfect for those who are watching their budget. Plus, it's quick and easy.
—Cary Letsche, Bradenton, Florida

2 pounds ground beef
1 large onion, chopped
1/2 teaspoon onion salt
1/2 teaspoon seasoned salt
8 ounces spaghetti, broken into 4-inch pieces
2 cans (10-3/4 ounces *each*) condensed tomato soup, undiluted
1 cup ketchup

In a skillet, brown ground beef; drain. Add onion, onion salt and seasoned salt; cook until onion is tender, about 5 minutes. Remove from the heat. In a large saucepan, cook spaghetti according to package directions; drain and return to pan. Add beef mixture, soup and ketchup; mix well. Simmer for 5-10 minutes. **Yield:** 6-8 servings.

— 🍷 🍷 🍷 —

Chicken with Mushroom Sauce

Chicken is my meat of choice. Besides barbecued chicken, this flavorful dish is one of my most tried-and-true recipes. —Philip Stent, Houston, Texas

1/2 pound fresh mushrooms, thinly sliced
1/2 cup butter *or* margarine
1/2 cup all-purpose flour
1/4 teaspoon ground nutmeg
Salt and pepper to taste
8 skinless boneless chicken breast halves
1/3 cup chicken broth *or* port wine
1-1/2 cups whipping cream
Minced fresh parsley, optional
Paprika, optional

In a skillet, saute mushrooms in butter until tender. With a slotted spoon, remove mushrooms and set aside. Reserve butter in the skillet. Combine flour, nutmeg, salt and pepper; coat chicken pieces and shake off excess. Brown chicken in skillet over medium heat. Add mushrooms. Add broth or wine to the remaining flour mixture; stir until smooth. Fold in cream. Pour over the chicken and mush-

rooms; bring to a boil. Reduce heat; cover and simmer for 20-25 minutes or until chicken is no longer pink. Garnish with parsley and paprika if desired. **Yield:** 8 servings.

— 🎺 🎺 🎺 —

Stuffed Sole

(Pictured above)

Seafood was a staple for my large family when I was growing up. Inspired by my mother's delicious meals, I developed this recipe. The fish is moist and flavorful, and the sauce is so good over rice. As I do when serving this dish, you'll get many compliments.
—*Winnie Higgins, Salisbury, Maryland*

- **1 cup chopped onion**
- **2 cans (4-1/4 ounces *each*) shrimp, rinsed and drained**
- **1 jar (4-1/2 ounces) sliced mushrooms, drained**
- **2 tablespoons butter *or* margarine**
- **1/2 pound fresh cooked *or* canned crabmeat, drained and cartilage removed**
- **8 sole *or* flounder fillets (2 to 2-1/2 pounds)**
- **1/2 teaspoon salt**
- **1/4 teaspoon pepper**
- **1/4 teaspoon paprika**
- **2 cans (10-3/4 ounces *each*) condensed cream of mushroom soup, undiluted**
- **1/3 cup chicken broth**
- **2 tablespoons water**
- **2/3 cup shredded cheddar cheese**
- **2 tablespoons minced fresh parsley**

Cooked wild, brown *or* white rice or a mixture, optional

In a saucepan, saute onion, shrimp and mushrooms in butter until onion is tender. Add crabmeat; heat through. Sprinkle fillets with salt, pepper and paprika. Spoon crabmeat mixture on fillets; roll up and fasten with a toothpick. Place in a greased 13-in. x 9-in. x 2-in. baking dish. Combine the soup, broth and water; blend until smooth. Pour over fillets. Sprinkle with cheese. Cover and bake at 400° for 30 minutes. Sprinkle with parsley; return to the oven, uncovered, for 5 minutes or until the fish flakes easily with a fork. Serve over rice if desired. **Yield:** 8 servings.

One serving equals 260 calories, 170 mg sodium, 76 mg cholesterol, 2 gm carbohydrate, 31 gm protein, 13 gm fat. **Diabetic Exchanges:** 3-1/2 lean meat, 1-1/2 fat.

Tangy Meatballs

This recipe originally came from my mother-in-law, then I made a few adjustments. These tender meatballs make a great entree. —*Ralph Wheat, Bedford, Texas*

    3 slices white bread, torn into small pieces
    1 cup milk
2-1/2 pounds ground beef
  1/2 pound bulk pork sausage
    1 medium onion, finely chopped
    1 tablespoon mustard seed
    2 teaspoons seasoned salt
    2 garlic cloves, minced
    1 egg, beaten
Salt and pepper to taste
    3 tablespoons vegetable oil
    2 bottles (10 ounces *each*) chili sauce
    1 jar (8 ounces) grape jelly
1-1/2 cups beef broth

In a large bowl, combine bread and milk. Squeeze excess milk out of bread; discard milk. To the bread, add beef, sausage, onion, mustard seed, seasoned salt, garlic, egg, salt and pepper; shape into 1-1/2-in. balls. In a large skillet, brown meatballs in oil; drain. In a large saucepan or Dutch oven, combine chili sauce, jelly and beef broth; slowly bring to a boil. Add meatballs; simmer for 30-45 minutes. **Yield:** 10 servings.

Quick Meatballs

Instead of taking the time to make meatballs, make "meat squares". Spread your meat mixture in a jelly roll pan and bake, then simply cut the meat into small squares.

Cranberry Pork Roast

Guests rave about this tender roast, and I love preparing it because it's so simple. The gravy is delicious over creamy mashed potatoes. —*Audrey Thibodeau Mesa, Arizona*

    1 boneless rolled pork loin roast (2-1/2 to 3 pounds)
    1 can (16 ounces) jellied cranberry sauce
  1/2 cup sugar
  1/2 cup cranberry juice

Marinated Flank Steak

(Pictured above)

I copied this recipe from a friend's collection years ago. Since then I've gotten married and had two children. Now whenever we make steak on the grill, this is the recipe we usually use. It's also a tempting dish to serve when entertaining. It's earned me many compliments. —*Debbie Bonczek, Tariffville, Connecticut*

☑ Uses less fat, sugar or salt. Includes Nutritional Analysis and Diabetic Exchanges.

    1 beef flank steak (about 2 pounds)
    3 tablespoons ketchup
    1 tablespoon vegetable oil
    1 tablespoon chopped onion
    1 teaspoon brown sugar
    1 teaspoon Worcestershire sauce
    1 garlic clove, minced
  1/8 teaspoon pepper

Place flank steak in an 11-in. x 7-in. x 2-in. glass dish. Combine remaining ingredients; pour over meat. Cover and refrigerate for at least 4 hours. Remove meat, discarding marinade. Grill over hot heat until meat reaches desired doneness (about 4 minutes per side for medium, 5 minutes per side for medium-well). Slice into thin strips across the grain to serve. **Yield:** 8 servings. **Nutritional Analysis:**

1 teaspoon ground mustard
1/4 teaspoon ground cloves
2 tablespoons cornstarch
2 tablespoons cold water
Salt to taste

Place pork roast in a slow cooker. In a medium bowl, mash cranberry sauce; stir in sugar, cranberry juice, mustard and cloves. Pour over roast. Cover and cook on low for 6-8 hours or until meat is tender. Remove roast and keep warm. Skim fat from juices; measure 2 cups, adding water if necessary, and pour into a saucepan. Bring to a boil over medium-high heat. Combine the cornstarch and cold water to make a paste; stir into gravy. Cook and stir until thickened. Season with salt. Serve with sliced pork. **Yield:** 4-6 servings.

— 🍷 🍷 🍷 —

Pan Burritos

Our family loves Mexican food, so this flavorful, satisfying casserole is a favorite. It's nice to have a way to get the taste of burritos and be able to cut servings any size you want.
—*Joyce Kent*
Grand Rapids, Michigan

2 packages (1-1/2 ounces *each*) enchilada sauce mix
3 cups water
1 can (12 ounces) tomato paste
1 garlic clove, minced
1/4 teaspoon pepper
Salt to taste
2 pounds ground beef
9 large flour tortillas (9-inch)
4 cups (16 ounces) shredded cheddar cheese *or* taco cheese
1 can (16 ounces) refried beans, warmed
Taco sauce, sour cream, chili peppers, chopped onion *and/or* guacamole, optional

In a saucepan, combine the first six ingredients; simmer for 15-20 minutes. In a skillet, brown the beef. Drain; stir in one-third of the sauce. Spread another third on the bottom of a greased 13-in. x 9-in. x 2-in. baking pan. Place three tortillas over sauce, tearing to fit bottom of pan. Spoon half of meat mixture over tortillas; sprinkle with 1-1/2 cups cheese. Add three more tortillas. Spread refried beans over tortillas; top with remaining meat. Sprinkle with 1-1/2 cups of cheese. Layer remaining tortillas; top with the remaining sauce. Sprinkle with remaining cheese. Bake, uncovered, at 350° for 35-40 minutes. Let stand 10 minutes before cutting. Serve with taco sauce, sour cream, chili peppers, chopped onion and/or guacamole if desired. **Yield:** 8-10 servings.

Sheepherder's Breakfast

(Pictured below)

My sister-in-law always made this delicious breakfast dish when we were camping. Served with toast, juice and milk or coffee, it's a sure hit with the breakfast crowd! One-dish casseroles like this were a big help while I was raising my nine children...now I've passed this recipe on to them.
—*Pauletta Bushnell*
Albany, Oregon

1 pound sliced bacon, diced
1 medium onion, chopped
32 ounces frozen shredded hash brown potatoes, thawed
7 eggs
Salt and pepper to taste
2 cups (8 ounces) shredded cheddar cheese, optional
Chopped fresh parsley

In a large skillet, cook bacon and onion until bacon is crisp. Drain all but 1/2 cup of the drippings. Add hash browns to skillet; mix well. Cook over medium heat for 10 minutes, turning when browned. Make 7 "wells" evenly spaced in the hash browns. Place one egg in each well. Sprinkle with salt and pepper. Sprinkle with cheese if desired. Cover and cook over low heat for about 10 minutes or until eggs are set. Garnish with parsley; serve immediately. **Yield:** 7 servings.

Streamlined Beef Classics

GREAT-TASTING beef dishes—shared by the National Cattlemen's Beef Association—are perfect for everyday meals or entertaining.

An old-fashioned favorite like Pot Roast with Vegetables uses an economical cut of beef that's simmered to fork-tenderness. With its festive look and zesty taste, Cheesy Spinach-Stuffed Meat Loaf is great for entertaining. And Updated Beef Stroganoff can fit into just about any dietary plan.

— 🝙 🝙 🝙 —

Pot Roast with Vegetables

(Pictured below)

✓ Uses less fat, sugar or salt. Includes Nutritional Analysis and Diabetic Exchanges.

   1 garlic clove, crushed
   1 teaspoon dried oregano
1/2 teaspoon lemon-pepper seasoning
   1 boneless beef chuck pot roast (3 pounds)
   1 tablespoon vegetable oil
3/4 cup water
   4 medium carrots, cut into 2-1/2-inch pieces
 16 small new potatoes, halved

   4 medium parsnips, cut into 2-1/2-inch pieces
   2 small leeks, cut into 1-1/2-inch pieces
   2 teaspoons cornstarch
   1 tablespoon cold water

Combine garlic, oregano and lemon pepper; rub over roast. In a Dutch oven, brown the roast in oil; drain. Add water; bring to a boil. Reduce heat; cover and simmer for 1-3/4 hours. Add vegetables; cover and simmer for 30 minutes or until beef and vegetables are tender. Remove to a serving platter and keep warm. Strain cooking liquid; skim fat. Return 1 cup liquid to pan; bring to a boil over medium-high heat. Dissolve cornstarch in cold water; add to pan. Cook and stir for 1 minute or until gravy is thickened and bubbly. Serve with roast and vegetables. **Yield:** 8 servings. **Nutritional Analysis:** One serving equals 287 calories, 48 mg sodium, 64 mg cholesterol, 28 gm carbohydrate, 27 gm protein, 7 gm fat. **Diabetic Exchanges:** 3 lean meat, 1-1/2 starch, 1 vegetable.

— 🝙 🝙 🝙 —

Cheesy Spinach-Stuffed Meat Loaf

✓ Uses less fat, sugar or salt. Includes Nutritional Analysis and Diabetic Exchanges.

3/4 cup soft bread crumbs
Egg substitute equivalent to 1 egg
   1 teaspoon salt
1/8 teaspoon pepper
1-1/2 pounds ground round
FILLING:
   1 package (10 ounces) frozen chopped spinach, thawed and well drained
1/2 cup shredded low-fat mozzarella cheese
   3 tablespoons grated Parmesan cheese
   1 teaspoon Italian seasoning
1/8 teaspoon garlic powder
TOPPING:
   3 tablespoons ketchup
1/4 cup shredded low-fat mozzarella cheese

In a large bowl, combine bread crumbs, egg substitute, salt and pepper. Add beef; mix well. On waxed paper, pat into a 14-in. x 10-in. rectangle. In a medium bowl, combine filling ingredients; mix well. Spread over rectangle, leaving 3/4 in. around edges. Starting at short end, roll up jelly-roll style. Press meat mixture over filling at both ends to seal. Place loaf, seam side down, on a rack in a roasting pan. Bake, uncovered, at 350° for 1 hour.

Spread ketchup on top; return to the oven for 15 minutes or until a meat thermometer reads 160°. Sprinkle with cheese; let stand a few minutes. Cut into 1-in.-thick slices. **Yield:** 6 servings. **Nutritional Analysis:** One serving equals 259 calories, 776 mg sodium, 39 mg cholesterol, 14 gm carbohydrate, 30 gm protein, 9 gm fat. **Diabetic Exchanges:** 3 lean meat, 1 starch, 1 vegetable.

Updated Beef Stroganoff

✓ Uses less fat, sugar or salt. Includes Nutritional Analysis and Diabetic Exchanges.

- 1-1/2 cups uncooked bow tie pasta
- 1 pound beef tenderloin tips, cut into 1-inch pieces
- 1/8 teaspoon pepper
- 1/2 pound mushrooms, sliced
- 1/3 cup coarsely chopped onion
- 2 teaspoons vegetable oil
- 1-1/2 tablespoons all-purpose flour
- 3/4 cup low-sodium beef broth
- 1 tablespoon sliced green onions
- 1/4 cup light sour cream

Cook the pasta according to package directions. Meanwhile, in a large skillet coated with nonstick cooking spray, cook and stir beef, half at a time, over medium-high heat for 1-2 minutes or until no longer pink. Season with pepper. Remove and keep warm. In the same skillet, saute mushrooms and onion in oil until tender. Stir in flour. Gradually add broth, stirring until blended. Bring to a boil; cook and stir for 2 minutes. Return beef to skillet and heat through. Drain pasta; top with beef mixture, green onions and sour cream. **Yield:** 4 servings. **Nutritional Analysis:** One serving equals 393 calories, 154 mg sodium, 87 mg cholesterol, 32 gm carbohydrate, 34 gm protein, 13 gm fat. **Diabetic Exchanges:** 4 lean meat, 1-1/2 starch, 1 vegetable.

'I Wish I Had That Recipe...'

"I HAD a wonderful meal of Jaeger Schnitzel with Spaetzle at the Essen Haus in Madison, Wisconsin," relates Lucy Peter of Janesville, Wisconsin.

According to manager Neil Hanson, "This schnitzel was originally made with venison. We use pork tenderloin instead. Spaetzle are German egg dumplings."

Essen Haus owner Bob Worm opened this ethnic dining establishment in an 1860s building that once housed German immigrants.

The restaurant—featuring Bavarian specialties like schnitzels, sauerbraten, beef rouladen and pork shanks—is decorated with antiques and beer steins.

You'll find Essen Haus not far from Wisconsin's State Capitol at 514 Wilson. Phone 1-608/255-4674.

Jaeger Schnitzel

- 1 pork tenderloin (6 to 7 ounces), trimmed
- 1 egg, lightly beaten
- 1/4 cup all-purpose flour
- 1/4 cup butter *or* margarine
- 1/2 cup sliced mushrooms
- 1/2 medium onion, thinly sliced
- 2 tablespoons white wine, optional
- 1-1/2 cups prepared brown gravy
- 2 tablespoons sour cream

Cut tenderloin in half lengthwise. Pound each half to 1/4-in. thickness. Dip into egg; coat with flour and shake off excess. In a skillet over medium heat, cook tenderloin in butter until no longer pink. Remove and keep warm. Add mushrooms and onion to skillet; cook until tender. Add wine if desired. Stir in the gravy and sour cream; mix well and heat through (do not boil). Serve with the tenderloin. **Yield:** 2 servings.

Spaetzle

- 1 cup all-purpose flour
- 1/2 teaspoon salt
- 1/2 teaspoon ground nutmeg
- Dash white pepper
- 2 eggs, lightly beaten
- 1/4 cup milk
- 4 quarts chicken broth *or* water
- 2 tablespoons butter *or* margarine
- Grated Parmesan cheese, optional

In a bowl, combine flour, salt, nutmeg and pepper. Add eggs and milk; stir to mix well (batter will be thick). In a Dutch oven or large kettle, bring chicken broth or water to a boil. Drop batter by 1/2 teaspoonfuls into boiling liquid. Boil until spaetzle rise to the surface; remove to ice water. Drain well. In a skillet, heat spaetzle in butter until lightly browned. Serve with schnitzel and gravy or with Parmesan cheese. **Yield:** 2 servings.

Mozzarella Meat Loaf

(Pictured above)

My children were not fond of meat loaf until I "dressed up" this recipe with pizza flavor. Now they're grown and have families of their own, and they make and serve this hearty, moist meat loaf. —Darlis Wilfer
Phelps, Wisconsin

> 2 eggs, lightly beaten
> 1 cup saltine cracker crumbs
> 1 cup milk
> 1/2 cup grated Parmesan cheese
> 1/2 cup chopped onion
> 1-1/2 teaspoons salt
> 1 teaspoon dried oregano
> 2 pounds lean ground beef
> 1 can (8 ounces) pizza sauce
> 3 slices mozzarella cheese, halved
> Green pepper rings and sliced mushrooms, optional
> 2 tablespoons butter *or* margarine, optional
> Fresh parsley sprigs, optional

In a bowl, combine eggs, crumbs, milk, Parmesan cheese, onion, salt and oregano. Add beef; mix well. Shape into a loaf and place in a greased 9-in. x 5-in. x 3-in. loaf pan. Bake at 350° for 1-1/4 hours or until meat is no longer pink and a meat thermometer reads 160°; drain. Spoon pizza sauce over loaf and top with mozzarella cheese slices. Return to the oven for 10 minutes or until the cheese is melted. Meanwhile, if desired, saute green pepper and mushrooms in butter; arrange on top of meat loaf. Garnish with parsley if desired. **Yield:** 8-10 servings.

— 🚩 🚩 🚩 —

Herbed Pork Roast

This recipe proves pork roasts don't have to be loaded with calories to be delicious. Even folks not on restricted diets will find it appealing. —Dianne Bettin
Truman, Minnesota

✓ Uses less fat, sugar or salt. Includes Nutritional Analysis and Diabetic Exchanges.

> 3 tablespoons finely chopped fresh parsley, *divided*
> 2 teaspoons paprika

2 teaspoons dried basil
2 teaspoons salt, optional
1 teaspoon pepper
1 teaspoon garlic powder
1 teaspoon dried oregano
1/2 teaspoon crushed fennel seed
1/2 teaspoon dried thyme
1 boneless extra-lean pork roast (about 2 pounds)

Combine half of the parsley with the herbs and seasonings. Rub over roast. Place in a shallow pan; cover with remaining parsley. Bake, uncovered, at 325° for 1 hour or until a meat thermometer reads 160°-170°. **Yield:** 6 servings. **Nutritional Analysis:** One serving (prepared without salt) equals 214 calories, 69 mg sodium, 83 mg cholesterol, trace carbohydrate, 32 gm protein, 8 gm fat. **Diabetic Exchanges:** 4 lean meat.

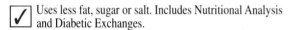

Applesauce Oatmeal Pancakes

This recipe makes light, fluffy pancakes that will have the entire family asking for seconds. They're wonderful for those on restricted diets. —Martha Cage
Wheeling, West Virginia

✓ Uses less fat, sugar or salt. Includes Nutritional Analysis and Diabetic Exchanges.

1 cup quick-cooking oats
1/4 cup whole wheat flour
1/4 cup all-purpose flour
1 tablespoon baking powder
1 cup skim milk
2 tablespoons unsweetened applesauce
4 egg whites

In a bowl, combine the oats, flours and baking powder. In another bowl, combine milk, applesauce and egg whites; add to dry ingredients and mix well. Pour batter by 1/4 cupfuls onto a heated griddle coated with nonstick cooking spray. Cook until bubbles appear on the top; turn and cook until lightly browned. **Yield:** 10 pancakes. **Nutritional Analysis:** One pancake equals 70 calories, 125 mg sodium, trace cholesterol, 12 gm carbohydrate, 5 gm protein, trace fat. **Diabetic Exchanges:** 1 starch.

Monterey Spaghetti

(Pictured at right)

I'm a working mother with two boys. Our family leads a very active life, so I make a lot of casseroles.

It's so nice to have a hearty, nutritious dish the kids will eat. Topped with cheese and french-fried onions, this tasty casserole is a hit at our house.
—Janet Hibler, Cameron, Missouri

4 ounces spaghetti, broken into 2-inch pieces
1 egg
1 cup (8 ounces) sour cream
1/4 cup grated Parmesan cheese
1/4 teaspoon garlic powder
2 cups (8 ounces) shredded Monterey Jack cheese
1 package (10 ounces) frozen chopped spinach, thawed and well drained
1 can (2.8 ounces) french-fried onions, *divided*

Cook spaghetti according to package directions. Meanwhile, in a medium bowl, beat egg. Add sour cream, Parmesan cheese and garlic powder. Drain spaghetti; add to egg mixture with Monterey Jack cheese, spinach and half of the onions. Pour into a greased 2-qt. baking dish. Cover and bake at 350° for 30 minutes or until heated through. Top with remaining onions; bake 5 minutes longer or until onions are golden brown. **Yield:** 6-8 servings.

French Banana Pancakes

(Pictured below)

These pancakes are a real breakfast favorite in our family. When they were younger, our daughters would make them all by themselves when they had friends spend the night. —Cheryl Sowers
Bakersfield, California

PANCAKES:
- 1 cup all-purpose flour
- 1/4 cup confectioners' sugar
- 1 cup milk
- 2 eggs
- 3 tablespoons butter *or* margarine, melted
- 1 teaspoon vanilla extract
- 1/4 teaspoon salt

FILLING:
- 1/4 cup butter *or* margarine
- 1/4 cup packed brown sugar
- 1/4 teaspoon ground cinnamon
- 1/4 teaspoon ground nutmeg
- 1/4 cup half-and-half cream
- 5 to 6 firm bananas, halved lengthwise

Whipped cream and additional cinnamon, optional

Sift flour and confectioners' sugar into a mixing bowl. Add milk, eggs, butter, vanilla and salt; beat until smooth. Heat a lightly greased 6-in. skillet; add about 3 tablespoons batter, spreading to almost cover bottom of skillet. Cook until lightly browned; turn and brown the other side. Remove to a wire rack. Repeat with remaining batter (makes 10-12 pancakes), greasing skillet as needed. For filling, melt butter in a large skillet. Stir in brown sugar, cinnamon and nutmeg. Stir in cream and cook until slightly thickened. Add half of the bananas at a time to skillet; heat for 2-3 minutes, spooning sauce over them. Remove from the heat. Roll a pancake around each banana half and place on a serving platter. Spoon sauce over pancakes. Top with whipped cream and cinnamon if desired. **Yield:** 5-6 servings.

Southern-Fried Baked Steak

When our family gets together, they often ask me to prepare this main course. They love its down-home flavor. —Howard Haug, Hewitt, Texas

- 2 pounds round steak, trimmed
- 1 teaspoon salt
- 1 teaspoon pepper
- 1-1/2 cups all-purpose flour
- 1/2 cup milk
- 1 egg, lightly beaten

Vegetable oil
- 1 onion, chopped
- 1 cup beef broth

Pound steak to tenderize; cut into serving-size pieces. Season with salt and pepper. Dust with flour. Combine milk and egg; dip meat into egg mixture and back into flour. In a skillet, brown meat on both sides in oil. Place onion in an ungreased 13-in. x 9-in. x 2-in. baking pan. Place meat over onion. Pour broth over all. Cover tightly and bake at 350° for 1-1/2 hours. Uncover; bake 20 minutes more. **Yield:** 6 servings.

Light Chicken Kabobs

These chicken kabobs are great for busy folks because they can be prepared the night before and grill in less than 30 minutes. —Margaret Balley
Coffeeville, Mississippi

✓ Uses less fat, sugar or salt. Includes Nutritional Analysis and Diabetic Exchanges.

- **6 boneless skinless chicken breast halves (1-1/2 pounds)**
- **1 bottle (8 ounces) fat-free Italian salad dressing**
- **1/4 cup light soy sauce**
- **1/4 cup Worcestershire sauce**
- **2 tablespoons lemon juice**
- **2 large green peppers, cut into 1-1/2-inch pieces**
- **2 large onions, cut into 18 wedges**
- **18 medium fresh mushrooms**

Cut each chicken breast half into three lengthwise strips. Combine the salad dressing, soy sauce, Worcestershire and lemon juice; set aside 1/3 cup for basting. Place remaining marinade in a large resealable plastic bag or glass bowl; add chicken and vegetables. Seal or cover and refrigerate 4 hours or overnight, turning occasionally. Drain and discard marinade. Thread chicken and vegetables alternately on 18 short skewers. Grill over medium-hot heat for 12-15 minutes or until chicken juices run clear, turning and basting with reserved marinade occasionally. **Yield:** 6 servings. **Nutritional Analysis:** One serving equals 182 calories, 588 mg sodium, 66 mg cholesterol, 13 gm carbohydrate, 29 gm protein, 2 gm fat. **Diabetic Exchanges:** 3 lean meat, 2 vegetable.

Perfect Pancakes

When making thin pancakes or crepes, use a meat baster to pick up the batter from the bowl. Then you can neatly pour it onto the hot griddle for perfectly shaped pancakes with no drippy mess.

Spicy Pork Tenderloin
(Pictured above)

A friend shared this recipe for marvelously flavorful pork years ago. It really sparks up a barbecue and has been popular whenever I've served it. I guarantee you'll get many requests for the recipe. —Diana Steger, Prospect, Kentucky

✓ Uses less fat, sugar or salt. Includes Nutritional Analysis and Diabetic Exchanges.

- **1 to 3 tablespoons chili powder**
- **1 teaspoon salt**
- **1/4 teaspoon ground ginger**
- **1/4 teaspoon ground thyme**
- **1/4 teaspoon pepper**
- **2 pork tenderloins (about 1 pound *each*)**

Combine the first five ingredients; rub over tenderloins. Cover and refrigerate for 2-4 hours. Grill over hot heat for 15 minutes per side or until juices run clear and a meat thermometer reads 160°. **Yield:** 8 servings. **Nutritional Analysis:** One serving equals 139 calories, 359 mg sodium, 73 mg cholesterol, 1 gm carbohydrate, 24 gm protein, 5 gm fat. **Diabetic Exchanges:** 3-1/2 lean meat.

5 minutes, stirring constantly. Stir in chicken. Pour into a greased 13-in. x 9-in. x 2-in. baking dish. For dumplings, combine biscuit mix and basil in a bowl. Stir in milk with a fork until moistened. Drop by tablespoonfuls onto casserole (12 dumplings). Bake, uncovered, at 350° for 30 minutes. Cover and bake 10 minutes more or until dumplings are done. **Yield:** 6-8 servings.

— 🍴 🍴 🍴 —

Slow-Cooked Pepper Steak

(Pictured on page 60)

After a long day in our greenhouse raising bedding plants for sale, I appreciate coming in to this hearty beef dish for supper. —Sue Gronholz
Columbus, Wisconsin

  1-1/2 to 2 pounds beef round steak
    2 tablespoons vegetable oil
    1/4 cup soy sauce
     1 cup chopped onion
     1 garlic clove, minced
     1 teaspoon sugar
    1/2 teaspoon salt
    1/4 teaspoon pepper
    1/4 teaspoon ground ginger
     4 tomatoes, cut into eighths *or* 1 can (14-1/2 ounces) diced tomatoes, undrained
     2 large green peppers, cut into strips
     1 tablespoon cornstarch
    1/2 cup cold water
Cooked noodles *or* rice

Cut beef into 3-in. x 1-in. strips; brown in oil in a skillet. Transfer to a slow cooker. Combine the next seven ingredients; pour over beef. Cover and cook on low for 5-6 hours or until meat is tender. Add tomatoes and green peppers; cook on low 1 hour longer. Combine the cornstarch and cold water until smooth; stir into liquid in slow cooker and cook on high until thickened. Serve over noodles or rice. **Yield:** 6-8 servings.

— 🍴 🍴 🍴 —

Chicken and Dumpling Casserole

(Pictured above)

This savory casserole is one of my husband's favorites. He loves the fluffy dumplings with plenty of gravy poured over them. The basil adds just the right touch of flavor and makes the whole house smell so good while this dish cooks. —Sue Mackey
Galesburg, Illinois

  1/2 cup chopped onion
  1/2 cup chopped celery
    2 garlic cloves, minced
  1/4 cup butter *or* margarine
  1/2 cup all-purpose flour
    2 teaspoons sugar
    1 teaspoon salt
    1 teaspoon dried basil
  1/2 teaspoon pepper
    4 cups chicken broth
    1 package (10 ounces) frozen green peas
    4 cups cubed cooked chicken
DUMPLINGS:
    2 cups buttermilk biscuit mix
    2 teaspoons dried basil
  2/3 cup milk

In a large saucepan, saute onion, celery and garlic in butter until tender. Add flour, sugar, salt, basil, pepper and broth; bring to a boil. Cook and stir for 1 minute; reduce heat. Add peas and cook for

Lamb's-Quarter Quiche

Lamb's-quarter greens taste like mild spinach and are loaded with vitamins. This delectable dish is fine to serve for any occasion. —Dorothy Holderbaum
Allegan, Michigan

    1 medium onion, chopped
    2 tablespoons vegetable oil
    4 cups chopped lamb's-quarter* (tender new leaves)
    3 eggs

1 can (12 ounces) evaporated milk *or* 1-2/3 cups milk
1/2 teaspoon salt
1/2 teaspoon pepper
2 cups (8 ounces) shredded cheddar cheese, *divided*
1 unbaked pastry shell (9 inches)

In a skillet, saute onion in oil until tender. Add lamb's-quarter; cook and stir until wilted. Cover and remove from the heat. In a mixing bowl, beat eggs and milk. Stir in salt, pepper, 1 cup cheese and lamb's-quarter mixture. Pour into pastry shell. Sprinkle with remaining cheese. Bake at 400° for 10 minutes. Reduce heat to 350°; bake 30 minutes more or until a knife inserted near the center comes out clean. Let stand for 5-10 minutes before cutting. **Yield:** 6-8 servings. ***Editor's Note:** 4 cups chopped fresh spinach can be substituted for the lamb's-quarter.

— 🍷 🍷 🍷 —

Sauerkraut 'n' Sausage

I've fixed this satisfying stovetop supper for dozens of group gatherings, and everyone enjoys the wonderful blend of flavors. Sweet and tart ingredients balance nicely, complemented with bacon and spices.
—Edna Hoffman, Hebron, Indiana

1 small onion, chopped
1 tablespoon butter *or* margarine
1 jar (32 ounces) sauerkraut, rinsed and drained
1 pound fully cooked Polish sausage, cut into 1/2-inch chunks
3-1/2 cups diced cooked peeled potatoes
1 cup apple juice
1 medium unpeeled apple, diced
2 tablespoons brown sugar
2 tablespoons all-purpose flour
1 tablespoon caraway seed
3 bacon strips, cooked and crumbled

In a large saucepan, saute onion in butter until tender. Add sauerkraut, sausage, potatoes, apple juice and apple. In a small bowl, combine the brown sugar, flour and caraway; stir into saucepan. Simmer for 35 minutes, stirring occasionally. Garnish with bacon. **Yield:** 10-12 servings.

— 🍷 🍷 🍷 —

Grilled Venison and Vegetables

(Pictured at right and on page 60)

My husband enjoys hunting, and it's my challenge to find new ways to serve venison. This recipe makes hearty kabobs perfect for grilling. The marinade reduces the "wild" taste, so guests often don't realize they're eating venison.
—Eva Miller-Videtich
Cedar Springs, Michigan

1/2 cup red wine vinegar
1/4 cup honey
1/4 cup soy sauce
2 tablespoons ketchup
Dash pepper
Dash garlic powder
1-1/2 pounds boneless venison steak, cut into 1-1/4-inch cubes
8 to 12 cherry tomatoes
8 to 12 fresh mushrooms, optional
1/2 medium green *or* sweet red pepper, cut into 1-1/2-inch pieces
1 to 2 small zucchini, cut into 1-inch chunks
1 large onion, cut into wedges
8 to 12 small new potatoes, parboiled

In a large resealable plastic bag or glass bowl, combine vinegar, honey, soy sauce, ketchup, pepper and garlic powder; set aside 1/4 cup for basting. Add meat; stir or shake to coat. Seal or cover and refrigerate for 4 hours. Drain and discard marinade. Thread meat and vegetables alternately on skewers. Brush with some of the reserved marinade. Grill over medium-hot heat, turning and basting often, for 15-20 minutes or until meat and vegetables reach desired doneness. Remove from skewers and serve. **Yield:** 4-6 servings.

Mexican Turkey Roll-Ups

(Pictured below)

This is the perfect recipe when you're hungry for a dish with Mexican flavor and want to use turkey. These roll-ups are fun and so tasty, even kids like them. It's a different use for leftover turkey.
—Marlene Muckenhirn, Delano, Minnesota

2-1/2 cups cubed cooked turkey
1-1/2 cups (12 ounces) sour cream, *divided*
   3 teaspoons taco seasoning, *divided*
   1 can (10-3/4 ounces) condensed cream of
      mushroom soup, undiluted, *divided*
1-1/2 cups (6 ounces) shredded cheddar cheese,
      divided
   1 small onion, chopped
1/2 cup salsa
1/4 cup sliced ripe olives
 10 flour tortillas (7 inches)
Shredded lettuce, chopped tomatoes and
   additional salsa and olives, optional

In a bowl, combine turkey, 1/2 cup sour cream, 1-1/2 teaspoons taco seasoning, half of the soup, 1 cup of cheese, onion, salsa and olives. Place 1/3 cup filling on each tortilla. Roll up and place, seam side down, in a greased 13-in. x 9-in. x 2-in. baking dish. Combine remaining sour cream, taco seasoning and soup; pour over roll-ups. Cover and bake at 350° for 30 minutes or until heated through. Sprinkle with the remaining cheese. Top with lettuce, tomatoes, salsa and olives if desired. **Yield:** 10 roll-ups.

Parsley Pasta Sauce

This cream-based sauce is a nice change of pace from more traditional red sauces. Use it as a topping for your favorite noodles or as the sauce in a deliciously different lasagna.
—Donna Barleen
Concordia, Kansas

   2 cups tightly packed fresh parsley leaves
1/2 cup vegetable oil
   1 teaspoon dried basil
   1 teaspoon dried oregano
   1 teaspoon dried marjoram
1/2 teaspoon salt
1/2 teaspoon garlic powder
1/2 teaspoon pepper
   1 cup (8 ounces) sour cream
1/2 cup grated Parmesan cheese
Hot cooked pasta *or* hot spaghetti squash
1/2 cup sunflower kernels, optional

In a blender, combine the first eight ingredients in order given; blend on high until smooth. Add sour cream and Parmesan cheese; blend on low just until mixed. Serve over pasta or spaghetti squash. Sprinkle with sunflower kernels if desired. **Yield:** 1-2/3 cups.

Glazed Chicken with Lemon Relish

(Pictured on page 60)

This moist tasty chicken has exceptional flair served with the sunny lemon relish. The dish combines two elements I like in a recipe—herbs and citrus fruit.
—Diane Hixon, Niceville, Florida

1/3 cup chicken broth
1/4 cup butter *or* margarine
1/4 cup chopped onion
   1 tablespoon honey
   1 teaspoon dried thyme
1/2 teaspoon salt
1/8 teaspoon pepper
   1 broiler/fryer chicken (about 3 pounds),
      cut up
LEMON RELISH:
   1 lemon
1/2 celery rib, chopped
1/4 small sweet red pepper, cut up
   2 green onions, chopped
1-1/2 teaspoons sugar
1/2 teaspoon salt
1/4 teaspoon hot pepper sauce

In a saucepan, combine the first seven ingredients; bring to a boil. Reduce heat and simmer, uncovered, for 5 minutes. Remove from the heat. Dip chicken pieces in glaze; place on broiler rack. Broil about 5 in. from the heat for 12 minutes, basting several times with the glaze. Turn chicken; broil 10-12 minutes more or until done. Meanwhile, trim outer portion of peel from lemon; set aside. Cut off and discard white membrane. Quarter lemon; discard seeds. Place lemon and peel in a food processor or blender; process until peel is finely chopped. Add remaining relish ingredients; process until vegetables are finely chopped. Serve with the chicken. **Yield:** 4-6 servings (about 3/4 cup relish).

——— 🥄 🥄 🥄 ———

Gingered Ham and Barley Roll-Ups

The National Barley Foods Council suggests these roll-ups make a tasty dish for a company-pleasing brunch.

> 2 **cups chicken broth**
> 1 **cup orange juice**
> 1 **cup pearl barley**
> 1 **medium orange**
> 1/2 **teaspoon salt**
> 1/3 **cup sliced green onions**
> 2 **tablespoons butter *or* margarine**
> 10 **thin slices deli ham**
> 1/2 **cup orange marmalade**
> 1/2 **teaspoon ground ginger**
> 1/4 **cup chopped pecans**

In a large saucepan, combine broth, orange juice and barley. Grate orange to make 1 teaspoon zest; add to the barley mixture with salt. Bring to a boil. Reduce heat; cover and simmer for 45-60 minutes or until liquid is absorbed and barley is tender. Peel orange; discard peel and chop the orange. Saute orange and onions in butter until tender. Add to the barley mixture. Spoon 1/4 cup of filling onto each ham slice. Roll up and place, seam side down, in a greased 13-in. x 9-in. x 2-in. baking dish. Spoon remaining barley mixture around roll-ups. Combine marmalade and ginger; spoon over the roll-ups. Sprinkle with pecans. Bake, uncovered, at 350° for 15-20 minutes or until heated through. **Yield:** 10 roll-ups.

Barley Basics

One cup uncooked barley yields about 3-1/2 cups cooked.

Regular pearl barley requires about 45 minutes cooking time, while quick-cooking barley takes 10 to 12 minutes.

Store uncooked barley in an airtight container.

Quick Mushroom Stew

(Pictured above)

Even with chunky vegetables and tender meat, the mushrooms star in this stick-to-your-ribs main dish. I got the recipe from my cousin and adapted it for my mushroom-loving family. —Cherie Sechrist
Red Lion, Pennsylvania

> 1 **can (10-3/4 ounces) condensed tomato soup, undiluted**
> 1 **can (10-3/4 ounces) condensed cream of mushroom soup, undiluted**
> 2-1/2 **cups water**
> 2 **pounds beef stew meat, cut into cubes**
> 2 **bay leaves**
> 3 **medium potatoes, peeled and cut into 1-inch chunks**
> 4 **carrots, cut into 1/2-inch slices**
> 1 **pound medium fresh mushrooms, halved**
> 1 **tablespoon quick-cooking tapioca**

In a Dutch oven, stir the soups and water until smooth. Add meat and bay leaves. Cover and bake at 325° for 1-1/2 hours. Stir in potatoes, carrots, mushrooms and tapioca. Cover and bake 1 hour longer or until the meat and vegetables are tender. Remove the bay leaves before serving. **Yield:** 6-8 servings.

Wild Goose with Giblet Stuffing

(Pictured above)

This recipe is one of our favorite ways to prepare goose, and it's especially nice for the holidays. My husband does a lot of hunting, so I'm always looking for new ways to fix game. —Louise Laginess
East Jordan, Michigan

1 wild goose (6 to 8 pounds dressed)
Lemon wedges
Salt
STUFFING:
Goose giblets
    2 cups water
  10 cups crumbled corn bread
    2 large Granny Smith apples, chopped
    1 large onion, chopped
  1/3 cup minced fresh parsley
    1 to 2 tablespoons rubbed sage
    1 teaspoon salt
  1/4 teaspoon pepper
  1/4 teaspoon garlic powder
Butter *or* margarine, softened

Rub inside goose cavity with lemon and salt; set aside. In a saucepan, cook giblets in water until tender, about 20-30 minutes. Remove giblets with a slotted spoon and reserve liquid. Chop giblets and place in a large bowl with the corn bread, apples, onion, parsley, sage, salt, pepper and garlic powder. Add enough of the reserved cooking liquid to make a moist stuffing; toss gently. Stuff the body and neck cavity; truss openings. Place goose, breast side up, on a rack in a shallow roasting pan. Spread with softened butter. Bake, uncovered, at 325° for 25 minutes *per pound* or until fully cooked and tender. If goose is an older bird, add 1 cup of water to pan and cover for the last hour of baking. **Yield:** 6-8 servings.

Improving Unstuffed Stuffing

Stuffing baked inside of a roasted bird is constantly steamed and basted with meat juices, so there will always be a difference in the moisture, texture and flavor compared to casserole-baked stuffing. To add moisture to casserole-baked stuffing, add extra broth or giblet cooking liquid and bake in a deep casserole. Dot the top of the stuffing with butter or margarine, and cover tightly so the stuffing can steam. Be careful not to overbake.

Vegetable Quiche

I've made and served this tasty dish for a long time. It has a unique rice crust and holds up well for cutting.
—Elnora Johnson, Union City, Tennessee

☑ Uses less fat, sugar or salt. Includes Nutritional Analysis and Diabetic Exchanges.

1-1/2 cups cooked brown rice, room
     temperature
Egg substitute equivalent to 3 eggs (3/4 cup),
    divided
  3/4 cup shredded reduced-fat mozzarella
    cheese, *divided*
1-1/2 cups chopped fresh broccoli
  3/4 cup sliced fresh mushrooms
  1/4 cup skim milk
    1 tablespoon margarine, melted

In a bowl, combine rice, 1/4 cup egg substitute and half of the cheese; mix well. Pat into the bottom and up the sides of a 9-in. pie plate coated with nonstick cooking spray; set aside. In another bowl, combine the broccoli, mushrooms, milk, margarine and remaining egg substitute. Pour into crust. Bake, uncovered, at 375° for 20-25 minutes or until a knife inserted near the center comes out clean. Sprinkle with the remaining cheese. Return to the oven until cheese melts. **Yield:** 8 servings.
Nutritional Analysis: One serving equals 124 calories, 119 mg sodium, 7 mg cholesterol, 11 gm carbohydrate, 7 gm protein, 6 gm fat. **Diabetic Exchanges:** 1 meat, 1 vegetable, 1/2 starch.

— 🍴 🍴 🍴 —

4-H Corn Special

I can trace this hearty main dish back to a 4-H cooking project. I liked the recipe immediately, and it has become a favorite with my children and husband. The only change I've made is to add extra seasonings.
—Donetta Brunner, Savanna, Illinois

    1 pound ground beef
    1 small onion, finely chopped
1-1/2 cups cooked rice
    2 cups seeded chopped fresh tomatoes
    or 1 can (14-1/2 ounces) diced tomatoes,
    undrained
    2 cups fresh, frozen *or* canned sweet corn
Salt and pepper to taste
    1 tablespoon Worcestershire sauce
    1 teaspoon hot pepper sauce
    1 cup crushed saltines
  1/4 cup butter *or* margarine, melted

In a large skillet, brown beef and onion; drain. Stir in rice, tomatoes, corn, salt, pepper, Worcestershire

sauce and hot pepper sauce. Pour into a greased 13-in. x 9-in. x 2-in. baking dish. Combine cracker crumbs and butter; sprinkle on top. Bake, uncovered, at 350° for 30 minutes. **Yield:** 6-8 servings.

— 🍴 🍴 🍴 —

Wheat Waffles
(Pictured below)

The nutty whole wheat taste comes through in these delicious waffles. Crispy and light with a subtle orange flavor, they make an appealing breakfast or supper when served with sausage. Topped with your favorite fruit and whipped cream, they even make a satisfying dessert.
—Phyllis Herlocker, Farlington, Kansas

    1 egg, *separated*
  3/4 cup milk
  1/3 cup vegetable oil
  1/4 cup orange juice
    1 cup whole wheat flour
    1 tablespoon sugar
    1 to 1-1/2 teaspoons grated orange peel
    1 teaspoon baking powder
  1/4 teaspoon salt

In a small mixing bowl, beat the egg white until stiff peaks form; set aside. In another small mixing bowl, beat egg yolk, milk, oil and orange juice. Combine flour, sugar, orange peel, baking powder and salt; stir into milk mixture. Fold in egg white. Bake in a preheated waffle iron according to manufacturer's directions until golden brown. **Yield:** 5 waffles (6-1/2 inches).

Cheddary Chicken Potpie

(Pictured below)

This is a comforting chicken dish that features a medley of flavorful cheeses. Some days I make it in the morning so I can just pop it in the oven for dinner or have my husband start it baking if I'm not home.
—Vicki Raatz, Waterloo, Wisconsin

        1 can (10-3/4 ounces) condensed cream of
            chicken soup, undiluted
        1 cup milk, *divided*
    1/2 cup chopped onion
        1 package (3 ounces) cream cheese,
            softened
    1/4 cup chopped celery
    1/4 cup shredded carrots
    1/4 cup grated Parmesan cheese
    1/2 teaspoon salt
        3 cups cubed cooked chicken
        1 package (10 ounces) frozen chopped
            broccoli, cooked and drained
        1 egg
        1 tablespoon vegetable oil
        1 cup buttermilk complete pancake mix
        1 cup (4 ounces) shredded sharp cheddar
            cheese
    1/4 cup sliced almonds, optional

In a large saucepan, combine soup, 1/2 cup of milk, onion, cream cheese, celery, carrots, Parmesan cheese and salt. Cook and stir until the mixture is hot and cream cheese is melted. Stir in the chicken and broccoli; heat through. Pour into an ungreased 2-qt. baking dish. In a bowl, combine the egg, oil and remaining milk. Add the pancake mix and cheddar cheese; blend well. Spoon over hot chicken mixture. Sprinkle with almonds if desired. Bake, uncovered, at 375° for 20-25 minutes or until golden brown. **Yield:** 6 servings.

Cream Can Dinner

My husband and I like to treat friends to this cowboy-style dinner. If you don't have a cream can, use a Dutch oven or large kettle on a gas grill.
—Nancy McDonald, Burns, Wyoming

        14 ears sweet corn with husks
          5 pounds medium red *or* white potatoes
    1-1/2 pounds carrots, peeled and halved
          2 large onions, quartered
          2 medium heads cabbage
        16 Polish sausages
          2 quarts water
    Salt and pepper, optional

Peel and clean corn, saving and washing enough husks to cover the bottom of a 5-gallon metal cream can or kettle. Layer all of the corn, half of the potatoes, carrots, onions and cabbage, then half of the sausages. Repeat layers with the rest of the vegetables and sausages, saving one or two potatoes for the top to test for doneness. Pour the water over and add salt and pepper if desired. Cover and bring to a boil on grate over a fire. Let steam for about 45 minutes or until the vegetables are tender. **Yield:** 10-12 servings.

Turkey Vegetable Skillet

As everyone who raises a garden knows, zucchini grows overnight! I never like to let anything go to waste, so I try adding this hearty squash to every recipe I can. —June Formanek, Belle Plaine, Iowa

✓ Uses less fat, sugar or salt. Includes Nutritional Analysis and Diabetic Exchanges.

        1 pound ground turkey breast
        1 small onion, chopped
        1 garlic clove, minced
        1 teaspoon vegetable oil
        1 pound fresh tomatoes, chopped
    1/4 pound zucchini, diced

1/4 cup chopped dill pickle
1 teaspoon dried basil
1/2 teaspoon pepper

In a large skillet over medium heat, cook turkey, onion and garlic in oil until meat is no longer pink. Add remaining ingredients. Simmer, uncovered, for 5-10 minutes or until the turkey is cooked and zucchini is tender. **Yield:** 6 servings. **Nutritional Analysis:** One serving equals 154 calories, 135 mg sodium, 47 mg cholesterol, 5 gm carbohydrate, 18 gm protein, 6 gm fat. **Diabetic Exchanges:** 3 lean meat, 1 vegetable.

Asparagus Cheese Strata

(Pictured on page 60)

One spring we visited old friends who served this egg dish for Sunday breakfast before church. I thought it was wonderful and full of flavor. Besides, it's easy to make ahead.   —Betty Jacques, Hemet, California

1-1/2 pounds fresh asparagus, cut into 2-inch
pieces
3 tablespoons butter *or* margarine, melted
1 loaf (1 pound) sliced bread, crusts
removed
3/4 cup shredded cheddar cheese, *divided*
2 cups cubed fully cooked ham
6 eggs, lightly beaten
3 cups milk
2 teaspoons dried minced onion
1/2 teaspoon salt
1/4 teaspoon ground mustard

Place asparagus in a saucepan and cover with water; cover and cook until crisp-tender. Drain and set aside. Lightly brush butter over one side of bread. Place half of the bread, buttered side up, in a greased 13-in. x 9-in. x 2-in. baking dish. Sprinkle with 1/2 cup cheese. Layer with asparagus and ham. Cover with remaining bread, buttered side up. Combine eggs, milk, onion, salt and mustard; pour over bread. Cover and refrigerate overnight. Remove from the refrigerator 30 minutes before baking. Bake, uncovered, at 325° for 50 minutes. Sprinkle with remaining cheese. Bake 10 minutes longer or until cheese is melted and a knife inserted near the center comes out clean. **Yield:** 10-12 servings.

Pleasing Cheese

If a hard cheese like cheddar becomes moldy, trim off 1/2 inch on all sides where mold is visible.

South Seas Chicken and Bananas

(Pictured above)

Your taste buds get a tropical vacation when you prepare a platter of this chicken! My father-in-law loves coconut, so this dish is one of his favorites. Whenever I serve this for dinner, everyone raves over it.
—Wendy Smith, Eagleville, Pennsylvania

1/4 cup lemon juice
1 can (14 ounces) sweetened condensed
milk
1/3 cup milk
1/2 cup flaked coconut
1/8 teaspoon ground cardamom
6 very firm bananas, halved lengthwise
3 cups cornflake crumbs
5 to 6 pounds chicken pieces
3/4 cup butter *or* margarine, melted, *divided*
Sliced kiwifruit and starfruit, optional

In a food processor or blender, blend the lemon juice, condensed milk, milk, coconut and cardamom until smooth. Pour into a bowl. Dip bananas into milk mixture; roll in cornflakes and set aside. Dip chicken into remaining milk mixture; roll in the remaining cornflakes and place in two greased 13-in. x 9-in. x 2-in. baking pans. Drizzle with 1/2 cup of the melted butter. Bake, uncovered, at 350° for 1 hour. Arrange bananas over the chicken. Drizzle with remaining butter. Bake 15 minutes longer or until chicken juices run clear. Garnish with fruit if desired. **Yield:** 6-8 servings.

into an ungreased 13-in. x 9-in. x 2-in. baking dish; arrange apples on top. In a bowl, beat eggs, milk and vanilla. Dip bread slices into the egg mixture for 1 minute; place over apples. Cover and refrigerate overnight. Remove from the refrigerator 30 minutes before baking. Bake, uncovered, at 350° for 35-40 minutes. Combine syrup ingredients in a saucepan; cook and stir until heated through. Serve with French toast. **Yield:** 9 servings.

🍴 🍴 🍴

Sage Dressing for Chicken

My family just loves this chicken stuffed with delicious sage dressing. They always ask for seconds.
—Bobbie Talbott, Veneta, Oregon

✓ Uses less fat, sugar or salt. Includes Nutritional Analysis and Diabetic Exchanges.

> 2 **cups unseasoned dry bread cubes**
> 1/2 **cup chopped onion**
> 1/4 **cup chopped fresh parsley**
> 3 **tablespoons chopped fresh sage *or* 1 tablespoon rubbed dried sage**
> 1 **egg, beaten**
> 1/2 to 3/4 **cup chicken broth**
> 1 **roasting chicken (3 to 4 pounds)**
> **Melted butter *or* margarine, optional**

In a large bowl, combine bread cubes, onion, parsley, sage and egg. Add enough broth until stuffing is moistened and holds together. Stuff loosely into chicken. Fasten with skewers to close. Place with breast side up on a shallow rack in roasting pan. Brush with butter if desired. Bake, uncovered, at 375° for 1-3/4 to 2-1/4 hours or until juices run clear. Baste several times with pan juices or butter. Prepare gravy if desired. **Yield:** 6 servings. **Nutritional Analysis:** One serving (prepared with egg substitute and low-sodium chicken broth, without butter or margarine, and with the skin removed after baking) equals 359 calories, 128 mg sodium, 85 mg cholesterol, 26 gm carbohydrate, 42 gm protein, 8 gm fat. **Diabetic Exchanges:** 4 lean meat, 2 starch, 1 vegetable.

🍴 🍴 🍴

Overnight Apple French Toast

(Pictured above)

My in-laws own and operate an orchard, so we have an abundance of fruit fresh from the trees. This dish includes fresh apples, apple jelly and applesauce all in one recipe. It's a warm, hearty breakfast for busy days.
—Debra Blazer, Hegins, Pennsylvania

> 1 **cup packed brown sugar**
> 1/2 **cup butter *or* margarine**
> 2 **tablespoons light corn syrup**
> 2 **large tart apples, peeled and sliced 1/4 inch thick**
> 3 **eggs**
> 1 **cup milk**
> 1 **teaspoon vanilla extract**
> 9 **slices day-old French bread (3/4 inch thick)**
> **SYRUP:**
> 1 **cup applesauce**
> 1 **jar (10 ounces) apple jelly**
> 1/2 **teaspoon ground cinnamon**
> 1/8 **teaspoon ground cloves**

In a small saucepan, cook brown sugar, butter and corn syrup until thick, about 5-7 minutes. Pour

Howard's Sauerbraten

Cooking for family and friends is a favorite pastime. People always seem to look forward to this tender beef roast with traditional tangy gravy. —Howard Koch
Lima, Ohio

> 2-1/2 **cups water**
> 1-1/2 **cups red wine vinegar**
> 1 **carrot, finely chopped**

1 celery rib, finely chopped
2 medium onions, sliced
8 whole cloves
4 bay leaves
1/2 teaspoon whole peppercorns
1 beef rump roast *or* eye of round (about 3 pounds)
1/4 cup butter *or* margarine
GINGERSNAP GRAVY:
1/2 cup water
2 tablespoons sugar
1/2 cup crushed gingersnaps (about 12 cookies)

In a saucepan, combine the first eight ingredients; bring to a boil. Place roast in a glass baking dish or large bowl. Pour hot marinade over roast; cover and refrigerate for 48 hours, turning meat twice each day. Remove roast, reserving marinade; pat dry with paper towel. In a Dutch oven, brown the roast on all sides in butter. Strain marinade; discard vegetables and seasonings. Add marinade to Dutch oven. Cover and simmer until meat is tender, about 3 hours. For gravy, remove 1-1/2 cups of the pan juices to a skillet; add water and sugar. Bring to a boil; cook until sugar is dissolved. Add gingersnap crumbs; simmer until gravy is thickened. Slice roast; serve with gravy. **Yield:** 8 servings.

＊ ＊ ＊

Beef Mushroom Stew

When cold winds blow here in Minnesota, there's nothing like sitting down to a steaming plate of savory stew.
—Marilyn Schroeder, St. Paul, Minnesota

1/4 cup all-purpose flour
1 teaspoon salt
1/8 teaspoon pepper
2-1/2 to 3 pounds beef round steak, cut into cubes
2 tablespoons vegetable oil
1 cup burgundy *or* beef broth
3/4 cup water
1 jar (8 ounces) whole mushrooms, drained
1/2 cup chopped onion
2 bay leaves
1 garlic clove, minced
1 tablespoon dried parsley flakes
Cooked rice *or* noodles

Place flour, salt and pepper in a plastic bag; add beef cubes and shake to coat on all sides. Brown beef in oil in a large saucepan. Stir in burgundy or broth, water, mushrooms, onion, bay leaves, garlic and parsley; bring to a boil. Reduce heat; cover and simmer for 1-1/2 hours or until meat is tender. Thicken if desired. Serve over rice or noodles. **Yield:** 8-10 servings.

Pork and Green Chili Casserole

(Pictured below)

I work at a local hospital and also part-time for some area doctors, so I'm always on the lookout for good, quick recipes to fix for my family. Some of my co-workers and I exchange recipes. This zippy casserole is one that was brought to a picnic at my house. People raved over it.
—Dianne Esposite
New Middletown, Ohio

1-1/2 pounds boneless pork, cut into 1/2-inch cubes
1 tablespoon vegetable oil
1 can (15 ounces) black beans, rinsed and drained
1 can (10-3/4 ounces) condensed cream of chicken soup, undiluted
1 can (14-1/2 ounces) diced tomatoes, undrained
2 cans (4 ounces *each*) chopped green chilies
1 cup quick-cooking brown rice
1/4 cup water
2 to 3 tablespoons salsa
1 teaspoon ground cumin
1/2 cup shredded cheddar cheese

In a large skillet, cook pork in oil until no longer pink; drain. Add the beans, soup, tomatoes, chilies, rice, water, salsa and cumin; cook and stir until bubbly. Pour into an ungreased 2-qt. baking dish. Bake, uncovered, at 350° for 30 minutes or until bubbly. Sprinkle with cheese; let stand a few minutes before serving. **Yield:** 6 servings.

ple and green pepper; cook until heated through and the green pepper is tender. Serve over noodles. **Yield:** 3-4 servings. ***Editor's Note:** Ground beef can be substituted for moose meat.

———— 🍴 🍴 🍴 ————

Catfish with Parsley Sauce

Catfish is abundant here in Mississippi and a staple on most menus. I was pleased when I first came across this recipe. I hope you enjoy it as much as we do.
— *Lee Bailey, Belzoni, Mississippi*

SAUCE:
   2 cups tightly packed fresh parsley leaves
   1/2 cup olive *or* vegetable oil
   1/2 cup chopped pecans
   1 garlic clove, minced
   1/2 cup grated Romano cheese
   1/2 cup grated Parmesan cheese
   2 tablespoons butter *or* margarine, cut into pieces
FILLETS:
   1 cup all-purpose flour
   1/2 to 1 teaspoon cayenne pepper
   1 teaspoon salt
   6 catfish fillets (6 to 8 ounces *each*)
   1 to 2 tablespoons vegetable oil
   1 to 2 tablespoons butter *or* margarine

In a food processor or blender, process parsley until coarsely chopped. Add remaining sauce ingredients; process until smooth. Refrigerate. Combine the flour, cayenne pepper and salt in a bowl. Dredge each fillet; shake off excess. In a skillet, heat 1 tablespoon each of oil and butter. Fry fillets for 4-5 minutes or until golden brown. Turn fillets; add remaining oil and butter if necessary. Divide the sauce and spread evenly on the cooked side of each fillet. Cover and cook for 5 minutes or until fish flakes easily with a fork. **Yield:** 6 servings.

———— 🍴 🍴 🍴 ————

Lasagna with White Sauce

I'm an old-fashioned country cook who loves preparing recipes like this one that uses staples I normally keep on hand. Unlike most lasagnas, this one doesn't call for precooking the noodles. It's so simple, my children would even make it after school and have it ready when I got home from work.
— *Angie Price*
Bradford, Tennessee

   1 pound ground beef
   1 large onion, chopped
   1 can (14-1/2 ounces) diced tomatoes, undrained

Moose Meatballs

(Pictured above)

Our family has found these meatballs in tangy sauce a great use for moose. I was glad to find a good recipe that incorporates ground moose meat, since we eat a lot of moose steaks and I like to use it differently for a change. —Janis Plourde, Smooth Rock Falls, Ontario

   1 egg, lightly beaten
   4 tablespoons cornstarch, *divided*
   1 teaspoon salt
   1/4 teaspoon pepper
   2 tablespoons chopped onion
   1 pound ground moose meat*
   1 tablespoon vegetable oil
   3 tablespoons vinegar
   1 can (8 ounces) pineapple chunks
   1/2 cup sugar
   1 tablespoon soy sauce
   1 medium green pepper, cut into strips
Hot cooked wide egg noodles

In a bowl, combine egg, 1 tablespoon cornstarch, salt, pepper and onion. Add meat; mix well. Shape into 1-1/2-in. balls. In a large skillet, brown meatballs in oil. Cover and cook over low heat for 10 minutes or until meat is no longer pink. In a saucepan, stir vinegar and remaining cornstarch until smooth. Drain pineapple, reserving juice. Set pineapple aside. Add enough water to juice to equal 1-1/2 cups; stir into vinegar mixture. Add sugar and soy sauce; cook and stir over medium heat until thickened. Add the meatballs, pineap-

2 tablespoons tomato paste
1 beef bouillon cube
1-1/2 teaspoons Italian seasoning
1 teaspoon salt
1/2 teaspoon pepper
1/4 teaspoon ground red *or* cayenne pepper
WHITE SAUCE:
2 tablespoons butter *or* margarine
3 tablespoons all-purpose flour
1 teaspoon salt
1/4 teaspoon pepper
2 cups milk
1-1/4 cups shredded mozzarella cheese, *divided*
10 to 12 uncooked lasagna noodles

In a Dutch oven, cook beef and onion over medium heat until meat is no longer pink and onion is tender; drain. Add tomatoes, tomato paste, bouillon and seasonings. Cover and cook over medium-low heat for 20 minutes, stirring occasionally. Meanwhile, melt butter in a medium saucepan; stir in flour, salt and pepper. Gradually add milk; bring to a boil, stirring constantly. Reduce heat and cook for 1 minute. Remove from the heat and stir in half of the cheese; set aside. Pour half of the meat sauce into an ungreased 13-in. x 9-in. x 2-in. baking dish. Cover with half of the lasagna noodles. Cover with remaining meat sauce. Top with remaining noodles. Pour white sauce over noodles. Sprinkle with remaining cheese. Cover and bake at 400° for 40 minutes or until noodles are done. **Yield:** 10-12 servings.

——— 🥄 🥄 🥄 ———

Mix 'n' Match Squash Casserole

Mix any kinds of summer squash you have on hand for this flavorful casserole. I serve it with a salad and hot rolls. —June Mullins, Livonia, Missouri

4 cups cubed summer squash (yellow, zucchini, pattypan *and/or* sunburst)
1 pound bulk pork sausage, cooked and drained
1 cup dry bread crumbs
1/4 cup chopped green pepper
1/4 cup chopped onion
1/2 cup grated Parmesan cheese
2 eggs, beaten
1/2 cup milk
1/2 teaspoon salt

Place squash and a small amount of water in a large saucepan; cover and cook for 8-10 minutes or until tender. Drain. Add all remaining ingredients; mix well. Transfer to a greased 11-in. x 7-in. x 2-in. baking dish. Bake, uncovered, at 325° for 30-35 minutes. **Yield:** 6-8 servings.

Chicken 'n' Hash Brown Bake

(Pictured below)

The first time I served this dish for company was to a family with five children. The kids and the adults loved it! This is one recipe I often make for potlucks—it goes a long way, and all ages enjoy it. —Ruth Andrewson
Peck, Idaho

1 package (32 ounces) frozen Southern-style hash brown potatoes
1 teaspoon salt
1/4 teaspoon pepper
4 cups diced cooked chicken
1 can (4 ounces) sliced mushrooms, drained
1 cup (8 ounces) sour cream
2 cups chicken broth *or* stock
1 can (10-3/4 ounces) condensed cream of chicken soup, undiluted
2 teaspoons chicken bouillon granules
2 tablespoons finely chopped onion
2 tablespoons finely chopped sweet red pepper
1 garlic clove, minced
Paprika
1/4 cup sliced almonds

Thaw hash browns overnight in refrigerator. Layer in an ungreased 13-in. x 9-in. x 2-in. baking dish. Sprinkle with salt and pepper. Place chicken and mushrooms over the hash browns. Stir together sour cream, broth, soup, bouillon, onion, red pepper and garlic; pour over chicken and mushrooms. Sprinkle with paprika and almonds. Bake, uncovered, at 350° for 50-60 minutes or until heated through. **Yield:** 8-10 servings.

Breads, Rolls & Muffins

With festive holiday breads, anytime muffins and delectable dinner rolls, this chapter offers a fresh-baked goody for any occasion.

BOUNTIFUL BREAD BASKET. Clockwise from upper left: Nutty Apple Muffins (p. 105), Russian Krendl (p. 106), Orange Date Bread (p. 102), Cheese Twists (p. 95), Chive Garden Rolls (p. 99) and Carrot Fruitcake (p. 108).

Grandma's Orange Rolls

(Pictured above)

Both our two children and grandchildren love these fine-textured sweet rolls. We have our own orange, lime and grapefruit trees, and it's such a pleasure to go out and pick fruit right off the tree. —Norma Poole Auburndale, Florida

    1 package (1/4 ounce) active dry yeast
1/4 cup warm water (110° to 115°)
    1 cup warm milk (110° to 115°)
1/4 cup shortening
1/4 cup sugar
    1 teaspoon salt
    1 egg, lightly beaten
3-1/2 to 3-3/4 cups all-purpose flour
FILLING:
    1 cup sugar
1/2 cup butter *or* margarine, softened
    2 tablespoons grated orange peel
GLAZE:
    1 cup confectioners' sugar
    4 teaspoons butter *or* margarine, softened
    4 to 5 teaspoons milk
1/2 teaspoon lemon extract

In a small bowl, dissolve yeast in water. In a large mixing bowl, mix milk, shortening, sugar, salt and egg. Add yeast mixture and blend. Stir in enough flour to form a soft dough. Knead on a lightly floured surface until smooth and elastic, about 6-8 minutes. Place in a greased bowl, turning once to grease top. Cover and let rise in a warm place until doubled, about 1 hour. Punch dough down; divide in half. Roll each half into a 15-in. x 10-in. rectangle. Mix filling ingredients until smooth. Spread half the filling on each rectangle. Roll up, jelly-roll style, starting with a long end. Cut each into 15 rolls. Place in two greased 11-in. x 7-in. x 2-in. baking pans. Cover and let rise until doubled, about 45 minutes. Bake at 375° for 20-25 minutes or until lightly browned. Mix glaze ingredients; spread over warm rolls. **Yield:** 30 rolls.

Give It a Rest

Some bread doughs are quite elastic and will quickly pull back when being rolled out. To "relax" the gluten in the dough and make it easier to roll out and shape, place an inverted bowl over the dough and let it rest 10 minutes after the dough has risen and you've punched it down.

If the dough continues to pull back, roll it and let it rest a few seconds, then continue to roll to the required measurements. You may need to repeat this short rest period several times.

Cheese Twists

(Pictured on page 92)

These impressive loaves take a little time to prepare, but they're well worth the effort. I've used the recipe for several years. I love making bread—there's no better way to work out life's little frustrations—and with such yummy results! —Michelle Beran
Claflin, Kansas

3-1/4 cups all-purpose flour
   2 packages (1/4 ounce *each*) active dry yeast
1-1/2 cups buttermilk
   3/4 cup butter *or* margarine
   1/2 cup sugar
   1/2 teaspoon salt
   5 eggs
3-1/2 to 4 cups whole wheat flour, *divided*
   2 cups (8 ounces) shredded cheddar cheese

In a large mixing bowl, combine all-purpose flour and yeast. In a saucepan, heat buttermilk, butter, sugar and salt to 120°-130°; add to flour mixture. Blend on low speed until moistened. Add eggs; beat on low for 30 seconds. Beat on high for 3 minutes. Stir in enough whole wheat flour to make a soft dough. Turn onto a floured board; knead until smooth and elastic, about 6-8 minutes. Place in a greased bowl, turning once to grease top. Cover and let rise in a warm place until nearly doubled, about 1 hour. Punch dough down; divide in half. On a lightly floured surface, roll each into a 12-in. x 9-in. rectangle. Cut each into three 12-in. x 3-in. strips. Combine cheese with 2 tablespoons of the remaining whole wheat flour; sprinkle 1/3 cup down center of each strip. Bring long edges together over cheese and pinch to seal. Place three strips seam side down on greased baking sheets. Braid strips together; secure ends. Cover and let rise until doubled, about 45 minutes. Bake at 375° for 20-25 minutes or until golden. Immediately remove from baking sheets to wire racks; cool. **Yield:** 2 loaves.

Rhubarb Coffee Cake

(Pictured at right)

My daughter gave me the recipe for this moist coffee cake. It mixes up quickly and is ideal for the family's weekend breakfast. The tangy rhubarb and crunchy nuts are nice accents. —Page Alexander
Baldwin City, Kansas

1/2 cup butter *or* margarine, softened
1/2 cup packed brown sugar
1/4 cup sugar

   1 egg
   1 teaspoon vanilla extract
1-1/4 cups all-purpose flour
   3/4 cup whole wheat flour
   1 teaspoon baking powder
   1/2 teaspoon baking soda
   1/4 teaspoon salt
   1/4 teaspoon ground cinnamon
   1 cup buttermilk
   2 cups diced fresh *or* frozen rhubarb
TOPPING:
   1/4 cup packed brown sugar
1-1/2 teaspoons ground cinnamon
   1/2 cup chopped walnuts

In a mixing bowl, cream the butter and sugars. Add egg and vanilla; beat until fluffy. Combine the flours, baking powder, baking soda, salt and cinnamon; add to creamed mixture alternately with buttermilk, mixing well after each addition. Stir in rhubarb. Pour into a greased 13-in. x 9-in. x 2-in. baking pan. Combine the topping ingredients; sprinkle evenly over batter. Bake at 350° for 35 minutes or until a toothpick inserted near the center comes out clean. Serve warm or at room temperature. **Yield:** 12-16 servings.

Delicious Potato Doughnuts

(Pictured below)

I first tried these tasty treats at my sister's house and thought they were the best I'd ever had. They're easy to make, and the fudge frosting tops them off well. When I make them for friends, the recipe is requested.
—Pat Davis, Beulah, Michigan

        2 cups hot mashed potatoes (mashed with milk and butter)
2-1/2 cups sugar
        2 cups buttermilk
        2 eggs, lightly beaten
        2 tablespoons butter *or* margarine, melted
        2 teaspoons baking soda
        2 teaspoons baking powder
        1 teaspoon ground nutmeg
    1/2 teaspoon salt
6-1/2 to 7 cups all-purpose flour
Cooking oil
FAST FUDGE FROSTING:
        4 cups (1 pound) confectioners' sugar
    1/2 cup baking cocoa
    1/4 teaspoon salt
    1/3 cup boiling water
    1/3 cup butter *or* margarine, melted
        1 teaspoon vanilla extract

In a large bowl, combine the potatoes, sugar, buttermilk and eggs. Stir in the butter, baking soda, baking powder, nutmeg, salt and enough of the flour to form a soft dough. Turn onto a lightly floured surface; pat out to 3/4-in. thickness. Cut with a 2-1/2-in. floured doughnut cutter. In an electric skillet, heat 1 in. of oil to 375°. Fry the doughnuts for 2 minutes per side or until browned. Place on paper towels. For frosting, sift sugar, cocoa and salt into a large bowl. Stir in the water, butter and vanilla. Dip tops of warm doughnuts in frosting. **Yield:** 4 dozen.

No More Greasy Doughnuts

To keep your homemade doughnuts from being too greasy, be sure to maintain a frying temperature of 375°F. It's also important not to overload the fryer or pan—fry just two or three doughnuts at a time to keep the temperature from dropping.

Bunny Biscuits

When our granddaughter Amanda was younger, she wanted to cook every time she visited. These biscuits are nice for snacking with a glass of juice or milk or a cup of hot chocolate.
—Flo Burtnett
Gage, Oklahoma

     1 tube (8 ounces) refrigerated biscuits
    10 raisins
     5 cinnamon candies *or* red candied cherries
    20 slivered almonds
     1 tube pink decorator icing

Separate biscuits; place five of them on a greased baking sheet about 2 in. apart. Cut remaining biscuits in half. Shape biscuit halves to form ears and firmly attach to whole biscuits. On each biscuit, press on two raisin eyes, one candy or cherry nose and four slivered almond whiskers. Bake at 375° for 8-10 minutes or until the biscuits are browned. Cool slightly; frost ears with icing. **Yield:** 5 biscuits.

Chocolate Zucchini Bread

I shred and freeze zucchini from my garden each summer so that I can make this bread all winter long. Our family loves this chocolaty treat. —Shari McKinney
Birney, Montana

    3 eggs
    1 cup vegetable oil
    2 cups sugar

1 tablespoon vanilla extract
2 cups shredded peeled zucchini (about 1
 medium)
2-1/2 cups all-purpose flour
1/2 cup baking cocoa
1 teaspoon salt
1 teaspoon baking soda
1 teaspoon ground cinnamon
1/4 teaspoon baking powder

In a mixing bowl, beat eggs, oil, sugar and vanilla. Stir in zucchini. Combine dry ingredients; add to zucchini mixture and mix well. Pour into two greased 8-in. x 4-in. x 2-in. loaf pans. Bake at 350° for 1 hour or until bread tests done. **Yield:** 2 loaves.

——— 🍃 🍃 🍃 ———

Poteca Nut Roll

(Pictured at right)

My mother-in-law brought this recipe from Yugoslavia in the early 1900s. It was a tradition in her family to serve it for holidays and special occasions. Now it's my tradition. Family members often help roll out the dough and add the filling. —Mrs. Anthony Setta
Saegertown, Pennsylvania

1 package (1/4 ounce) active dry yeast
1/4 cup warm water (110° to 115°)
3/4 cup warm milk (110° to 115°)
1/4 cup sugar
1 teaspoon salt
1 egg, lightly beaten
1/4 cup shortening
3 to 3-1/2 cups all-purpose flour
FILLING:
1/2 cup butter *or* margarine, softened
1 cup packed brown sugar
2 eggs, lightly beaten
1 teaspoon vanilla extract
1 teaspoon lemon extract, optional
4 cups ground *or* finely chopped walnuts
Milk
1/2 cup confectioners' sugar, optional

In a mixing bowl, dissolve yeast in water. Add milk, sugar, salt, egg, shortening and 1-1/2 cups flour; beat until smooth. Add enough remaining flour to form a soft dough. Turn onto a floured surface; knead until smooth and elastic, about 6-8 minutes. Place in a greased bowl, turning once to grease top. Cover and let rise in a warm place until doubled, about 1 hour. Combine butter, brown sugar, eggs, vanilla, lemon extract if desired and nuts. Add milk until mixture is of spreading consistency, about 1/2 cup; set aside. Punch dough down. Roll into a 30-in. x 20-in. rectangle. Spread filling to within 1 in. of edges. Roll up from one long side; pinch seams and ends to seal. Place on a greased baking sheet; shape into a tight spiral. Cover and let rise until nearly doubled, about 1 hour. Bake at 350° for 35 minutes or until golden brown. Cool on a wire rack. If desired, brush with a glaze of confectioners' sugar and milk. **Yield:** 1 coffee cake.

Jam-Filled Muffins

Kids and adults alike love the sweet surprise inside these muffins. They make a nice breakfast with fresh fruit and also complement a luncheon salad.
—Jessie MacLeod, St. Stephen, New Brunswick

1-3/4 cups all-purpose flour
1/2 cup sugar
1 tablespoon baking powder
1/2 teaspoon salt
2 eggs
2/3 cup milk
1/3 cup butter *or* margarine, melted
1 teaspoon grated lemon peel
1/2 cup raspberry *or* strawberry jam

In a large bowl, combine flour, sugar, baking powder and salt. In a small bowl, lightly beat eggs; add milk, butter and lemon peel. Pour into dry ingredients and stir just until moistened. Spoon half of the batter into 12 greased or paper-lined muffin cups. Make a well in the center of each; add jam. Spoon remaining batter over jam. Bake at 400° for 20-25 minutes or until golden. **Yield:** 1 dozen.

topping; cover with remaining batter and topping. Bake at 350° for 60-65 minutes or until done. Cool for 10 minutes. Loosen edges and remove sides of pan. Run a knife around the bottom of the tube pan. Cool for 10 minutes on a wire rack. Carefully invert onto a serving platter. Spread preserves over top. Garnish with toasted almonds if desired. Serve warm. **Yield:** 10-12 servings. **Editor's Note:** Only a springform pan with tube insert will work for this recipe. Do not use a bundt or angel food cake pan.

— ▼ ▼ ▼ —

Butter Nut Twists

My mother has been using this recipe for more than 45 years. She taught my sister and me how to make the twists so we can carry on the tradition for our families.
 —*Joyce Hallisey, Mt. Gilead, North Carolina*

    2 **packages (1/4 ounce *each*) active dry yeast**
1/4 **cup warm water (110° to 115°)**
    1 **cup butter *or* margarine**
    4 **cups all-purpose flour**
    2 **eggs, beaten**
3/4 **cup sour milk***
    1 **cup sugar**
1/2 **teaspoon salt**
FILLING:
    1 **pound ground walnuts**
    2 **cups flaked coconut**
3/4 **cup sugar**
    3 **tablespoons butter *or* margarine, melted**

Dissolve yeast in warm water; set aside. In a large bowl, cut butter into flour until crumbly. Add the yeast mixture, eggs, milk, sugar and salt; mix lightly. Divide dough into thirds. Cover and refrigerate overnight. Take out one piece at a time from refrigerator; roll out on a sugared board to a 12-in. x 9-in. rectangle. Combine all filling ingredients. Sprinkle 1/3 cup filling on half of the 12-in. edge of dough. Fold over lengthwise and seal, forming a 12-in. x 4-1/2-in. rectangle. Pat out to press filling into dough. Sprinkle another 1/3 cup of filling on half of the 12-in. edge of dough. Fold over lengthwise, forming a 12-in. x 2-in. rectangle. Pat down to 12 in. x 4 in. Slice 1/2-in. pieces down the 12-in. side of dough. Repeat with remaining two portions of dough. Twist each slice and roll in remaining filling. Place on greased baking sheets. Bake at 350° for 15-18 minutes or until golden brown. Serve warm or at room temperature. **Yield:** 5-6 dozen. ***Editor's Note:** To sour milk, place 2 teaspoons white vinegar in a measuring cup. Add enough milk to equal 3/4 cup.

Apricot Almond Coffee Cake

(Pictured above)

This cake looks beautiful on a silver serving plate with holly leaves and red berries around it. Delicious and elegant, it won a blue ribbon at the Oklahoma State Fair. —*Peggy Phelps, Oklahoma City, Oklahoma*

TOPPING:
    1 **cup sliced *or* slivered toasted almonds**
    2 **tablespoons sugar**
    1 **teaspoon ground cinnamon**
CAKE:
    1 **cup butter *or* margarine, softened**
    2 **cups sugar**
    2 **eggs**
    1 **teaspoon almond extract**
1-1/2 **cups cake flour**
1-1/2 **teaspoons baking powder**
1/2 **teaspoon salt**
    1 **cup (8 ounces) sour cream**
    1 **jar (6 ounces) apricot preserves**
Additional toasted almonds, optional

Combine topping ingredients; sprinkle a third of mixture in the bottom of a well-greased and floured 9-in. springform pan with a flat bottom tube pan insert (not fluted). In a mixing bowl, cream butter and sugar. Add eggs and extract; mix well. Combine flour, baking powder and salt; add to creamed mixture alternately with sour cream. Spoon half over topping in pan. Sprinkle with another third of the

Chive Garden Rolls

(Pictured on page 92)

I never seem to have enough of these light, flavorful rolls on hand. Folks like the subtle taste of the chives.
—Joanie Elbourn, Gardner, Massachusetts

✓ Uses less fat, sugar or salt. Includes Nutritional Analysis and Diabetic Exchanges.

    1 egg
    1 cup (8 ounces) fat-free cottage cheese
  1/4 cup vegetable oil
    2 teaspoons honey
    1 teaspoon salt
    1 package (1/4 ounce) active dry yeast
  1/2 cup warm water (110° to 115°)
  1/4 cup wheat germ
2-3/4 to 3-1/4 cups all-purpose flour
    3 tablespoons chopped fresh _or_ dried chives
TOPPING:
    1 egg, beaten
    1 small onion, finely chopped

In a mixing bowl, combine the egg, cottage cheese, oil, honey and salt. Dissolve yeast in warm water; add to egg mixture. Add wheat germ and 1-1/2 cups flour. Mix on medium speed for 3 minutes. Add chives and enough remaining flour to form a soft dough. Turn onto a floured surface; knead until smooth and elastic, about 10 minutes. Place in a greased bowl, turning once to grease top. Cover and let rise in a warm place until doubled, about 1 hour. Punch dough down; roll out to 3/4-in. thickness. Cut with a 3-in. round cutter and place on greased baking sheets. Cover and let rise until doubled, about 45 minutes. Brush tops with egg and sprinkle with onion. Bake at 350° for 15-20 minutes or until the rolls are golden brown. **Yield:** about 1 dozen. **Nutritional Analysis:** One serving (1 roll) equals 190 calories, 291 mg sodium, 35 mg cholesterol, 27 gm carbohydrate, 8 gm protein, 6 gm fat. **Diabetic Exchanges:** 1-1/2 starch, 1 fat.

— 🍴 🍴 🍴 —

Honey Wheat Bread

(Pictured at right)

This recipe produces two beautiful, high loaves that have wonderful texture and slice very well. The tempting aroma of this bread baking can cut the chill from a cool autumn day. It's a tribute to the goodness of wheat. —Dorothy Anderson, Ottawa, Kansas

✓ Uses less fat, sugar or salt. Includes Nutritional Analysis and Diabetic Exchanges.

2-1/2 to 3 cups all-purpose flour
3-1/2 cups whole wheat flour, _divided_
    2 packages (1/4 ounce _each_) active dry yeast
    1 cup milk
1-1/4 cups water
  1/4 cup honey
    3 tablespoons butter _or_ margarine
    1 tablespoon salt

In a large mixing bowl, combine 2 cups all-purpose flour, 2 cups whole wheat flour and yeast. In a saucepan, heat milk, water, honey, butter and salt to 120°-130°; add to flour mixture. Blend on low speed until moistened; beat on medium for 3 minutes. Gradually stir in remaining whole wheat flour and enough of the remaining all-purpose flour to form a soft dough. Turn onto a floured surface; knead until smooth and elastic, about 6-8 minutes. Place in a greased bowl, turning once to grease top. Cover and let rise in a warm place until doubled, about 1 hour. Punch dough down. Shape into two loaves; place in greased 8-in. x 4-in. x 2-in. loaf pans. Cover and let rise until doubled, about 1 hour. Bake at 375° for 40-45 minutes. Remove from pans to cool on wire racks. **Yield:** 2 loaves. **Nutritional Analysis:** One 1/2-inch slice (prepared with skim milk and margarine) equals 99 calories, 235 mg sodium, 0 cholesterol, 19 gm carbohydrate, 3 gm protein, 1 gm fat. **Diabetic Exchanges:** 1 starch.

BAKING THE BEST holiday breads begins with Eggnog Bread, Candy Cane Rolls, Christmas Stollen and Cherry Almond Wreath (shown above, clockwise from bottom right).

Cherry Almond Wreath

(Pictured above)

My daughter and I enjoy making specialty breads like this as Christmas gifts. —Gwen Roffler
Grassy Butte, North Dakota

  1 **package (1/4 ounce) active dry yeast**
1/2 **cup warm milk (110° to 115°)**
1/4 **cup warm water (110° to 115°)**
  3 **to 4-1/4 cups all-purpose flour**
  2 **eggs**
1/4 **cup butter *or* margarine, softened**
  3 **tablespoons sugar**
1-1/2 **teaspoons salt**
  1 **teaspoon grated lemon peel**
1/2 **teaspoon ground cardamom**
FILLING:
1/4 **cup butter *or* margarine, softened**
1/4 **cup all-purpose flour**
  2 **tablespoons sugar**
  1 **teaspoon almond extract**
1/2 **teaspoon grated lemon peel**
2/3 **cup finely chopped blanched almonds**
1/2 **cup chopped red and green candied cherries**
GLAZE:
2/3 **cup confectioners' sugar**
  2 **teaspoons lemon juice**
  1 **teaspoon water**

In a large mixing bowl, dissolve yeast in milk and water. Add 2 cups flour, eggs, butter, sugar, salt, lemon peel and cardamom; beat until smooth. Add enough remaining flour to form a soft dough. Turn onto a floured surface; knead until smooth and elastic, about 6-8 minutes. Place in a greased bowl, turning once to grease top. Cover and let rise in a warm place until doubled, about 1-1/2 hours. In a small mixing bowl, beat butter, flour, sugar, extract and lemon peel. Stir in almonds and cherries. Refrigerate until needed. Punch dough down. Roll into a 30-in. x 9-in. rectangle. Crumble filling over dough. Starting with the 30-in. edge, roll up and seal edge. Place, seam side down, on a greased baking sheet. With a sharp knife, cut roll in half lengthwise; carefully turn cut sides up. Loosely twist strips around each other, keeping cut sides up.

Shape into a ring and pinch ends together. Cover and let rise 1 hour. Bake at 350° for 35-40 minutes or until browned. Cool 15 minutes. Combine glaze ingredients; drizzle over warm coffee cake. Cool completely. **Yield:** 1 coffee cake.

——— 🍶 🍶 🍶 ———

Candy Cane Rolls

(Pictured at left)

These festive rolls will delight children of all ages.
—Janice Peterson, Huron, South Dakota

     1 package (1/4 ounce) active dry yeast
 1/4 cup warm water (110° to 115°)
 3/4 cup warm milk (110° to 115°)
 1/4 cup sugar
 1/4 cup shortening
     1 teaspoon salt
     1 egg, lightly beaten
3-1/4 to 3-3/4 cups all-purpose flour
     1 cup red candied cherries, quartered
     1 cup confectioners' sugar
     1 tablespoon milk

In a large mixing bowl, dissolve yeast in warm water. Add warm milk, sugar, shortening, salt, egg and 2 cups flour; beat until smooth. Stir in cherries. Add enough of the remaining flour to form a soft dough. Turn onto a floured surface; knead until smooth and elastic, about 6-8 minutes. Place in a greased bowl, turning once to grease top. Cover and let rise in a warm place until doubled, about 1 hour. Punch dough down; let rest for 10 minutes. Divide in half. Roll each half into a 12-in. x 7-in. rectangle. Cut twelve 1-in. strips from each rectangle. Twist each strip and place 2 in. apart on greased baking sheets, shaping one end like a cane. Cover and let rise until doubled, about 45 minutes. Bake at 375° for 12-15 minutes or until golden brown. Cool completely. Combine confectioners' sugar and milk; frost rolls. **Yield:** 2 dozen.

——— 🍶 🍶 🍶 ———

Christmas Stollen

(Pictured above left)

I like to make and share this rich bread dotted with colorful candied fruit and nuts. —*Sharon Hasty*
New London, Missouri

 3/4 cup raisins
 1/2 cup chopped mixed candied fruit
 1/4 cup orange juice
     1 package (1/4 ounce) active dry yeast
 1/4 cup warm water (110° to 115°)
 3/4 cup warm milk (110° to 115°)

 1/2 cup butter *or* margarine, melted
 1/4 cup sugar
     2 eggs, lightly beaten
     2 tablespoons grated orange peel
     1 tablespoon grated lemon peel
     1 teaspoon salt
5-1/4 to 5-3/4 cups all-purpose flour
 1/2 cup chopped almonds
Confectioners' sugar

Soak raisins and fruit in orange juice; set aside. In a large mixing bowl, dissolve yeast in water. Add milk, butter, sugar, eggs, orange and lemon peel, salt and 3 cups flour; beat until smooth. Add raisin mixture and almonds. Add enough remaining flour to form a soft dough. Turn onto a floured surface; knead until smooth and elastic, about 6-8 minutes. Place in a greased bowl, turning once to grease top. Cover and let rise in a warm place until doubled, about 1-1/2 hours. Punch dough down; let rest for 10 minutes. Divide in half; roll each half into a 10-in. x 7-in. oval. Fold one of the long sides over to within 1 in. of the opposite side; press edges lightly to seal. Place on greased baking sheets. Cover and let rise until nearly doubled, about 1 hour. Bake at 375° for 25-30 minutes or until golden brown. Cool on a wire rack. Just before serving, dust with confectioners' sugar. **Yield:** 2 loaves.

——— 🍶 🍶 🍶 ———

Eggnog Bread

(Pictured at far left)

This bread is a Christmas tradition at my home here in the foothills of the Blue Ridge Mountains.
—Ruth Bickel, Hickory, North Carolina

 1/4 cup butter *or* margarine, melted
 3/4 cup sugar
     2 eggs, beaten
2-1/4 cups all-purpose flour
     2 teaspoons baking powder
     1 teaspoon salt
     1 cup dairy *or* canned eggnog
 1/2 cup chopped pecans
 1/2 cup raisins
 1/2 cup chopped red and green candied
        cherries

In a large bowl, combine butter, sugar and eggs; mix well. Combine the flour, baking powder and salt. Stir into the butter mixture alternately with eggnog; mix only until dry ingredients are moistened. Fold in pecans, raisins and cherries. Spoon into a greased 8-in. x 4-in. x 2-in. loaf pan. Bake at 350° for 70 minutes or until bread tests done. **Yield:** 1 loaf.

In a mixing bowl, cream butter and sugar. Add eggs; mix well. Combine bananas and buttermilk. Combine the flour, baking powder, baking soda and salt; add to creamed mixture alternately with banana mixture. Stir in bran, apricots and nuts. Pour into a greased 9-in. x 5-in. x 3-in. loaf pan. Bake at 350° for 55-60 minutes or until a toothpick inserted near the center comes out clean. Cool 10 minutes before removing from pan to a wire rack. **Yield:** 1 loaf.

— 🍶 🍶 🍶 —

Orange Date Bread

(Pictured on page 92)

I loved visiting my aunt—she was an excellent baker, and her kitchen always smelled great. With her inspiration, I now bake this moist yummy bread every holiday season. —Joann Wolfe, Sunland, California

        1 cup butter *or* margarine, softened
        2 cups sugar
        3 eggs, beaten
        4 cups all-purpose flour
        1 teaspoon baking soda
        1 teaspoon salt
1-1/3 cups buttermilk
        1 cup chopped walnuts
        1 cup chopped dates
        1 tablespoon grated orange peel
GLAZE:
        1/4 cup orange juice
        1/2 cup sugar
        2 tablespoons grated orange peel

In a mixing bowl, cream the butter and sugar. Add eggs; mix well. Combine the flour, baking soda and salt; add to creamed mixture alternately with buttermilk. Fold in walnuts, dates and orange peel. Pour into two greased and floured 8-in. x 4-in. x 2-in. loaf pans. Bake at 350° for 60-65 minutes or until a toothpick inserted near the center comes out clean. Combine glaze ingredients; spoon half over hot bread. Cool for 10 minutes. Remove from pans; spoon remaining glaze over bread. **Yield:** 2 loaves.

— 🍶 🍶 🍶 —

Nutty Sweet Potato Biscuits

Back in the 1920s and '30s, Mom always had something good for us to eat when we got home from school. Her wood range had an apron right by the firebox, and Mom often left a plate of these warm wonderful biscuits waiting for us. What a treat!
—Mrs. India Thacker, Clifford, Virginia

Apricot Banana Bread

(Pictured above)

Making this delightfully different twist on traditional banana bread is fun. It tastes excellent spread with cream cheese or butter. When I take this bread to bake sales, it really goes fast. I also make it in small loaf pans to give as gifts. I discovered the recipe in 1955 and have been making it since. —Betty Hull Stoughton, Wisconsin

        1/3 cup butter *or* margarine, softened
        2/3 cup sugar
           2 eggs
           1 cup mashed ripe bananas (2 to 3 medium)
        1/4 cup buttermilk
1-1/4 cups all-purpose flour
           1 teaspoon baking powder
        1/2 teaspoon baking soda
        1/2 teaspoon salt
           1 cup 100% bran cereal (not flakes)
        3/4 cup chopped dried apricots (about 6 ounces)
        1/2 cup chopped walnuts

2-3/4 cups all-purpose flour
   4 teaspoons baking powder
1-1/4 teaspoons salt
  1/2 teaspoon ground cinnamon
  1/2 teaspoon ground nutmeg
  3/4 cup chopped nuts
   2 cups mashed cooked sweet potatoes
  3/4 cup sugar
  1/2 cup butter *or* margarine, melted
   1 teaspoon vanilla extract

In a large mixing bowl, combine flour, baking powder, salt, cinnamon, nutmeg and nuts. In another bowl, combine sweet potatoes, sugar, butter and vanilla; add to flour mixture and mix well. Turn onto a lightly floured surface; knead slightly. Roll dough to 1/2-in. thickness. Cut with a 2-1/2-in. biscuit cutter and place on lightly greased baking sheets. Bake at 450° for 12 minutes or until golden brown. **Yield:** 1-1/2 to 2 dozen.

Whole Wheat Hamburger Buns

I never baked much bread—much less hamburger buns—until I worked as a baker at a ranch camp. This recipe from the camp files has become a favorite of mine. —Dawn Fagerstrom, Warren, Minnesota

   2 packages (1/4 ounce *each*) active dry yeast
1-3/4 cups warm water (110° to 115°)
1-1/4 cups whole wheat flour
  1/4 cup nonfat dry milk powder
   3 tablespoons sugar
   2 teaspoons salt
   2 teaspoons lemon juice
   5 tablespoons butter *or* margarine, melted, *divided*
3-1/2 to 4 cups all-purpose flour

In a large mixing bowl, dissolve yeast in warm water; let stand 5 minutes. Add wheat flour, dry milk, sugar, salt, lemon juice, 3 tablespoons butter and 1 cup all-purpose flour. Beat until smooth. Add enough of the remaining all-purpose flour to form a soft dough. Turn onto a floured surface; knead until smooth and elastic, about 10 minutes. Place in a greased bowl, turning once to grease top. Cover and let rise in a warm place until doubled, about 1 hour. Punch down. Shape into 14 buns, about 3-1/2 in. in diameter. Place on greased baking sheets; brush with 1 tablespoon of the remaining butter. Cover and let rise until doubled, about 30 minutes. Bake at 375° for 14-16 minutes. Remove from baking sheets; brush with remaining butter. Cool on wire racks. **Yield:** 14 buns.

'I Wish I Had That Recipe...'

"INSTEAD of the usual rolls, Heritage House in Chesaning, Michigan serves delicious blueberry muffins with their lunches," relates Carole Mulder of Perry, Michigan. "Those muffins are tops, and I would appreciate it if *Taste of Home* could get the recipe."

Glad to oblige, Carole! Bonnie Ebenhoeh, owner of Heritage House with husband Howard, tells us, "I combined a favorite yellow cake recipe with a muffin recipe to come up with this light, sweet muffin when we first opened the restaurant in 1980. At that time, we were the only ones in the area who served muffins," she recalls.

"Now many restaurants feature homemade muffins, but somehow my blueberry variety has always remained a favorite with our guests. I'm honored to share the recipe!"

Known for generous portions of home-cooked food at family prices, Heritage House is in a stately mansion on historic Broad Street Boulevard in downtown Chesaning MI 48616; 1-517/845-7700.

Bonnie's Blueberry Muffins

   2 cups all-purpose flour
  2/3 cup sugar
   1 tablespoon baking powder
  1/2 teaspoon salt
   2 eggs
   1 cup milk
  1/3 cup butter *or* margarine, melted
   1 teaspoon ground nutmeg
   1 teaspoon vanilla extract
   2 cups fresh *or* frozen blueberries*
Additional butter *or* margarine, melted
Additional sugar

In a mixing bowl, combine flour, sugar, baking powder and salt. In another bowl, beat eggs. Blend in milk, butter, nutmeg and vanilla; pour into dry ingredients and mix just until moistened. Fold in blueberries. Fill greased or paper-lined muffin cups two-thirds full. Bake at 375° for 20-25 minutes. Brush tops with melted butter and sprinkle with sugar. **Yield:** 1 dozen. ***Editor's Note:** If using frozen berries, do not thaw before adding to batter.

The Magic of Bread Machines

PRACTICALLY with the touch of a button, you can create oven-fresh bread in your own kitchen. That's the beauty of bread machines!

— 🥤 🥤 🥤 —

Onion Dill Bread

(Pictured below)

Moist and flavorful, this bread owes its richness to cottage cheese and sour cream. —Ruth Andrewson
Leavenworth, Washington

>   2 teaspoons active dry yeast
> 3-1/2 cups bread flour
>   1 teaspoon salt
>   1 egg
>   3/4 cup cream-style cottage cheese
>   3/4 cup sour cream
>   3 tablespoons sugar
>   3 tablespoons minced dried onion
>   2 tablespoons dill seed
> 1-1/2 tablespoons butter *or* margarine

In bread machine pan, place first four ingredients in order suggested by manufacturer. In a saucepan, combine remaining ingredients and heat just until warm (do not boil). Pour into bread pan. Select the basic bread setting. Choose crust color and loaf size if available. Bake according to bread machine directions. **Yield:** 1 loaf (1-1/2 pounds). **Editor's Note:** Use of the timer feature is not recommended for this recipe.

— 🥤 🥤 🥤 —

Oatmeal Bread

This bread has a lightly sweet flavor with good texture and crust. —Ruth Andrewson

>   1 package (1/4 ounce) active dry yeast
>   1 cup quick-cooking oats
>   3 cups bread flour
>   1 teaspoon salt
>   1/2 cup molasses
>   1 tablespoon vegetable oil
>   1 cup water (70° to 80°)

In bread machine pan, place ingredients in order suggested by manufacturer. Select the basic bread setting. Choose crust color and loaf size if available. Bake according to bread machine directions. **Yield:** 1 loaf (2 pounds).

— 🥤 🥤 🥤 —

Buttermilk Wheat Bread

This bread has a wonderful texture and attractive golden crust. —Mary Jane Cantrell, Turlock, California

> 1-1/4 cups buttermilk
> 1-1/2 tablespoons butter *or* margarine
>   2 tablespoons sugar
>   1 teaspoon salt
>   3 cups bread flour
>   1/3 cup whole wheat flour
>   2 teaspoons active dry yeast

In bread machine pan, place all ingredients in order suggested by manufacturer. Select the basic bread setting. Choose crust color and loaf size if available. Bake according to bread machine directions. **Yield:** 1 loaf (2 pounds). **Editor's Note:** Use of the timer feature is not recommended for this recipe.

For the Best Breads

Check the dough after 5 minutes of mixing. If the dough seems dry or cracked, add 1 to 2 tablespoons water. If the dough is wet-looking or flat, add 1 to 2 tablespoons flour.

Easy Bran Muffins

Because this recipe's ingredients are measured in whole amounts, it's perfect for kids to make. My grand-daughter Kelsey entered these muffins in a baking contest at age 4! —Peggy Reed, Vergennes, Vermont

  6 cups bran cereal (not flakes)
  2 cups boiling water
  1 cup butter *or* margarine, softened
  3 cups sugar
  4 eggs
  5 cups all-purpose flour
  5 teaspoons baking soda
  1 teaspoon salt
  1 quart buttermilk

Combine cereal and water; let stand 10 minutes. In a mixing bowl, cream butter and sugar. Add the eggs, one at a time, beating well after each addition. Combine flour, baking soda and salt; add to creamed mixture alternately with buttermilk. Fold in cereal mixture. Fill greased or paper-lined muffin cups two-thirds full. Bake at 400° for 15-20 minutes or until a toothpick inserted near the center comes out clean. **Yield:** 5-6 dozen. **Editor's Note:** Muffin batter will keep in the refrigerator for 1 week.

Pumpkin Bread

I keep my freezer stocked with home-baked goodies like this deliciously spicy pumpkin-rich quick bread.
                    —Joyce Jackson, Bridgetown, Nova Scotia

1-1/2 cups sugar
  1 cup cooked *or* canned pumpkin
  1/2 cup vegetable oil
  1/2 cup water
  2 eggs
1-2/3 cups all-purpose flour
  1 teaspoon baking soda
  1 teaspoon ground cinnamon
  3/4 teaspoon salt
  1/2 teaspoon baking powder
  1/2 teaspoon ground nutmeg
  1/4 teaspoon ground cloves
  1/2 cup chopped walnuts
  1/2 cup raisins, optional

In a mixing bowl, combine sugar, pumpkin, oil, water and eggs; beat well. Combine dry ingredients; gradually add to pumpkin mixture and mix well. Stir in nuts and raisins if desired. Pour into a greased 9-in. x 5-in. x 3-in. loaf pan. Bake at 350° for 65-70 minutes or until a toothpick inserted near the center comes out clean. Cool 10 minutes in pan before removing to a wire rack. **Yield:** 1 loaf.

Nutty Apple Muffins

(Pictured above and on page 92)

I teach quick-bread making for 4-H, and I'm always on the lookout for good new recipes. My sister-in-law shared this recipe with me for a slightly different kind of muffin. With apples and coconut, they are moist, chewy and tasty. —Gloria Kaufmann, Orrville, Ohio

1-1/2 cups all-purpose flour
1-1/2 teaspoons baking soda
  3/4 teaspoon salt
  1/2 teaspoon ground nutmeg
  2 eggs
  1 cup plus 2 tablespoons sugar
  1/3 cup vegetable oil
  2 cups diced peeled apples
1-1/2 cups chopped walnuts
  3/4 cup flaked coconut

In a large bowl, combine the flour, baking soda, salt and nutmeg. In another bowl, beat eggs, sugar and oil. Stir in apples, nuts and coconut. Stir into dry ingredients just until moistened. Fill 18 greased muffin cups three-fourths full. Bake at 350° for 25-30 minutes or until a toothpick inserted near the center comes out clean. Cool in pan 10 minutes before removing to a wire rack. **Yield:** 1-1/2 dozen.

20-25 minutes or until golden brown. Remove from pans to cool on wire racks. **Yield:** 45 rolls.

Russian Krendl

(Pictured on page 92)

While dining with a Russian immigrant family, I jumped at the chance to add this wonderful bread they served to my collection. I never turn down hugs from my grandchildren when I make this special bread!
—*Ann Sodman, Evans, Colorado*

FILLING:
   2 tablespoons butter *or* margarine
   2 tablespoons sugar
   1/3 cup chopped prunes
   1/3 cup finely chopped dried apricots
   1 large apple, peeled and chopped
   1 cup apple juice
   2/3 cup finely chopped dried apple
BREAD:
   1 package (1/4 ounce) active dry yeast
   5 tablespoons sugar, *divided*
   3/4 cup warm half-and-half cream *or* milk
      (110° to 115°)
   1/4 cup butter *or* margarine, softened
   1/2 teaspoon salt
1-1/2 teaspoons vanilla extract
   2 egg yolks
2-3/4 to 3-1/4 cups all-purpose flour
Additional butter *or* margarine, melted
   1/2 teaspoon ground cinnamon
Confectioners' sugar

In a saucepan, combine filling ingredients. Simmer, stirring occasionally, for 30 minutes or until fruit is tender and mixture has jam-like consistency. Cool to room temperature. In a large mixing bowl, dissolve yeast and 3 tablespoons sugar in cream or milk. Add butter, salt, vanilla, egg yolks and 1-1/2 cups of the flour; beat until smooth. Add enough remaining flour to form a soft dough. Turn onto a floured surface; knead until smooth and elastic, about 6-8 minutes. Place in a greased bowl, turning once to grease top. Cover and let rise until doubled, about 1 hour. Punch dough down. Roll into a 32-in. x 10-in. rectangle. Brush with melted butter. Combine cinnamon and remaining sugar; sprinkle over butter. Spread filling to within 1 in. of edges. Roll up from one of the long sides; pinch seams and ends to seal. Place on a greased baking sheet; form into a pretzel shape. Cover and let rise until nearly doubled, about 30 minutes. Bake at 350° for 45 minutes or until golden brown. Cool on a wire rack. Dust with confectioners' sugar. **Yield:** 1 coffee cake.

Easy Potato Rolls

(Pictured above)

After I discovered this recipe, it became a mainstay for me. I make the dough ahead of time when company is coming, and I try to keep some in the refrigerator to make for "hay hands" on our cattle ranch. Leftover mashed potatoes are sure to go into these rolls.
—*Jeanette McKinney, Belleview, Missouri*

   2/3 cup sugar
   2/3 cup shortening
   1 cup mashed potatoes
2-1/2 teaspoons salt
   2 eggs
   2 packages (1/4 ounce *each*) active dry
      yeast
1-1/3 cups warm water (110° to 115°), *divided*
   6 to 6-1/2 cups all-purpose flour

In a large mixing bowl, cream sugar and shortening. Add potatoes, salt and eggs. In a small bowl, dissolve yeast in 2/3 cup of warm water; add to creamed mixture. Beat in 2 cups of flour and remaining water. Add enough remaining flour to form a soft dough. Shape into a ball; do not knead. Place in a greased bowl; turn once to grease top. Cover and let rise in a warm place until doubled, about 1 hour. Punch dough down; divide into thirds. Shape each portion into 15 balls; arrange in three greased 9-in. round baking pans. Cover and let rise until doubled, about 30 minutes. Bake at 375° for

Raspberry Buttermilk Muffins

For a morning lift, the Washington Red Raspberry Commission shares these delicious eye-openers. They're easy to stir up and bake.

2 cups all-purpose flour
1/2 cup sugar
2 teaspoons baking powder
1 teaspoon salt
6 tablespoons cold butter *or* margarine
1 egg, lightly beaten
1 cup buttermilk
1 cup fresh *or* frozen raspberries*

In a bowl, combine flour, sugar, baking powder and salt. Cut in butter until mixture resembles coarse crumbs. Add egg and buttermilk; mix just until dry ingredients are moistened. Fold in berries. Fill greased or paper-lined muffin cups two-thirds full. Bake at 400° for 25 minutes or until browned. **Yield:** 12-15 muffins. ***Editor's Note:** If using frozen berries, do not thaw before adding to batter.

— 🥄 🥄 🥄 —

Poppy Seed Snack Bread

A slice of this moist bread is a great between-meal snack. We like to slather slices with peanut butter or a variety of jams.
— *Kathy Scott*
Hemingford, Nebraska

1 package (18-1/2 ounces) white cake mix without pudding
1 package (3.4 ounces) instant coconut cream pudding mix
4 eggs, lightly beaten
1 cup hot water
1/2 cup vegetable oil
2 tablespoons poppy seeds

In a mixing bowl, combine cake and pudding mixes, eggs, water and oil; beat 2 minutes. Fold in poppy seeds. Pour into two greased and floured 8-in. x 4-in. x 2-in. loaf pans. Bake at 350° for 35-40 minutes or until golden. Cool 10 minutes before removing from pans. **Yield:** 2 loaves.

— 🥄 🥄 🥄 —

Cranberry Fruit Bread

(Pictured at right)

My family looks forward to this combination of cranberry bread and fruitcake for the holidays. Baked in smaller pans, the pretty loaves make nice gifts. The bread also freezes well. I got this recipe from a woman at church before my husband retired as minister.
— *Ellen Puotinen, Tower, Minnesota*

1 bag (12 ounces) fresh *or* frozen cranberries, halved
2 cups pecan halves
1 cup chopped mixed candied fruit
1 cup chopped dates
1 cup golden raisins
1 tablespoon grated orange peel
4 cups all-purpose flour, *divided*
2 cups sugar
1 tablespoon baking powder
1 teaspoon baking soda
1/4 teaspoon salt
2 eggs
1 cup orange juice
1/4 cup shortening, melted
1/4 cup warm water

Combine cranberries, pecans, fruit, dates, raisins and orange peel with 1/4 cup flour; set aside. In another bowl, combine sugar, baking powder, baking soda, salt and remaining flour; set aside. In a large mixing bowl, beat eggs. Add orange juice, shortening and water. Add flour mixture; stir just until combined. Fold in cranberry mixture. Spoon into three greased and waxed paper-lined 8-in. x 4-in. x 2-in. loaf pans. Bake at 350° for 60-65 minutes or until a toothpick inserted near the center comes out clean. Cool 10 minutes in pans. Remove to a wire rack. Remove waxed paper and continue to cool on the rack. **Yield:** 3 loaves.

Cheesy Garlic Bread

(Pictured below)

I find this crisp bread smothered in a full-flavored topping adds zip to an ordinary meal. It's also a satisfying snack or appetizer. A friend shared this recipe a while back. I always come home with an empty plate when I take it to a gathering. —Judy Skaar
Pardeeville, Wisconsin

1-1/2 cups mayonnaise
   1 cup (4 ounces) shredded sharp cheddar cheese
   1 cup thinly sliced green onions with tops
   3 garlic cloves, minced
   1 loaf French bread (about 20 inches), halved lengthwise
  1/3 cup minced fresh parsley, optional
Paprika, optional

Mix mayonnaise, cheese, onions and garlic; spread on bread halves. If desired, sprinkle with parsley and paprika. Wrap each half in foil. Refrigerate for 1-2 hours or freeze. Unwrap and place on a baking sheet. Bake at 400° for 8-10 minutes (20-25 minutes if frozen) or until puffed but not brown. Cut into slices. **Yield:** 12-15 servings.

Peach Upside-Down Muffins

I love to showcase our state's fine peach crop in these novel muffins. They make pretty individual servings for breakfast, a snack or even dessert.
—Geraldine Grisdale, Mt. Pleasant, Michigan

   2 cups all-purpose flour
1-1/2 cups sugar
   1 tablespoon baking powder
  1/2 teaspoon salt
  1/4 cup shortening, melted
   2 eggs, lightly beaten
   1 cup milk
   6 tablespoons butter *or* margarine
   1 cup plus 2 tablespoons packed brown sugar
   3 cups sliced peeled ripe peaches

In a mixing bowl, combine flour, sugar, baking powder and salt. Add shortening, eggs and milk; mix until smooth. In the bottom of 18 greased muffin cups, place 1 teaspoon of butter and 1 tablespoon brown sugar. Place in a 375° oven for 5 minutes. Arrange peaches in the muffin cups. Fill each half full with batter. Bake at 375° for 25 minutes or until browned. Turn out of pans immediately. **Yield:** 1-1/2 dozen.

Carrot Fruitcake

(Pictured on page 92)

Even those who don't care for fruitcake will love this special version. —Ann Parden, Chunchula, Alabama

1-1/2 cups chopped nuts
   1 cup chopped mixed candied fruit
   1 cup chopped dates
   1 cup raisins
   3 cups all-purpose flour, *divided*
   2 cups sugar
1-1/2 cups vegetable oil
   4 eggs
   2 teaspoons baking powder
   2 teaspoons baking soda
   2 teaspoons ground cinnamon
   1 teaspoon salt
   3 cups finely shredded carrots
Confectioners' sugar icing

Combine nuts, fruit, dates and raisins with 1/2 cup flour; set aside. In a large mixing bowl, combine sugar and oil; mix well. Add eggs, one at a time, beating well after each addition. Combine baking powder, baking soda, cinnamon, salt and remaining flour; gradually add to sugar mixture, beating until smooth. (Batter will be stiff.) Fold in carrots and fruit mixture. Spoon into a greased and floured 10-in. tube pan. Bake at 350° for 1 hour and 20 minutes or until a toothpick inserted near the center comes out clean. Cool for 15 minutes before removing from pan to cool on a wire rack. Drizzle with confectioners' sugar icing when cooled. **Yield:** 12-16 servings.

Southern Sweet Potato Bread

Sweet potatoes lend to the moistness in this quick bread from the North Carolina Sweet Potato Commission. Plus, a creamy orange spread delightfully dresses up every slice.

- 1/4 cup butter *or* margarine, softened
- 1/2 cup packed brown sugar
- 2 eggs, lightly beaten
- 1 cup mashed cooked sweet potatoes
- 3 tablespoons milk
- 1 teaspoon grated orange peel
- 2 cups self-rising flour*
- 1/4 teaspoon ground allspice
- 1/4 teaspoon ground nutmeg
- 1/4 cup chopped pecans

ORANGE CREAM SPREAD:
- 1 package (3 ounces) cream cheese, softened
- 1 teaspoon orange juice
- 1 teaspoon grated orange peel

In a mixing bowl, cream butter and brown sugar. Add eggs; mix well. Add sweet potatoes, milk and orange peel; mix well. Combine flour, allspice and nutmeg; add to creamed mixture. Mix just until combined. Fold in nuts. Pour into a greased 9-in. x 5-in. x 3-in. loaf pan. Bake at 350° for 40-45 minutes or until a toothpick inserted near the center comes out clean. Cool in pan for 10 minutes before removing to a wire rack. Cool completely. In a mixing bowl, combine spread ingredients; beat until smooth. Serve with bread. **Yield:** 1 loaf. ***Editor's Note:** 2 cups of all-purpose flour, 1 tablespoon baking powder and 1 teaspoon salt may be substituted for self-rising flour.

Orange Biscuits

(Pictured above right)

These biscuits are a special treat with a ham dinner, but they're also delicious just by themselves. They're often requested by my five children and seven grandchildren. —Winifred Brown, Wilmette, Illinois

- 1/2 cup orange juice
- 3/4 cup sugar, *divided*
- 1/4 cup butter *or* margarine
- 2 teaspoons grated orange peel
- 2 cups all-purpose flour
- 1 tablespoon baking powder
- 1/2 teaspoon salt
- 1/4 cup shortening
- 3/4 cup milk
- Additional butter *or* margarine, melted
- 1/2 teaspoon ground cinnamon

In a saucepan, combine orange juice, 1/2 cup of sugar, butter and orange peel. Cook and stir over medium heat for 2 minutes. Divide among 12 muffin cups; set aside. In a large bowl, combine flour, baking powder and salt. Cut in shortening until mixture resembles coarse crumbs. With a fork, stir in milk until mixture forms a ball. On a lightly floured surface, knead the dough 1 minute. Roll into a 9-in. square, about 1/2 in. thick. Brush with melted butter. Combine the cinnamon and remaining sugar; sprinkle over butter. Roll up. Cut into 12 slices, about 3/4 in. thick. Place slices, cut side down, over orange mixture in muffin cups. Bake at 450° for 12-16 minutes. Cool for 2-3 minutes; remove from pan. **Yield:** 1 dozen.

Perfect Biscuits

Biscuits that don't rise and seem heavy are generally over-kneaded. Limit your kneading to 10-12 strokes, and don't overwork the scraps. Gently pat or roll dough before cutting biscuits. Also, make sure your baking powder is fresh.

Cakes, Cookies & Candies

*Nothing quite satisfies a craving for something sweet
like a generous slice of cake, cookie-jar classics,
a bounty of bars or homemade candies.*

SWEET TREATS. Clockwise from upper left: Soda Cracker Chocolate Candy (p. 114), Frosted Banana Bars (p. 120), Chocolate Marshmallow Cookies (p. 113), Banana Nut Layer Cake (p. 126) and Saucy Apple Cake (p. 117).

Banana Squares

(Pictured above)

When we were first married, my husband was in the Navy. Stationed in Puerto Rico, we had banana trees growing in our yard, so I found ways to use dozens of ripe bananas at a time. I made these squares often. They freeze well and make a great snack to have on hand. —Susan Miller, Raleigh, North Carolina

> **2 eggs,** *separated*
> **2/3 cup shortening**
> **1-1/2 cups sugar**
> **1 cup mashed ripe bananas (2 to 3 medium)**
> **1-1/2 cups all-purpose flour**
> **1 teaspoon baking soda**
> **1/4 cup sour milk***
> **1/2 teaspoon vanilla extract**
> **1/2 cup chopped walnuts, optional**
> **Whipped cream and sliced bananas, optional**

In a small mixing bowl, beat egg whites until soft peaks form; set aside. In a large mixing bowl, cream shortening and sugar. Beat in egg yolks; mix well. Add bananas. Combine flour and baking soda; add to creamed mixture alternately with milk, beating well after each addition. Add vanilla. Fold in egg whites. Fold in nuts if desired. Pour into a greased 13-in. x 9-in. x 2-in. baking pan. Bake at 350° for 45-50 minutes or until a toothpick inserted near the center comes out clean. Cool on a wire rack. If desired, garnish with a dollop of whipped cream and a few banana slices. **Yield:** 12-16 servings. ***Editor's Note:** To sour milk, place 1 teaspoon white vinegar in a measuring cup. Add enough milk to equal 1/4 cup.

Apricot Almond Bars

My friend Edie Mueller brought these beautiful bars to my Christmas cookie exchange, and I wouldn't let her leave without passing on the recipe! —Arliene Hillinger, Rancho Palos Verdes, California

CRUST:
> **1-1/2 cups all-purpose flour**
> **3/4 cup confectioners' sugar**
> **1/2 cup butter** *or* **margarine, softened**
> **1/4 cup shortening**

TOPPING:
> **1 egg, lightly beaten**
> **1/2 cup sugar**
> **1/2 cup apricot preserves**
> **1 tablespoon butter** *or* **margarine, softened**
> **1/2 teaspoon vanilla extract**
> **1 cup sliced almonds**

In a mixing bowl, beat the flour, sugar, butter and shortening. Pat into the bottom and 1/2 in. up the sides of an ungreased 13-in. x 9-in. x 2-in. baking pan. Bake at 350° for 15-18 minutes or until lightly browned. For topping, beat egg, sugar, preserves, butter and vanilla in a mixing bowl until smooth. Spread over hot crust. Sprinkle with almonds. Bake at 350° for 15-20 minutes. Cool. **Yield:** 2-1/2 to 3 dozen.

Spice Cake

I enjoy cake decorating and sometimes decorate one for a family member's birthday. I've even encouraged nieces and nephews to help me bake this cake. —Robin Perry, Seneca, Pennsylvania

> **2 cups sugar**
> **1 cup butter** *or* **margarine, softened**
> **4 eggs, beaten**
> **3 cups all-purpose flour**
> **1 teaspoon baking powder**
> **1 teaspoon baking soda**
> **1 teaspoon ground cinnamon**
> **1 teaspoon ground cloves**
> **1 teaspoon ground nutmeg**
> **1 cup buttermilk**

BUTTER CREAM FROSTING:
> **1/2 cup shortening**
> **1/2 cup butter** *or* **margarine, softened**
> **1 teaspoon vanilla extract**
> **4 cups confectioners' sugar**
> **3 tablespoons milk**

In a mixing bowl, cream sugar and butter. Add eggs; beat well. Combine dry ingredients; add to creamed mixture alternately with buttermilk. Mix well. Pour into a greased and floured 13-in. x 9-

in. x 2-in. baking pan. Bake at 350° for 35-40 minutes or until a toothpick inserted near the center comes out clean. Cool. For frosting, cream shortening and butter in a mixing bowl. Add vanilla. Gradually beat in sugar. Add milk; beat until light and fluffy. Frost cake. **Yield:** 12-16 servings.

— 🥄 🥄 🥄 —

Chocolate Marshmallow Cookies

(Pictured below and on page 110)

What fun—these double-chocolaty delights have a surprise inside! Atop the chocolate cookie base, marshmallow peeks out under chocolate icing. Kids love them! —*June Formanek, Belle Plaine, Iowa*

   1/2 **cup butter** *or* **margarine, softened**
   1 **cup sugar**
   1 **egg**
   1/4 **cup milk**
   1 **teaspoon vanilla extract**
1-3/4 **cups all-purpose flour**
   1/3 **cup baking cocoa**
   1/2 **teaspoon baking soda**
   1/2 **teaspoon salt**
   16 **to 18 large marshmallows**
ICING:
   6 **tablespoons butter** *or* **margarine**
   2 **tablespoons baking cocoa**
   1/4 **cup milk**
1-3/4 **cups confectioners' sugar**
   1/2 **teaspoon vanilla extract**
Pecan halves

In a mixing bowl, cream butter and sugar. Add egg, milk and vanilla; mix well. Combine flour, cocoa, baking soda and salt; beat into creamed mixture. Drop by rounded teaspoonfuls onto ungreased cookie sheets. Bake at 350° for 8 minutes. Meanwhile, cut marshmallows in half. Press a marshmallow half, cut side down, onto each cookie. Return to the oven for 2 minutes. Cool completely on a wire rack. For icing, combine butter, cocoa and milk in a saucepan. Bring to a boil; boil for 1 minute, stirring constantly. Cool slightly; transfer to a small mixing bowl. Add confectioners' sugar and vanilla; beat well. Spread over the cooled cookies. Top each with a pecan half. **Yield:** about 3 dozen.

Cooks Choose Chocolate!

CHOCOLATE knows no season. Sweet sensations like the favorites featured here from fellow cooks might be just the thing to delight the chocolate lover closest to your heart!

🌶 🌶 🌶

Soda Cracker Chocolate Candy

(Pictured below and on page 110)

My husband and I make several batches of these chocolaty nut squares for holiday gifts. Most people are surprised to learn the recipe includes soda crackers.
—*Margery Bryan, Royal City, Washington*

35 **to 40 soda crackers**
1 **cup butter** *or* **margarine**
1 **cup packed brown sugar**
1-1/2 **cups semisweet chocolate chips**
1-1/2 **cups coarsely chopped walnuts**

Line a 15-in. x 10-in. x 1-in. baking pan with foil and coat with nonstick cooking spray. Place crackers in rows on foil. In a saucepan, melt butter; add the brown sugar and bring to a boil. Boil for 3 minutes. Pour over crackers and spread until completely covered. Bake at 350° for 5 minutes (crackers will float). Remove from the oven. Turn oven off. Sprinkle chocolate chips and walnuts over crack-

CELEBRATE with chocolaty sweets like Sandy's Chocolate Cake, Double Chocolate Chip Cookies and Soda Cracker Chocolate Candy (shown above, clockwise from upper left).

ers. Return to the oven until chocolate is melted, about 3-5 minutes. Remove from the oven; using a greased spatula, press walnuts into chocolate. Cut into 1-in. squares while warm. Cool completely; remove candy from foil. **Yield:** about 5 dozen.

— 🥄 🥄 🥄 —

Double Chocolate Chip Cookies

(Pictured below left)

Cocoa in the batter gets the credit for the double dose of chocolate in these treats, which disappear fast from the cookie jar!   *—Diane Hixon*
Niceville, Florida

      1 cup butter *or* margarine, softened
      1 cup sugar
  1/2 cup packed dark brown sugar
      1 teaspoon vanilla extract
      1 egg
  1/3 cup baking cocoa
      2 tablespoons milk
1-3/4 cups all-purpose flour
  1/4 teaspoon baking powder
      1 cup chopped walnuts
      1 cup (6 ounces) semisweet chocolate chips

In a large mixing bowl, cream the butter, sugars and vanilla. Beat in egg. Add cocoa and milk. Combine flour and baking powder; fold into creamed mixture with walnuts and chocolate chips. Roll teaspoonfuls of dough into balls; place 2 in. apart on ungreased baking sheets. Bake at 350° for 10-12 minutes. Cool for 5 minutes before removing to wire racks to cool. **Yield:** 3-4 dozen.

— 🥄 🥄 🥄 —

Sandy's Chocolate Cake

(Pictured at left)

I held this velvety, rich cake on my lap during the 4-1/2-hour drive to the Greatest Cocoa Cake Contest at the Pennsylvania Farm Show several years ago. By the time we got to the judges table, I was almost too tired to care if I won. But win I did! Topping 59 other entries, this impressive layer cake with creamy frosting took first place!   *—Sandy Johnson, Tioga, Pennsylvania*

      1 cup butter *or* margarine, softened
      3 cups packed brown sugar
      4 eggs
      2 teaspoons vanilla extract
2-2/3 cups all-purpose flour
  3/4 cup baking cocoa
      1 tablespoon baking soda
  1/2 teaspoon salt

1-1/3 cups sour cream
1-1/3 cups boiling water
FROSTING:
  1/2 cup butter (no substitutes)
      3 squares (1 ounce *each*) unsweetened chocolate
      3 squares (1 ounce *each*) semisweet chocolate
      5 cups confectioners' sugar
      1 cup (8 ounces) sour cream
      2 teaspoons vanilla extract

In a mixing bowl, cream butter and brown sugar. Add eggs, one at a time, beating well after each addition. Beat on high speed until light and fluffy. Blend in vanilla. Combine flour, cocoa, baking soda and salt; add alternately with sour cream to creamed mixture. Mix on low just until combined. Stir in water until blended. Pour into three greased and floured 9-in. round baking pans. Bake at 350° for 35 minutes or until a toothpick inserted near the center comes out clean. Cool in pans 10 minutes; remove to wire racks to cool completely. For frosting, in a medium saucepan, melt butter and chocolate over low heat. Cool several minutes. In a mixing bowl, combine sugar, sour cream and vanilla. Add chocolate mixture and beat until smooth. Frost cooled cake. **Yield:** 12-14 servings.

— 🥄 🥄 🥄 —

Packable Chocolate Chip Cake

I used this easy recipe frequently when I made brown-bag lunches for our children years ago. This recipe doesn't call for frosting, so slices travel well. Sour cream in the batter makes each piece deliciously moist. You're sure to enjoy this recipe.   —Barbara Hofstede
Waukesha, Wisconsin

      1 box (18-1/2 ounces) yellow cake mix with pudding
      1 cup (8 ounces) sour cream
  1/2 cup vegetable oil
  1/4 cup water
      4 eggs, lightly beaten
      1 to 1-1/2 cups semisweet chocolate chips
Confectioners' sugar

In a mixing bowl, combine the cake mix, sour cream, oil, water and eggs. Beat for 2 minutes. Fold in the chocolate chips. Pour into a greased 10-in. fluted tube pan. Bake at 350° for 45-50 minutes or until a toothpick inserted near the center comes out clean. Cool in pan for 20 minutes before removing to a wire rack. Just before serving, dust with confectioners' sugar. **Yield:** 12-16 servings.

Fudge Brownies

(Pictured above)

True to their name, these rich frosted bars are BIG on fudgy chocolate flavor! My family enjoys this special treat. —Inez Orsburn, Demotte, Indiana

- 1-1/4 cups butter *or* margarine, softened
-     4 cups sugar
-     8 eggs
-     2 cups all-purpose flour
- 1-1/4 cups baking cocoa
-     1 teaspoon salt
-     2 teaspoons vanilla extract
-     2 cups chopped walnuts

ICING:
-   1/2 cup butter (no substitutes)
- 1-1/2 squares (1-1/2 ounces) unsweetened chocolate
-     3 cups confectioners' sugar
-     5 tablespoons milk
-     1 teaspoon vanilla extract

Additional chopped walnuts, optional

In a mixing bowl, cream butter and sugar. Add eggs. Combine flour, cocoa and salt; add to creamed mixture and mix well. Stir in vanilla and walnuts. Spread into a greased 15-in. x 10-in. x 1-in. baking pan. Bake at 325° for 40-45 minutes or until a toothpick inserted near the center comes out clean. Cool for 10 minutes. Meanwhile, for icing, melt the butter and chocolate. Place in a mixing bowl. Add half of the confectioners' sugar; mix well. Add milk, vanilla and remaining sugar and beat until smooth. Spread immediately over warm brownies. Sprinkle with nuts if desired. **Yield:** about 3 dozen.

— 🥤 🥤 🥤 —

Oatmeal Cookies

Most folks can't believe that these chewy, lightly sweet cookies are low in fat. —Laura Letobar
Livonia, Michigan

✓ Uses less fat, sugar or salt. Includes Nutritional Analysis and Diabetic Exchanges.

-     3 cups quick-cooking oats
-   2/3 cup all-purpose flour
-   2/3 cup sugar
-   1/3 cup packed brown sugar
-     1 teaspoon baking powder
-   1/4 teaspoon salt
-   1/2 cup egg substitute
-   1/3 cup light corn syrup
-     1 teaspoon vanilla extract

In a mixing bowl, mix oats, flour, sugars, baking powder and salt. Add egg substitute, corn syrup and vanilla; mix. Drop by rounded teaspoonfuls onto cookie sheets coated with nonstick cooking spray. Bake at 350° for 10-12 minutes. **Yield:** 2 dozen. **Nutritional Analysis:** One serving (1 cookie) equals 101 calories, 47 mg sodium, trace cholesterol, 21 gm carbohydrate, 3 gm protein, 1 gm fat. **Diabetic Exchanges:** 1 starch, 1/2 fat.

Triple-Layer Cookie Bars

My family just loves these chewy chocolate and peanutty bars. They're perfect for dessert and snacks. I make them whenever I get a craving for something sweet. —Diane Bradley, Sparta, Michigan

CRUST:
1-1/4 cups all-purpose flour
  2/3 cup sugar
  1/3 cup baking cocoa
  1/4 cup packed brown sugar
    1 teaspoon baking powder
  1/4 teaspoon salt
  1/2 cup butter *or* margarine
    2 eggs, lightly beaten
TOPPING:
    1 package (7 ounces) flaked coconut
    1 can (14 ounces) sweetened condensed milk
    2 cups (12 ounces) semisweet chocolate chips
  1/2 cup creamy peanut butter

In a mixing bowl, combine the first six ingredients. Cut in butter until crumbly. Add eggs; mix well. Spread in a greased 13-in. x 9-in. x 2-in. baking pan. Bake at 350° for 8 minutes. Sprinkle coconut on top. Drizzle sweetened condensed milk evenly over coconut. Return to the oven for 20-25 minutes or until lightly browned. In a saucepan over low heat, melt chocolate chips and peanut butter, stirring until smooth. Spread over bars. Cool. **Yield:** 2-3 dozen.

No More Clumps
Spritz nonstick cooking spray on the beaters before mixing cake and cookie batters to prevent clumping.

Saucy Apple Cake
(Pictured at right and on page 110)

I found this recipe in a Midwestern cookbook. My friends and family consider it one of their favorite desserts. I like it because it's so easy to make. One delectable slice calls for another! —DeEtta Twedt Mesa, Arizona

    1 cup sugar
  1/4 cup shortening
    1 egg, lightly beaten
    1 cup all-purpose flour
    1 teaspoon baking soda
  1/2 teaspoon ground cinnamon
  1/4 teaspoon salt
    2 cups shredded peeled tart apples
  1/4 cup chopped walnuts
VANILLA SAUCE:
    1 cup sugar
    2 tablespoons cornstarch
  1/2 cup half-and-half cream
  1/2 cup butter *or* margarine
1-1/2 teaspoons vanilla extract

In a mixing bowl, cream sugar and shortening. Add egg and mix well. Add the dry ingredients; mix well. Fold in the apples and walnuts. Spread in a greased 8-in. square baking pan. Bake at 350° for 35-40 minutes or until a toothpick inserted near the center comes out clean. For sauce, combine sugar, cornstarch and cream in a saucepan. Bring to a boil over medium heat; boil for 2 minutes. Remove from the heat. Add butter and vanilla; stir until butter is melted. Serve warm over warm cake. **Yield:** 9 servings.

Sour Cream Cutouts

(Pictured below)

These soft buttery cookies make a comforting after-noon or evening snack. They have a delicious, delicate flavor and cake-like texture that pairs well with the sweet frosting. —Marlene Jackson
Kingsburg, California

    1 cup butter *or* margarine, softened
1-1/2 cups sugar
    3 eggs
    1 cup (8 ounces) sour cream
    2 teaspoons vanilla extract
3-1/2 cups all-purpose flour
    2 teaspoons baking powder
    1 teaspoon baking soda
FROSTING:
    1/3 cup butter *or* margarine, softened
    2 cups confectioners' sugar
    2 to 3 tablespoons milk
1-1/2 teaspoons vanilla extract
    1/4 teaspoon salt

In a mixing bowl, cream butter and sugar. Beat in eggs. Add sour cream and vanilla; mix well. Combine flour, baking powder and baking soda; add to the creamed mixture and mix well. Chill dough at least 2 hours or overnight. Roll on a heavily floured board to 1/4-in. thickness. Cut with a 3-in. cutter. Place on lightly greased cookie sheets. Bake at 350° for 10-12 minutes or until cookie springs back when lightly touched. Cool. Mix all frosting ingredients until smooth; spread over cookies. **Yield:** about 3-1/2 dozen.

— 🍵 🍵 🍵 —

Chewy Maple Bars

I've been making maple syrup for over 50 years and have collected many recipes. These bars, which my wife, Sue, prepares often, are the best I've ever eaten. —Wilson "Bill" Clark, Wells, Vermont

1/2 cup sugar
1/2 cup shortening
1/2 cup maple syrup
    1 egg
2/3 cup all-purpose flour
1/2 teaspoon baking powder
    1 teaspoon vanilla extract
    1 cup rolled oats
    1 cup chopped walnuts

In a mixing bowl, cream sugar and shortening. Add syrup and egg and beat well. Combine flour and baking powder; add to creamed mixture. Add vanilla and mix well. Stir in oats and walnuts. Pour into a greased 9-in. square baking pan. Bake at 350° for 35 minutes. Cut into squares while warm. Cool on a wire rack. **Yield:** about 2 dozen.

— 🍵 🍵 🍵 —

Raisin Granola Mini-Bites

Our family enjoys these cookies because they're not too sweet. Whenever we'll be doing some traveling, I'm sure to bring these along for the ride. —Germaine Stank, Pound, Wisconsin

    1 cup raisins
1/2 cup butter *or* margarine
    1 can (6 ounces) frozen apple juice
        concentrate
    1 egg, lightly beaten
1-1/4 cups all-purpose flour
    1 teaspoon baking soda
1/2 teaspoon ground cinnamon
1/2 teaspoon grated orange peel
    2 cups granola, lightly crushed

In a saucepan over medium heat, cook raisins, butter and apple juice concentrate until the butter and concentrate are melted; cool. Beat in egg. In a bowl, combine flour, baking soda, cinnamon and orange peel; add raisin mixture and blend well. Stir in granola. Let stand for 5-10 minutes. Drop by rounded teaspoonfuls onto ungreased cookie sheets. Bake at 350° for 8-10 minutes or until lightly browned. Cool on a wire rack. **Yield:** 3 dozen.

Chocolate Potato Cake

(Pictured above)

Potatoes are the secret ingredient in this moist rich cake, which is terrific for a special occasion. The white fluffy frosting goes perfectly with the dark chocolate cake. —Jill Kinder, Richlands, Virginia

- 3/4 cup butter *or* margarine, softened
- 1-1/2 cups sugar, *divided*
- 4 eggs, *separated*
- 1 cup hot mashed *or* riced potatoes (no milk, butter or seasoning added)
- 1-1/2 cups all-purpose flour
- 1/2 cup baking cocoa
- 2 teaspoons baking powder
- 1 teaspoon ground cinnamon
- 1/2 teaspoon salt
- 1/2 teaspoon ground nutmeg
- 1/4 teaspoon ground cloves
- 1 cup milk
- 1 teaspoon vanilla extract
- 1 cup chopped nuts

FLUFFY WHITE FROSTING:
- 2 egg whites
- 1-1/2 cups sugar
- 1/3 cup water
- 2 teaspoons light corn syrup
- 1/8 teaspoon salt
- 1 teaspoon vanilla extract

In a mixing bowl, cream butter and 1 cup sugar. Add egg yolks; beat well. Add potatoes and mix thoroughly. Combine flour, cocoa, baking powder, cinnamon, salt, nutmeg and cloves; add to the creamed mixture alternately with milk, beating until smooth. Stir in vanilla and nuts. In a mixing bowl, beat egg whites until foamy. Gradually add remaining sugar; beat until stiff peaks form. Fold into batter. Pour into a greased and floured 13-in. x 9-in. x 2-in. baking pan. Bake at 350° for 40-45 minutes or until a toothpick inserted near the center comes out clean. Cool. Combine first five frosting ingredients in top of a double boiler. Beat with electric mixer for 1 minute. Place over boiling water; beat constantly for 7 minutes, scraping sides of pan occasionally. Remove from heat. Add vanilla; beat 1 minute. Frost cake. **Yield:** 16-20 servings. **Editor's Note:** Cake is moist and has a firm texture.

Crumb-Free Frosting

To keep chocolate cake crumbs from getting into white frosting, first ice the cake with a very thin layer, then freeze the cake for 5 minutes or refrigerate for 15 minutes until the icing is set. Then frost with the remaining icing. The crumbs get caught in the first layer, and your top layer is lovely and crumb-free.

Frosted Banana Bars

(Pictured above and on page 110)

These bars are always a hit at potlucks here in the small rural farming community where my husband and I live. I also like to provide them for coffee hour after church. They're so moist and delicious that wherever I take them, they don't last long. —Karen Dryak
Niobrara, Nebraska

    1/2 cup butter *or* margarine, softened
      2 cups sugar
      3 eggs
1-1/2 cups mashed ripe bananas (about 3
          medium)
      1 teaspoon vanilla extract
      2 cups all-purpose flour
      1 teaspoon baking soda
Pinch salt
FROSTING:
    1/2 cup butter *or* margarine, softened
      1 package (8 ounces) cream cheese,
          softened
      4 cups confectioners' sugar
      2 teaspoons vanilla extract

In a mixing bowl, cream butter and sugar. Beat in eggs, bananas and vanilla. Combine flour, baking soda and salt. Add to creamed mixture; mix well. Pour into a greased 15-in. x 10-in. x 1-in. baking pan. Bake at 350° for 25 minutes or until a toothpick inserted near the center comes out clean. Cool. For frosting, cream butter and cream cheese in a mixing bowl. Gradually add sugar and vanilla; beat well. Spread over bars. **Yield:** 3 dozen.

———— 🥤 🥤 🥤 ————

Mom's Chocolate Chip Cookies

When I was growing up, Mom often brightened my brown-bag lunches with these yummy cookies. Instant pudding mix makes them nice and soft. —Tammy Orr
Wharton, New Jersey

      1 cup butter *or* margarine, softened
    3/4 cup packed brown sugar
    1/4 cup sugar
      1 package (3.4 ounces) instant vanilla
          pudding mix
      2 eggs, lightly beaten

1 teaspoon vanilla extract
2-1/4 cups all-purpose flour
1 teaspoon baking soda
2 cups (12 ounces) semisweet chocolate
chips

In a mixing bowl, cream butter and sugars. Add pudding mix, eggs and vanilla. Combine flour and baking soda; add to creamed mixture and mix well. Fold in chocolate chips. Drop by teaspoonfuls onto ungreased baking sheets. Bake at 375° for 10-12 minutes or until lightly browned. **Yield:** 4 dozen.

—— 🍴 🍴 🍴 ——

No-Bake Raisin Bars

Hearty bars like these make a terrific take-along breakfast or afternoon snack. Plus, they take little time to prepare. —*Dawn Fagerstrom, Warren, Montana*

3 cups miniature marshmallows
1/4 cup butter *or* margarine
5 cups multi-grain puffed rice cereal
1 cup raisins
1/2 cup chopped walnuts
1/4 teaspoon ground cinnamon

In a large saucepan or microwave-safe bowl, heat marshmallows and butter over low until melted; mix well. Stir in the cereal, raisins, walnuts and cinnamon. Pat into a greased 13-in. x 9-in. x 2-in. baking pan. Cool. Cut into bars. **Yield:** 2 dozen.

—— 🍴 🍴 🍴 ——

Oatmeal Chip Cookies

These delicious, nutritious cookies use lots of oatmeal. They're crisp on the outside and sweet, chewy inside. —*Ruth Ann Stelfox, Raymond, Alberta*

2 cups butter *or* margarine, softened
2 cups sugar
2 cups packed brown sugar
4 eggs
2 teaspoons vanilla extract
6 cups quick-cooking oats
3 cups all-purpose flour
2 teaspoons baking soda
1 teaspoon salt
2 cups (12 ounces) semisweet chocolate
chips

In a mixing bowl, cream butter, sugars, eggs and vanilla. Combine oats, flour, baking soda and salt; stir into creamed mixture. Add chocolate chips and mix well. Chill dough for 1 hour or until firm. Roll dough into 1-1/2-in. balls; place on greased cook-

ie sheets. Bake at 350° for 11-13 minutes or until lightly browned. **Yield:** about 7 dozen.

—— 🍴 🍴 🍴 ——

Chewy Brownie Cookies

(Pictured below)

Biting into these chocolaty cookies reveals they're like chewy brownies inside. —*Jonie Adams*
Albion, Michigan

2/3 cup shortening
1-1/2 cups packed brown sugar
1 tablespoon water
1 teaspoon vanilla extract
2 eggs
1-1/2 cups all-purpose flour
1/3 cup baking cocoa
1/2 teaspoon salt
1/4 teaspoon baking soda
2 cups (12 ounces) semisweet chocolate
chips
1/2 cup chopped walnuts *or* pecans, optional

In a large mixing bowl, cream shortening, sugar, water and vanilla. Beat in the eggs. Combine flour, cocoa, salt and baking soda; gradually add to creamed mixture and beat just until blended. Stir in chocolate chips and nuts if desired. Drop by rounded teaspoonfuls 2 in. apart on ungreased baking sheets. Bake at 375° for 7-9 minutes; do not overbake. Cool 2 minutes before removing to wire racks. **Yield:** 3 dozen.

Favorites from Grandma's Pantry

RECALL when the best holiday cookies came from Grandma's cozy kitchen? She made them with love and served them up with a warm smile...and didn't mind a bit if you polished off the entire batch!

Recapture that great feeling with these all-time-favorite cookie recipes from some special Grandmas.

— ☕ ☕ ☕ —

Cutout Christmas Cookies

(Pictured below)

These old-fashioned cookies have been a tradition in my family for many years. It was always a joy to make these cookies for my children, and now I have little grandchildren who will soon be enjoying them, too.
—Carolyn Moseley, Charleston, South Carolina

1 cup butter *or* margarine, softened
1 cup sugar
2 eggs
1-1/2 teaspoons vanilla extract
3-1/2 cups all-purpose flour
1 teaspoon ground cinnamon
1/2 teaspoon baking powder
1/2 teaspoon salt
1/4 teaspoon ground cloves
1/4 teaspoon ground nutmeg
1 egg white, beaten
Colored decorating sugars

In a mixing bowl, cream butter and sugar. Add eggs and vanilla. Combine flour, cinnamon, baking powder, salt, cloves and nutmeg; gradually add to creamed mixture and mix well. Chill for at least 1

OLD-FASHIONED FLAVORS star in nostalgic Cutout Christmas Cookies, Granny's Spice Cookies and Date Swirls (shown above, clockwise from upper right).

hour. On a lightly floured surface, roll dough, a portion at a time, to 1/8-in. thickness. Cut into desired shapes. Place on ungreased baking sheets. Bake at 350° for 12-14 minutes or until edges begin to brown. Carefully brush with egg white; sprinkle with colored sugar. Return to the oven for 3-5 minutes or until lightly browned. **Yield:** about 6 dozen (2-inch cookies).

Granny's Spice Cookies

(Pictured below left)

Granny always had a batch of these delicious, crispy cookies waiting for us at her house. She lives far away, so when I miss her more than usual, I make these cookies and let the aroma fill my house and heart.
—*Valerie Hudson, Mason City, Iowa*

1 cup butter *or* margarine, softened
1-1/2 cups sugar
1 egg, lightly beaten
2 tablespoons light corn syrup
2 tablespoons grated orange peel
1 tablespoon cold water
3-1/4 cups all-purpose flour
2 teaspoons baking soda
2 teaspoons ground cinnamon
1 teaspoon ground ginger
1/2 teaspoon ground cloves
Red-hot candies, nonpareils *and/or* sprinkles

In a mixing bowl, cream butter and sugar. Add egg, corn syrup, orange peel and cold water. Combine flour, baking soda, cinnamon, ginger and cloves; add to creamed mixture and mix well. Chill for at least 1 hour. On a lightly floured surface, roll dough, a portion at a time, to 1/8-in. thickness. Cut into desired shapes. Place on greased baking sheets. Decorate as desired. Bake at 375° for 6-8 minutes or until lightly browned. **Yield:** about 4 dozen (3-inch cookies).

Date Swirls

(Pictured at left)

Years ago, our granddaughter nicknamed my mother "Cookie Grandma" because she always made wonderful cookies. Mom made these crisp and chewy cookies every Christmas without fail. —*Donna Grace Clancy, Montana*

FILLING:
2 cups chopped dates
1 cup water
1 cup sugar
1 cup chopped nuts
2 teaspoons lemon juice
DOUGH:
1 cup butter *or* margarine, softened
1 cup packed brown sugar
1 cup sugar
3 eggs
1 teaspoon lemon extract
4 cups all-purpose flour
1 teaspoon salt
3/4 teaspoon baking soda

In a saucepan, combine all the filling ingredients. Cook over medium-low heat, stirring constantly, until mixture becomes stiff, about 15-20 minutes. Chill. For dough, cream the butter and sugars in a mixing bowl. Add eggs, one at a time, beating well after each addition. Add extract. Combine the flour, salt and baking soda; gradually add to creamed mixture and mix well. Chill for at least 1 hour. On a lightly floured surface, roll out half of the dough to a 12-in. x 9-in. rectangle, about 1/4 in. thick. Spread with half of the filling. Roll up, starting with the long end. Repeat with the remaining dough and filling. Wrap with plastic wrap; chill overnight. Cut rolls into 1/4-in. slices. Place 2 in. apart on greased baking sheets. Bake at 375° for 8-10 minutes or until lightly browned. Cool on wire racks. **Yield:** 4 dozen.

Raisin Bran Chewies

I created this recipe when I was trying to use up some Raisin Bran cereal. Now I buy the cereal just to make these cookies! —*Ione Perkins, Rawlins, Wyoming*

1 cup shortening
1 cup packed brown sugar
1/2 cup sugar
2 eggs, lightly beaten
2 tablespoons honey
2 teaspoons vanilla extract
2-1/4 cups all-purpose flour
1/2 teaspoon baking soda
1/4 teaspoon salt
3 cups Raisin Bran cereal
3/4 cup raisins
1/2 cup chopped walnuts

In a mixing bowl, cream shortening and sugars. Add eggs, honey and vanilla; mix well. Combine flour, baking soda and salt; add to creamed mixture. Stir in cereal. Fold in raisins and walnuts. Drop by teaspoonfuls onto greased baking sheets. Bake at 350° for 12-14 minutes or until a toothpick inserted near the center comes out clean. **Yield:** 4 dozen.

1/2 cup shortening
1 cup packed brown sugar
2 eggs
1 cup mashed ripe bananas (2 to 3 medium)
2 cups all-purpose flour
2 teaspoons baking powder
1/2 teaspoon ground cinnamon
1/4 teaspoon baking soda
1/4 teaspoon ground cloves
1/4 teaspoon salt
1/2 cup chopped walnuts
1/2 cup raisins

In a mixing bowl, cream shortening and brown sugar. Add eggs and bananas; mix well. Combine dry ingredients; add to creamed mixture and mix well. Stir in nuts and raisins. Chill (dough will be very soft). Drop by rounded teaspoonfuls onto greased baking sheets. Bake at 350° for 8-10 minutes or until lightly browned. **Yield:** 3 dozen.

Cookie Jar Gingersnaps

(Pictured above)

My grandma kept two cookie jars in her pantry. One of the jars, which I now have, always had these crisp and chewy gingersnaps in it. They're still my favorite. My daughter, Becky, used this recipe for a 4-H fair when she was 11 years old and won a blue ribbon.
—Deb Handy, Pomona, Kansas

3/4 cup shortening
1 cup sugar
1 egg
1/4 cup molasses
2 cups all-purpose flour
2 teaspoons baking soda
1-1/2 teaspoons ground ginger
1 teaspoon ground cinnamon
1/2 teaspoon salt
Additional sugar

In a large mixing bowl, cream the shortening and sugar. Beat in the egg and molasses. Combine flour, baking soda, ginger, cinnamon and salt; gradually add to the creamed mixture. Roll teaspoonfuls of dough into balls. Dip one side of each ball into sugar; place with sugar side up on a greased baking sheet. Bake at 350° for 12-15 minutes or until lightly browned and crinkly. **Yield:** 3-4 dozen.

🍃 🍃 🍃

Banana Spice Cookies

My grandkids love these tasty, soft cookies. They're a fun and different way to use up overripe bananas.
—Peggy Burdick, Burlington, Michigan

Measuring Sticky Ingredients

Before measuring ingredients such as molasses, honey or syrup, first lightly spray the measuring spoon or cup with nonstick cooking spray. The sticky ingredient easily slides right out with no mess on the measuring spoon or cup.

Praline Brownies

I created these brownies as a tribute to the luscious candy that is so popular in the Deep South. Dark brown sugar adds to the richness.
—Mindy Weiser
Southport, North Carolina

1/2 cup packed dark brown sugar
3/4 cup butter *or* margarine, *divided*
2 tablespoons evaporated milk
1/2 cup coarsely chopped pecans
2 cups packed light brown sugar
2 eggs
1-1/2 cups all-purpose flour
1 teaspoon vanilla extract
1/2 teaspoon salt

In a saucepan, combine the dark brown sugar, 1/4 cup butter and milk. Stir over low heat just until butter is melted. Pour into an ungreased 8-in. square baking pan; sprinkle evenly with pecans. In a mixing bowl, cream light brown sugar and remaining butter; add eggs. Stir in flour, vanilla and salt until moistened. Spread over pecans. Bake at 350° for 40-45 minutes or until a toothpick inserted near the center comes out clean. Cool 5 minutes in pan; invert onto a tray or serving plate. Cool slightly before cutting. **Yield:** 16 brownies.

Black-Bottom Banana Bars

(Pictured below)

These bars stay very moist, and their rich banana and chocolate flavor is even better the second day. My mother-in-law gave me this recipe, and it's a big favorite with both my husband and two sons.
—Renee Wright, Ferryville, Wisconsin

    1/2 cup butter *or* margarine, softened
      1 cup sugar
      1 egg
      1 teaspoon vanilla extract
    1-1/2 cups mashed ripe bananas (about 3 medium)
    1-1/2 cups all-purpose flour
      1 teaspoon baking powder
      1 teaspoon baking soda
    1/2 teaspoon salt
    1/4 cup baking cocoa

In a mixing bowl, cream butter and sugar. Add egg and vanilla; beat until thoroughly combined. Blend in the bananas. Combine the flour, baking powder, baking soda and salt; add to creamed mixture and mix well. Divide batter in half. Add cocoa to half; spread into a greased 13-in. x 9-in. x 2-in. baking pan. Spoon remaining batter on top and swirl with a knife. Bake at 350° for 25 minutes or until a toothpick inserted near the center comes out clean. Cool. **Yield:** 2-1/2 to 3 dozen.

Dipped Peanut Butter Sandwich Cookies

A tin of these chocolate-coated cookies is a tempting treat you'll love to give. The recipe is almost too simple to believe! —Jackie Howell, Gordo, Alabama

    1/2 cup creamy peanut butter
      1 sleeve (4 ounces) round butter-flavored crackers
      1 cup (6 ounces) white, semisweet *or* milk chocolate chips
      1 tablespoon shortening

Spread peanut butter on half of the crackers; top with remaining crackers to make sandwiches. Refrigerate. In a double boiler over simmering water, melt chocolate chips and shortening, stirring until smooth. Dip sandwiches and place on waxed paper until chocolate hardens. **Yield:** 1-1/2 dozen.

Banana Nut Layer Cake

(Pictured above and on page 110)

This cake is the top choice of the "birthday child" in our family! —Patsy Howard, Bakersfield, California

    1/2 cup shortening
      2 cups sugar
      1 egg plus 1 egg white
      1 cup buttermilk
      1 cup mashed ripe bananas
      2 cups all-purpose flour
      1 teaspoon baking soda
      1 teaspoon salt
      1 teaspoon vanilla extract
    1/2 cup chopped walnuts
FILLING:
    1/4 cup butter *or* margarine
    1/2 cup packed brown sugar
    1/4 cup all-purpose flour
Pinch salt
    3/4 cup milk
      1 egg yolk
      1 teaspoon vanilla extract
    1/2 cup chopped walnuts
Confectioners' sugar

In a mixing bowl, cream shortening and sugar. Beat in egg and egg white. Add buttermilk and bananas; mix well. Combine flour, baking soda and salt; stir into the creamed mixture. Add vanilla and nuts. Pour into two greased and floured 9-in. round baking pans. Bake at 350° for 35 minutes or until a toothpick inserted near the center comes out clean. Cool in pans 10 minutes before removing to a wire rack. For filling, melt butter and brown sugar in a saucepan over medium heat. In a small bowl, combine flour and salt with a small amount of milk; stir until smooth. Add the remaining milk gradually. Add egg yolk and mix well; stir into saucepan. Cook and stir over medium heat until very thick, about 10 minutes. Add vanilla and nuts. Cool. Spread between cake layers. Dust with confectioners' sugar. Store in the refrigerator. **Yield:** 10-12 servings.

Buttery Black Walnut Brittle

Here in the Ozarks, black walnuts are very plentiful and are often called "Black Gold". We usually start harvesting the nuts from the trees on our property in

the beginning of October so I can use them to make this Christmas candy. —Anne Medlin, Bolivar, Missouri

- 1 cup sugar
- 1/2 cup corn syrup
- 1/4 cup water
- 1/2 cup butter (no substitutes)
- 1 to 1-1/2 cups black walnuts
- 1/2 teaspoon baking soda

In a saucepan, cook sugar, corn syrup and water until sugar dissolves and mixture comes to a boil. Add butter; cook until mixture reaches 280° (soft-crack stage) on a candy thermometer. Stir in walnuts; cook until 300° (hard-crack stage). Remove from the heat and stir in baking soda. Spread immediately into a greased 15-in. x 10-in. x 1-in. baking pan. When cool, break into pieces. Store in an airtight container. **Yield:** 1-1/4 pounds.

Handy Homemade Mixes

When you make a cake, prepare a few homemade cake mixes. As you measure the dry ingredients into the mixing bowl, put the same amounts into plastic storage bags. Then label the bags with the recipe name, what to add and baking instructions. Keep a supply of mixes on hand to use whenever you need a quick dessert.

Persimmon Pudding Cake

I put up jams and jellies featuring persimmons, but also use that delectable fruit in desserts. I think you'll savor this moist cake with a bit of spice. It tastes great served with a dollop of whipped cream.
—Ralph Wheat, Bedford, Texas

- 4 eggs
- 1 cup milk
- 2-1/4 cups sugar
- 1 teaspoon vanilla extract
- 1-1/2 teaspoons salt
- 4-1/2 tablespoons butter *or* margarine, softened
- 3 cups all-purpose flour
- 1-1/2 teaspoons ground cinnamon
- 1 teaspoon baking soda
- 3 cups ripe persimmon pulp
- 1 cup chopped dates
- 1 cup flaked coconut
- 1 cup chopped walnuts *or* pecans
Whipped cream, optional

In a bowl, beat eggs. Add milk, sugar, vanilla and salt; mix well. Stir in butter. Combine flour, cinnamon and baking soda; add to milk mixture. Fold in persimmon pulp, dates, coconut and nuts. Pour

into a greased 13-in. x 9-in. x 2-in. baking pan. Bake at 325° for 1 hour or until a toothpick inserted near center comes out clean. Serve warm or at room temperature with whipped cream if desired. **Yield:** 20-24 servings.

Pumpkin Chocolate Chip Cookies

I'm one of the cooking project leaders for my daughter's 4-H club, where these soft delicious cookies were a great hit with the kids. —Marietta Slater, Augusta, Kansas

- 1 cup butter *or* margarine, softened
- 3/4 cup packed brown sugar
- 3/4 cup sugar
- 1 egg
- 1 teaspoon vanilla extract
- 2 cups all-purpose flour
- 1 cup quick-cooking oats
- 1 teaspoon baking soda
- 1 teaspoon ground cinnamon
- 1 cup cooked *or* canned pumpkin
- 1-1/2 cups semisweet chocolate chips

In a mixing bowl, cream butter and sugars. Beat in egg and vanilla. Combine flour, oats, baking soda and cinnamon; stir into creamed mixture alternately with pumpkin. Fold in chocolate chips. Drop by tablespoonfuls onto greased baking sheets. Bake at 350° for 12-13 minutes or until lightly browned. **Yield:** 4 dozen.

Picnic Cupcakes

These moist cupcakes don't need frosting, so they're perfect for taking along to a picnic. Kids and adults love them. —Florence Leinweber, Endicott, Washington

- 1 package (18-1/2 ounces) chocolate *or* yellow cake mix
FILLING:
- 1 package (8 ounces) cream cheese, softened
- 1 egg, lightly beaten
- 1/3 cup sugar
- 1 cup (6 ounces) semisweet chocolate chips

Mix cake according to package directions. Spoon batter into 24 greased or paper-lined muffin cups, filling two-thirds full. In a mixing bowl, beat cream cheese, egg and sugar until smooth. Fold in the chips. Drop by tablespoonfuls into batter. Bake at 350° for 20 minutes or until a toothpick inserted near the center comes out clean. **Yield:** 2 dozen.

In a large mixing bowl, combine the dry ingredients. Add the eggs, water, oil, vinegar and vanilla; mix well. Pour into 18 greased or paper-lined muffin cups. For filling, beat cream cheese and sugar in another mixing bowl. Add egg and salt; mix well. Fold in the chocolate chips. Drop by tablespoonfuls into center of each cupcake. Sprinkle with nuts. Bake at 350° for 25-30 minutes or until a toothpick inserted near the center comes out clean. **Yield:** 1-1/2 dozen.

— 🝙 🝙 🝙 —

Chocolate Macadamia Nut Cookies

This recipe is from my daughter, who's a terrific cook. The caramel glaze makes it impossible to eat just one.
—Arliene Hillinger
Rancho Palos Verdes, California

    10 tablespoons butter (no substitutes),
       softened
   3/4 cup packed brown sugar
     1 teaspoon vanilla extract
     1 egg, lightly beaten
     1 cup all-purpose flour
   3/4 teaspoon baking powder
   1/8 teaspoon baking soda
   1/8 teaspoon salt
 1-1/2 cups semisweet chocolate chips
   3/4 cup coarsely chopped macadamia nuts
   3/4 cup coarsely chopped pecans
CARAMEL GLAZE:
    12 caramel candies
     2 tablespoons whipping cream

In a mixing bowl, cream the butter, sugar and vanilla. Add egg. Combine the flour, baking powder, baking soda and salt; add to creamed mixture and mix well. Fold in chocolate chips and nuts. Drop by teaspoonfuls 2 in. apart onto greased baking sheets. Bake at 350° for 10-12 minutes or until golden. Cool on a wire rack. For glaze, melt the caramels and cream in a saucepan over low heat, stirring until smooth. Drizzle over cooled cookies. **Yield:** 2 dozen.

— 🝙 🝙 🝙 —

Creamy Chocolate Cupcakes

(Pictured above)

The "surprise" inside these rich chocolate cupcakes is their smooth cream cheese filling.
—Mrs. Walter Jacobson, Ashland, Ohio

 1-1/2 cups all-purpose flour
     1 cup sugar
   1/4 cup baking cocoa
     1 teaspoon baking soda
   1/2 teaspoon salt
     2 eggs, lightly beaten
   3/4 cup water
   1/3 cup vegetable oil
     1 tablespoon vinegar
     1 teaspoon vanilla extract
FILLING:
     1 package (8 ounces) cream cheese,
       softened
   1/3 cup sugar
     1 egg, lightly beaten
   1/8 teaspoon salt
     1 cup (6 ounces) semisweet chocolate chips
     1 cup chopped walnuts

Icebox Cookies

(Pictured at right)

This cookie recipe from my grandmother was my grandfather's favorite. She still makes them and sends us home with the dough so we can make more whenever we want. I love to make a fresh batch when company drops in. *—Chris Paulsen, Glendale, Arizona*

   1/2 cup butter *or* margarine, softened

1 cup packed brown sugar
1 egg, beaten
1/2 teaspoon vanilla extract
2 cups all-purpose flour
1/2 teaspoon baking soda
1/2 teaspoon cream of tartar
1/2 teaspoon salt
1 cup chopped walnuts, optional

In a mixing bowl, cream the butter and brown sugar. Add egg and vanilla; beat well. Combine dry ingredients; add to creamed mixture. Stir in nuts if desired. On a lightly floured surface, shape the dough into three 10-in. x 1-in. rolls. Tightly wrap each roll in waxed paper. Freeze for at least 12 hours. Cut into 3/8-in. slices and place on greased baking sheets. Bake at 350° for 6-8 minutes. Remove to a wire rack to cool. **Yield:** about 7 dozen.

Sugar-Free Raisin Bars

My mother is diabetic, so I keep these moist, golden bars on hand for dessert. I even serve them during the holidays. They're a nice light snack for everyone.
—Betty Ruenholl, Syracuse, Nebraska

✓ Uses less fat, sugar or salt. Includes Nutritional Analysis and Diabetic Exchanges.

1/2 cup water
1 cup raisins
1/4 cup margarine, softened

1 egg
3/4 cup unsweetened applesauce
1 teaspoon vanilla extract
1 cup all-purpose flour
Sugar substitute equivalent to 1 tablespoon sugar
1 teaspoon ground cinnamon
1/4 teaspoon baking soda
1/4 teaspoon salt
1/8 teaspoon ground nutmeg

In a saucepan, bring water to a boil. Add raisins, then remove from the heat. Let stand for 10 minutes; drain well and set aside. In a bowl, cream margarine. Beat in egg and applesauce. Add vanilla. In a bowl, combine the flour, sugar substitute, cinnamon, baking soda, salt and nutmeg. Stir into applesauce mixture just until moistened. Stir in reserved raisins. Pour into an 8-in. square baking dish coated with nonstick cooking spray. Bake at 350° for 25-30 minutes or until toothpick inserted near center comes out clean. Cool in pan on wire rack. **Yield:** 16 bars. **Nutritional Analysis:** One bar equals 89 calories, 150 mg sodium, 13 mg cholesterol, 15 gm carbohydrate, 1 gm protein, 3 gm fat. **Diabetic Exchanges:** 1/2 starch, 1/2 fruit, 1/2 fat.

Chilled Cookie Dough Slices
To quickly and easily cut rolled and chilled cookie dough, use your electric knife. It makes perfect cookies every time.

Pies & Desserts

*Family and friends will sing your praises when
fresh and fruity pies, cool creamy puddings and a host of
other desserts make an appearance on the dinner table.*

FINISHING TOUCHES. Clockwise from upper left:
Candy Apple Pie (p. 138), Chocolate Trifle (p. 145),
Lemony Apple Dumplings (p. 134), Ambrosia
Dessert Bowl (p. 135) and Fruit Pizza (p. 146).

Creamy Banana Pie

(Pictured below)

When friends ask me to share a recipe using bananas, I know instantly this is the dessert to pass along. This delectable pie is from a recipe I found years ago, and everyone who tastes it enjoys its delicious old-fashioned flavor.
—Rita Pribyl
Indianapolis, Indiana

    1 **envelope unflavored gelatin**
1/4 **cup cold water**
3/4 **cup sugar**
1/4 **cup cornstarch**
1/2 **teaspoon salt**
2-3/4 **cups milk**
    4 **egg yolks, beaten**
    2 **tablespoons butter *or* margarine**
    1 **tablespoon vanilla extract**
    4 **medium firm bananas**
    1 **cup whipping cream, whipped**
    1 **pastry shell (10 inches), baked**
Juice and grated peel of 1 lemon
1/2 **cup apple jelly**

Soften the gelatin in cold water; set aside. In a saucepan, combine sugar, cornstarch and salt. Blend in the milk and egg yolks; cook over low

BANANAS AT THEIR BEST! Fruitful favorites like Creamy Banana Pie and Banana Bread Pudding (shown above, top to bottom) have real taste "a-peel".

heat, stirring constantly, until thickened and bubbly, about 20-25 minutes. Remove from the heat; stir in softened gelatin until dissolved. Stir in butter and vanilla. Cover the surface of custard with plastic wrap and chill until no longer warm. Slice 3 bananas; fold into custard with whipped cream. Spoon into pie shell. Chill until set, about 4-5 hours. Shortly before serving time, place lemon juice in a small bowl and slice the remaining banana into it. Melt jelly in a saucepan over low heat. Drain banana; pat dry and arrange on top of pie. Brush banana with the jelly. Sprinkle with grated lemon peel. Serve immediately. **Yield:** 8 servings. **Editor's Note:** The filling is very light in color. It is not topped with additional whipped cream.

— 🍷 🍷 🍷 —

Banana Bread Pudding

(Pictured at left)

When I visited my grandmother in summer, I always looked forward to the comforting pudding she'd make. With its crusty golden top, custard-like inside and smooth vanilla sauce, this bread pudding is a real homespun dessert. Now I make it for my grandchildren.
—_Mary Detweiler, West Farmington, Ohio_

       4 cups cubed day-old French _or_ sourdough
          bread (1-inch pieces)
    1/4 cup butter _or_ margarine, melted
       3 eggs
       2 cups milk
    1/2 cup sugar
       2 teaspoons vanilla extract
    1/2 teaspoon ground cinnamon
    1/2 teaspoon ground nutmeg
    1/2 teaspoon salt
       1 cup sliced firm bananas (1/4-inch pieces)
SAUCE:
       3 tablespoons butter _or_ margarine
       2 tablespoons sugar
       1 tablespoon cornstarch
    3/4 cup milk
    1/4 cup light corn syrup
       1 teaspoon vanilla extract

Place the bread cubes in a greased 2-qt. casserole; pour butter over and toss to coat. In a medium bowl, lightly beat eggs; add milk, sugar, vanilla, cinnamon, nutmeg and salt. Stir in bananas. Pour over bread cubes and stir to coat. Bake, uncovered, at 375° for 40 minutes or until a knife inserted near the center comes out clean. Meanwhile, for sauce, melt butter in a small saucepan. Combine sugar and cornstarch; add to butter. Stir in milk and corn syrup. Cook and stir over medium heat until the mixture comes to a full boil. Boil for

1 minute. Remove from the heat; stir in the vanilla. Serve warm sauce over warm pudding. **Yield:** 6 servings.

— 🍷 🍷 🍷 —

Peach Praline Pie

Peach pie gets a delightful twist with a nutty layer beneath and atop the sliced fruit. It's a dessert that always draws compliments!   —_Clarice Schweitzer_
                                    Sun City, Arizona

       4 cups sliced peeled ripe peaches
       1 cup sugar, _divided_
       2 tablespoons quick-cooking tapioca
       1 teaspoon lemon juice
    1/2 cup all-purpose flour
    1/2 cup chopped pecans _or_ walnuts
    1/4 cup butter _or_ margarine
       1 unbaked pastry shell (9 inches)
Whipped cream _or_ ice cream, optional

In a large bowl, combine peaches, 1/4 cup sugar, tapioca and lemon juice; mix well. In a small bowl, combine flour, nuts and remaining sugar; cut in butter until crumbly. Sprinkle a third of the crumbs into pie shell; cover with peaches. Sprinkle remaining crumbs on top. Bake at 450° for 10 minutes. Reduce heat to 350°; bake for 30 minutes or until the peaches are tender and topping is golden brown. Serve with whipped cream or ice cream if desired. **Yield:** 6-8 servings.

— 🍷 🍷 🍷 —

Frozen Chocolate Torte

In summer, this cool make-ahead dessert is one of my favorites.   —_Tammy Neubauer, Ida Grove, Iowa_

       1 package (10-1/2 ounces) miniature
          marshmallows
       1 cup (6 ounces) semisweet chocolate chips
       1 can (12 ounces) evaporated milk
       1 cup flaked coconut
    1/2 cup butter _or_ margarine
       2 cups graham cracker crumbs
    1/2 gallon vanilla ice cream, softened

In a saucepan over low heat, melt marshmallows and chocolate chips with milk. Remove from the heat; cool. In a skillet, cook and stir coconut in butter until browned. Remove from the heat; stir in crumbs. Pat three-fourths into a 13-in. x 9-in. x 2-in. baking pan; cool. Spoon half of the ice cream onto crust. Top with half of the chocolate mixture. Layer with remaining ice cream and chocolate. Sprinkle with remaining crumbs. Cover and freeze for at least 2 hours. **Yield:** 12 servings.

Combine flour and 1 teaspoon salt. Cut in shortening until crumbly. Stir in milk until pastry forms a ball; set aside. Stir brown sugar, butter, cinnamon and remaining salt to form a paste. Divide and press into center of each apple; pat any extra filling on outside of apples. On a floured surface, roll pastry into a 14-in. square. Cut into four 7-in. squares. Place one apple in center of each square. Brush edges of pastry with egg white. Fold up corners to center; pinch to seal. Place in a greased 9-in. square baking dish. Bake at 375° for 35-40 minutes or until golden brown. Meanwhile, combine sugar and cornstarch in a saucepan. Stir in water. Bring to a boil; boil 2 minutes. Remove from heat; stir in remaining ingredients until smooth. Serve warm sauce over warm dumplings. **Yield:** 4 servings.

🝡 🝡 🝡

Best-Ever Cheesecake

I've passed this recipe on to dozens of folks. My daughter was so fond of it that she wanted it served for her wedding instead of traditional cake. —Howard Koch
Lima, Ohio

1-1/4 cups graham cracker crumbs
  1/3 cup butter *or* margarine, melted
  1/4 cup sugar
FILLING/TOPPING:
    2 packages (8 ounces *each*) cream cheese, softened
    2 eggs, lightly beaten
  2/3 cup sugar, *divided*
    2 teaspoons vanilla extract, *divided*
Pinch salt
    1 cup (8 ounces) sour cream

In a bowl, combine the graham cracker crumbs, butter and sugar; mix well. Pat evenly into the bottom and up the sides of a 9-in. pie plate. Chill. For filling, beat cream cheese and eggs in a mixing bowl on medium speed for 1 minute. Add 1/3 cup sugar, 1 teaspoon of vanilla and salt. Continue beating until well blended, about 1 minute. Pour into crust. Bake at 350° for 35 minutes. Cool for 10 minutes. For topping, combine the sour cream, and remaining sugar and vanilla in a small bowl; spread evenly over cheesecake. Return to the oven for 10 minutes. Cool completely on a wire rack. Refrigerate 3 hours or overnight. **Yield:** 8 servings.

Lemony Apple Dumplings

(Pictured above and on page 130)

The first time I made this recipe, I was serving guests who had two little daughters. The girls weren't sure about eating a dessert that looked so different. But after just one bite, they proclaimed the treat "yummy" and cleaned their plates. The smooth lemon sauce adds a bit of zip. —Kristy Deloach, Baker, Louisiana

1-1/2 cups all-purpose flour
1-1/4 teaspoons salt, *divided*
  1/3 cup shortening
    4 to 5 tablespoons cold milk
  1/2 cup packed brown sugar
    3 tablespoons butter *or* margarine, softened
  1/2 teaspoon ground cinnamon
    4 medium baking apples, peeled and cored
    1 egg white, beaten
LEMON SAUCE:
  1/2 cup sugar
    4 teaspoons cornstarch
    1 cup water
    3 tablespoons butter *or* margarine
    4 teaspoons lemon juice
    2 teaspoons grated lemon peel
  1/8 teaspoon salt

Avoid Cracks in Cheesecake

For a perfect-looking cheesecake, place a shallow pan of water in the oven while baking. The moisture helps prevent cracking.

Pumpkin Bread Pudding

This comforting dessert is old-fashioned but never out of style. I got this favorite pumpkin recipe from an elderly aunt. —Lois Fetting, Nelson, Wisconsin

    4 cups cubed day-old whole wheat bread
  1/2 cup chopped dates *or* raisins
  1/2 cup chopped pecans, *divided*
    2 cups milk
    1 cup cooked *or* canned pumpkin
    2 eggs, *separated*
  2/3 cup packed brown sugar
1-1/2 teaspoons ground cinnamon
  3/4 teaspoon ground nutmeg
  1/4 teaspoon salt
  1/8 teaspoon ground cloves
Half-and-half cream *or* whipped cream,
  optional

Combine bread cubes, dates and 1/3 cup pecans; place in a greased 2-qt. shallow baking dish. In a mixing bowl, combine the milk, pumpkin, egg yolks, brown sugar, cinnamon, nutmeg, salt and cloves; beat well. In a small mixing bowl, beat egg whites until stiff; fold into pumpkin mixture. Pour over bread cubes and toss gently. Sprinkle with remaining nuts. Bake, uncovered, at 350° for 1 hour or until a knife inserted near the center comes out clean. Serve warm or chilled with cream if desired. **Yield:** 6-8 servings.

Sweet Potato Pie

The North Carolina Sweet Potato Commission contends that any day's a holiday for sweet potatoes. Instead of serving traditional pumpkin pie at Thanksgiving, try this creamy dessert that's subtly spiced and slices beautifully.

  1/3 cup butter *or* margarine, softened
  1/2 cup sugar
    2 eggs, lightly beaten
  3/4 cup evaporated milk
    2 cups mashed sweet potatoes
    1 teaspoon vanilla extract
  1/2 teaspoon ground cinnamon
  1/2 teaspoon ground nutmeg
  1/4 teaspoon salt
    1 unbaked pastry shell (9 inches)

In a mixing bowl, cream butter and sugar. Add eggs; mix well. Add milk, sweet potatoes, vanilla, cinnamon, nutmeg and salt; mix well. Pour into pie shell. Bake at 425° for 15 minutes. Reduce heat to 350°; bake 35-40 minutes longer or until a knife inserted near the center comes out clean. Cool. Store in refrigerator. **Yield:** 6-8 servings.

Ambrosia Dessert Bowl

(Pictured below and on page 130)

I'm happy to share this wonderful recipe that uses fresh oranges. I've had it a long time. As a volunteer wildlife rehabilitator, I keep busy throughout the year. It's nice to treat myself to a light, refreshing dessert. —Donna Morris, Weirsdale, Florida

  20 large marshmallows
    2 cups whipping cream, *divided*
    2 tablespoons sugar
    2 teaspoons vanilla extract
  1/2 teaspoon almond extract
    1 can (20 ounces) crushed pineapple, well drained
    1 cup flaked coconut
    1 loaf (10-3/4 ounces) frozen pound cake, thawed and cubed (about 4 cups)
    5 to 6 large navel oranges, peeled and sectioned
  1/4 cup slivered almonds, toasted

Place marshmallows and 1/4 cup cream in the top of a double boiler; heat over boiling water until marshmallows are melted and mixture is smooth. Cool completely. Meanwhile, whip remaining cream until thick. Add sugar. Fold into marshmallow mixture. Fold in extracts, pineapple and coconut. Place half of the pound cake cubes in the bottom of a 2-1/2- to 3-qt. clear glass bowl. Top with half of the orange sections. Top with half of the cream mixture. Repeat layers. Sprinkle with almonds. Chill until serving time. **Yield:** 10-12 servings.

Fresh Peach Pie

I enthusiastically share this fruit-filled recipe with customers at my family's Schreiman Orchards. This favorite recipe is reprinted annually in our cookbook.
—*Judy Marshall, Waverly, Missouri*

1 cup sugar
2 tablespoons cornstarch
1 cup water
1 package (3 ounces) peach gelatin
3 cups sliced peeled ripe peaches
1 pastry shell (9 inches), baked
Whipped cream, optional

In a saucepan, combine sugar, cornstarch and water until smooth. Cook and stir over medium heat until bubbly and thickened. Remove from the heat; stir in gelatin until dissolved. Cool. Arrange peaches in crust; pour filling over peaches. Chill until set, about 2 hours. Serve with whipped cream if desired. **Yield:** 6-8 servings.

— 🝙 🝙 🝙 —

Old-Fashioned Raisin Pie

(Pictured below)

My family came to Texas from Virginia after the Civil War. Two brothers helped drive a herd of cattle up the Chisholm Trail to Abilene, Kansas. The boys decided to stay in Kansas and open a meat market. They did well. One brother sent for his girlfriend back in Texas to come and marry him. She did, and she brought along this recipe. The family has been making this pie ever since. —*Debra Ayers, Cheyenne, Wyoming*

2 eggs
1 cup (8 ounces) sour cream
2 cups raisins
1 cup packed brown sugar
1 teaspoon ground cinnamon
1/2 teaspoon ground nutmeg
1/4 teaspoon salt
Pastry for double-crust pie (9 inches)
Additional nutmeg, optional

In a bowl, beat eggs. Add sour cream. Stir in raisins, brown sugar, cinnamon, nutmeg and salt. Place bottom pastry in a pie plate; pour in filling. Top with a lattice crust. Bake at 450° for 10 minutes. Reduce the heat to 350°; bake for about 25 minutes more or until filling is set. If desired, sprinkle with nutmeg. **Yield:** 8 servings.

— 🝙 🝙 🝙 —

Low-Fat Vanilla Pudding

I assure you won't miss the fat and calories in this good-for-you pudding. It's a cool, creamy dessert or anytime snack. —*Laura Letobar, Livonia, Michigan*

✓ Uses less fat, sugar or salt. Includes Nutritional Analysis and Diabetic Exchanges.

1 cup skim milk
1 cup plain nonfat yogurt
1 cup light nonfat vanilla yogurt
1 package (1 ounce) instant sugar-free vanilla pudding mix
1/2 teaspoon vanilla extract
Maraschino cherries, optional
Mint leaves, optional

In a mixing bowl, combine milk, yogurt, pudding mix and vanilla. Beat on high speed for 2 minutes. Spoon into serving dishes. Chill. If desired, garnish with cherries and mint. **Yield:** 6 servings. **Nutritional Analysis:** One 1/2-cup serving (without garnish) equals 88 calories, 275 mg sodium, 3 mg cholesterol, 15 gm carbohydrate, 5 gm protein, 1 gm fat. **Diabetic Exchanges:** 1/2 skim milk, 1/2 starch.

Cherry Pie

A generous slice of this pretty cherry pie makes for a traditionally delicious treat. —Frances Poste
Wall, South Dakota

PASTRY:
1-1/2 cups all-purpose flour
1/2 teaspoon salt
1/2 cup shortening
1/4 cup ice water
FILLING:
2 cans (16 ounces _each_) tart cherries
1 cup sugar
3 tablespoons quick-cooking tapioca
1/4 teaspoon almond extract
1/4 teaspoon salt
Red food coloring, optional
1 tablespoon butter _or_ margarine

In a bowl, combine flour and salt; cut in shortening until crumbly. Gradually add water, tossing with a fork until dough forms a ball. Divide dough in half. Roll out one half to fit a 9-in. pie plate for bottom crust. Drain cherries, reserving 1/4 cup juice. Mix cherries, juice, sugar, tapioca, extract, salt and food coloring if desired; pour into the crust. Dot with butter. Top with a lattice crust. Bake at 375° for 55-60 minutes. **Yield:** 6-8 servings.

Apple Turnovers with Custard

(Pictured above right)

When I was working on the apple section of my own cookbook, I knew I had to include this recipe. With the flaky turnovers and rich sauce, it outshines every other apple recipe I make! —Leora Muellerleile
Turtle Lake, Wisconsin

CUSTARD:
1/3 cup sugar
2 tablespoons cornstarch
2 cups milk _or_ half-and-half cream
3 egg yolks, lightly beaten
1 tablespoon vanilla extract

TURNOVERS:
4 medium baking apples, peeled and cut into 1/4-inch slices
1 tablespoon lemon juice
2 tablespoons butter _or_ margarine, diced
1/3 cup sugar
3/4 teaspoon ground cinnamon
1 tablespoon cornstarch
Pastry for double-crust pie
Milk

Combine sugar and cornstarch in a saucepan. Stir in milk until smooth. Cook and stir over medium-high heat until thickened and bubbly. Reduce heat; cook and stir for 2 minutes. Remove from heat; stir 1 cup into yolks. Return all to pan. Bring to a gentle boil; cook and stir for 2 minutes. Remove from heat; stir in vanilla. Cool slightly. Cover surface of custard with waxed paper; chill. Place apples in a bowl; sprinkle with lemon juice. Add butter. Combine sugar, cinnamon and cornstarch; mix with apples and set aside. Divide pastry into eight portions; roll each into a 5-in. square. Spoon filling off-center on each. Brush edges with milk. Fold over to form a triangle; seal. Crimp with tines of fork. Make steam vents in top. Place on greased baking sheets. Chill 15 minutes. Brush with milk. Bake at 400° for 35 minutes. Serve warm with custard. **Yield:** 8 servings.

'I Wish I Had That Recipe...'

"ONE Mother's Day, the family treated me to dinner at Stoney's Restaurant in Mankato, Minnesota," recalls Esther Fahning of nearby Wells.

"I especially enjoyed a refreshing rhubarb crisp served attractively in a large sherbet dish."

Taste of Home contacted Stoney's owner, Ray Swegman, who willingly shared the recipe and told us, "Stoney's Famous Rhubarb Crisp is one of my mother's recipes. It's been in the family for over 40 years.

"We serve it warm in a footed tulip sundae glass, topped with real whipped cream. Our guests really enjoy its rhubarb tang and old-fashioned goodness, and they have made it an often-requested specialty here."

This is one of many family recipes on the American-Italian menu at this popular dining spot.

"Our goal here at Stoney's is to make each customer's dining experience with us a special one by preparing fresh food daily from our own recipes, served in casual comfort by a concerned staff," adds Ray.

Lunches and dinners are served from 11 a.m. to 10 p.m. daily in a friendly, relaxed atmosphere at Stoney's, 900 N. Riverfront Dr., Mankato MN 56001; 1-507/387-4813.

Stoney's Famous Rhubarb Crisp

1 cup sugar
3/4 cup all-purpose flour, *divided*
3/4 teaspoon ground cinnamon
4 cups chopped fresh *or* frozen rhubarb
3/4 cup packed brown sugar
1/2 teaspoon baking powder
1/2 teaspoon baking soda
1/3 cup butter *or* margarine, melted

In a bowl, combine sugar, 1 tablespoon flour and cinnamon. Add rhubarb; toss. Place in a greased 13-in. x 9-in. x 2-in. baking dish. In a bowl, combine brown sugar, baking powder, baking soda and remaining flour; stir in butter. Sprinkle over rhubarb. Bake at 350° for 40 minutes or until rhubarb is tender. **Yield:** 10-12 servings.

Candy Apple Pie

(Pictured on page 130)

This is the only apple pie my husband will eat, but that's all right since he makes it as often as I do. Like a combination of apple and pecan pie, it's a sweet treat that usually tops off our holiday meals from New Year's all the way through to Christmas! —Cindy Kleweno, Burlington, Colorado

6 cups thinly sliced peeled baking apples
2 tablespoons lime juice
3/4 cup sugar
1/4 cup all-purpose flour
1/2 teaspoon ground cinnamon *or* nutmeg
1/4 teaspoon salt
Pastry for double-crust pie (9 inches)
2 tablespoons butter *or* margarine
TOPPING:
1/4 cup butter *or* margarine
1/2 cup packed brown sugar
2 tablespoons whipping cream
1/2 cup chopped pecans

In a large bowl, toss apples with lime juice. Combine dry ingredients; add to the apples and toss lightly. Place bottom pastry in a 9-in. pie plate; fill with apple mixture. Dot with butter. Cover with top crust. Flute edges high; cut steam vents. Bake at 400° for 40-45 minutes or until golden brown and apples are tender. Meanwhile, for topping, melt butter in a small saucepan. Stir in brown sugar and cream; bring to a boil, stirring constantly. Remove from the heat and stir in pecans. Pour over top crust. Return to the oven for 3-4 minutes or until bubbly. Serve warm. **Yield:** 8 servings.

Black Walnut Pie

Most years, I have a large supply of black walnuts and am always looking for new ways to use them up. This dessert, which is similar to traditional pecan pie, has been a favorite for years. —Shirley Sutton, Garnavillo, Iowa

1 cup light corn syrup
1/2 cup packed brown sugar
1/2 cup plus 1 tablespoon sugar, *divided*
3 tablespoons butter *or* margarine
3 eggs
1 cup chopped black walnuts
1 tablespoon all-purpose flour
1 unbaked pastry shell (9 inches)

In a saucepan, combine the corn syrup, brown sugar and 1/2 cup sugar; bring to a boil. Remove from the heat; stir in butter until melted. In a mixing bowl, beat eggs. Gradually stir in hot mixture; mix well. Add walnuts. Combine flour and remaining sugar; sprinkle over bottom of pastry shell. Pour walnut mixture into shell. Bake at 350° for 45-50 minutes or until browned. **Yield:** 6-8 servings.

— 🍷 🍷 🍷 —

Apple Tart
(Pictured below)

For 15 years my husband, daughter and I owned and operated an apple orchard, where we raised 27 varieties of apples on 2,200 trees. Through the years, this recipe has become my personal favorite. My family even prefers this wonderful tart over traditional apple pie. I hope you enjoy it, too. —Marilyn Begres *Dexter, Michigan*

  1 cup sugar, *divided*
  2 tablespoons all-purpose flour
1/2 teaspoon ground cinnamon
  6 medium baking apples, peeled
     and thinly sliced
  1 tablespoon butter *or* margarine
Pastry for a single-crust pie

In a small skillet, heat 3/4 cup sugar, stirring constantly until it is liquefied and just golden. Remove from the heat and quickly pour into a 10-in. pie plate; set aside. In a small bowl, combine flour, cinnamon and remaining sugar. Arrange half of the apples in a single layer in a circular pattern in pie plate. Sprinkle with half of the sugar mixture. Arrange half of the remaining apples in a circular pattern over sugar; sprinkle with the remaining sugar mixture. Place remaining apples over all, keeping the top as level as possible. Dot with butter. Roll out pastry to 9 in.; place over apples, pressing gently to completely cover. Do not flute. Bake at 400° for 50 minutes or until golden brown and apples are tender. As soon as tart comes out of the oven, carefully invert onto a large serving plate and remove pie plate. Cool. **Yield:** 8 servings.

Seven-Minute Pudding

This rich, smooth pudding couldn't be quicker to make, and it has such nice homemade flavor.
—Renee Schwebach, Dumont, Minnesota

    1/3 cup sugar
    2 tablespoons cornstarch
    2 cups milk
    2 egg yolks
    2 tablespoons butter *or* margarine
    1 teaspoon vanilla extract

In a microwave-safe mixing bowl, combine sugar and cornstarch. With a hand mixer, beat in milk and egg yolks until smooth. Microwave on medium for 5 minutes. Beat well with mixer. Microwave on high for 2 minutes or until a thermometer reads 160°; stir. Blend in butter and vanilla. Pour into serving dishes; cool. **Yield:** 3-4 servings. **Editor's Note:** This recipe was tested in a 700-watt microwave.

Peach Shortcake

(Pictured at far right and on front cover)

When blushing fresh peaches are in plentiful supply, this appealing layered dessert can't be beat. Brown sugar and ginger give the shortcake its mellow, sweet-spicy flavor. —Karen Owen, Rising Sun, Indiana

    2 cups all-purpose flour
    2 tablespoons brown sugar
    1 tablespoon baking powder
    1/2 teaspoon salt
    1/2 teaspoon ground ginger
    1/2 cup butter *or* margarine
    2/3 cup milk
FILLING:
1-1/2 pounds ripe fresh peaches *or* nectarines, peeled and thinly sliced
    6 tablespoons brown sugar, *divided*
    1/4 teaspoon ground ginger
    1 cup whipping cream
    1/4 cup chopped pecans, toasted

Combine the first five ingredients in a bowl; cut in butter until mixture resembles coarse crumbs. Add milk, stirring only until moistened. Turn onto a lightly floured surface; knead 10 times. Pat evenly into a greased 8-in. round baking pan. Bake at 425° for 20-25 minutes or until golden brown. Remove from pan to cool on a wire rack. Just before serving, combine peaches, 4 tablespoons brown sugar and ginger. Whip cream with remaining brown sugar until stiff. Split shortcake into two layers; place bottom layer on a serving

platter. Spoon half of the peach mixture over cake; top with half of the cream. Cover with second cake layer and remaining peach mixture. Garnish with remaining cream; sprinkle with pecans. **Yield:** 8-10 servings.

Vanilla Custard Ice Cream

(Pictured at right)

When we were growing up on the farm, homemade ice cream was our favorite dessert. I now make it for my own family. Enjoy this recipe "solo" or topped with sauce, fruit or nuts for a spectacular sundae.
—Lucile Proctor, Panguitch, Utah

    1 tablespoon butter *or* margarine
    6 cups milk
2-1/4 cups sugar, *divided*
    6 tablespoons all-purpose flour
    6 eggs, *separated*
    3 cups whipping cream
    1 tablespoon vanilla extract
Sliced strawberries *or* other fresh fruit, optional

In a large kettle, melt butter to coat the bottom. Pour in milk and 1 cup of sugar. Bring to a boil over medium-high heat, stirring occasionally. Combine flour and remaining sugar; add to kettle. Bring to a boil, stirring constantly. Cook and stir for 2 minutes; remove from the heat. In a mixing bowl, beat egg whites until stiff peaks form. While beating, gradually add yolks. Stir in 1 cup of hot milk mixture. Return all to kettle; cook and stir for 2 minutes (do not boil). Chill. Add cream and vanilla; mix well. Freeze in an ice cream maker according to manufacturer's directions. Serve with fruit if desired. **Yield:** about 3 quarts.

Keeping Ice Cream Fresh

To keep ice cream fresh, don't allow it to repeatedly soften and refreeze; otherwise, lumps of ice will form. Store it in the main part of the freezer, not on the door where temperatures fluctuate.

Turtle Sundae Dessert

(Pictured above right)

This treat is sure to please children and chocolate lovers of all ages! A convenient cake mix starts the stellar surprise my six grandchildren endorse.
—Bethel Walters, Willow River, Minnesota

    1 package (18-1/4 ounces) German chocolate cake mix

SCRUMPTIOUS AND SHOWY Turtle Sundae Dessert, Peach Shortcake and Vanilla Custard Ice Cream (shown above, clockwise from upper right) make up this delicious medley of treats.

   1 package (14 ounces) caramels
1/2 cup evaporated milk
   6 tablespoons butter *or* margarine
   1 cup chopped pecans
   1 cup (6 ounces) semisweet chocolate chips
Vanilla ice cream and pecan halves, optional

Mix the cake according to package directions. Set aside half of the batter; pour remaining batter into a greased and floured 13-in. x 9-in. x 2-in. baking pan. Bake at 350° for 18 minutes. Meanwhile, in a saucepan over low heat, melt the caramels, milk and butter. Remove from the heat and add nuts. Pour over cake. Sprinkle with chocolate chips. Pour the reserved batter over the top. Bake 20-25 minutes more or until cake springs back when lightly touched. Cool. Cut into squares. If desired, top each square with a scoop of ice cream and a pecan half. **Yield:** 20 servings.

Roll pastry to fit a 12-in. pizza pan; fold under or flute the edges. Combine sugar, flour and cinnamon in a bowl. Add apples and toss. Arrange the apples in a single layer in a circular pattern to completely cover pastry. Combine the first five topping ingredients; sprinkle over apples. Bake at 350° for 35-40 minutes or until apples are tender. Remove from the oven and immediately drizzle with caramel topping or dip. Serve warm with ice cream if desired. **Yield:** 12 servings.

— 🏆 🏆 🏆 —

Butterscotch Pie

I've been cooking since I was a young boy. Now I enjoy preparing foods like this for my wife.
—Cary Letsche, Bradenton, Florida

       6 **tablespoons butter** *or* **margarine**
       6 **tablespoons all-purpose flour**
   1-1/2 **cups packed brown sugar**
       2 **cups milk**
     1/4 **teaspoon salt**
       3 **eggs yolks, beaten**
       1 **teaspoon vanilla extract**
       1 **pastry shell (9 inches), baked**
  MERINGUE:
       3 **egg whites**
     1/4 **teaspoon cream of tartar**
     1/2 **cup sugar**

In a saucepan, melt the butter. Remove from the heat; add flour and stir until smooth. Stir in brown sugar. Return to heat; gradually add milk and salt, stirring constantly. Cook and stir over medium-high heat until thickened and bubbly. Reduce heat; cook and stir 2 minutes more. Remove from the heat. Stir about 1 cup into the egg yolks; return all to the saucepan. Bring to a gentle boil. Cook and stir for 2 minutes. Remove from the heat and add vanilla. Pour into the pastry shell. Immediately make the meringue: In a small bowl, beat egg whites with cream of tartar until soft peaks form. Gradually add sugar, about 1 tablespoon at a time, beating until stiff and glossy. Spread evenly over filling, sealing meringue to crust. Bake at 350° for 12-15 minutes or until golden. Cool on a wire rack. Store, covered, in the refrigerator. **Yield:** 6-8 servings.

Apple Crisp Pizza

(Pictured above)

While visiting a Wisconsin apple orchard bakery, I tried this tempting treat. At home, I put together this recipe. My family thinks it tastes better than the one used by the bakery. As it bakes, the enticing aroma fills my kitchen, and friends and family linger waiting for a sweet sample. —Nancy Preussner, Delhi, Iowa

  Pastry for a single-crust pie
     2/3 **cup sugar**
       3 **tablespoons all-purpose flour**
       1 **teaspoon ground cinnamon**
       4 **medium baking apples, peeled and cut**
          into 1/2-inch slices
  TOPPING:
     1/2 **cup all-purpose flour**
     1/3 **cup packed brown sugar**
     1/3 **cup rolled oats**
       1 **teaspoon ground cinnamon**
     1/4 **cup butter** *or* **margarine**
     1/4 **to 1/2 cup caramel ice cream topping** *or*
          caramel apple dip
  Vanilla ice cream, optional

Making Meringue

For maximum volume, let egg whites stand at room temperature for 30 minutes before beating. Once they're beaten, they should be spread on a hot filling. Always be sure to spread the meringue so it extends out to the edge of your crust.

Layered Lemon Dessert

(Pictured below)

Add sunshine to a meal's end with this refrigerator dessert. —*Dorothy Pritchett, Wills Point, Texas*

    6 tablespoons butter *or* margarine
    1 cup all-purpose flour
1/2 cup finely chopped pecans
FILLING:
    1 package (8 ounces) cream cheese, softened
1-1/2 cups confectioners' sugar
1-1/2 cups whipped topping
    2 cups sugar
1/3 cup cornstarch
1/4 teaspoon salt
    2 cups water, *divided*
    3 eggs
1/4 cup vinegar
1/4 cup lemon juice
    1 tablespoon butter *or* margarine
    1 teaspoon lemon extract

Cut butter into flour until crumbly. Stir in pecans. Press into the bottom of an ungreased 13-in. x 9-in. x 2-in. baking pan. Bake at 350° for 15 minutes. Cool. Beat cream cheese and confectioners' sugar until fluffy. Fold in whipped topping. Spread over crust; chill. In a saucepan, combine sugar, cornstarch and salt. Add 1/4 cup water and stir until smooth. Add eggs and mix well. Add vinegar, lemon juice and the remaining water; stir until smooth. Bring to a boil over medium heat, stirring constantly; boil for 1 minute. Remove from the heat; add butter and extract. Cool. Spread over cream cheese layer. Chill 2 hours or overnight. **Yield:** 12-16 servings.

Pear Pie

With our 12 acres of fruit trees, fruit pies are popular at our house! One of my favorites is this recipe because it showcases pears simply and wonderfully. —*Jean Lauer, Summerland, British, Columbia*

    1 cup sugar, *divided*
    2 tablespoons lemon juice
1/2 teaspoon grated lemon peel
1/4 teaspoon ground coriander
    6 cups sliced peeled ripe pears
    1 unbaked pastry shell (9 inches)
1/2 cup all-purpose flour
1/2 teaspoon ground cinnamon
1/4 teaspoon ground mace
1/3 cup butter *or* margarine
Vanilla ice cream, optional

In a bowl, combine 1/2 cup sugar, lemon juice and peel and coriander. Add pears and toss. Spoon into pie shell. In a bowl, combine flour, cinnamon, mace and remaining sugar; cut in butter until mixture resembles coarse crumbs. Sprinkle over pears. Bake at 400° for 45 minutes or until pears are tender. Serve warm or cold with ice cream if desired. **Yield:** 6-8 servings.

Revel in Raspberries

DELICATE fresh raspberries are the ultimate taste of summer for fruit lovers far and wide. The berries' brilliant, deep red adds a pretty touch to any plate, and their flavor distinctively balances sweet and tart.

The Washington Red Raspberry Commission shares several recipes in which the crop takes a delicious bow.

Raspberry Royal Pie—the producer group's "signature pie"—showcases the jewel-toned fruit. Its shortbread type crust is a change of pace, and pecans pair nicely with the berries.

Apples take on a summertime twist in versatile Raspberry Baked Apples. This colorful combination may be served warm or cold as a side dish or dessert the whole family would enjoy.

Choosing Fresh Raspberries

When buying fresh raspberries, look for deep red color and fruit that is slightly firm to the touch. Inspect the bottom of the basket. Any juice weeping through the container means some of the berries may be crushed.

The bulk of the berry crop is frozen or used in preserves, toppings and juices.

Besides raspberries frozen in syrup, many grocery stores now carry "individually quick-frozen" raspberries, which remain separate so you can conveniently measure out as many berries as you need.

You can also freeze fresh berries "loose" for later use. Here's how: Lightly rinse raspberries under a fine faucet mist in a colander and spread on a cookie sheet or tray just one layer deep. Put the tray in your freezer until berries are solid (about 2 hours). Store frozen berries in airtight plastic bags.

— 🦃 🦃 🦃 —

Raspberry Royal Pie

CRUST:
1-1/4 cups all-purpose flour
1/2 cup pecans, finely chopped
1/2 cup butter *or* margarine, softened
1/4 cup confectioners' sugar
1/2 teaspoon vanilla extract
1/8 teaspoon salt
FILLING:
2 packages (10 ounces *each*) frozen raspberries, thawed
1/3 cup sugar
1/4 cup cornstarch
1/3 cup water
Whipped cream

In a mixing bowl, beat all of the crust ingredients until well mixed. Refrigerate for 30 minutes. Pat into an ungreased 9-in. pie pan. Bake at 400° for 10-12 minutes or until golden brown. Cool. Drain the raspberries, reserving syrup; set aside. Combine the sugar and cornstarch in a saucepan; add water and raspberry syrup. Simmer until thick, stirring constantly. Remove from the heat and fold in berries. Pour into the crust. Chill for 2 hours or until firm. Garnish with whipped cream. **Yield:** 6-8 servings.

— 🦃 🦃 🦃 —

Raspberry Baked Apples

1/2 cup sugar
1 tablespoon quick-cooking tapioca
1/3 cup water
3 cups fresh raspberries
6 medium tart apples, quartered
Cream

In a bowl, combine sugar and tapioca. Stir in water and berries. Cut a lengthwise strip of peel from the center of each apple quarter; discard peel and stir apples into raspberry mixture. Pour into a greased shallow 3-qt. baking dish. Cover and bake at 350° for 1 hour or until apples are tender, spooning sauce over apples every 15 minutes. Serve warm with cream. **Yield:** 8-10 servings.

Peach Crumble

Old-fashioned, delicious and easy to make describe this dessert. It's wonderful served with ice cream.
—Nancy Horsburgh, Everett, Ontario

    6 cups sliced peeled ripe peaches
  1/4 cup packed brown sugar
    3 tablespoons all-purpose flour
    1 teaspoon lemon juice
  1/2 teaspoon grated lemon peel
  1/2 teaspoon ground cinnamon
TOPPING:
    1 cup all-purpose flour
    1 cup sugar
    1 teaspoon baking powder
  1/4 teaspoon salt
  1/4 teaspoon ground nutmeg
    1 egg, beaten
  1/2 cup butter *or* margarine, melted and
      cooled
Vanilla ice cream, optional

Place peaches in a greased shallow 2-1/2-qt. baking dish. Combine brown sugar, flour, lemon juice and peel and cinnamon; sprinkle over the peaches. In a bowl, combine flour, sugar, baking powder, salt and nutmeg. Stir in egg until the mixture resembles coarse crumbs. Sprinkle over the peaches. Pour butter evenly over topping. Bake at 375° for 35-40 minutes. Serve with ice cream if desired. **Yield:** 10-12 servings.

— 🍴 🍴 🍴 —

Butter Pecan Crunch

"Elegant but easy" is my favorite description of this frozen treat my mother first made decades ago.
—Julie Sterchi, Flora, Illinois

    2 cups graham cracker crumbs
  1/2 cup butter *or* margarine, melted
    2 packages (3.4 ounces *each*) instant vanilla
      pudding mix
    2 cups milk
    1 quart butter pecan ice cream, softened
      slightly
    1 carton (8 ounces) frozen whipped
      topping, thawed
    2 Heath bars (1.4 ounces *each*), crushed

In a bowl, combine crumbs and butter. Pat into the bottom of an ungreased 13-in. x 9-in. x 2-in. pan. Refrigerate. In a mixing bowl, beat pudding mixes and milk until well blended, about 1 minute. Fold in the ice cream and whipped topping. Spoon over crust. Sprinkle with crushed candy bars. Freeze. Remove from the freezer 20 minutes before serving. **Yield:** 12-16 servings.

Chocolate Trifle

(Pictured above and on page 130)

For a fabulous finale when entertaining, this lovely layered trifle is a winner! It's a do-ahead dessert that serves a group, and it even tastes great the next day.
—Pam Botine, Goldsboro, North Carolina

    1 package (18-1/4 ounces) chocolate fudge
      cake mix
    1 package (6 ounces) instant chocolate
      pudding mix
  1/2 cup strong coffee
    1 carton (12 ounces) frozen whipped
      topping, thawed
    6 Heath bars (1.4 ounces *each*), crushed

Bake cake according to package directions. Cool. Prepare pudding according to package directions; set aside. Crumble cake; reserve 1/2 cup. Place half of the remaining cake crumbs in the bottom of a 4-1/2- or 5-qt. trifle dish or decorative glass bowl. Layer with half of the coffee, half of the pudding, half of the whipped topping and half of the crushed candy bars. Repeat the layers of cake, coffee, pudding and whipped topping. Combine remaining crushed candy bars with reserved cake crumbs; sprinkle over top. Refrigerate 4-5 hours before serving. **Yield:** 8-10 servings.

Fruit Pizza

(Pictured above and on page 130)

This pretty dessert is a hit every time I serve it for dinner guests. —Janet O'Neal, Poplar Bluff, Missouri

> 1 package (20 ounces) refrigerated sugar cookie dough
> 1 package (8 ounces) cream cheese, softened
> 1/4 cup confectioners' sugar
> 1 carton (8 ounces) frozen whipped topping, thawed
> 2 to 3 kiwifruit, peeled and thinly sliced
> 1 to 2 firm bananas, sliced
> 1 can (11 ounces) mandarin oranges, drained
> 1/2 cup red grape halves
> 1/4 cup sugar
> 1/4 cup orange juice
> 2 tablespoons water
> 1 tablespoon lemon juice
> 1-1/2 teaspoons cornstarch
> Pinch salt

Pat cookie dough into an ungreased 14-in. pizza pan. Bake at 375° for 10-12 minutes or until browned; cool. In a mixing bowl, beat the cream cheese and confectioners' sugar until smooth. Fold in whipped topping. Spread over crust. Arrange fruit on top. In a saucepan, bring sugar, orange juice, water, lemon juice, cornstarch and salt to a boil, stirring constantly for 2 minutes or until thickened. Cool; brush over fruit. Chill. Store in refrigerator. **Yield:** 16-20 servings.

Freezer Pumpkin Pie

This wonderful do-ahead dessert puts a cool twist on the traditional. Gingersnaps and pecans form the delicious baked crust for this pie's pumpkin and ice cream filling. —Vera Reid, Laramie, Wyoming

> 1 cup ground pecans
> 1/2 cup ground gingersnaps
> 1/4 cup sugar
> 1/4 cup butter *or* margarine, softened
> **FILLING:**
> 1 cup cooked *or* canned pumpkin
> 1/2 cup packed brown sugar
> 1/2 teaspoon salt
> 1/2 teaspoon ground cinnamon
> 1/2 teaspoon ground ginger
> 1/4 teaspoon ground nutmeg
> 1 quart vanilla ice cream, softened slightly

In a bowl, combine the pecans, gingersnaps, sugar and butter; mix well. Press into a 9-in. pie pan; bake at 450° for 5 minutes. Cool completely. In a mixing bowl, beat first six filling ingredients. Stir in ice cream and mix until well blended. Spoon into crust. Freeze until firm, at least 2-3 hours. Store in freezer. **Yield:** 6-8 servings.

❦ ❦ ❦

Delicious Apple Pie

My mother taught me to make this delectable apple pie. I've yet to find a recipe that tastes better than this! —Howard Haug, Hewitt, Texas

3 tablespoons water
4 teaspoons cornstarch
1 egg, beaten
3/4 cup half-and-half cream
3/4 cup sugar
1 teaspoon ground cinnamon
1/4 teaspoon ground nutmeg
4 medium Red Delicious apples, peeled and sliced
Pastry for double-crust pie (9 inches)
2 tablespoons butter *or* margarine
1 tablespoon milk
1 tablespoon cinnamon-sugar

In a small bowl, mix the water and cornstarch until dissolved. Add egg, cream, sugar, cinnamon and nutmeg. Place apples in a large bowl; pour cream mixture over and stir to coat. Line a 9-in. pie pan with the bottom pastry. Pour apple mixture into the crust; dot with butter. Top with remaining pastry; flute edges and cut slits in top. Brush with milk and sprinkle with cinnamon-sugar. Bake at 350° for 55 minutes or until golden brown. **Yield:** 6-8 servings.

Creamy Pineapple Pie

My father and I have a bumper crop of pineapple here in central Florida. I'm often asked for this recipe whenever I make it for family and friends. You can either use fresh or canned fruit to sample this refreshing treat that's one of our special favorites.
—Bonnie Sandlin, Lakeland, Florida

1/4 cup sugar
3 tablespoons cornstarch
1-1/3 cups pineapple juice
1 egg yolk
2 cups fresh pineapple chunks* (1/2-inch pieces)
1 pastry shell (9 inches), baked
1/4 cup flaked coconut, toasted

In a saucepan, combine sugar and cornstarch. Add pineapple juice; bring to a boil, stirring occasionally. Boil for 2 minutes. In a small bowl, beat egg yolk; stir in 1/4 cup of the hot mixture. Return all to pan; cook and stir for 1 minute. Remove from the heat; stir in pineapple. Pour into crust. Chill for 2 hours or until firm. Store in the refrigerator. Sprinkle with coconut just before serving. **Yield:** 6-8 servings. ***Editor's Note:** Canned pineapple can be substituted for fresh. Use one 20-ounce can and one 8-ounce can of pineapple tidbits. Drain, reserving juice. Add additional pineapple juice if necessary to equal 1-1/3 cups. Prepare the recipe as directed.

Layered Banana Pudding

(Pictured below)

My mother gave me this recipe, which an old friend had shared with her. When my children were still at home, we enjoyed this satisfying pudding often, and now I make it for company. There's no comparison between this recipe and the instant pudding mixes from the grocery store!
—Esther Matteson
Bremen, Indiana

1/3 cup all-purpose flour
2/3 cup packed brown sugar
2 cups milk
2 egg yolks, beaten
2 tablespoons butter *or* margarine
1 teaspoon vanilla extract
1 cup whipping cream, whipped
4 to 6 firm bananas, sliced
Chopped walnuts, optional

In a medium saucepan, combine the flour and brown sugar; stir in milk. Cook and stir over medium heat until thickened and bubbly; cook and stir 1 minute more. Remove from the heat. Gradually stir about 1 cup hot mixture into egg yolks. Return all to the saucepan. Bring to a gentle boil; cook and stir for 2 minutes. Remove from the heat; stir in butter and vanilla. Cool to room temperature, stirring occasionally. Fold in the whipped cream. Layer a third of the pudding in a 2-qt. glass bowl; top with half of the bananas. Repeat layers. Top with remaining pudding. Sprinkle with nuts if desired. Cover and chill at least 1 hour before serving. **Yield:** 8 servings.

Country-Style Condiments

*You and your family
will relish every bite
when your favorite foods
are topped with any of
these dressings, glazes, jams,
jellies, sauces and more.*

ENJOYABLE EXTRAS. Clockwise from upper left: Banana Poppy Seed Dressing (p. 151), Golden Granola (p. 155), Chunky Fruit and Nut Relish (p. 155), Dill Mustard (p. 154), Low-Fat Ranch Dressing (p. 152) and Tangy Barbecue Sauce (p. 153).

Herbed Salad Dressing

I'm an avid gardener, and thyme is one of my favorite things to grow. A few years ago, I even published a cookbook featuring herb tips and recipes. In this recipe, aromatic thyme really shines. —Marge Clark
West Lebanon, Indiana

    1 to 1-1/3 cups tarragon vinegar
    1 cup vegetable oil
  2/3 cup olive oil
    4 teaspoons mayonnaise
    3 garlic cloves, minced
    1 tablespoon minced fresh thyme *or* 1 teaspoon dried thyme
    2 teaspoons Dijon mustard
1-1/2 teaspoons minced fresh tarragon *or* 1/2
     teaspoon dried tarragon
    1 teaspoon brown sugar
    1 teaspoon salt

In a jar with tight-fitting lid, combine all ingredients; shake well. Serve over salad greens. Refrigerate leftovers. **Yield:** 3 cups.

Sweet Dill Refrigerator Pickles

Dill and cucumbers are natural companions in a number of dishes. I turn to this recipe every summer when my garden is in full bloom. My family can hardly wait to eat these pickles. —Kay Curtis
Guthrie, Oklahoma

Glazes Make Ham Holiday-Special

ADD festive Yuletide color and flavor to your holiday ham with fruity glazes!

Glazes are so simple and economical that you may decide to serve several different ones along with your Christmas ham or on a party buffet.

Tangy cranberries are a "natural" with ham, says Hormel's chef, Horst Kruppa. His Elegant Holiday Ham Glaze mixes whole cranberries in a fruity medley with just a hint of mustard.

Another even simpler recipe, Fruity Ham Glaze features your homemade or purchased cranberry-orange sauce with peach or apricot preserves for a jewel-toned look and traditional taste your dinner crowd will savor.

Pineapple, a longtime favorite flavor with ham, combines with cloves and Dijon mustard in Zesty Pineapple Ham Glaze. It stirs up in a wink and is sure to perk up the palate.

Elegant Holiday Ham Glaze

Juice and grated peel of 1 orange
Juice and grated peel of 1 lemon
    1 cup sweet red wine *or* cranberry juice
  1/2 cup light corn syrup
  1/2 teaspoon ground mustard
    1 can (16 ounces) whole-berry cranberry sauce
Drippings from a baked ham, optional
    2 tablespoons cornstarch, optional
    2 tablespoons cold water, optional

In a saucepan, combine orange and lemon juices and peel, wine or cranberry juice, corn syrup and mustard. Simmer for 30 minutes. Add the cranberry sauce and ham drippings if desired; heat through. If a thicker glaze is desired, bring just to a boil. Combine cornstarch and water; add to glaze. Cook and stir until slightly thickened. Serve warm over sliced ham. **Yield:** 3-1/2 cups.

Fruity Ham Glaze

1/4 cup cranberry-orange sauce
1/4 cup apricot *or* peach preserves

Combine ingredients in a small bowl. About 30 minutes before ham is done, remove from the oven. Score surface; spoon glaze over entire ham. Return to the oven, basting occasionally during the last 30 minutes of baking. **Yield:** 1/2 cup.

Zesty Pineapple Ham Glaze

1/2 cup crushed pineapple
1/4 cup Dijon mustard
Dash ground cloves

Combine all ingredients in a small bowl. About 30 minutes before ham is done, remove from the oven. Score surface; spoon glaze over entire ham. Return to the oven, basting occasionally during the last 30 minutes of baking. **Yield:** 1/2 cup.

2 cups sugar
2 cups vinegar
2 cups water
1/4 cup salt
3 quarts sliced unpeeled cucumbers
1 large onion, sliced
3/4 to 1 cup minced fresh dill

In a saucepan, combine sugar, vinegar, water and salt. Bring to a boil and boil 1 minute. In a large nonmetallic container, combine cucumbers, onion and dill. Pour dressing over; cool. Cover and refrigerate at least 3 days before serving. Stir occasionally. **Yield:** 3-1/2 quarts.

—— 🍴 🍴 🍴 ——

Sugar-Free Strawberry Jam

My husband has been a diabetic for almost 20 years and is very careful about what he eats. He was tired of eating the flavorless jams and jellies for diabetics in the grocery store, so I came up with this recipe. With its fresh flavor, it makes a nice gift. —*Rita Christ Wauwatosa, Wisconsin*

☑ Uses less fat, sugar or salt. Includes Nutritional Analysis and Diabetic Exchanges.

3/4 cup diet lemon-lime soda
1 package (.3 ounce) sugar-free strawberry gelatin
1 cup mashed fresh *or* unsweetened frozen strawberries
1-1/2 teaspoons lemon juice

In a saucepan, bring soda to a boil. Remove from the heat; stir in gelatin until dissolved. Stir in strawberries and lemon juice. Pour into jars or plastic containers; cover and refrigerate up to 3 weeks. Do not freeze. **Yield:** 1-3/4 cups. **Nutritional Analysis:** One 2-tablespoon serving equals 8 calories, 18 mg sodium, 0 cholesterol, 2 gm carbohydrate, trace protein, trace fat. **Diabetic Exchanges:** Free food.

—— 🍴 🍴 🍴 ——

Wild Plum Jelly

I've had this recipe for ages. Each year when the wild plums are ripe, I'll fill my pail and make this jelly. It's so good served with toast, pancakes or waffles! —*Ludell Heuser, Mt. Horeb, Wisconsin*

5 pounds wild plums, halved and pitted
4 cups water
1 package (1-3/4 ounces) powdered fruit pectin
7-1/2 cups sugar

In a large kettle, simmer plums and water until ten-der, about 30 minutes. Pour through a damp jelly bag, allowing juice to drip into a bowl. Measure 5-1/2 cups of juice; return to the kettle. Add pectin; stir and bring to a boil. Add sugar; bring to a full rolling boil. Boil for 1 minute, stirring constantly. Remove from the heat; skim off any foam. Pour hot mixture into hot jars, leaving 1/4-in. headspace. Adjust caps. Process for 5 minutes in a boiling-water bath. **Yield:** about 8 half-pints.

Banana Poppy Seed Dressing
(Pictured above and on page 148)

Here's a lightly sweet, refreshing dressing that lets the flavor of banana come through. A homemaker with four grown children, I have an extensive recipe collection. This dressing is so good over crisp greens or fresh orange and grapefruit sections. Give it a try! —*Gloria Kirchman, Eden Prairie, Minnesota*

1 ripe banana
1 cup (8 ounces) sour cream
1/4 cup sugar
1 tablespoon poppy seeds
1 tablespoon lemon juice
1 teaspoon ground mustard
3/4 teaspoon salt

In a small bowl, finely mash banana. Add sour cream, sugar, poppy seeds, lemon juice, mustard and salt. Chill for at least 30 minutes before serving. **Yield:** 1-3/4 cups.

Low-Fat Ranch Dressing

(Pictured above and on page 149)

This creamy, rich-tasting dressing is a very deceiving low-fat alternative! —Cindy Bertrand
Floydada, Texas

✓ Uses less fat, sugar or salt. Includes Nutritional Analysis and Diabetic Exchanges.

**1 package (2 ounces) reduced-fat ranch
salad dressing mix**
1-1/2 cups skim milk
1/4 cup nonfat sour cream
1/4 cup fat-free mayonnaise

In a small bowl, combine all ingredients until smooth. Cover and chill. Serve over salad greens. Refrigerate leftovers. **Yield:** 2 cups. **Nutritional Analysis:** One 2-tablespoon serving equals 30 calories, 263 mg sodium, 1 mg cholesterol, 4 gm carbohydrate, 1 gm protein, trace fat. **Diabetic Exchanges:** Free food.

———— 🏺 🏺 🏺 ————

Sugarless Applesauce

A friend gave me this delicious recipe more than 20 years ago, and I've made applesauce this way ever since. We grow a lot of apples in this area and have fun putting this crop to good use. —Margery Bryan
Royal City, Washington

✓ Uses less fat, sugar or salt. Includes Nutritional Analysis and Diabetic Exchanges.

8 cups sliced peeled tart apples
1/2 to 1 can (12 ounces) diet lemon-lime soda
1/2 to 1 teaspoon ground cinnamon

In a saucepan over medium heat, cook apples, soda and cinnamon until apples are tender, about 45 minutes. Serve warm or cold. **Yield:** 8 servings. **Nutritional Analysis:** One 1/2-cup serving equals 74 calories, 6 mg sodium, 0 cholesterol, 21 gm carbohydrate, trace protein, trace fat. **Diabetic Exchanges:** 1-1/2 fruit.

———— 🏺 🏺 🏺 ————

Cranberry Apple Relish

Give this tart, rose-colored relish a try. It's a special dish even for those who can have sugar.
—Carla Hodenfield, Mandan, North Dakota

✓ Uses less fat, sugar or salt. Includes Nutritional Analysis and Diabetic Exchanges.

2 cups ground fresh *or* frozen cranberries
1/2 cup diced peeled apple
1/4 cup raisins
Sugar substitute equivalent to 3/4 cup sugar
1/4 cup chopped walnuts, optional

In a bowl, combine all ingredients. Refrigerate for at least 2 hours. **Yield:** 10 servings. **Nutritional Analysis:** One 1/4-cup serving (prepared without walnuts) equals 24 calories, 1 mg sodium, 0 cholesterol, 6 gm carbohydrate, trace protein, trace fat. **Diabetic Exchanges:** 1/2 fruit.

Berry Good Topping

The natural sweetness of fresh berries comes through in this sauce. It's a versatile condiment that can be used to top pancakes, ice cream and yogurt.
—*Martha Balser, Cincinnati, Ohio*

✓ Uses less fat, sugar or salt. Includes Nutritional Analysis and Diabetic Exchanges.

- **1 pint fresh raspberries, *divided***
- **1/4 cup unsweetened apple juice**
- **2 tablespoons unsweetened apple juice concentrate**
- **2 teaspoons cornstarch**
- **1/4 teaspoon vanilla extract**

In a blender, puree 1 cup of the berries with apple juice. In a small saucepan, combine apple juice concentrate and cornstarch; stir until smooth. Add pureed berries. Cook over low heat, stirring constantly, until thickened. Cool. Add vanilla and remaining raspberries. Serve over yogurt, ice cream or pancakes. **Yield:** 8 servings (1-1/2 cups). **Nutritional Analysis:** One 3-tablespoon serving equals 29 calories, 1 mg sodium, 0 cholesterol, 8 gm carbohydrate, trace protein, trace fat. **Diabetic Exchanges:** 1/2 fruit.

Savory Steak Rub

Marjoram stars in this recipe. I use the rub on a variety of beef cuts...it locks in the natural juices of the meat for mouth-watering results. —*Donna Brockett Kingfisher, Oklahoma*

- **1 tablespoon dried marjoram**
- **1 tablespoon dried basil**
- **2 teaspoons garlic powder**
- **2 teaspoons dried thyme**
- **1 teaspoon dried rosemary, crushed**
- **3/4 teaspoon dried oregano**

Combine all ingredients; store in a covered container. Rub over steaks before grilling or broiling. Will season four to five steaks. **Yield:** 1/4 cup.

Sauerkraut Hot Dog Topping

You'll relish this zesty condiment! For years, I stirred this up "by guess and by golly" before finally figuring out the proper measure of ingredients so I could share the recipe. It's great to have on hand anytime that you grill hot dogs or smoked sausages.
—*Erlene Cornelius, Spring City, Tennessee*

- **1 can (15 ounces) sauerkraut, rinsed and drained**

- **1/4 cup sweet pickle relish**
- **2 tablespoons brown sugar**
- **1 tablespoon prepared mustard**
- **1/2 teaspoon caraway seed**

Combine all ingredients in a saucepan; cook on low heat until heated through. Serve over hot dogs or sausages. **Yield:** 2 cups.

Tangy Barbecue Sauce

(Pictured below and on page 148)

My mother-in-law created this recipe, and we just can't get enough of her delectable sauce! I always keep a little out of the basting dish prior to using it on the grill so we have some to serve at the table. It tastes terrific on any grilled meat. —*Mary Kaye Rackowitz Marysville, Washington*

- **1 cup ketchup**
- **2 tablespoons lemon juice**
- **2 tablespoons cider vinegar**
- **1/4 cup packed brown sugar**
- **2 teaspoons prepared mustard**
- **1 teaspoon salt**
- **1/2 to 1 teaspoon hot pepper sauce**
- **1 bay leaf**
- **1 garlic clove, minced**
- **1/2 cup water**
- **2 teaspoons Worcestershire sauce**

Combine all of the ingredients in a small saucepan; bring to a boil, stirring occasionally. Reduce heat; cover and simmer for 30 minutes. Discard bay leaf. Use as a basting sauce when grilling chicken, pork or beef. **Yield:** 1-1/2 cups.

Homemade Holiday Gifts

PRESENTS you make yourself are always appreciated—especially when they come from the kitchen.

Try one or more of these sensational seasonal gifts and solve some gift-giving dilemmas without even untying your apron!

☕ ☕ ☕

Dill Mustard

(Pictured below and on page 149)

I pick up small, decorative canning jars at rummage sales or in hardware stores to fill with the zesty mustard I make to give to friends. —Sue Braunschweig
Delafield, Wisconsin

1 cup ground mustard
1 cup cider vinegar
3/4 cup sugar
1/4 cup water
2 teaspoons salt
1-1/2 teaspoons dill weed
2 eggs, lightly beaten

In the top of a double boiler, combine mustard, vinegar, sugar, water, salt and dill. Cover and let stand at room temperature for 4 hours. Bring water in bottom of double boiler to a boil. Add eggs to mustard mixture. Cook and stir until thickened, about 10 minutes. Cool. Store in the refrigerator. **Yield:** about 2 cups.

PRETTILY PACKAGED Chunky Fruit and Nut Relish (in glass-topped jars), Dill Mustard and Golden Granola (shown above, clockwise from upper right) make great gifts throughout the year and taste terrific.

Golden Granola

(Pictured below left and on page 148)

This crunchy granola—which may be used to top ice cream or fruit or eaten as cereal —makes a welcome gift. Package it in a tin or jar decked with a festive bow.
—Maxine Smith, Owanka, South Dakota

        4 cups old-fashioned oats
        1 cup flaked coconut
    1/2 cup wheat germ
    1/2 cup sesame seeds
    1/2 cup sunflower seeds
    1/2 cup slivered almonds
1-1/2 teaspoons salt
1-1/2 teaspoons ground cinnamon
    1/2 cup vegetable oil
    1/4 cup packed brown sugar
    1/3 cup honey
    1/3 cup water
        1 tablespoon vanilla extract
    1/2 cup golden raisins *or* chopped dried
        apricots

In a large bowl, combine the first eight ingredients; mix well. In a saucepan, heat oil, brown sugar, honey, water and vanilla until sugar is dissolved. Pour over dry ingredients and mix well. Spoon into a greased 13-in. x 9-in. x 2-in. baking pan. Bake at 275° for 1 hour or until golden, stirring every 15 minutes. Cool completely. Stir in raisins or apricots. **Yield:** about 9 cups.

Chunky Fruit and Nut Relish

(Pictured at left and on page 149)

This colorful relish's tasty medley of fruits and nuts is delicious served with ham or poultry.
—Donna Brockett, Kingfisher, Oklahoma

        2 packages (12 ounces *each*) fresh *or* frozen
        cranberries
1-1/2 cups sugar
        1 cup orange juice
        1 can (16 ounces) sliced peaches, drained
        and cut up
        1 can (8 ounces) pineapple tidbits, drained
        1 cup chopped pecans
    1/2 cup golden raisins

In a large saucepan, bring cranberries, sugar and orange juice to a boil, stirring occasionally. Reduce heat and simmer, uncovered, for 8-10 minutes or until the berries burst. Remove from the heat; stir in peaches, pineapple, pecans and raisins. Cool. Cover and refrigerate at least 3 hours. **Yield:** about 6 cups.

Aroma's Sweet... But Don't Eat!

THE WARM SCENT of cinnamon and other spices helps make the holidays merry for Mary Kay Dixson in her Catlin, Illinois home.

Mary Kay shares her recipe for *non-edible* Crafty Cinnamon Cookie Ornaments to hang on a tree or decorate packages. "Sometimes I give them as a set with the cookie cutter," she relates.

Try Mary Kay's "scent-sational" recipe...and be sure to keep these decorative cookies out of the reach of pets and small children.

Crafty Cinnamon Cookie Ornaments

        1 cup ground cinnamon
        1 tablespoon ground cloves
        1 tablespoon ground nutmeg
    3/4 cup applesauce
        2 tablespoons Aleene's Tacky Glue
Ribbon *or* gold cord

In a medium bowl, combine cinnamon, cloves and nutmeg. Stir in applesauce and glue. Work mixture with hands for 2-3 minutes to form a ball. If mixture is too dry, add more applesauce; if too wet, add more cinnamon. Knead on a cinnamon-sprinkled surface until dough holds together well. Divide into four equal portions; roll out each to 1/4-in. thickness. Cut with cookie cutters. Place on cookie sheets. Use a pencil to make a small hole in the top of each for hanging, being sure hole goes all the way through. Air-dry ornaments. Turn over from time to time to ensure even drying (it will take about 4-5 days). For faster results, place ornaments in sunlight or dry in a warm oven (250°-300°) for several hours. When ornaments are dry, insert ribbon or gold cord through hole and tie ends into a knot. If desired, tie another length into a bow near ornament top. **Yield:** 8 ornaments (6 inches). **Editor's Note:** These ornaments are *not edible.*

Potluck Pleasers

***When you need large-quantity recipes for a picnic,
family reunion or church function, turn to these tried-and-true
main courses, side dishes, salads, desserts and more.***

—— 🍲 🍲 🍲 ——

GOOD FOR GATHERINGS. Clockwise from upper left: Sweet Peanut Treats (p. 168), Classic Beef Stew (p. 172), Tangy Tomato Slices (p. 164), Broccoli Rice Casserole (p. 169) and Chicken Spinach Bake (p. 160).

HARVEST HELPINGS like Caramel Apple Cake, Cranberry Conserve and Turkey with Sausage Stuffing (shown above, clockwise from top) are perfect for any function in fall.

Turkey with Sausage Stuffing

(Pictured above)

Here's a super way to savor roast turkey and stuffing without having to cook the big holiday bird. The stuffing is hearty, and the meat is juicy and tender.
—Aura Lee Johnson, Vermilion, Ohio

1 whole bone-in turkey breast (5 to 7 pounds)
1/4 cup butter *or* margarine, melted
2 packages (12 ounces *each*) bulk pork sausage
2 cups sliced celery
2 medium onions, chopped
4 cups dry bread cubes
2 cups pecan halves
1 cup raisins
2/3 cup chicken broth
2 eggs, beaten
1 teaspoon salt
1/2 teaspoon rubbed sage
1/4 teaspoon pepper

Rinse turkey breast and pat dry. Place with breast side up in a shallow baking dish. Brush with butter.

Bake, uncovered, at 325° for 2 to 2-1/2 hours or until the internal temperature reaches 170°. Cover loosely with foil to prevent excess browning if necessary. Meanwhile, in a skillet, cook sausage, celery and onions until the sausage is browned and vegetables are tender; drain. Remove from the heat; add all remaining ingredients and mix well. Spoon into a greased 3-qt. casserole. Cover and bake at 325° for 1 hour. Serve with sliced turkey. **Yield:** 15-20 servings.

Cranberry Conserve

(Pictured at left)

I can still remember my grandmother from Germany making this lovely, delicious conserve for the holidays. She'd give it to family members and friends. It tastes great served as a relish alongside meat or even spread on biscuits. —Mildred Marsh Banker
Austin, Texas

4 cups fresh *or* frozen cranberries, halved
1 tablespoon grated orange peel
2 oranges, peeled, sliced and quartered
1 cup raisins
1-1/4 cups water
1 cup chopped pecans
2-1/2 cups sugar

In a large saucepan, combine cranberries, orange peel, oranges, raisins and water. Cover and simmer over medium heat until cranberries are soft. Add pecans and sugar; stir well. Simmer, uncovered, for 10-15 minutes, stirring often. Cool. Spoon into covered containers. Refrigerate. Serve as a relish with poultry or pork, or spread on biscuits or rolls. **Yield:** 3 pints.

Caramel Apple Cake

(Pictured at left)

When I go to potlucks, family gatherings or on hunting and fishing trips with my husband and son, this cake is one of my favorite desserts to bring. The flavorful cake stays moist as long as it lasts, which isn't long!
—Marilyn Paradis, Woodburn, Oregon

1-1/2 cups vegetable oil
1-1/2 cups sugar
1/2 cup packed brown sugar
3 eggs
3 cups all-purpose flour
2 teaspoons ground cinnamon
1/2 teaspoon ground nutmeg
1 teaspoon baking soda
1/2 teaspoon salt
3-1/2 cups diced peeled apples
1 cup chopped walnuts
2 teaspoons vanilla extract
CARAMEL ICING:
1/2 cup packed brown sugar
1/3 cup half-and-half cream
1/4 cup butter *or* margarine
Dash salt
1 cup confectioners' sugar
Chopped walnuts, optional

In a mixing bowl, combine oil and sugars. Add eggs, one at a time, beating well after each addition. Combine dry ingredients; add to batter and stir well. Fold in apples, walnuts and vanilla. Pour into a greased and floured 10-in. tube pan. Bake at 325° for 1-1/2 hours or until cake tests done. Cool in pan 10 minutes; remove to a wire rack to cool completely. In the top of a double boiler over simmering water, heat brown sugar, cream, butter and salt until sugar is dissolved. Cool to room temperature. Beat in confectioners' sugar until smooth; drizzle over cake. Sprinkle with nuts if desired. **Yield:** 12-16 servings.

Hot Potato Salad for 100

Folks are surprised to see pickles in this potato salad. They really pair well with the other flavors. Why not try it for yourself? —Jene Cain
Northridge California

45 pounds potatoes
7 pounds bacon, chopped
5 cups all-purpose flour
3-1/2 quarts vinegar
3-1/2 quarts water
6 cups sugar
1 cup salt
4 teaspoons pepper
3-1/2 quarts chopped onion (about 4-1/2 pounds)
1-1/2 quarts chopped pickles

Cook potatoes until tender. Meanwhile, in a large skillet, cook bacon until crisp; remove to paper towels to drain. Add flour to drippings; cook and stir until bubbly. In a large kettle, heat vinegar, water and sugar to boiling. Gradually add flour mixture; cook and stir until thickened. Add salt, pepper, onion and pickles; mix well. Drain, peel and slice potatoes; place in serving pans. Divide sauce among pans and stir to coat. Sprinkle with bacon. **Yield:** 100 servings (7 gallons).

Chicken Spinach Bake

(Pictured below and on page 156)

A good friend shared this recipe with me years ago, and I've used it often. With the creamy sauce and love-ly look of this dish, even people who aren't very fond of spinach seem to enjoy it served this way.
—Sue Braunschweig, Delafield, Wisconsin

    3 packages (10 ounces *each*) frozen
      chopped spinach, thawed
    3 eggs
1/2 teaspoon onion salt
1/2 teaspoon ground nutmeg
3/4 cup grated Parmesan cheese, *divided*
3/4 cup Italian-seasoned bread crumbs
   16 boneless skinless chicken breast halves
Salt and pepper to taste
    5 tablespoons butter *or* margarine, melted
CHEESE SAUCE:
    6 tablespoons butter *or* margarine, *divided*
1/4 cup all-purpose flour
1/2 teaspoon salt
    2 cups milk
    2 cups (8 ounces) shredded cheddar cheese
    1 cup sliced fresh mushrooms

Drain and squeeze out excess moisture from spinach. Beat eggs, onion salt and nutmeg. Add spinach and 1/4 cup Parmesan cheese; mix well. Combine bread crumbs and remaining Parmesan. Sprinkle chicken with salt and pepper; coat with crumb mixture. Place in two greased 13-in. x 9-in. x 2-in. baking pans. Spread 2 tablespoons spinach mixture onto each breast. Sprinkle with re-maining crumb mixture; drizzle with butter. Bake at 350° for 35-40 minutes or until chicken juices run clear. For sauce, melt 4 tablespoons butter; blend in flour and salt. Stir to form a smooth paste. Add milk; cook and stir until thickened and bubbly. Add cheese and stir until melted. Saute mushrooms in remaining butter. Stir into cheese mixture. Carefully pour sauce over chicken, or pour into a serving bowl and pass. **Yield:** 16 servings.

Barbecued Bean Salad

This tangy hearty salad is a refreshing dish to serve at a summertime picnic. Mild spices blend nicely with the beans and garden ingredients. Be prepared to bring home an empty bowl.
—Linda Ault
Newberry, Indiana

    1 package (16 ounces) dry pinto beans,
      rinsed
    1 medium onion, chopped
    1 medium green pepper, diced
    1 medium sweet red pepper, diced
    1 can (17 ounces) whole kernel corn,
      drained
DRESSING:
1/4 cup ketchup
1/4 cup cider vinegar
1/4 cup olive oil
    3 tablespoons brown sugar
    1 tablespoon Worcestershire sauce
    1 tablespoon chili powder
    5 teaspoons Dijon mustard
    1 teaspoon ground cumin
    1 teaspoon salt
1/4 teaspoon pepper

In a large kettle, cover beans with water; bring to a boil. Boil for 2 minutes. Remove from the heat and let stand 1 hour. Drain and rinse beans; re-turn to the kettle. Cover with water again and bring to a boil. Reduce heat; cover and simmer for 1-1/2 hours or until beans are tender. Drain and rinse beans; place in a large bowl and cool to room tem-perature. Add the onion, peppers and corn; toss. In a saucepan, combine all dressing ingredients; simmer for 10 minutes. Pour over vegetables and mix well. Cover and chill. **Yield:** 16-20 servings.

Sausage Mozzarella Supper

I've used this recipe for many church meals, and it's always a hit. Everyone loves the combination of sausage, mushrooms, cheese and noodles.
—Clara Honeyager, Mukwonago, Wisconsin

- 20 pounds link *or* bulk Italian sausage, sliced *or* crumbled
- 3 gallons spaghetti sauce
- 16 cups sliced fresh mushrooms
- 1-1/2 quarts tomato juice
- 3 large onions, chopped
- 3 tablespoons Italian seasoning
- 2 tablespoons salt
- 1 tablespoon pepper
- 12 pounds corkscrew noodles, cooked and drained
- 5 pounds mozzarella cheese, sliced
- 8 pounds mozzarella cheese, shredded

Brown sausage; drain fat. Mix with the spaghetti sauce, mushrooms, tomato juice, onions, Italian seasoning, salt and pepper. Grease eight 6-qt. baking pans. Layer half of the noodles, sliced cheese and meat sauce in pans. Repeat layers. Sprinkle shredded cheese equally over each pan. Cover and bake at 350° for 1 hour. Uncover and bake 15 minutes longer or until cheese is melted. **Yield:** 150-175 servings.

Escalloped Potatoes

I belong to a group of women who help put on big meals for church functions, weddings and more. This large-quantity recipe, featuring tender sliced red potatoes in a creamy sauce, is always a hit.
—Bernice Hartje, Cavalier, North Dakota

- 25 to 30 pounds red potatoes, sliced
- 1 pound butter *or* margarine
- 2 cups all-purpose flour
- 2-1/2 teaspoons salt
- 2-1/2 teaspoons pepper
- 2-1/2 quarts milk
- 2-1/2 quarts whipping cream
- 4 medium onions, sliced

Cover potatoes with cold water; refrigerate overnight. In a large kettle, melt butter; add flour, salt and pepper. Cook until thickened, stirring constantly. Gradually add milk and cream. Cook and stir until thickened and bubbly. Drain potatoes; place in eight 3-qt. baking pans. Add onions. Pour the sauce over and stir gently. Cover and bake at 300° for 2 hours and 15 minutes. Uncover and bake 15 minutes longer. **Yield:** 70-80 servings.

Nutty O's

(Pictured above)

Almonds add a nice nutty flavor to this tasty snack. It's perfect for potlucks and not too sweet. Served in a decorative dish, basket or tin, it has a golden holiday look.
—Karen Buchholz, Sitka, Alaska

- 1 cup packed brown sugar
- 1 cup dark corn syrup
- 1/2 cup butter *or* margarine
- 12 cups Cheerios
- 2 cups pecan halves
- 1 cup whole almonds

In a large saucepan, heat brown sugar, corn syrup and butter until sugar is dissolved. Stir in cereal and nuts; mix well. Spread onto greased 15-in. x 10-in. x 1-in. baking pans. Bake at 325° for 15 minutes. Cool for 10 minutes; stir to loosen from pan. Cool completely. Store in an airtight container. **Yield:** 16 cups.

Cookie Capers

If you plan on taking cookies to a potluck but won't have time to fuss beforehand, make the dough ahead of time, form into balls and freeze. Pull them out of the freezer the day of the event and bake a little longer than usual.

Salted Nut Squares

A favorite of young and old, this recipe is delicious. There's no need to keep it warm or cold, so it's perfect for the potluck that has you traveling longer distances. —Kathy Tremel, Earling, Iowa

> 3 cups salted peanuts without skins, *divided*
> 2-1/2 tablespoons butter *or* margarine
> 2 cups (12 ounces) peanut butter chips
> 1 can (14 ounces) sweetened condensed milk
> 2 cups miniature marshmallows

Place half of the peanuts in an ungreased 11-in. x 7-in. x 2-in. baking pan; set aside. In a saucepan, melt butter and peanut butter chips over low heat. Remove from the heat. Add milk and marshmallows; stir until melted. Pour over peanuts. Sprinkle the remaining peanuts on top. Cover and refrigerate. Cut into squares. **Yield:** 5-6 dozen.

Worry-Free Serving Tray

To make a handy disposable tray for carrying bars or cookies to potlucks or bake sales, cut the front out of a large empty cereal box, tape up the sides and cover with wrapping paper. You don't have to worry about getting it back or bringing it home.

Baked Spaghetti

(Pictured at far right)

Every time that I make this cheesy dish, I get requests for the recipe. It puts a different spin on spaghetti and is great for any meal. The leftovers, if there are any, also freeze well for a quick meal later on in the week. —Ruth Koberna, Brecksville, Ohio

> 1 cup chopped onion
> 1 cup chopped green pepper
> 1 tablespoon butter *or* margarine
> 1 can (28 ounces) diced tomatoes, undrained
> 1 can (4 ounces) mushroom stems and pieces, drained
> 1 can (2-1/4 ounces) sliced ripe olives, drained
> 2 teaspoons dried oregano
> 1 pound ground beef, browned and drained, optional
> 12 ounces spaghetti, cooked and drained
> 2 cups (8 ounces) shredded cheddar cheese
> 1 can (10-3/4 ounces) condensed cream of mushroom soup, undiluted
> 1/4 cup water
> 1/4 cup grated Parmesan cheese

In a large skillet, saute onion and green pepper in butter until tender. Add tomatoes, mushrooms, olives and oregano. Add ground beef if desired. Simmer, uncovered, for 10 minutes. Place half of the spaghetti in a greased 13-in. x 9-in. x 2-in. baking dish. Top with half of the vegetable mixture. Sprinkle with 1 cup of cheddar cheese. Repeat layers. Mix the soup and water until smooth; pour over casserole. Sprinkle with Parmesan cheese. Bake, uncovered, at 350° for 30-35 minutes or until heated through. **Yield:** 12 servings.

Fluffy Fruit Salad

(Pictured at right)

I like to bring my mom's fruit salad to potlucks. Its smooth sauce combined with all the colorful fruit makes it different than any other salad I've tried. I've given out the recipe more times than I can remember. —Anne Heinonen, Howell, Michigan

> 2 cans (20 ounces *each*) crushed pineapple
> 2/3 cup sugar
> 2 tablespoons all-purpose flour
> 2 eggs, lightly beaten
> 1/4 cup orange juice
> 3 tablespoons lemon juice
> 1 tablespoon vegetable oil
> 2 cans (17 ounces *each*) fruit cocktail, drained
> 2 cans (11 ounces *each*) mandarin oranges, drained
> 2 bananas, sliced
> 1 cup whipping cream, whipped

Drain pineapple, reserving 1 cup juice in a small saucepan. Set pineapple aside. To saucepan, add sugar, flour, eggs, orange juice, lemon juice and oil. Bring to a boil, stirring constantly. Boil for 1 minute; remove from the heat and let cool. In a salad bowl, combine the pineapple, fruit cocktail, oranges and bananas. Fold in the whipped cream and cooled sauce. Chill for several hours. **Yield:** 12-16 servings.

Peanut Butter Pie

(Pictured at right)

I entered this pie in our county fair, and it was selected Grand Champion. Who can resist a tempting chocolate crumb crust and the creamy filling with big peanut butter taste? Be prepared to take an empty pan home when you serve this pie. —Doris Doherty, Albany, Oregon

CRUST:
1-1/4 cups chocolate cookie crumbs (20 cookies)
  1/4 cup sugar
  1/4 cup butter *or* margarine, melted
FILLING:
  1 package (8 ounces) cream cheese, softened
  1 cup creamy peanut butter
  1 cup sugar
  1 tablespoon butter *or* margarine, softened
  1 teaspoon vanilla extract
  1 cup whipping cream, whipped
Grated chocolate *or* chocolate cookie crumbs, optional

Combine crust ingredients; press into a 9-in. pie plate. Bake at 375° for 10 minutes. Cool. In a mixing bowl, beat cream cheese, peanut butter, sugar, butter and vanilla until smooth. Fold in whipped cream. Gently spoon into crust. Garnish with chocolate or cookie crumbs if desired. Refrigerate. **Yield:** 8-10 servings.

YOUR GANG will eagerly crowd around the buffet table when Baked Spaghetti, Peanut Butter Pie and Fluffy Fruit Salad (shown above, clockwise from upper right) are served.

qt. casserole; sprinkle with cheese if desired. Bake, uncovered, at 375° for 40-45 minutes or until heated through. **Yield:** 6-8 servings.

Meat Loaf for 120

A friend of mine gave me this recipe, which was a favorite at 4-H camp. People are pleasantly surprised to see such a down-home entree offered to a large group.
—Joanne Shew Chuk
St. Benedict, Saskatchewan

  16 eggs, lightly beaten
   8 cups old-fashioned oats
   5 cups tomato juice
   3 large onions, chopped
1/3 cup salt
   2 tablespoons pepper
  40 pounds ground beef
SAUCE:
   3 cups water
1-1/2 cups ketchup
   6 tablespoons vinegar
   2 tablespoons prepared mustard
   2 tablespoons brown sugar

Combine the first six ingredients. Add beef; mix well. Form into 16 loaves. Place in 9-in. x 5-in. x 3-in. loaf pans. Combine sauce ingredients; pour 3 tablespoons over each loaf. Bake at 350° for 1-1/2 to 2 hours or until no pink remains, basting once with remaining sauce. **Yield:** 120 servings.

Make Your Mark on Meat Loaf

When making meat loaf for a potluck, score across the top of the raw meat in the loaf pan where each serving is to be sliced. When cooked, there's no question about the size or number of servings.

Turkey Tetrazzini

(Pictured above)

This recipe comes from a cookbook our church compiled. It's convenient because it can be made ahead and frozen. After the holidays, we use leftover turkey to prepare a meal for university students. They clean their plates!
—Gladys Waldrop
Calvert City, Kentucky

   1 box (7 ounces) spaghetti, broken into
     2-inch pieces
   2 cups cubed cooked turkey
   1 cup (4 ounces) shredded cheddar cheese
   1 can (10-3/4 ounces) condensed cream of
     mushroom soup, undiluted
   1 medium onion, chopped
   2 cans (4 ounces *each*) sliced mushrooms,
     drained
1/3 cup milk
1/4 cup chopped green pepper
   1 jar (2 ounces) chopped pimientos, drained
1/4 teaspoon salt
1/8 teaspoon pepper
Additional shredded cheddar cheese, optional

Cook spaghetti according to package directions; drain. Transfer to a large bowl; add the next 10 ingredients and mix well. Spoon into a greased 2-1/2-

Tangy Tomato Slices

(Pictured on page 156)

Fresh garden tomatoes are a treat at a picnic or family gathering. The zesty flavor of this dish is a crowd-pleaser, and it's a colorful addition to the buffet.
—Lois Fetting, Nelson, Wisconsin

   1 cup vegetable oil
1/3 cup vinegar
1/4 cup minced fresh parsley
   3 tablespoons minced fresh basil *or* 1
     tablespoon dried basil
   1 tablespoon sugar
   1 teaspoon salt

1/2 teaspoon pepper
1/2 teaspoon ground mustard
1/2 teaspoon garlic powder
1 medium sweet onion, thinly sliced
6 large tomatoes, thinly sliced

In a small bowl or a jar with a tight-fitting lid, mix the first nine ingredients. Layer onion and tomatoes in a shallow glass dish. Pour the marinade over; cover and refrigerate for several hours. **Yield:** 12 servings.

—— 🝆 🝆 🝆 ——

Big-Batch Bean Soup

When I was a cook in the service, I learned all I could from the cooks in the galley. This soup was a favorite among the men. —Jene Cain, Northridge, California

6 pounds dry white beans (about 3-1/2 quarts)
7 gallons ham *or* chicken stock
8 ham bones
2-3/4 cups shredded carrots (about 1 pound)
4-1/2 cups finely chopped onion (about 2 pounds)
2 teaspoons pepper
2 cups all-purpose flour
3 cups cold water

Rinse beans. Place in a large kettle with stock and ham bones; bring to a boil. Reduce heat; cover and simmer for 2-3 hours or until the beans are tender. Stir in carrots, onion and pepper; cover and simmer for 30 minutes. Combine flour and cold water until smooth; gradually stir into soup. Cook for 10 minutes. If too thick, add additional water. **Yield:** 100 servings (6-1/4 gallons).

—— 🝆 🝆 🝆 ——

Cocoa for a Crowd

For a large gathering during the winter, this cocoa really hits the spot. Combine the sugar, baking cocoa and salt ahead of time and store in an airtight container until ready to use.
—Pat Monson
Stewartville, Minnesota

4 cups sugar
3 cups baking cocoa
1/2 teaspoon salt
1 quart warm water
2 quarts boiling water
4 gallons hot milk

In a large kettle, combine sugar, cocoa, salt and warm water; mix well. Add boiling water; boil for 10 minutes. Remove from the heat; stir in hot milk. **Yield:** 100 servings.

Herbed Spinach Bake

(Pictured below)

This is a special side dish my mother liked to serve at church dinners. She was recognized by family and friends as an outstanding cook. It's a pleasure to share her recipe with you.
—Nancy Frank
Lake Ariel, Pennsylvania

2 packages (10 ounces *each*) frozen chopped spinach
2 cups cooked rice
2 cups (8 ounces) shredded cheddar cheese
4 eggs, beaten
2/3 cup milk
1/4 cup butter *or* margarine, softened
1/4 cup chopped onion
2 teaspoons salt
1 teaspoon Worcestershire sauce
1 teaspoon ground thyme

Cook spinach according to package directions; drain well, squeezing out excess liquid. Combine spinach with remaining ingredients in a large bowl. Pour into a greased 13-in. x 9-in. x 2-in. baking dish. Cover and bake at 350° for 20 minutes. Uncover and bake 5 minutes more or until set. **Yield:** 16 servings.

Picnic Coleslaw

(Pictured below)

I usually prepare this distinctive, colorful coleslaw for picnics, block parties and potlucks. No matter where I take this tasty dish, people are always asking for the recipe. The bacon adds rich flavor to the fresh crisp carrots and cabbage. Plus, it travels well.
—Karen Page, St. Louis, Missouri

6 cups shredded cabbage
2 cups shredded carrots
8 bacon strips, cooked and crumbled
12 green onions with tops, thinly sliced
1/2 cup cider vinegar
1/3 cup vegetable oil
1/3 cup sugar
1 teaspoon salt

In a bowl, combine cabbage, carrots, bacon and onions. In a jar with tight-fitting lid, mix vinegar, oil, sugar and salt; shake well. Just before serving, pour dressing over cabbage mixture and toss. **Yield:** 12-16 servings.

A SUCCESSFUL SUMMER PICNIC includes a scrumptious spread of Fourth of July Bean Casserole, Onion Cheese Ball and Picnic Coleslaw (shown above, clockwise from upper right).

Onion Cheese Ball

(Pictured below left)

This hearty cheese ball is as wonderful to eat as it is beautiful to serve. A delicious combination of cheeses makes it a real crowd-pleaser, and it's so quick and easy to make—perfect for open houses and wedding receptions. —Anna Mayer, Fort Branch, Indiana

> 2 cups (8 ounces) shredded cheddar cheese, room temperature
> 3 to 4 ounces blue cheese, room temperature
> 4 packages (3 ounces *each*) cream cheese, softened
> 3 tablespoons dried minced onion
> 1 tablespoon Worcestershire sauce
> 1 cup minced fresh parsley

Crackers

In a mixing bowl, beat cheeses, onion and Worcestershire sauce until well mixed. Shape into a ball and roll in parsley. Chill. Serve with crackers. **Yield:** 1 cheese ball (4 inches).

— ☕ ☕ ☕ —

Fourth of July Bean Casserole

(Pictured at left)

The outstanding barbecue taste of these beans makes them a favorite for cook-outs all summer and into the fall. It's a popular dish with everyone—even kids. Having meat in with the beans is so much better than plain pork and beans. —Donna Fancher
Indianapolis, Indiana

> 1/2 pound sliced bacon, diced
> 1/2 pound ground beef
> 1 cup chopped onion
> 1 can (28 ounces) pork and beans
> 1 can (17 ounces) lima beans, rinsed and drained
> 1 can (15 to 16 ounces) kidney beans, rinsed and drained
> 1/2 cup barbecue sauce
> 1/2 cup ketchup
> 1/2 cup sugar
> 1/2 cup packed brown sugar
> 2 tablespoons prepared mustard
> 2 tablespoons molasses
> 1 teaspoon salt
> 1/2 teaspoon chili powder

In a large skillet, cook bacon, beef and onion until meat is browned and onion is tender; drain. Transfer to a greased 2-1/2-qt. baking dish; add all of the beans and mix well. In a small bowl, combine the remaining ingredients; stir into beef and bean mixture. Cover and bake at 350° for 45 minutes. Uncover; bake 15 minutes longer. **Yield:** 12 servings.

— ☕ ☕ ☕ —

Ample Brown Betty

Not only is the country-style dessert tasty, it's also a great way to use up leftover bread. No one can resist this sweet treat wherever I take it. —Evelyn Kennell
Roanoke, Illinois

> 2 loaves (20 ounces *each*) white bread with crusts, cut into 1-inch cubes (about 32 cups)
> 2 cups butter *or* margarine, melted
> 40 cups (about 12 pounds) sliced peeled apples
> 3 cups packed brown sugar, *divided*
> 2 cups sugar
> 2 teaspoons ground nutmeg
> 2 teaspoons ground cinnamon
> 4 cups water
> 3 tablespoons lemon juice

Toss bread cubes with butter; divide half of the cubes among four greased 13-in. x 9-in. x 2-in. baking pans. Arrange apples over bread, using 10 cups per pan. Mix 2 cups of brown sugar, sugar, nutmeg and cinnamon; divide into fourths and sprinkle over the apples. Mix water and lemon juice; pour a fourth into each pan. Top with remaining bread cubes. Sprinkle remaining brown sugar equally over pans. Cover and bake at 375° for 30 minutes. Uncover and bake 25-30 minutes longer. **Yield:** 50-60 servings.

— ☕ ☕ ☕ —

Barbecued Beef Sandwiches

These savory barbecued sandwiches are one of my specialties. They really capture the flavor of foods we serve here in "Big Sky Country". When we're invited to a potluck, I'm asked to bring these sandwiches. —Lorraine Elvbakken, Billings, Montana

> 2 beef briskets, trimmed (about 12 pounds)
> 6 cups barbecue sauce
> 2 cups water
> 40 to 50 hamburger buns

Place briskets in a large roasting pan. Combine barbecue sauce and water; pour over meat. Cover tightly and bake at 325° for 4 to 4-1/2 hours or until fork-tender. Remove meat from juices; cool. Skim fat from juices. Thinly slice meat; return to pan and heat in juices. Serve on buns. **Yield:** 40-50 servings.

Sweet Peanut Treats

(Pictured below and on page 156)

We sold tempting bars almost like these at the refreshment stand at a Minnesota state park where I worked in the '70s, and they were a favorite of employees and visitors alike. Now I make this recipe when I want to serve a special treat. —Phyllis Smith
Olympia, Washington

2 cups (12 ounces) semisweet chocolate chips
2 cups (12 ounces) butterscotch chips
1 jar (18 ounces) creamy peanut butter
1 cup butter *or* margarine
1 can (5 ounces) evaporated milk
1/4 cup vanilla cook-and-serve pudding mix
1 bag (2 pounds) confectioners' sugar
1 pound salted peanuts

In the top of a double boiler over simmering water, melt chocolate chips, butterscotch chips and peanut butter; stir until smooth. Spread half into a greased 15-in. x 10-in. x 1-in. baking pan. Chill until firm. Meanwhile, in a saucepan, bring butter, milk and pudding mix to a boil. Cook and stir for 2 minutes. Remove from the heat; add confectioners' sugar and beat until smooth. Spread over chocolate mixture in pan. Stir peanuts into remaining chocolate mixture; mix well. Carefully spread over pudding layer. Refrigerate. Cut into 1-in. squares. **Yield:** 10 dozen.

Macaroni Salad for 100

Whenever I make this traditional pasta salad, hungry guests leave few leftovers. I've been relying on this classic recipe for years. —Judy Depree
Thief River Falls, Minnesota

5 to 6 pounds macaroni, cooked and drained
5 to 6 pounds fully cooked ham, cubed
3 pounds shredded cheddar cheese
2 bags (20 ounces *each*) frozen peas, thawed
2 bunches celery, chopped (about 12 cups)
2 large onions, chopped (2 to 2-1/2 cups)
2 cans (5-3/4 ounces *each*) pitted ripe olives, drained and sliced
DRESSING:
2 quarts mayonnaise
1 bottle (8 ounces) Western *or* French salad dressing
1/4 cup vinegar
1/4 cup sugar
1 cup half-and-half cream
1-1/2 teaspoons onion salt
1-1/2 teaspoons garlic salt
1 teaspoon salt
1 teaspoon pepper

Combine the first seven ingredients. Combine all dressing ingredients; pour over the macaroni mixture and toss. Refrigerate. **Yield:** 100 servings.

— ☕ ☕ ☕ —

Chicken Supreme with Gravy

A group of friends and I have met often throughout the years to swap our favorite recipes. This tried-and-true dish has always been well received. —Bernice Hartje, Cavalier, North Dakota

1-1/2 celery stalks, diced (about 6 cups)
6 medium onions, diced (about 4 cups)
1 pound butter *or* margarine
3 loaves (1-1/2 pounds *each*) white bread
3 tablespoons ground sage
3 tablespoons salt
1 tablespoon baking powder
2 teaspoons pepper
12 eggs
9 cups milk
24 cups diced cooked chicken (about 6 chickens)
3 cans (14-1/2 ounces *each*) chicken broth
GRAVY:
8 cans (10-3/4 ounces *each*) condensed creamy chicken mushroom soup, undiluted
9 to 10 cups water

In a large skillet, saute celery and onions in butter. Break bread into small pieces into a large bowl. Add sage, salt, baking powder and pepper; toss to coat. Add celery and onions; mix well. Beat eggs and milk; add to bread mixture. Divide half the chicken in four 13-in. x 9-in. x 2-in. greased baking pans. Cover with half the bread mixture. Repeat layers. Pour broth into each pan. Cover and bake at 300° for 1 hour and 45 minutes or until broth is absorbed; uncover and bake 15 minutes more. For gravy, combine soup and water in a large saucepan; mix well. Simmer about 10 minutes. Serve with the chicken dish. **Yield:** 70-80 servings.

— 🍴 🍴 🍴 —

Party Punch

Here's a traditional fruity punch I've come to rely on when serving crowds. It's a refreshing beverage with tropical flair. —*Donna Long, Searcy, Arkansas*

    3 cups warm water
    2 cups sugar
    3 ripe bananas, sliced
    1 can (46 ounces) pineapple juice
1-1/2 cups orange juice
  1/4 cup lemon juice
    3 quarts ginger ale, chilled

In a blender or food processor, blend the water, sugar and bananas until smooth. Pour into a large container. Add pineapple juice, orange juice and lemon juice; mix well. Freeze, stirring occasionally, until slushy. Add ginger ale when ready to serve. **Yield:** about 24 servings.

— 🍴 🍴 🍴 —

Broccoli Rice Casserole

(Pictured above right and on page 156)

This hearty casserole is my favorite dish to make for a potluck. With the green of the broccoli and the rich cheese sauce, it's pretty to serve, and it makes a tasty side dish for almost any kind of meat.
—*Margaret Mayes, La Mesa, California*

    1 small onion, chopped
  1/2 cup chopped celery
    1 package (10 ounces) frozen chopped broccoli, thawed
    1 tablespoon butter *or* margarine
    1 jar (8 ounces) process cheese spread
    1 can (10-3/4 ounces) condensed cream of mushroom soup, undiluted
    1 can (5 ounces) evaporated milk
    3 cups cooked rice

In a large skillet over medium heat, saute onion, celery and broccoli in butter for 3-5 minutes. Stir in cheese, soup and milk until smooth. Place rice in a greased 8-in. square baking dish. Pour cheese mixture over; do not stir. Bake, uncovered, at 325° for 25-30 minutes or until hot and bubbly. **Yield:** 8-10 servings.

Hawaiian Baked Beans

I made these one-of-a-kind baked beans for my daughter's wedding reception. The guests really enjoyed the sweet-and-sour flavor. —*Charlene Laper Lakeview, Michigan*

    4 jars (48 ounces *each*) great northern beans, rinsed and drained
    4 cups chopped onion
    1 bag (2 pounds) dark brown sugar
    2 pounds cubed fully cooked ham
    1 bottle (28 ounces) ketchup
    1 can (20 ounces) crushed pineapple, drained
  1/2 cup prepared mustard
  1/3 cup vinegar

Combine all ingredients; mix well. Divide among four greased 13-in. x 9-in. x 2-in. baking pans. Cover tightly; bake at 350° for 1-1/2 hours. Uncover and bake 20-30 minutes more. **Yield:** 80-100 servings.

Honey Mustard Dressing

It's nice to offer people a simple green salad at gatherings. This dressing adds the right amount of zip.
—*Judy Roehrman, Phoenix, Arizona*

 2 quarts mayonnaise
 4 cups (32 ounces) sour cream
 12 ounces honey
 12 ounces Dijon mustard
 6 tablespoons mustard seed
Salad greens

Combine the mayonnaise, sour cream, honey, mustard and mustard seed until smooth. Serve over salad greens. **Yield:** 100 servings (about 4 quarts).

— ☕ ☕ ☕ —

Ham-Stuffed Manicotti

(Pictured at far right)

Here's a fun and different use for ham. It's unexpected combined with the manicotti, yet delicious. The creamy cheese sauce makes this casserole perfect for chilly days. I'm always asked for the recipe whenever I serve it. —*Dorothy Anderson, Ottawa, Kansas*

 8 manicotti shells
 1/2 cup chopped onion
 1 tablespoon vegetable oil
 3 cups (1 pound) ground fully cooked ham
 1 can (4 ounces) sliced mushrooms, drained
 1 cup (4 ounces) shredded Swiss cheese, *divided*
 3 tablespoons grated Parmesan cheese
 1/4 to 1/2 cup chopped green pepper
 3 tablespoons butter *or* margarine
 3 tablespoons all-purpose flour
 2 cups milk
Paprika
Chopped fresh parsley

Cook manicotti according to package directions; set aside. In a large skillet, saute onion in oil until tender. Remove from the heat. Add ham, mushrooms, half of the Swiss cheese and Parmesan; set aside. In a saucepan, saute green pepper in butter until tender. Stir in flour until thoroughly combined. Add milk; cook, stirring constantly, until thickened and bubbly. Mix a quarter of the sauce into ham mixture. Stuff each shell with about 1/3 cup of filling. Place in a greased 11-in. x 7-in. x 2-in. baking dish. Top with remaining sauce; sprinkle with paprika. Cover and bake at 350° for 30 minutes or until heated through. Sprinkle with parsley and remaining Swiss cheese before serving. **Yield:** 8 servings. **Editor's Note:** Recipe can easily be doubled for a larger group.

Sauerkraut Soup

(Pictured at right)

The medley of tomato, sauerkraut and smoked sausage gives this savory soup old-world flavor. It's enjoyable to make and serve, especially during the cold months. The tangy taste and aroma really warm you up!
—*Jean Marie Cornelius, Whitesville, New York*

 1 pound smoked Polish sausage, cut into 1/2-inch pieces
 5 medium potatoes, peeled and cubed
 2 medium onions, chopped
 2 carrots, cut into 1/4-inch slices
 3 cans (14-1/2 ounces *each*) chicken broth
 1 can (32 ounces) sauerkraut, rinsed and drained
 1 can (6 ounces) tomato paste

In a large saucepan or Dutch oven, combine sausage, potatoes, onions, carrots and chicken broth; bring to a boil. Reduce heat; cover and simmer for 30 minutes or until potatoes are tender. Add sauerkraut and tomato paste; mix well. Return to a boil. Reduce heat; cover and simmer 30 minutes longer. If a thinner soup is desired, add water or additional broth. **Yield:** 8-10 servings (2-1/2 quarts).

— ☕ ☕ ☕ —

Four-Fruit Compote

(Pictured at right)

A beautiful side dish, this compote spotlights wonderful fruit like bananas, apples, oranges and pineapple. Best of all, it can be made anytime of year. I'm sure you'll get as many smiles as I do when I bring out this refreshing salad. —*Donna Long, Searcy, Arkansas*

 1 can (20 ounces) pineapple chunks
 1/2 cup sugar
 2 tablespoons cornstarch
 1/3 cup orange juice
 1 tablespoon lemon juice
 1 can (11 ounces) mandarin oranges, drained
 3 to 4 unpeeled apples, chopped
 2 to 3 bananas, sliced

Drain pineapple, reserving 3/4 cup juice. In a saucepan, combine sugar and cornstarch. Add pineapple juice, orange juice and lemon juice. Cook and stir over medium heat until thickened and bubbly; cook and stir 1 minute longer. Remove from the heat; set aside. In a bowl, combine pineapple chunks, oranges, apples and bananas. Pour warm sauce over the fruit; stir gently to coat. Cover and refrigerate. **Yield:** 12-16 servings.

CHASE AWAY cold-weather chills with heartwarming recipes like Four-Fruit Compote, Pecan Sandies, Ham-Stuffed Manicotti and Sauerkraut Soup (shown above, clockwise from upper right).

Pecan Sandies

(Pictured above)

Whenever Mother made these cookies, there never seemed to be enough! Even now when I make them, they disappear quickly. These melt-in-your-mouth treats are great with milk or hot chocolate.
—Debbie Carlson, San Diego, California

2 cups butter *or* margarine, softened
1 cup confectioners' sugar
2 tablespoons water
4 teaspoons vanilla extract
4 cups all-purpose flour
2 cups chopped pecans
Additional confectioners' sugar

In a mixing bowl, cream butter and sugar. Add water and vanilla; mix well. Gradually add flour; fold in pecans. Roll dough into 1-in. balls. Place on ungreased baking sheets and flatten with fingers. Bake at 300° for 20-25 minutes. Cool on a wire rack. When cool, dust with confectioners' sugar. **Yield:** about 5 dozen.

In a Dutch oven, brown the beef, half at a time, in oil. Drain. Return all meat to pan. Add onion, tomatoes, beef broth, tapioca, garlic, parsley, salt, pepper and bay leaf. Bring to a boil; remove from the heat. Cover and bake at 350° for 1-1/2 hours. Stir in carrots, potatoes and celery. Bake, covered, 1 hour longer or until meat and vegetables are tender. Remove bay leaf before serving. **Yield:** 6-8 servings.

— 🥄 🥄 🥄 —

Crowd Chicken Casserole

Here's a no-fuss feast that will bring you rave reviews. It's a creamy, comforting casserole that appeals to everyone. —Marna Dunn, Bullhead City, Arizona

- 10 cups diced cooked chicken
- 10 cups chopped celery
- 2 bunches green onions with tops, sliced
- 2 cans (4 ounces *each*) chopped green chilies
- 1 can (5-3/4 ounces) pitted ripe olives, drained and sliced
- 2 cups slivered almonds
- 5 cups (20 ounces) shredded cheddar cheese, *divided*
- 2 cups mayonnaise
- 2 cups (16 ounces) sour cream
- 5 cups crushed potato chips

Combine the first six ingredients. Add 2 cups of cheese. Mix mayonnaise and sour cream; add to chicken mixture and toss. Spoon into two greased 13-in. x 9-in. x 2-in. baking dishes. Sprinkle with potato chips. Top with remaining cheese. Bake, uncovered, at 350° for 20-25 minutes or until heated through. **Yield:** 24 servings.

— 🥄 🥄 🥄 —

Tapioca Pudding

The best thing about this creamy, old-fashioned pudding is that it's made the night before. That's a real plus when cooking for a crowd. —Bernice Hartje Cavalier, North Dakota

- 4 packages (3 ounces *each*) tapioca pudding mix
- 4 cups milk
- 1 carton (16 ounces) frozen whipped topping, thawed
- 2 cans (22 ounces *each*) lemon pie filling
- 1 package (10-1/2 ounces) pastel *or* white miniature marshmallows
- 4 cans (17 ounces *each*) fruit cocktail, drained

Classic Beef Stew

(Pictured above and on page 156)

Here's a good old-fashioned stew with rich beef gravy that lets the flavor of the potatoes and carrots come through. This is the perfect hearty dish for a blustery winter day. I make it often when the weather turns cooler. —Alberta McKay, Bartlesville, Oklahoma

- 2 pounds beef stew meat, cut into 1-inch cubes
- 1 to 2 tablespoons vegetable oil
- 1-1/2 cups chopped onion
- 1 can (14-1/2 ounces) diced tomatoes, undrained
- 1 can (10-1/2 ounces) condensed beef broth, undiluted
- 3 tablespoons quick-cooking tapioca
- 1 garlic clove, minced
- 1 tablespoon dried parsley flakes
- 1 teaspoon salt
- 1/4 teaspoon pepper
- 1 bay leaf
- 6 medium carrots, cut into 2-inch pieces
- 3 medium potatoes, peeled and cut into 2-inch pieces
- 1 cup sliced celery (1-inch pieces)

4 cans (15 ounces *each*) mandarin oranges, drained
1 can (20 ounces) crushed pineapple, drained

In a large saucepan, cook pudding and milk according to package directions; cool. In a large bowl, fold whipped topping into pie filling. Add the remaining ingredients; stir gently. Fold in pudding. Refrigerate overnight. **Yield:** 70-80 servings.

— 🥤 🥤 🥤 —

Clam Chowder for 60

When my mobile home park put on a "Soup Day" potluck, this is the recipe I made. Everyone agreed it tasted as good—if not better!—than the version so popular in New England. —Gretchen Draeger
Santa Cruz, California

30 cans (6-1/2 ounces *each*) minced clams
8 cups diced onions
1-1/2 pounds butter *or* margarine
2 cups all-purpose flour
3 quarts milk
3 bunches celery, sliced
3 cups minced fresh parsley
12 pounds potatoes, peeled and cubed
3 pounds sharp cheddar cheese, shredded
Salt and pepper to taste

Drain and rinse clams, reserving juice; set aside. In a large kettle, saute onions in butter until tender. Add flour; stir to form a smooth paste. Gradually add the milk, stirring constantly until slightly thickened (do not boil). Add the celery, parsley and potatoes; cook until tender, about 45 minutes. Add the clams and cheese; cook until cheese is melted and soup is heated through. Add reserved clam juice and salt and pepper. **Yield:** 60 servings (15 quarts).

— 🥤 🥤 🥤 —

Tropical Carrot Cake

(Pictured at right)

I look forward to August because our family reunion means fun and great food, like this cake with the special flair it gets from pineapple. My great-aunt gave me this recipe, and I always make it for the reunion.
—Victoria Teeter-Casey, Enterprise, Oregon

3 eggs
3/4 cup vegetable oil
3/4 cup buttermilk
2 cups all-purpose flour
2 cups sugar

2 teaspoons baking soda
2 teaspoons ground cinnamon
1/2 teaspoon salt
2 teaspoons vanilla extract
2 cups finely shredded carrots
1 cup raisins
1 can (8 ounces) crushed pineapple, undrained
1 cup chopped walnuts
1 cup flaked coconut
FROSTING:
1 package (8 ounces) cream cheese, softened
4 to 4-1/2 cups confectioners' sugar
1 to 2 tablespoons whipping cream
1 teaspoon vanilla extract

In a large mixing bowl, beat eggs, oil and buttermilk. Combine flour, sugar, baking soda, cinnamon and salt; add to egg mixture and mix well. Stir in vanilla, carrots, raisins, pineapple, walnuts and coconut; mix well. Pour into a greased 13-in. x 9-in. x 2-in. baking pan. Bake at 350° for 45-50 minutes or until cake tests done. Cool. Combine frosting ingredients in a mixing bowl; beat until smooth. Frost cake. **Yield:** 12-16 servings.

Cooking for One or Two

These smaller-serving recipes are packed with big flavor, making them perfect whether you're cooking for one when the clan is away or for you two empty nesters.

— ♟ ♟ ♟ —

PERFECTLY PORTIONED. Clockwise from upper left: Orange-Kissed Beets and Midget Pot Roast (p. 184); Dan's Peppery London Broil, Italian Herb Salad Dressing and Mini White Breads (p. 186); Pasta with Tomatoes and Basil Buttered Beans (p. 182); Zesty Ham Sandwich and Cool Lime Salad (p. 180).

Singling Out Good Food

YOU NEEDN'T BE SINGLE to appreciate single-serving recipes—even folks with large families are singled out at suppertime. (You'll find more singular sensations on the following four pages. And starting on page 182, there are nine perfectly portioned foods for just the two of you.)

Dottye Wolf of Rolla, Missouri assures you don't have to skip dessert—or reach for ordinary store-bought sweets—just because you're cooking for one. Plus, being on a restricted diet, she often makes two single-serving recipes, one for her and a different one for her husband.

"Yogurt Parfait is a delicious breakfast or luncheon treat, especially because it's prepared with assorted fresh fruit," states Dottye. "Even my husband is tempted to try some for himself!"

With her family's hectic schedule, Sherry Krenz of Woodworth, North Dakota cooks for one quite frequently, and a dessert is sure to appear on the menu.

"My Mini Apple Crisp is so simple to make. It works equally well as a single-serving dessert for me or as an afternoon snack for one of our children," says Sherry.

But what about when you need to make a main dish for one? From Royal City, Washington, Margery Bryan shares her festive Ham for One recipe.

"Growing up, our children didn't care for turkey on holidays," explains Margery. "So I'd make these ham slices just for them. The kids loved them so much, they asked me to make them throughout the year."

— 🏺 🏺 🏺 —

Yogurt Parfait

✓ Uses less fat, sugar or salt. Includes Nutritional Analysis and Diabetic Exchanges.

   1 carton (6 ounces) flavored yogurt
1/4 cup granola
1/2 cup sliced fresh fruit (apple, strawberries, banana, etc.)

In a parfait glass or large glass mug, layer one-third of the yogurt, half of the granola and then half of the fruit. Repeat layers. Top with the remaining yogurt. **Yield:** 1 serving. **Nutritional Analysis:** One serving (prepared with light nonfat yogurt and low-fat granola) equals 298 calories, 134 mg sodium, 14 mg cholesterol, 59 gm carbohydrate, 10 gm pro-tein, 3 gm fat. **Diabetic Exchanges:** 1-1/2 starch, 1 skim milk, 1 fat, 1/2 fruit.

— 🏺 🏺 🏺 —

Mini Apple Crisp

   1 medium apple, peeled and sliced
1 tablespoon all-purpose flour
2 tablespoons brown sugar
1 tablespoon butter *or* margarine

2 tablespoons quick-cooking oats
1/8 teaspoon ground cinnamon
Cream, optional

Place apple slices in a small greased baking dish. In a small bowl, combine flour and brown sugar; cut in butter until mixture resembles coarse crumbs. Add oats and cinnamon. Sprinkle over apple slices. Bake, uncovered, at 350° for 35-40 minutes or until tender. Serve with cream if desired. **Yield:** 1 serving.

Ham for One

(Not pictured)

1 small ham steak
1 tablespoon brown sugar
2 tablespoons crushed pineapple with juice

Line a 9-in. pie pan with foil. Place ham in pan; sprinkle with brown sugar. Top with pineapple. Bake, uncovered, at 350° for 20-25 minutes or until heated through. **Yield:** 1 serving.

SOMETIMES, the phrase "Dining alone?" can be music to your ears. After all, you can cook what *you* like, you can serve just as much as you want when you want it, and you're always sure to eat in good company!

With that in mind, we think you'll agree the delightful duet featured here is a symphony of fabulous flavor to your taste buds.

Mary Jo Amos of Noel, Missouri shares her tempting recipe for Tomato Strip Salad, which was passed on by her mother.

"At the height of tomato-growing season, everyone in the family could depend on Mom to make this colorful salad," recalls Mary Jo. "I can still picture her setting it on the table in a pretty yellow bowl.

"Even though our children are grown and gone, I'm as busy as ever working and volunteering for different committees," she states. "With my hectic schedule, I'm often cooking for one. I frequently rely on Mom's scaled-down recipe."

One-Serving Cheese Puff comes from Sharon McClatchey of Muskogee, Oklahoma. "This is an easy and delicious main dish for one," assures Sharon. "It's perfect for breakfast, lunch and even dinner, and it bakes to a pretty golden brown every time."

Tomato Strip Salad

✓ Uses less fat, sugar or salt. Includes Nutritional Analysis and Diabetic Exchanges.

   1 tomato, peeled, seeded and cut into strips
1/4 cup fresh *or* frozen peas, parboiled
   2 tablespoons fresh green chili strips
1/2 teaspoon lemon juice
1/2 teaspoon minced fresh cilantro *or* parsley
Lettuce leaves

In a bowl, toss tomato strips, peas, chili strips, lemon juice and cilantro or parsley. Cover and chill. Serve on a bed of lettuce. **Yield:** 1 serving. **Nutritional Analysis:** 76 calories, 20 mg sodium, 0 cholesterol, 16 gm carbohydrate, 3 gm protein, 1 gm fat. **Diabetic Exchanges:** 1 vegetable, 1/2 starch.

One-Serving Cheese Puff

1-1/2 slices white *or* whole wheat bread, buttered
   1 egg
1/4 cup shredded process American cheese
1/2 cup milk
1/8 teaspoon onion salt
1/8 teaspoon salt
   6 to 8 drops hot pepper sauce

Cut the bread into strips; place with buttered sides down along the sides and on the bottom of a 10-oz. custard cup. In a bowl, lightly beat the egg; add the cheese, milk, onion salt, salt and hot pepper sauce. Pour into the custard cup. Place on a baking sheet. Bake at 350° for 35-40 minutes or until puffy and golden brown. Serve immediately. **Yield:** 1 serving.

Single-Serving Suggestions

COOKING for one can be just as satisfying as cooking for a group. Check out these strategies from readers:

• It's very simple to make one cup of brewed coffee without all the fuss of using the coffeepot. Just put a level tablespoon of coffee in a tea strainer, place in a cup and add boiling water. —C.M. Wegner
Minneapolis, Minnesota

• I enjoy a soft-boiled egg on toast. For a perfect egg, I carefully prick an egg at each end with a pin, then gently place it in boiling water for 4 minutes. For me, this is the perfect meal.
—*Sister Barbara Ann, Dearborn, Michigan*

• I make a puree with tomatoes and other garden vegetables. I pour it into ice cube trays and freeze, then pop the cubes out into a plastic bag to store in the freezer. I use one or two as a base for soups or stews when cooking for myself. —*Mrs. Alex Vajda*
Lakewood, Ohio

JUST BECAUSE you find yourself alone at lunchtime doesn't meal you have to forgo food altogether or even rely on a single-portion frozen dinner. Instead, rely on these single-serving recipes featured here. They give new meaning to fast food!

For a refreshing side dish, try Cool Lime Salad, a favorite of Elnora Johnson of Union City, Tennessee. "I've made this recipe for many years," remarks Elnora. "Since my husband is diabetic, one-portion recipes work out well for us."

Zesty Ham Sandwich comes from Mara McAuley of Hinsdale, New York. "My mother's garden was producing abundantly, and I'd been reading about the Italian origins of American pizza," Mara recalls.

"I learned that in Rome and other parts of the Italy, pizza simply started out as bread with oil and herbs on it. In some locales, cheese, tomato and grilled meat were added.

"With the basic original pizza ingredients surrounding me, I was inspired to make a modern version of an ancient food, and this recipe was born," explains Mara.

Another single-serving sandwich is Turkey Reuben from Patricia Rutherford of Winchester, Illinois. "This recipe combines a nice medley of flavors for a delicious Reuben taste even without the corned beef," assures Patricia.

So next time you're dining alone and want a well-rounded but easy-to-fix meal, this "solo so good" sensation is sure to please!

Cool Lime Salad

1/2 cup undrained canned crushed pineapple
2 tablespoons lime gelatin
1/4 cup cottage cheese
1/4 cup whipped topping

In a small saucepan, bring pineapple to a boil. Remove from the heat and stir in gelatin until dissolved. Cool to room temperature. Stir in cottage cheese and whipped topping. Chill until set. **Yield:** 1 serving.

Zesty Ham Sandwich

1 submarine roll (6 to 7 inches)
2 to 3 thin slices fully cooked ham
3 to 4 slices mozzarella cheese
1 small tomato, thinly sliced
4 sprigs fresh parsley, chopped
4 fresh basil leaves, chopped *or* 1/2 teaspoon dried basil

1 tablespoon prepared Italian *or* Caesar salad dressing

Split roll enough to open (don't cut all the way through); place open-faced on a baking sheet. Layer remaining ingredients in order listed over roll. Bake at 350° for 10 minutes or until the cheese is melted and sandwich is warm. Fold top of roll over and serve immediately. **Yield:** 1 serving.

Turkey Reuben

(Not pictured)

1 slice white bread, toasted
1 teaspoon prepared mustard
2 ounces thinly sliced cooked turkey breast
1/8 teaspoon caraway seed
1/2 cup sauerkraut
1 slice Swiss cheese

Green pepper rings, optional

Place the toast on an ungreased baking sheet; spread the top with mustard. Arrange turkey over mustard. Sprinkle with caraway seed; top with the sauerkraut and cheese. Broil about 4 in. from the heat for 3 minutes or until cheese is bubbly and lightly browned. Top with pepper rings if desired. **Yield:** 1 serving.

Cooking for 'Just the Two of Us'

WHETHER you're a young married couple just starting out or empty-nesters learning to scale down recipe yields, it can be a challenge to find recipes that work well for two people. Here and on the following four pages, we provide recipes especially tailored for two.

Earlene Ertelt of Woodburn, Oregon found the recipe for Pasta with Tomatoes in the newspaper many years ago and has used it frequently ever since. "My husband, Charles, and I are busy on our farm and with other activities, so quick and easy dishes like this one are very important to me," Earlene asserts.

She adds, "Fresh basil is a simply delicious way to bring out the naturally terrific flavor of homegrown tomatoes. This light main course appears on our summer menus a few times a month."

Basil Buttered Beans is shared by Laura Porter of Sheridan, Oregon. "This small-portioned, fresh-tasting side dish goes great with any meat entree," Laura confirms. "I sometimes double the recipe because it gets gobbled up so quickly!"

In Phoenix, Arizona, Sharon Balzer often depends on Tuna Salad for Two. "We have long, hot summers here in the desert Southwest, so I try to get creative with salads and come up with cool dinners for my husband, Roger, and me," explains Sharon. "I think it's the easy homemade dressing that lends to this salad's special flavor."

— 🏺 🏺 🏺 —

Pasta with Tomatoes

  2 **large tomatoes, chopped**
  2 **tablespoons snipped fresh basil** *or* 2
     teaspoons dried basil
  1 **garlic clove, minced**
1/2 **teaspoon salt**
1/4 **teaspoon pepper**
  4 **ounces bow tie pasta** *or* **spaghetti, cooked**
     and drained
Fresh basil and grated Parmesan cheese, optional

Combine the tomatoes, basil, garlic, salt and pepper. Set aside at room temperature for several hours. Serve over hot pasta. If desired, garnish with basil and sprinkle with Parmesan cheese. **Yield:** 2 servings.

Basil Buttered Beans

    2 **cups fresh green beans, cut into 2-inch**
       pieces
    2 **tablespoons chopped onion**
    2 **tablespoons chopped celery**
  1/4 **cup water**
    2 **tablespoons butter** *or* **margarine, melted**
1-1/2 **teaspoons minced fresh basil** *or* 1/2
       teaspoon dried basil
  1/4 **teaspoon salt**
  1/8 **teaspoon pepper**

In a saucepan, combine beans, onion, celery and water. Cover and cook 5 minutes or until beans are tender. Drain. Add the butter, basil, salt and pepper; stir to coat. **Yield:** 2 servings.

— 🥄 🥄 🥄 —

Tuna Salad for Two

(Not pictured)

2 cups torn lettuce
1 package (5 ounces) corkscrew macaroni,
    cooked and drained
1 can (6-1/8 ounces) tuna, drained and
    flaked
1 medium tomato, cut into wedges
1 celery rib, sliced
1 carrot, peeled and sliced
1 small cucumber, sliced
1/4 cup green pepper strips
1 cup broccoli florets

1/2 cup julienned Provolone *or* mozzarella
    cheese
DRESSING:
    1/4 cup olive *or* vegetable oil
    1 tablespoon lemon juice
    1 small garlic clove, minced
1-1/2 teaspoons white wine vinegar
    3/4 teaspoon Italian seasoning
    1/4 teaspoon salt
    1/8 teaspoon pepper

On two salad plates, arrange the first 10 ingredients in the order listed. In a jar with a tight-fitting lid, combine the dressing ingredients; shake well. Pour over salads and serve immediately. **Yield:** 2 servings.

DO YOU REMEMBER the old-fashioned pot roasts Grandma used to make? Now just the two of you can enjoy that terrific flavor.

From Sequim, Washington, Marian Platt shows how you can make a delicious down-home dinner without feeding an army!

"Instead of a chuck roast, Midget Pot Roast calls for beef shanks, which you can purchase in a much smaller amount," explains Marian. "With big old-fashioned flavor, this is a savory dish I enjoy making for husband Art and me."

A great side dish, Orange-Kissed Beets comes from Bonnie Baumgardner of Sylva, North Carolina. "This is an original recipe I developed a few years ago," Bonnie shares. "It's my husband's favorite."

For Alpha and Thomas Wilson in Roswell, New Mexico, Baked Custard for Two makes the perfect amount. "We don't need to worry about over-indulging with this scaled-down recipe," Alpha says.

Midget Pot Roast

  2 **beef shanks (about 1-1/2 pounds)**
  3 **tablespoons all-purpose flour,** *divided*
1-1/2 **cups cold water,** *divided*
 1/2 **cup beef broth**
  1 **tablespoon dry onion soup mix**
  1 **garlic clove, minced**
  1 **teaspoon Worcestershire sauce**
 1/4 **teaspoon dried thyme**
  1 **large potato, peeled and cut into eighths**
  2 **carrots, cut into 2-inch lengths**
  6 **boiling onions**
Salt and pepper to taste

Sprinkle meat with 1 tablespoon flour; place in a shallow 2-qt. baking dish. Mix 1 cup water, broth, soup mix, garlic, Worcestershire sauce and thyme; pour over meat. Cover and bake at 325° for 1-1/2 hours. Turn meat; add potato, carrots and onions. Cover; return to the oven for 30-45 minutes or until meat and vegetables are tender. Remove meat and vegetables and keep warm. To prepare gravy, skim fat from pan juices. Measure 1 cup of the juices and place in a small saucepan. Combine remaining flour and cold water; stir into juices. Cook and stir until thickened and bubbly; cook and stir 1 minute longer. Season with salt and pepper. Serve with meat and vegetables. **Yield:** 2 servings.

Saving Soup Mix

When you only use a portion of dry onion soup mix in a recipe, place the leftovers in a resealable plastic bag and freeze for another use.

Orange-Kissed Beets

1/3 **cup orange juice**
  2 **tablespoons light brown sugar**
  1 **tablespoon butter** *or* **margarine**
1/2 **teaspoon cornstarch**
1/8 **teaspoon ground ginger**
1/8 **teaspoon salt**
1/8 **teaspoon pepper**
  1 **can (8-1/4 ounces) sliced beets, drained**
  2 **tablespoons golden raisins**
Strips of orange peel

In a saucepan over medium heat, cook and stir orange juice, brown sugar, butter, cornstarch, ginger, salt and pepper until thick. Add the beets and raisins; heat through. Garnish with orange peel. **Yield:** 2 servings.

——— 🍴 🍴 🍴 ———

Baked Custard for Two

(Not pictured)

1 egg

1 cup milk
3 tablespoons sugar
3/4 teaspoon vanilla extract
1/8 teaspoon salt
1/8 teaspoon ground nutmeg

In a bowl, lightly beat the egg. Add milk, sugar, vanilla and salt. Pour into two ungreased 6-oz. custard cups. Sprinkle with nutmeg. Set in a pan containing 1/2 to 1 in. of hot water. Bake at 350° for 35 minutes or until set and a knife inserted near the center comes out clean. **Yield:** 2 servings.

IF YOU HAVE a taste for beef but are only cooking for two, don't reach for a roast! Instead, this steak dinner will satisfy your hearty appetite without leaving you lots of leftovers.

Dan's Peppery London Broil comes from Dan Wright of San Jose, California. "I was bored making the usual London broil, so I got a little creative and sparked up the flavor with crushed red pepper, garlic and Worcestershire sauce," explains Dan.

To round out the meal, Dan prepares a tossed salad featuring his savory Italian Herb Salad Dressing. It's a delicious dressing that he likes to keep on hand for topping a variety of salad greens.

When Dan was single, he enjoyed cooking but not eating alone. "Now that I'm married, I think it's twice as nice to prepare meals for my lovely wife, Cookie," he adds.

To round out this menu, Nila Towler of Baird, Texas shares her recipe for Mini White Breads. These small, perfectly portioned loaves have a wonderful flavor and texture.

These three recipes make one delicious meal two people are sure to enjoy!

Dan's Peppery London Broil

1 beef flank steak (about 3/4 pound)
1 garlic clove, minced
1/2 teaspoon seasoned salt
1/8 teaspoon crushed red pepper flakes
1/4 cup Worcestershire sauce

With a meat fork, poke holes in both sides of meat. Make a paste with garlic, seasoned salt and red pepper flakes; rub over both sides of meat. Place the steak in a resealable gallon-size plastic bag. Add Worcestershire sauce and close bag. Refrigerate for at least 4 hours, turning once. Remove meat; discard marinade. Broil or grill over hot heat until meat reaches desired doneness, about 4-5 minutes on each side. To serve, slice thinly across the grain. **Yield:** 2 servings.

Italian Herb Salad Dressing

3/4 cup olive *or* vegetable oil
1/2 cup red wine vinegar
1 tablespoon grated Parmesan *or* Romano cheese
1 garlic clove, minced
1/2 teaspoon salt
1/2 teaspoon sugar
1/2 teaspoon dried oregano
Pinch pepper

In a jar with a tight-fitting lid, combine all ingredients; shake well. Refrigerate. Shake well again before serving over greens. **Yield:** 1-1/4 cups.

Mini White Breads

✓ Uses less fat, sugar or salt. Includes Nutritional Analysis and Diabetic Exchanges.

1 package (1/4 ounce) active dry yeast
1 tablespoon sugar

1/3 cup warm water (110° to 115°)
2-1/4 to 2-1/2 cups all-purpose flour
  1 teaspoon salt
1/2 cup milk
  2 teaspoons butter *or* margarine, melted
Additional melted butter *or* margarine

Combine yeast, sugar and water in a large mixing bowl. Add 1-1/2 cups of flour, salt, milk and butter. Mix for 3 minutes on medium speed. Add enough remaining flour to form a soft dough. Turn onto a floured board; knead until smooth and elastic, 6-8 minutes. Place in a greased bowl, turning once to grease top. Cover and let rise in a warm place until doubled, about 45 minutes. Punch dough down. Divide in half; shape into two loaves and place in greased 5-3/4-in. x 3-in. x 2-in. pans. Cover and let rise until doubled, about 30 minutes. Bake at 375° for 30 minutes or until golden brown. Remove from pans; cool on wire racks. Brush tops with melted butter. **Yield:** 2 mini loaves. **Nutritional Analysis:** One 1/2-inch slice (prepared with margarine) equals 75 calories, 156 mg sodium, 0 cholesterol, 14 gm carbohydrate, 2 gm protein, 1 gm fat. **Diabetic Exchanges:** 1 starch.

'My Mom's Best Meal'

Six cooks go back in taste and time when they make one of their mom's special meals.

MEMORIES OF MOM include, clockwise from upper left: A Dinner to Delight Dad (p. 194), Farm-Style Chicken Dinner (p. 198), New Year's Fare (p. 190) and Meat-and-Potatoes Meal (p. 210).

To ring in the start of a new year, her mom added extra love and attention to prepare traditional dishes that remain family favorites today.

By Ruby Williams, Bogalusa, Louisiana

ALL 10 of my sisters and brothers agree that our mom's best meal was this one that she cooked on New Year's Day. It sure started the year off right!

With such a large family, Mom cooked simple, nourishing meals for the most part. No matter what she prepared, it was always delicious (and never lasted long in our house of hungry kids!).

We were brought up to appreciate family and friends, and Mom made sure we were generous with our hospitality. So when we rang in the New Year with guests, this is the meal she'd prepare.

Mom never followed recipes. And I was always amazed that she knew just how much of everything to add to make meals taste terrific. After watching her cook this special-occasion meal from scratch for years, I finally decided to record the recipes.

The aroma of Garlic Pork Roast as it bakes is absolutely heavenly. It turns out moist and tasty every time and is a no-fuss favorite.

In the South, no New Year's celebration is complete without hearty helpings of traditional Black-Eyed Peas with Bacon.

Cabbage Casserole is a comforting side dish that gets its mild flavor from cream of mushroom soup and American cheese.

Dotted with raisins and pecans, Pumpkin Raisin Cake is surely one of Mom's best dessert recipes.

Of course, now when I make this dinner for my family, I also add the "special" ingredient Mom generously added to every recipe…love!

⎯⎯ 🥤 🥤 🥤 ⎯⎯

PICTURED AT LEFT: Garlic Pork Roast, Black-Eyed Peas with Bacon, Cabbage Casserole and Pumpkin Raisin Cake (recipes are on the next page).

Black-Eyed Peas with Bacon

A real Southern favorite, black-eyed peas are traditionally served on New Year's Day to bring good luck. My mother's recipe with bacon, garlic and thyme makes them extra special.

- 1 pound black-eyed peas, rinsed and sorted
- 1/2 pound bacon, cooked and crumbled
- 1 large onion, chopped
- 1 garlic clove, minced
- 1 tablespoon butter *or* margarine
- 1/2 teaspoon dried thyme

Salt to taste
Additional crumbled bacon, optional

Place peas, bacon and enough water to cover in a large kettle; bring to a boil. Boil for 2 minutes. Remove from the heat; cover and let stand for 1 hour. Do not drain. In a skillet, saute onion and garlic in butter until tender. Add to pea mixture with thyme and salt. Return to the heat; simmer, covered, for 30 minutes or until peas are soft. Top with crumbled bacon if desired. **Yield:** 6-8 servings.

Garlic Pork Roast

Mom cooked for 11 children, so her menus usually featured basic, simple foods. But on New Year's Day, she always treated us to this special pork roast. All of us kids agree this was our mom's best meal!

- 1 pork loin roast (about 5 pounds), backbone loosened
- 1/2 medium green pepper, finely chopped
- 1/2 cup thinly sliced green onions
- 1/2 cup chopped celery
- 8 garlic cloves, minced
- 1 teaspoon salt
- 1/4 teaspoon cayenne pepper

With a sharp knife, cut a deep pocket between each rib on meaty side of roast. Combine green pepper, green onions, celery and garlic; stuff deeply into pockets. Season roast with salt and cayenne pepper. Place roast, rib side down, in a shallow roasting pan. Bake, uncovered, at 325° for 2-3 hours or until a meat thermometer reads 170°. Let stand for 15 minutes before carving. **Yield:** 6-8 servings.

Separating Bacon Strips

To easily separate packaged bacon strips, first roll up the whole package as tightly as you can the long way. You'll be amazed at how easily the strips come apart.

Pumpkin Raisin Cake

This nutty, golden cake is one of my mom's best. It's a wonderfully different use for pumpkin. With a holiday taste and beautiful look, it's bound to become a favorite with your family, too.

    2 cups all-purpose flour
    2 cups sugar
    2 teaspoons pumpkin pie spice
    2 teaspoons baking powder
    1 teaspoon baking soda
  1/2 teaspoon salt
    4 eggs
    1 can (15 ounces) solid-pack pumpkin
  3/4 cup vegetable oil
    2 cups bran cereal (not flakes)
    1 cup chopped pecans
    1 cup raisins
Confectioners' sugar, optional

Combine the flour, sugar, pumpkin pie spice, baking powder, baking soda and salt; set aside. In a large bowl, beat eggs. Add pumpkin and oil; stir in cereal just until moistened. Add dry ingredients and stir just until combined. Fold in pecans and raisins. Pour into a greased 10-in. tube pan. Bake at 350° for 60-65 minutes or until the cake tests done. Cool in pan for 10 minutes before removing to a wire rack to cool completely. Dust with confectioners' sugar before serving if desired. **Yield:** 12-16 servings.

Cabbage Casserole

Even those who don't care for cabbage will enjoy it made this way. This tangy, creamy, comforting side dish goes exceptionally well with pork roast. When the roast is done, just turn up the temperature and pop the casserole in the oven for about 20 minutes.

  1 large head cabbage, shredded (about 12 cups)
  1 onion, chopped
  6 tablespoons butter *or* margarine, *divided*
  1 can (10-3/4 ounces) condensed cream of mushroom soup, undiluted
  8 ounces process American cheese, cubed
Salt and pepper to taste
  1/4 cup dry bread crumbs

Cook cabbage in boiling salted water until tender; drain thoroughly. In a large skillet, saute onion in 5 tablespoons butter until tender. Add soup and mix well. Add cheese; cook and stir until melted. Remove from the heat. Stir in the cabbage, salt and pepper. Transfer to an ungreased 2-qt. baking dish. In a small skillet, melt the remaining butter. Cook and stir bread crumbs in butter until lightly browned; sprinkle over casserole. Bake, uncovered, at 350° for 20-30 minutes or until heated through. **Yield:** 6-8 servings.

***Although the foods
she enjoyed as a child
were anything but fancy,
this cook recalls how her
mom made even the most
simple meals special.***

By Ruth Ann Stelfox, Raymond, Alberta

WHENEVER I prepare this mouth-watering meal (pictured at left) for my own family these days, the wonderful aromas of the homemade foods never fail to remind me of my happy childhood and how our large family often gathered around the big kitchen table with Dad at the head.

He especially loved the Sweet-and-Sour Spareribs with their thick, tangy sauce. Mom liked them, too, because the sauce was no hassle to make. Baking the ribs for hours keeps the meat tender and delicious. These ribs never lasted long around our house!

Confetti Rice is a classic dish that's stood the test of time. Much to our disappointment—and Mom's amazement—there never seemed to be any left over …no matter how much she made!

This colorful recipe combines rice and vegetables for a nutritious side dish that Mom was glad we gobbled up.

It seemed that Creamy Pineapple Salad made frequent appearances on our dinner table, but we kids didn't mind. Whenever we saw Mom preparing this cool, sweet salad, we couldn't wait to eat.

After all of these delicious dished were served up, we knew Raisin Custard Pie was sure to follow. Cutting the pie into seven equal pieces was tricky, though we didn't hear any complaints from Dad.

Mom felt it was important for us to eat together as a family, and that fostered a closeness we've tried to carry over to our homes today. Now you, too, can make some happy memories with this meal!

PICTURED AT LEFT: Sweet-and-Sour Spareribs, Confetti Rice, Creamy Pineapple Salad and Raisin Custard Pie (recipes are on the next page).

Sweet-and-Sour Spareribs

Just the tempting aroma of these ribs reminds me of many simple but delicious meals my mom made. Dad especially loved these tender tasty ribs with their thick, tangy sauce. Mom liked them because the sauce was no fuss to make.

    5 to 6 pounds pork spareribs *or* pork loin
        back ribs
1/2 cup packed brown sugar
1/2 cup sugar
    2 tablespoons cornstarch
    1 cup ketchup
2/3 cup vinegar
1/2 cup cold water

Place ribs on a rack in a large shallow roasting pan. Bake, uncovered, at 350° for 1-1/2 hours. Meanwhile, combine sugars and cornstarch in a medium saucepan. Stir in ketchup, vinegar and water; bring to a boil. Cook and stir until thickened and clear. Remove ribs and rack from pan. Discard fat. Place ribs back in roasting pan; pour about 1-1/2 cups of the sauce over ribs. Bake 30 minutes longer. Cut ribs into serving-size pieces; brush with remaining sauce. **Yield:** 6-8 servings.

Confetti Rice

I still enjoy the superb combination of bacon and rice in this dish. The peas add color and a bit of a crunch. It's so easy to make, and so good! It cooks on the stovetop, keeping the oven open for the ribs.

1/2 pound sliced bacon, diced
    1 cup long grain rice, cooked
    1 cup diced carrots, parboiled
    1 cup diced celery, parboiled
1/2 cup fresh *or* frozen peas
Soy sauce, optional

In a large skillet, cook bacon until crisp. Remove to paper towels; drain all but 3 tablespoons of the drippings. Cook rice, carrots, celery and peas in drippings until heated through, about 5-7 minutes. Stir in bacon. Serve with soy sauce if desired. **Yield:** 6-8 servings.

─── 🍷 🍷 🍷 ───

Creamy Pineapple Salad

Mom made this slightly sweet, fruity salad often. It was a favorite because the cool and creamy texture tasted so good paired with her zesty spareribs. We kids couldn't wait to eat when we saw this salad appear on the table. As an added plus, it can be prepared the night before, so it's convenient, too.

Storing Vinegar

Store vinegar in a cool, dry place. Unopened, it will keep almost indefinitely. Once opened, store vinegar at room temperature for about 6 months.

1 can (20 ounces) crushed pineapple
1 package (3 ounces) lemon gelatin
1 cup whipping cream
1/4 cup sugar
1 cup cottage cheese

Drain pineapple, reserving the juice in a small saucepan. Set pineapple aside. Add enough water to juice to make 1-1/3 cups; bring to a boil. Place gelatin in a bowl; add boiling liquid and stir to dissolve. Cool until slightly thickened. In a mixing bowl, whip cream; gradually beat in sugar. Fold into the gelatin mixture. Stir in pineapple and cottage cheese; blend well. Pour into a 1-1/2-qt. serving bowl; chill at least 3 hours or overnight. **Yield:** 8-10 servings.

Raisin Custard Pie

A comforting, old-fashioned dessert, this custard pie is one of my mom's best. The raisins are a nice surprise, and the fluffy meringue makes it look so special. But for a variation, you can skip the meringue. Just cool the pie filling in the crust completely, and then refrigerate. Just before serving, top with whipped cream instead of meringue. It's just as delicious.

1/2 cup sugar
3 tablespoons cornstarch
3 egg yolks
2 cups milk
2 teaspoons lemon juice
1/2 cup raisins
1 pastry shell (9 inches), baked

MERINGUE:
3 egg whites
1/4 cup sugar

In a medium saucepan, combine sugar and cornstarch. Whisk in the egg yolks and milk until thoroughly combined. Cook over medium heat, stirring constantly, until mixture comes to a boil; boil for 1 minute. Remove from the heat. Add lemon juice and raisins. Pour into pie shell. For meringue, beat egg whites in a small bowl until foamy. Gradually add sugar, about 1 tablespoon at a time, beating until stiff and glossy. Spread over warm pie, making sure meringue covers all of the filling. Bake at 350° for 10-15 minutes or until light golden brown. Serve warm or cold. Store leftovers in the refrigerator. **Yield:** 8 servings.

Basic Pie Crust Recipe

To make a single-crust pie, combine 1-1/4 cups all-purpose flour and 1/2 teaspoon salt in a bowl; cut in 1/3 cup shortening until crumbly. Gradually add 4 to 5 tablespoons cold water, tossing with a fork, until a ball forms. Roll out pastry to fit a 9-inch pie plate; transfer pastry to pie plate. Trim and flute edges.

***Full of old-fashioned
goodness, this family-style
chicken dinner with
flaky biscuits is reminiscent
of down-home dinners
on the farm.***

By Vera Reid, Laramie, Wyoming

AS A TRUE farm wife, my mom has always been a great cook. She worked hard to prepare delicious meals for Dad, my two sisters and me that would satisfy our hungry appetites after doing a variety of chores.

Of all the terrific foods Mom prepared, I remember her crispy Buttermilk Fried Chicken the most. Served with a wonderful savory gravy, it was one of her many main meals guaranteed to make our mouths water.

As the plate of chicken was passed, we girls knew not to touch until Dad and Mom had each selected their favorites. We could hardly resist snatching a piece as the plate passed us by, but there was always plenty of chicken to go around.

I can still see Mom pulling the fluffy Buttermilk Biscuits out of the oven. They always seemed to disappear too quickly, especially when we slathered each delectable bite with sweet, creamy butter.

With crisp radishes and smoky bacon bits, Wilted Lettuce Salad looked and tasted so tempting. It was the only salad we wanted her to make, and she was happy to watch us devour the nutritious greens.

We couldn't wait for Mom to bring dessert to the table. Her Hot Fudge Cake was a rich, satisfying end to a perfect meal. Mom served it with a scoop of ice cream or cream poured over the top.

Living on a farm is not easy. But growing up there with all the cool green grass, the endless blue sky and Mom's home cooking, we knew we were safe and loved.

That's something I wish every child was able to experience. This memorable meal helps capture the comforting flavor of farm life!

—— 🍴 🍴 🍴 ——

PICTURED AT LEFT: Buttermilk Fried Chicken with Gravy, Mom's Buttermilk Biscuits, Wilted Lettuce Salad and Hot Fudge Cake (recipes are on the next page).

move chicken and keep warm. Drain all but 1/4 cup drippings in skillet; stir in flour until bubbly. Add milk and 1-1/2 cups water; cook and stir until thickened and bubbly. Cook 1 minute more. Add remaining water if needed. Season with salt and pepper. Serve with chicken. **Yield:** 4-6 servings.

Wilted Lettuce Salad

(Also pictured on front cover)

Fresh, colorful and lightly coated with a delectable dressing, this salad is perfect for a special meal or Sunday dinner. Mom made it look so tempting with the crisp radishes and crumbled bacon.

>   1 **bunch leaf lettuce, torn**
>   6 **to 8 radishes, thinly sliced**
>   4 **to 6 green onions with tops, thinly sliced**
> **DRESSING:**
>   4 **to 5 bacon strips**
>   2 **tablespoons red wine vinegar**
>   1 **tablespoon lemon juice**
>   1 **teaspoon sugar**
> 1/2 **teaspoon pepper**

Toss lettuce, radishes and onions in a large salad bowl; set aside. In a skillet, cook bacon until crisp. Remove to paper towels to drain. To the hot drippings, add vinegar, lemon juice, sugar and pepper; stir well. Immediately pour dressing over salad; toss gently. Crumble the bacon and sprinkle on top. Serve immediately. **Yield:** 6-8 servings.

Buttermilk Fried Chicken With Gravy

We raised our own meat and vegetables when I was a girl. This golden chicken reminds me of Mom and home…there's nothing quite like a crispy piece smothered in creamy gravy.

>   1 **broiler/fryer chicken (2-1/2 to 3 pounds),** **cut up**
>   1 **cup buttermilk**
>   1 **cup all-purpose flour**
> 1-1/2 **teaspoons salt**
>   1/2 **teaspoon pepper**
> **Vegetable oil for frying**
> **GRAVY:**
>   3 **tablespoons all-purpose flour**
>   1 **cup milk**
> 1-1/2 **to 2 cups water**
> **Salt and pepper to taste**

Place chicken in a large flat dish. Pour buttermilk over; cover and refrigerate for 1 hour. Combine flour, salt and pepper in a double-strength paper bag. Drain chicken pieces; toss, one at a time, in flour mixture. Shake off excess; place on waxed paper for 15 minutes to dry. Heat 1/8 to 1/4 in. of oil in a large skillet; brown chicken on all sides. Cover and simmer, turning occasionally, for 40-45 minutes, or until juices run clear and chicken is tender. Uncover and cook 5 minutes longer. Re-

Leftover Biscuits?

If you have leftover biscuits, wrap them in foil and store at room temperature for up to 3 days. To reheat, place the foil packet in a 300° oven for about 10 minutes or until warm.

Mom's Buttermilk Biscuits

These fluffy biscuits are so tasty served warm, slathered with butter or used to mop up every last drop of gravy off your plate. I can still see Mom pulling these tender biscuits out of the oven.

      2 cups all-purpose flour
      2 teaspoons baking powder
  1/2 teaspoon baking soda
  1/2 teaspoon salt
  1/4 cup shortening
  3/4 cup buttermilk

In a bowl, combine the flour, baking powder, baking soda and salt; cut in shortening until the mixture resembles coarse crumbs. Stir in buttermilk; knead dough gently. Roll out to 1/2-in. thickness. Cut with a 2-1/2-in. biscuit cutter and place on a lightly greased baking sheet. Bake at 450° for 10-15 minutes or until golden brown. **Yield:** 10 biscuits.

Hot Fudge Cake

Here's a wonderful way to top off a great meal—a rich, chocolaty cake that's not overly sweet. Mom served it with a scoop of ice cream or cream poured over. I'd always have room for a serving of this dessert.

      1 cup all-purpose flour
  3/4 cup sugar
      6 tablespoons baking cocoa, *divided*
      2 teaspoons baking powder
  1/4 teaspoon salt
  1/2 cup milk
      2 tablespoons vegetable oil
      1 teaspoon vanilla extract
      1 cup packed brown sugar
1-3/4 cups hot water
Whipped cream *or* ice cream, optional

In a medium bowl, combine flour, sugar, 2 tablespoons cocoa, baking powder and salt. Stir in the milk, oil and vanilla until smooth. Spread in an ungreased 9-in. square baking pan. Combine brown sugar and remaining cocoa; sprinkle over batter. Pour hot water over all; do not stir. Bake at 350° for 35-40 minutes. Serve warm. Top with whipped cream or ice cream if desired. **Yield:** 9 servings.

***The cozy kitchen
in her childhood home
was bustling with lots
of activity and was the place
where her mom and grandma
made many memorable meals.***

By Sally Holbrook, Pasadena, California

I HAVE many fond memories of my years growing up in a household where the kitchen was the center of activity.

Ours was a large, sunny kitchen with a work table in the center. It was a wonderful place where my mother and grandmother would spend hours lovingly preparing delicious meals, from simple family fare to delectable party dishes, filling the house with appealing aromas.

My parents and grandparents often entertained friends on the patio overlooking the bay. A long wooden table, spread with a blue and white cloth, was topped with a treasure of flavorful foods that friends and family couldn't wait to dig into.

Hungry guests enjoyed a hearty casserole Mom called Sausage Pie, featuring pork sausage links and produce found in her own garden.

As a special treat, Mom would give salad greens an added punch by preparing zippy Creamy Garlic Dressing. To save time, prepare this dressing and wash, cut and dry all salad ingredients the night before. You'll appreciate the extra time you have to spend visiting with guests.

Mom dressed up thick slices of Buttery French Bread with some simple seasonings and real butter.

For a fantastic finale, Mom's Peach Pie would overflow with fresh peach flavor, making it a delightful treat.

Now when my brother, sisters and I get together with friends and family in our homes, we still use all these wonderful recipes from Mom's delicious menu!

— 🥄 🥄 🥄 —

PICTURED AT LEFT: Sausage Pie, Creamy Garlic Dressing, Buttery French Bread and Mom's Peach Pie (recipes are on the next page).

Sausage Pie

When I was growing up, Mom made this tasty casserole often in summer for our family and guests. People would comment on the pretty color of this casserole. This recipe is a great way to use garden vegetables, and the sausage adds comforting flavor. I'm sure you'll enjoy it as much as we do. With rice, it truly is a meal-in-one, but Mom was sure to pair it with her other favorite foods.

- 16 small fresh pork sausage links (about 1 pound)
- 1/2 medium green pepper, chopped
- 1/2 medium sweet red pepper, chopped
- 1 tablespoon vegetable oil
- 3 cups cooked long grain rice
- 4 to 5 medium tomatoes, peeled and chopped
- 1 package (10 ounces) frozen corn, thawed
- 1 cup (4 ounces) shredded cheddar cheese
- 1 tablespoon Worcestershire sauce
- 1 teaspoon salt
- 2 tablespoons chopped fresh parsley
- 1 teaspoon dried basil
- 1 cup soft bread crumbs
- 2 tablespoons butter *or* margarine, melted

Place sausages on a rack in a baking pan; bake at 350° for 15 minutes or until lightly browned. Cut into 1-in. pieces; set aside. In a skillet, saute peppers in oil for 3 minutes. Place in a 3-qt. casserole; add the sausages and the next eight ingredients. Combine bread crumbs and butter; sprinkle on top of casserole. Bake, uncovered, at 350° for 30-40 minutes or until heated through. **Yield:** 6-8 servings.

Buttery French Bread

Instead of always having to make bread from scratch, Mom would frequently dress up plain purchased French bread with this interesting, delicious recipe. The combination of paprika, celery seed and butter makes for a full-flavored bread. Wrapping the bread in foil before baking keeps the crust nice and tender. Then bake it uncovered for just a few minutes to give it a lovely golden brown color.

- 1/2 cup butter *or* margarine, softened
- 1/4 teaspoon paprika
- 1/4 teaspoon celery seed
- 1 loaf French bread (about 20 inches), sliced

In a small bowl, combine butter, paprika and celery seed; spread between bread slices and over top.

Wrap bread tightly in foil. Bake at 375° for 15 minutes. Open the foil and bake 5 minutes longer. **Yield:** 6-8 servings.

— 🏺 🏺 🏺 —

Creamy Garlic Dressing

This zippy dressing gives a refreshing warm-weather salad added punch. The wonderful garlic taste comes through as this creamy mixture coats the lettuce beautifully.

   1 cup vegetable oil
1/2 cup sour cream
1/4 cup whipping cream
1/4 cup cider vinegar
   1 teaspoon salt
   1 large garlic clove, minced
Salad greens

In a small bowl, combine oil, sour cream, whipping cream, vinegar, salt and garlic; stir until smooth. Chill. Serve over salad greens. Refrigerate leftovers. **Yield:** 1-2/3 cups.

Mom's Peach Pie

A delightful summertime pie, this dessert is overflowing with fresh peach flavor. Each sweet slice is packed with old-fashioned appeal. The streusel topping makes this pie a little different than the ordinary and adds homemade flair.

   1 egg white
   1 unbaked pastry shell (9 inches)
3/4 cup all-purpose flour
1/2 cup packed brown sugar
1/3 cup sugar
1/4 cup chilled butter *or* margarine, cut into 6 pieces
   6 cups sliced peeled fresh peaches

Beat egg white until foamy; brush over the bottom and sides of the pastry. In a small bowl, combine flour and sugars; cut in butter until mixture resembles fine crumbs. Sprinkle two-thirds into the bottom of the pastry; top with peaches. Sprinkle with remaining crumb mixture. Bake at 375° for 40-45 minutes or until filling is bubbly and peaches are tender. **Yield:** 6-8 servings.

Peach Pointers

Purchase very fragrant peaches that give slightly to pressure; avoid those with soft spots. A pound (about 4 peaches) yields 2-3/4 cups sliced.

To easily remove the skin from a peach, dip the peach into boiling water for 20 to 30 seconds; remove with a slotted spoon and immediately plunge into a bowl of ice water. Remove the skin with a paring knife.

***Although Mom
was busy, she found
the time to prepare
memorable family meals
that were packed with
old-fashioned goodness.***

By Bernice Morris, Marshfield, Missouri

THINKING BACK to my childhood, I often wonder just how my mom ever found the time to cook three meals a day!

Not only did she tend to the children, clean the house, do laundry and help Dad milk the cows, she did her best to watch the family budget by planting a large vegetable garden each year.

Still, she somehow managed to set a pretty table laden with delicious food for the family and the hired hands at noon.

Every meal Mom prepared was wonderful because it was made with love. But I'd have to rank the meal featured here as one of my all-time favorites.

Packed with hearty ingredients and flavorful seasonings, Pork Chops with Scalloped Potatoes was always a welcome sight at the table. The thick chops in this all-in-one entree turn out moist and tender every time as they bake on top of the bubbling potatoes.

Pineapple Beets may seem unusual to you. But after one taste, their slightly sweet flavor will have you wanting more. This side dish dresses up ordinary beets with pineapple and adds eye-appealing color to the table.

Fresh-from-the oven Make-Ahead Butterhorns (pictured on page 209) really completed the meal. Given her hectic schedule, Mom often relied on this recipe that lets you shape and freeze the unbaked rolls until needed.

For dessert, Mom would cut hearty slices of Banana Cream Pie and top each with rich whipped cream from our own Guernsey cows.

Fortified with a meal like this, we could tackle afternoon chores with smiles on our faces!

————— ▼ ▼ ▼ —————

PICTURED AT LEFT: Pork Chops with Scalloped Potatoes, Pineapple Beets and Banana Cream Pie (recipes are on the next page).

utes longer or until potatoes are tender. If desired, sprinkle with paprika and parsley before serving. **Yield:** 6 servings.

— 🏆 🏆 🏆 —

Pineapple Beets

This is a special way to dress up beets. Paired with pineapple, they have a fresh, slightly sweet taste that has even people who don't usually like beets taking second helpings.

    2 **tablespoons brown sugar**
    1 **tablespoon cornstarch**
  1/4 **teaspoon salt**
    1 **can (8 ounces) pineapple tidbits, undrained**
    1 **can (16 ounces) sliced beets, drained**
    1 **tablespoon butter *or* margarine**
    1 **tablespoon lemon juice**

In a saucepan, combine brown sugar, cornstarch and salt; add pineapple and bring to a boil, stirring constantly until thick, about 2 minutes. Add the beets, butter and lemon juice; cook over medium heat for 5 minutes, stirring occasionally. **Yield:** 4 servings.

Pork Chops with Scalloped Potatoes

Mom always managed to put a delicious hearty meal on the table for us and for our farmhands. This all-in-one main dish has a comforting flavor.

    3 **tablespoons butter *or* margarine**
    3 **tablespoons all-purpose flour**
1-1/2 **teaspoons salt**
  1/4 **teaspoon pepper**
    1 **can (14-1/2 ounces) chicken broth**
    6 **rib *or* loin pork chops (3/4 inch thick)**
    2 **tablespoons vegetable oil**
Additional salt and pepper, optional
    6 **cups thinly sliced peeled potatoes (about 4 pounds)**
    1 **medium onion, sliced**
Paprika and chopped fresh parsley, optional

In a saucepan, melt butter; stir in flour, salt and pepper. Add chicken broth; cook and stir constantly until mixture boils. Cook for 1 minute; remove from the heat and set aside. In a skillet, brown pork chops in oil; season with additional salt and pepper if desired. In a greased 13-in. x 9-in. x 2-in. baking dish, layer potatoes and onion. Pour the broth mixture over. Place pork chops on top. Cover and bake at 350° for 1 hour; uncover and bake 30 min-

Removing Beet Stains

If you get a little beet juice on your hands when making Pineapple Beets, remove the stain by rubbing your hands with half a lemon.

sheets; thaw 5 hours or until doubled in size. Bake at 375° for 12-15 minutes or until lightly browned. Remove from baking sheets and serve immediately or cool on wire racks. **Yield:** 32 rolls.

Banana Cream Pie

Made from our farm-fresh dairy products, this pie was a sensational creamy treat anytime that Mom served it. Her recipe is a real treasure, and I've never found one that tastes better!

     3/4 cup sugar
     1/3 cup all-purpose flour
     1/4 teaspoon salt
       2 cups milk
       3 egg yolks, lightly beaten
       2 tablespoons butter *or* margarine
       1 teaspoon vanilla extract
       3 medium firm bananas
       1 pastry shell (9 inches), baked
Whipped cream and additional sliced bananas

In a saucepan, combine sugar, flour and salt; stir in milk and mix well. Cook over medium heat, stirring constantly, until the mixture thickens and comes to a boil; boil for 2 minutes. Remove from the heat. Stir a small amount into egg yolks; return all to saucepan. Cook for 2 minutes, stirring constantly; remove from the heat. Add butter and vanilla; cool slightly. Slice the bananas into pastry shell; pour filling over. Cool. Before serving, garnish with whipped cream and bananas. Refrigerate any leftovers. **Yield:** 6-8 servings.

Make-Ahead Butterhorns

Mom loved to prepare these lightly sweet, golden rolls. They're beautiful and impressive to serve and have a wonderful homemade taste. It's so handy to be able to bake and freeze them ahead.

       2 packages (1/4 ounce *each*) active dry yeast
     1/3 cup warm water (110° to 115°)
       9 cups all-purpose flour, *divided*
       2 cups warm milk (110° to 115°)
       1 cup shortening
       1 cup sugar
       6 eggs
       2 teaspoons salt
       3 to 4 tablespoons butter *or* margarine, melted

In a large mixing bowl, dissolve yeast in water. Add 4 cups flour, milk, shortening, sugar, eggs and salt; beat for 2 minutes or until smooth. Add enough remaining flour to form a soft dough. Turn onto a floured board; knead lightly. Place in a greased bowl, turning once to grease top. Cover and let rise in a warm place until doubled, about 2-3 hours. Punch dough down; divide into four equal parts. Roll each into a 9-in. circle; brush with butter. Cut each circle into eight pie-shaped wedges; roll up each wedge from wide edge to tip of dough and pinch to seal. Place rolls with tip down on baking sheets; freeze. When frozen, place in freezer bags and seal. Store in the freezer for up to 4 weeks. To bake, place on greased baking

*Her mom's reputation
among family and
friends for making terrific
beef roasts has been
relished—and unrivaled
—for decades.*

By Linda Gaido, New Brighton, Pennsylvania

FOR YEARS, Mom has had a reputation among family and friends for making the very best roast beef. And that honor still stands today.

Mom was one of those people born to be a good cook. She rarely measures anything, and everything she makes tastes wonderful.

When my two older sisters and I were growing up, the house smelled simply heavenly on those chilly fall days when Mom's Roast Beef was cooking on the stovetop.

People always ask Mom what her secret ingredients are. And they're surprised to hear that the rich flavor comes from brewed coffee! Hard as I try to follow Mom's recipe step-by-step, I can never make it taste just like hers.

To make Country Green Beans, Mom added garlic, chopped ham and onion. These additions blend so well with the beans and really complement the beef.

The melt-in-your-mouth Oven-Roasted Potatoes round out this meat-and-potatoes meal. They're also convenient because they can share the oven with the Baked Apples Slices.

Mom enjoyed serving this updated version of baked apples over cool, creamy vanilla ice cream. But you could also top individual servings with whipped cream. It's an easy recipe to double when cooking for more people.

Mom and I are now thrilled to pass on the treasured family recipes for this warm, satisfying meal to you and your family. Why not give these dishes a try when cooler weather has you craving hearty old-fashioned foods?

PICTURED AT LEFT: Mom's Roast Beef, Oven-Roasted Potatoes, Country Green Beans and Baked Apple Slices (recipes are on the next page).

Mom's Roast Beef

Everyone loves slices of this fork-tender roast beef and its savory gravy. This well-seasoned roast is Mom's specialty. People always ask what her secret ingredients are. Now you know the secret of what makes this our favorite meat dish!

   1 tablespoon vegetable oil
   1 eye of round beef roast (about 2-1/2 pounds)
   1 medium onion, chopped
   1 cup brewed coffee
   1 cup water, *divided*
   1 beef bouillon cube
   2 teaspoons dried basil
   1 teaspoon dried rosemary, crushed
   1 garlic clove, minced
   1 teaspoon salt
1/2 teaspoon pepper
1/4 cup all-purpose flour

Heat oil in a Dutch oven; brown roast on all sides. Add onion and cook until transparent. Add coffee, 3/4 cup water, bouillon, basil, rosemary, garlic, salt and pepper. Cover and simmer for 2-1/2 hours or until meat is tender. Combine flour and remaining water until smooth; stir into pan juices. Cook and stir until thickened and bubbly. Remove roast and slice. Pass the gravy. **Yield:** 8 servings.

Oven-Roasted Potatoes

These golden, melt-in-your-mouth potatoes go perfectly with roast beef. They make a homey side dish that's also convenient because they can share the oven with the baked apple slices Mom serves for dessert.

   4 baking potatoes (about 2 pounds)
   2 tablespoons butter *or* margarine, melted
   2 teaspoons paprika
   1 teaspoon salt
1/2 teaspoon pepper

Peel potatoes and cut into large chunks; place in a shallow 2-qt. baking pan. Pour butter over and toss until well coated. Sprinkle with paprika, salt and pepper. Bake, uncovered, at 350° for 45-60 minutes or until potatoes are tender. **Yield:** 4 servings.

Country Green Beans

This deliciously different way to dress up green beans is sure to become a family favorite at your house, too. The garlic, chopped ham and onion blend so well with the beans. It's a beautiful and tasty side dish that has real country appeal.

   1 pound fresh green beans, trimmed
1/4 cup chopped onion
1/4 cup chopped fully cooked ham
1/4 cup butter *or* margarine
1/4 cup water
   1 garlic clove, minced
1/2 teaspoon salt
1/4 teaspoon pepper

In a saucepan, combine all ingredients. Cover and simmer for 15-20 minutes or until beans are tender. **Yield:** 4 servings.

   1 tablespoon ground cinnamon
1/4 teaspoon ground nutmeg
1/4 teaspoon ground ginger
1/4 cup apple cider
1/2 cup butter *or* margarine
1/2 cup walnuts *or* raisins
Vanilla ice cream

Place apples in a greased 1-qt. baking dish. Combine sugar, cinnamon, nutmeg, ginger and apple cider; pour over apples. Dot with butter. Sprinkle with nuts or raisins. Bake, uncovered, at 350° for 45-60 minutes or until apples are tender. Serve warm over ice cream. **Yield:** 4 servings.

Baked Apple Slices

Nothing beats these warm tender apple slices over ice cream for satisfying harvest flavor. This old-fashioned treat gives a new twist to traditional baked apples. They are also excellent served over waffles or with ham. I make sure to save room for dessert when this is the featured finale!

   3 large baking apples, peeled and sliced
3/4 cup sugar

Good Gravy

To avoid lumps in your gravy, whisk the hot liquid rapidly as you gradually add the flour-based paste to the hot liquid.

For a little richer color and flavor, stir in a teaspoon or two of instant coffee powder or unsweetened cocoa powder.

When making a big family dinner, make your gravy as usual and then keep it warm on the low setting in a slow cooker. It's easy to refill the gravy boat with hot gravy throughout the meal.

Editors' Meals

Taste of Home magazine is edited by 1,000 cooks across North America. On the following pages, six of those cooks share a favorite meal you can make for your family!

TREASURED MEALS include, clockwise from upper left: Tried-and-True Menu (p. 236), Down-Home Ham Dinner (p. 220), Pleasing Pasta Supper (p. 228) and "Berry Special Luncheon" (p. 224).

Country Christmas Eve dinner and gift exchange at her Rocky Mountain ranch is a feast for family and friends.

By Lucy Meyring, Walden, Colorado

ON OUR RANCH high in the Rockies, 750 cows, 500 yearlings and several horses must be fed and tended every day…even Christmas Day.

That's why my husband, Danny, and I celebrate on Christmas Eve instead, inviting his folks and several neighbors for a gift exchange and festive dinner. As our merry group begins to gather, we sip delicious cupfuls of fruity Holiday Wassail.

Special occasions call for special meals, of course, so on Christmas Eve I serve Standing Rib Roast with all the trimmings. This elegant but easy-to-prepare feast is Danny's absolute favorite.

The seasoning "rub" I use on my roast is delicious on other beef cuts as well. It flavors the meat without much fuss, and you'll love the way the herbs season the pan juices. Serve the juices on the side to add extra flavor to this special meat entree.

Stuffed Baked Potatoes make the perfect accompaniment to the roast. I got the recipe for this simple side dish from my mother-in-law, Ruth, one of the best cooks in the area.

I sometimes bake and stuff the potatoes ahead, then freeze them until I need them. Simply allow additional time for reheating.

To add color and crunch to our holiday meal, I serve a Green Salad with Dill Dressing. This creamy dressing turns an ordinary salad into a real taste treat and has been a favorite of mine for years.

Baked Cranberry Pudding, a recipe I found in a holiday entertaining cookbook, does take some time to prepare, but it's worth it! Every bite reminds me of the wonderful puddings and custards my mother made when I was a child. This delightful dessert is our traditional Yuletide finale.

— 🎺 🎺 🎺 —

PICTURED AT LEFT: Standing Rib Roast, Stuffed Baked Potatoes, Baked Cranberry Pudding, Holiday Wassail and Green Salad with Dill Dressing (recipes are on the next page).

Standing Rib Roast

For any special occasion, treat your family to tender slices of standing rib roast.

  1 tablespoon lemon-pepper seasoning
  1 tablespoon paprika
1-1/2 teaspoons garlic salt
  1 teaspoon dried rosemary, crushed
  1/2 teaspoon cayenne pepper
  1 standing beef rib roast (6 to 7 pounds)
  2 cups boiling water
  1 teaspoon instant beef bouillon granules

Combine lemon-pepper, paprika, garlic salt, rosemary and cayenne pepper; rub over roast. Place roast with fat side up in a large roasting pan. Bake, uncovered, at 325° until meat reaches desired doneness. Allow 23-25 minutes *per pound* for rare (140° on a meat thermometer), 27-30 minutes for medium (160°) and 32-35 minutes for well-done (170°). Remove to serving platter and keep warm. Let stand 15 minutes before carving. Pour meat juices from roasting pan into a glass measuring cup; skim off fat. Add boiling water and bouillon to roasting pan and stir to remove drippings. Stir in meat juices. Serve with the roast. **Yield:** 10-12 servings.

Stuffed Baked Potatoes

You'll receive raves over these rich, creamy potatoes.

  8 baking potatoes (about 3 pounds)
Vegetable oil
  1/3 cup butter *or* margarine, softened
  1/4 cup chopped fresh chives *or* 2 tablespoons
      dried chives
  1 teaspoon salt
  1/4 teaspoon pepper
  1/3 to 1/2 cup evaporated milk
Paprika

Rub the potato skins with oil; prick with a fork. Bake at 400° for 1 hour or until tender. Allow potatoes to cool to the touch. Slice a small portion off the top of each potato. Carefully scoop out pulp, leaving a thin shell. In a large bowl, mash the pulp with butter, chives, salt, pepper and enough milk to obtain desired consistency. Carefully stuff shells; sprinkle with paprika. Place on an ungreased baking sheet. Bake at 325° for 30 minutes or until heated through. **Yield:** 8 servings.

Holiday Wassail

(Pictured on page 216)

This richly colored beverage tastes of Christmastime.

  1 quart hot tea
  1 cup sugar
  1 bottle (32 ounces) cranberry juice
  1 bottle (32 ounces) apple juice
  2 cups orange juice
  3/4 cup lemon juice
  2 cinnamon sticks (3 inches *each*)
 24 whole cloves, *divided*
  1 orange, sliced

In a large kettle, combine tea and sugar. Add juices, cinnamon sticks and 12 of the cloves. Bring to a boil and boil for 2 minutes. Remove from the heat. Serve warm or cool. Garnish punch bowl with orange slices studded with remaining cloves. **Yield:** 12-16 servings (1 gallon).

Green Salad with Dill Dressing

With a big holiday meal, a light salad is the perfect side dish, especially with this flavorful dressing.

   1 head Boston lettuce, torn
1/2 bunch romaine, torn
   4 green onions, sliced
   3 radishes, sliced
   1 large green pepper, cut into strips
   1 large tomato, diced
   1 carrot, shredded
   1 small cucumber, sliced
DILL DRESSING:
   2 tablespoons cider *or* red wine vinegar
   1 teaspoon Dijon mustard
   2 tablespoons sour cream
1/4 cup vegetable oil
   3 tablespoons olive oil
1/4 teaspoon salt, optional
   2 teaspoons dill weed

In a large bowl, combine the first eight ingredients. Refrigerate. For dressing, whisk the vinegar and mustard in a small bowl. Whisk in remaining ingredients. Refrigerate for at least 30 minutes. Stir well before serving with the salad. **Yield:** 8 servings (about 3/4 cup dressing). **Nutritional Analysis:** One serving with 1 tablespoon dressing (prepared with light sour cream and without added salt) equals 134 calories, 32 mg sodium, 0 cholesterol, 7 gm carbohydrate, 3 gm protein, 12 gm fat. **Diabetic Exchanges:** 2 fat, 1 vegetable.

Baked Cranberry Pudding

This old-fashioned pudding is a cranberry lover's delight. Serve with whipped cream if you like.

   1 cup packed brown sugar

   2 eggs, *separated*
1/2 cup whipping cream
   2 teaspoons vanilla extract
   1 teaspoon ground cinnamon
1/2 teaspoon ground nutmeg
1-1/2 cups all-purpose flour
   3 tablespoons grated orange peel
   1 teaspoon baking powder
1/2 teaspoon cream of tartar, *divided*
1/8 teaspoon salt
   3 cups coarsely chopped cranberries
1/4 cup butter *or* margarine, melted
TOPPING:
1-1/2 cups sugar
1/2 cup orange juice
2-1/2 cups whole cranberries

In a bowl, combine brown sugar and egg yolks. Add whipping cream, vanilla, cinnamon and nutmeg; set aside. In a large bowl, combine flour, orange peel, baking powder, 1/4 teaspoon cream of tartar and salt. Stir in chopped cranberries and completely coat them. Add brown sugar mixture and butter; mix well. (Batter will be very stiff.) Beat egg whites until foamy. Add remaining cream of tartar; beat until soft peaks form. Fold into batter. Pour into a greased 9-in. springform pan. Bake at 350° for 45-50 minutes or until a toothpick inserted near center comes out clean. Meanwhile, for topping, bring sugar and orange juice to a boil in a saucepan. Cook for 3 minutes or until sugar dissolves. Reduce heat; add cranberries and simmer 6-8 minutes or until berries begin to burst. Remove from heat and cover. When pudding tests done, place springform pan on a jelly roll pan. Spoon warm cranberry sauce evenly over top. Return to the oven for 10 minutes. Cool for 10 minutes before removing sides of springform pan. Cool at least 1 hour or overnight. Before serving, reheat at 350° for 10 minutes. **Yield:** 8-10 servings.

When spring makes its debut, this farm wife welcomes the season with a fresh-tasting feast.

By Eunice Stoen, Decorah, Iowa

EVERYDAY MEALS can be hurried here on the dairy and grain farm husband Wilbur and I (everyone calls me "Euny") operate with our son, Bill. But now and then, I enjoy preparing a special feast.

My farm background, Norwegian heritage and love of sharing recipes all come through in this mouth-watering menu. Ham is my meat of choice—we used to raise hogs, and I'm a big promoter of Iowa farm products.

Not only is my Baked Ham with Cumberland Sauce easy to prepare, but it looks so impressive. When you've fixed a beautiful roast like this, I think it's nice to put it on your largest platter and take it to the table before carving it. Then pass around a platter with thick slices of the ham and a bowl of the fruity sauce.

My Asparagus with Sesame Butter recipe retains the color and shape of the spears, accentuating the fresh flavor and adding some crunch.

And a delicious simple side dish like Norwegian Parsley Potatoes goes well with the ham and honors my heritage. I also like to serve warm rolls, a relish tray and a make-ahead salad.

Hawaiian Dessert is a perfect refreshing end to this meal. It makes two large pans, so there's one to serve and another to freeze—or better yet—to share with your neighbor.

Preparing as much of my meal as possible the day before allows me to enjoy our guests and the food, too. I dish up all the food, then sit where I can reach the bowls and platters and pass them for "seconds".

Our guests often say that I make putting on a meal like this look easy. I gratefully respond that my secret to success is planning and preparing ahead of time... and, of course, using these never-fail recipes!

— 🍴 🍴 🍴 —

PICTURED AT LEFT: Baked Ham with Cumberland Sauce, Asparagus with Sesame Butter, Norwegian Parsley Potatoes and Hawaiian Dessert (recipes are on the next page).

Baked Ham with Cumberland Sauce

The centerpiece of a beautiful spring family dinner, this golden ham with tangy jewel-toned sauce is impressive to serve.

> **1/2 fully cooked ham with bone (4 to 5 pounds)**
> **1/2 cup packed brown sugar**
> **1 teaspoon ground mustard**
> **Whole cloves**
> **CUMBERLAND SAUCE:**
> **1 cup red currant *or* apple jelly**
> **1/4 cup orange juice**
> **1/4 cup lemon juice**
> **1/4 cup red wine *or* apple juice**
> **2 tablespoons honey**
> **1 tablespoon cornstarch**

Remove skin from ham; score the surface with shallow diagonal cuts, making diamond shapes. Mix brown sugar and mustard; rub into fat of ham. Insert a whole clove in center of each diamond. Place ham in a large roaster with a baking rack. Bake, uncovered, at 325° for 20-22 minutes per pound or until ham is heated through and thermometer reads 140°. For sauce, combine all of the ingredients in a medium saucepan. Cook over medium heat until thickened, stirring often. Serve over the sliced ham. (Sauce recipe can be doubled if desired.) **Yield:** 8-10 servings (1-3/4 cups sauce).

Norwegian Parsley Potatoes

I love to use parsley in many dishes, and it suits the fresh taste of small red potatoes well. Even though they're easy to prepare, they look fancy and go great with baked ham.

> **2 pounds small red new potatoes**
> **1/2 cup butter *or* margarine**
> **1/4 cup chopped fresh parsley**
> **1/4 teaspoon dried marjoram**

Cook potatoes in boiling salted water for 15 minutes or until tender. Cool slightly. With a sharp knife, remove one narrow strip of skin around the middle of each potato. In a large skillet, melt butter; add parsley and marjoram. Add the potatoes and stir gently until coated and heated through. **Yield:** 6-8 servings.

Asparagus with Sesame Butter

The first fresh asparagus is a delightful springtime treat. This light butter sauce lets the asparagus flavor come through, and the sprinkling of sesame seeds adds a delicate crunch. This is a simple yet delicious dish.

> **2 pounds fresh asparagus**
> **1 cup boiling water**

1/2 teaspoon salt
1 tablespoon cornstarch
1/4 cup cold water
1/4 cup butter *or* margarine
3 tablespoons sesame seeds, toasted

Place asparagus spears in a large skillet; add boiling water and salt. Cook for 5-7 minutes or until tender. Remove asparagus and keep warm. Drain cooking liquid, reserving 1/2 cup in a small saucepan. Combine cornstarch and cold water; stir into liquid. Cook and stir over medium heat until thickened and bubbly; cook and stir 1 minute more. Stir in butter until melted. Spoon over asparagus; sprinkle with sesame seeds and serve immediately. **Yield:** 6-8 servings.

Asparagus Tips

When buying asparagus, look for stalks that are brittle enough to snap and fairly uniform in circumference. The tips should be tightly closed.

Store the spears loose in a plastic bag in the crisper compartment of your refrigerator.

When fresh asparagus is plentiful, blanch some and freeze it for later. Keep asparagus frozen until you're ready to use it. Don't defrost before cooking. If the asparagus thaws, cook it right away and don't refreeze. Frozen asparagus should be used within 8 months.

Hawaiian Dessert

A chilled fluffy dessert like this one is a satisfying way to finish off a big meal. I got the recipe from a woman I happened to meet in a department store one day. Leftovers taste just as good the next day, and this dessert can also be frozen. I like to keep a pan in the freezer to take to a last-minute potluck.

1 package (18-1/4 ounces) yellow cake mix
3 packages (3.4 ounces *each*) instant vanilla pudding mix
4 cups cold milk
1-1/2 teaspoons coconut extract
1 package (8 ounces) cream cheese, softened
1 can (20 ounces) crushed pineapple, well drained
2 cups whipping cream, whipped and sweetened
2 cups flaked coconut, toasted

Mix cake batter according to package directions. Pour into two greased 13-in. x 9-in. x 2-in. baking pans. Bake at 350° for 15 minutes or until the cakes test done. Cool completely. In a large mixing bowl, combine pudding mixes, milk and coconut extract; beat for 2 minutes. Add the cream cheese and beat well. Stir in pineapple. Spread over the cooled cakes. Top with whipped cream; sprinkle with coconut. Chill for at least 2 hours. **Yield:** 24 servings. **Editor's Note:** Prepared dessert can be covered and frozen for up to 1 month.

This Illinois cook's colorful "Berry Special Luncheon" is big on eye appeal and terrific taste.

By Janet Moonberry, Peoria, Illinois

SINCE "berry" is part of my last name, it's not surprising that bright strawberries and raspberries top my list of favorite spring and summertime ingredients!

As an avid cook, I find there's nothing more satisfying than making simple recipes look elegant. So I'm proud to share my menu for a "Berry Special Luncheon". I devised this fresh meal many years ago for a cooking class I taught at a gourmet cooking shop where I worked. The class loved it! Since then I've served this menu myself countless times.

To start things off, I ladle up some sparkly, refreshing Springtime Punch. Its blend of lemon, orange and pineapple juices defines the sunny color and fruity flavor, while ginger ale adds zesty fizz.

Cool Raspberry Soup is the first course to this meal. Most people are pleasantly surprised by this flavorful chilled soup. One sweet-tart spoonful usually elicits delighted exclaims of, "Oh, I like this!"

To complement the fruit soup, I bring out a basket of Cinnamon Twists. Twisting the strips of dough for these sweet breadsticks spirals the brown sugar mixture for a fancier presentation than ordinary rolls.

My recipe for Spinach Chicken Salad evolved from a recipe given to me by a special friend. With an eye for color, I jazzed up the salad by adding a few extra ingredients I like.

Desserts are my forte! I like them elegant-looking but easy. I've never had anyone turn down a slice of Sky-High Strawberry Pie, which is my own creation. Husband Scott thinks it's such a wonderfully special dessert that he requests it each year for his birthday instead of the traditional cake!

This luncheon menu works beautifully for a shower or for any spring or summer gathering.

⎯⎯ 🏆 🏆 🏆 ⎯⎯

PICTURED AT LEFT: Springtime Punch, Spinach Chicken Salad, Cool Raspberry Soup, Sky-High Strawberry Pie and Cinnamon Twists (recipes are on the next page).

Spinach Chicken Salad

Dazzle your hungry visitors with this crunchy salad. It showcases an interesting mixture of chicken, pasta, spinach and other vegetables. The delectable dressing complements the colorful ingredients.

> 5 cups cubed cooked chicken (about 3 whole breasts)
> 2 cups green grape halves
> 1 cup snow peas
> 2 cups packed torn spinach
> 2-1/2 cups sliced celery
> 7 ounces corkscrew pasta *or* elbow macaroni, cooked and drained
> 1 jar (6 ounces) marinated artichoke hearts, drained and quartered
> 1/2 large cucumber, sliced
> 3 green onions with tops, sliced
> Large spinach leaves, optional
> Orange slices, optional
> DRESSING:
> 1/2 cup vegetable oil
> 1/4 cup sugar
> 2 tablespoons white wine vinegar
> 1 teaspoon salt
> 1/2 teaspoon dried minced onion
> 1 teaspoon lemon juice
> 2 tablespoons minced fresh parsley

In a large bowl, combine chicken, grapes, peas, spinach, celery, pasta, artichoke hearts, cucumber and green onions. Cover and refrigerate. Combine all dressing ingredients in a jar or small bowl; mix well and refrigerate. Just before serving, pour dressing over salad and toss. If desired, serve on a spinach leaf and garnish with oranges. **Yield:** 8-10 servings.

Cool Raspberry Soup

An exquisite combination of spices and a rich berry flavor make this beautiful soup so refreshing. It's a lovely and tasty way to begin a luncheon. Your guests will rave about the special treat.

> 1 bag (20 ounces) frozen raspberries, thawed
> 1-1/4 cups water
> 1/4 cup white wine, optional
> 1 cup cran-raspberry juice
> 1/2 cup sugar
> 1-1/2 teaspoons ground cinnamon
> 3 whole cloves
> 1 tablespoon lemon juice
> 1 carton (8 ounces) raspberry-flavored yogurt
> 1/2 cup sour cream

In a blender, puree raspberries, water and wine if desired. Transfer to a large saucepan; add the cran-raspberry juice, sugar, cinnamon and cloves. Bring just to a boil over medium heat. Remove from the heat; strain and allow to cool. Whisk in lemon juice and yogurt. Refrigerate. To serve, pour into small bowls and top with a dollop of sour cream. **Yield:** 4-6 servings.

Springtime Punch

(Pictured on page 225)

Floating fresh whole strawberries in the punch bowl adds flair to this beverage.

> 2 cups sugar
> 2-1/2 cups water
> 1 cup fresh lemon juice (3 to 4 lemons)

1 cup fresh orange juice (2 to 3 oranges)
1 can (6 ounces) frozen pineapple juice
   concentrate, thawed
2 quarts ginger ale, chilled

In a saucepan, bring sugar and water to a boil. Boil for 10 minutes; remove from the heat. Stir in the lemon, orange and pineapple juices. Refrigerate. Just before serving, combine with ginger ale in a large punch bowl. **Yield:** 16-20 servings (3 quarts).

Cinnamon Twists

Brown sugar and cinnamon give these golden twists a delicate spicy flavor. It's a good thing the recipe makes a big batch...people can rarely eat just one.

1 package (1/4 ounce) active dry yeast
3/4 cup warm water (110° to 115°), *divided*
4 to 4-1/2 cups all-purpose flour
1/4 cup sugar
1-1/2 teaspoons salt
1/2 cup warm milk (110° to 115°)
1/4 cup butter *or* margarine, softened
1 egg
FILLING:
1/4 cup butter *or* margarine, melted
1/2 cup packed brown sugar
4 teaspoons ground cinnamon

In a large mixing bowl, dissolve yeast in 1/4 cup warm water. Add 2 cups of flour, sugar, salt, milk, butter, egg and remaining water; beat on medium speed for 2 minutes. Stir in enough remaining flour to form a soft dough. Turn onto a floured board; knead until smooth and elastic, about 6-8 minutes. Place in a greased bowl, turning once to grease top. Cover and let rise in a warm place until doubled,

about 1 hour. Punch down. Roll into a 16-in. x 12-in. rectangle. Brush with butter. Combine brown sugar and cinnamon; sprinkle over butter. Let dough rest for 6 minutes. Cut lengthwise into three 16-in. x 4-in. strips. Cut each strip into sixteen 4-in. x 1-in. pieces. Twist and place on greased baking sheets. Cover and let rise until doubled, about 30 minutes. Bake at 350° for 15 minutes or until golden. **Yield:** 4 dozen.

Sky-High Strawberry Pie

This pie is my specialty. It's fairly simple to make but so dramatic to serve. I've had many requests to bring this luscious pie to gatherings.

3 quarts fresh strawberries, *divided*
1-1/2 cups sugar
6 tablespoons cornstarch
2/3 cup water
Red food coloring, optional
1 deep-dish pastry shell (10 inches), baked
1 cup whipping cream
1-1/2 tablespoons instant vanilla pudding mix

In a large bowl, mash enough strawberries to equal 3 cups. In a saucepan, combine the sugar and cornstarch. Stir in the mashed berries and water; mix well. Bring to a boil over medium heat, stirring constantly. Cook and stir for 2 minutes. Remove from the heat; add food coloring if desired. Pour into a large bowl. Refrigerate for 20 minutes, stirring occasionally, until mixture is just slightly warm. Fold in the remaining berries. Pile into pie shell. Refrigerate for 2-3 hours. In a small mixing bowl, whip cream until soft peaks form. Sprinkle pudding mix over cream and whip until stiff; serve with the pie. **Yield:** 8-10 servings.

With a family of 14 to feed, she looks for thrifty meals big on flavor ...like her savory spaghetti dinner.

By Anne Heinonen, Howell, Michigan

FRIENDS with smaller families say that cooking for my crew must be like having company every day! But to me, planning and preparing meals for husband and our 12 children is a joy.

I'm always looking for new recipes we all like. Fortunately, Fred and the kids are open to trying different foods and like it when I serve something new.

A hit with everyone in the family is my Savory Spaghetti Sauce, especially when I add fresh basil and oregano from our herb garden.

I double or triple the recipe and serve it family-style, putting out a big bowl of pasta, a dish of steaming sauce and freshly grated Parmesan cheese to sprinkle on top. The hearty sauce is similar to what my mom served me and my 10 brothers and sisters. But Mom never had fresh herbs, which make the biggest flavor difference in my variation.

Fred and I are both of Finnish descent, and my Finnish Flat Bread (rieska) is a satisfying staple we grew up eating. The combination of white and wheat flours adds old-world appeal, and the buttermilk makes it extra tasty.

Mandarin Almond Salad is our family's favorite, hands down! I clipped the recipe from a magazine some years ago and vary it with different garden greens. The sweet crunch of the caramelized almonds always makes this salad seem special.

I got the recipe for Chocolate Walnut Squares from a friend with whom I often trade recipes. The combination of chocolate, vanilla and nuts raises these bars above the ordinary. The secret to their creamy frosting is a cooked milk and flour blend.

I hope that you receive lots of compliments when you try my favorite meal in your home!

— ▼ ▼ ▼ —

PICTURED AT LEFT: Savory Spaghetti Sauce, Finnish Flat Bread, Mandarin Almond Salad and Chocolate Walnut Squares (recipes are on the next page).

Savory Spaghetti Sauce

This fresh-tasting spaghetti sauce is a real crowd-pleaser. With a husband and 12 kids to feed every day, I rely on this flavorful recipe often. It tastes especially good in the summer made with fresh garden herbs.

> 1 pound ground beef
> 1 large onion, chopped
> 2 cans (15 ounces *each*) tomato sauce
> 1 garlic clove, minced
> 1 bay leaf
> 1 tablespoon minced fresh basil *or* 1 teaspoon dried basil
> 2 teaspoons minced fresh oregano *or* 3/4 teaspoon dried oregano
> 2 teaspoons sugar
> 1/2 to 1 teaspoon salt
> 1/2 teaspoon pepper
> Hot cooked spaghetti
> Fresh oregano, optional

In a Dutch oven, cook ground beef and onion until meat is browned and onion is tender; drain. Add the next eight ingredients; bring to a boil. Reduce heat; cover and simmer for 1 hour, stirring occasionally. Remove the bay leaf. Serve over spaghetti. Garnish with oregano if desired. **Yield:** 4-6 servings (about 1 quart).

Finnish Flat Bread

My husband and I have eaten this simple-to-make bread for years. It's so nice to have homemade bread with spaghetti, and it's even nicer when you don't have to fuss.

> 1-1/2 cups all-purpose flour
> 3/4 cup whole wheat flour
> 2 tablespoons sugar
> 1-1/2 teaspoons baking powder
> 1 teaspoon salt
> 1/2 teaspoon baking soda
> 1/4 cup shortening
> 1 cup buttermilk

In a bowl, combine flours, sugar, baking powder, salt and baking soda. Cut in shortening until the mixture resembles coarse crumbs. Add buttermilk and mix just until dough is moistened. Knead on a floured surface for 3-5 minutes. Pat onto an ungreased 12-in. pizza pan. Bake at 350° for 30 minutes or until golden. Cool for 10 minutes before removing to a wire rack. Cut into pieces. **Yield:** 6-8 servings.

— 🥄 🥄 🥄 —

Mandarin Almond Salad

Here's a refreshing salad that's always a hit at our house. Crisp greens, bright oranges and red onion add pretty color to your meal, and the sweet caramelized almonds provide a unique crunch.

    4 tablespoons sugar, *divided*
  1/2 cup slivered almonds
  1/4 cup vegetable oil
    2 tablespoons vinegar
    1 tablespoon minced fresh parsley
  1/2 teaspoon salt
  1/8 teaspoon pepper
  1/8 teaspoon hot pepper sauce
    1 bunch red leaf lettuce, torn
    1 can (11 ounces) mandarin oranges, drained
    1 small red onion, sliced

In a small skillet, melt 3 tablespoons of sugar over low heat. Add almonds and stir until coated. Cool; break into small pieces and set aside. In a jar with a tight-fitting lid, combine the oil, vinegar, parsley, salt, pepper, hot pepper sauce and remaining sugar; shake well. Just before serving, combine the lettuce, oranges, onion and almonds in a large salad bowl. Shake dressing; pour over salad and toss. **Yield:** 4-6 servings.

Chocolate Walnut Squares

Rich and satisfying, these bars create a symphony of flavors with every bite. The nutty crust, exquisite chocolate layer and the creamy frosting make this dessert one of my personal favorites. It's fun to take these treats to a potluck.

    1 cup butter *or* margarine, softened
    2 cups sugar
    4 eggs, lightly beaten
    1 tablespoon vanilla extract*
    2 cups all-purpose flour
  1/2 teaspoon salt
    2 cups chopped walnuts
    2 squares (1 ounce *each*) unsweetened chocolate, melted
FROSTING:
    5 tablespoons all-purpose flour
    1 cup milk
    1 cup butter *or* margarine, softened
    1 cup confectioners' sugar
    2 teaspoons vanilla extract

In a mixing bowl, cream butter and sugar. Beat in eggs and vanilla. Add flour and salt; mix well. Fold in walnuts. Spread half of the batter into a greased 13-in. x 9-in. x 2-in. baking pan. Add chocolate to the remaining batter; mix well. Carefully spread over batter in pan. Bake at 350° for 30-35 minutes or until cake tests done. Cool completely. For frosting, mix flour and milk in a saucepan. Cook and stir over medium heat until a thick paste forms, about 10 minutes. Cool completely. In a mixing bowl, cream butter and confectioners' sugar. Add vanilla and mix well. Gradually add the milk mixture; beat for 5 minutes. Frost cake. Store in the refrigerator. **Yield:** 20-24 servings.
*Editor's Note: The amount of vanilla is correct.

In a Nutshell

You can store unshelled walnuts in a cool, dry place indefinitely. Shelled nuts should be stored in an airtight container in the refrigerator for 6 months or in the freezer for a year.

This football fan's feast is a winner at pregame "tailgate parties" and will draw cheers at your picnics.

By Rita Reifenstein, Evans City, Pennsylvania

SEPTEMBER is my favorite month—it brings bounty from the garden *and* football season!

On fall Saturdays for over 20 years, I've attended Penn State University home football games with my father, Martin Marburger. Since I married Rick, he's happily joined in those traditional outings.

For me, planning good food for our "tailgate parties" at the stadium is part of the fun!

On game day, we leave bright and early in Dad's motor home. Our enthusiastic group can vary from four to 16, and I love trying out new recipes on them. But my Glazed Corned Beef Sandwiches score so high that I serve them often during the season.

I prepare the beef brisket a day or two ahead, simmering it with peppercorns and spices until it's wonderfully tender. The glaze is rubbed into the meat while it's still warm and can best absorb the zesty flavor.

Two colorful dishes I like to serve with these hearty sandwiches were inspired by my garden's bounty.

Stuffed Cherry Tomatoes make refreshing appetizers to munch during our pregame banter. You can fix these tasty bites ahead—just hollow out firm cherry tomatoes and spoon or pipe in the creamy filling.

Sweet corn, fresh-cut from the cob or frozen, gives my Corn Salad its sunny appeal. The recipe has a winning combination of garden ingredients.

No tailgate meal would be complete without a sweet ending like Apple Cobbler. This treasured family dessert was a staple when I was growing up.

I hope you decide to try my recipes for a fall or summer picnic or any time you need tasty food that travels well.

— 🏆 🏆 🏆 —

PICTURED AT LEFT: Glazed Corned Beef Sandwiches, Stuffed Cherry Tomatoes, Corn Salad and Apple Cobbler (recipes are on the next page).

Glazed Corned Beef Sandwiches

Fans of good food will cheer when you bring out these full-flavored, hearty sandwiches! Made of tender corned beef and a special sweet and spicy seasoning, they're always a hit.

  1 **corned beef brisket (3 to 4 pounds)**
12 **peppercorns**
  4 **bay leaves**
  3 **garlic cloves, minced**
  2 **cinnamon sticks (3 inches), broken**
  1 **tablespoon crushed red pepper flakes**
Sandwich buns
GLAZE:
  1/2 **cup packed brown sugar**
  1/2 **teaspoon ground cloves**
  1/2 **teaspoon ground ginger**
  1/2 **teaspoon ground mustard**
  1/4 **teaspoon celery salt**
  1/4 **teaspoon caraway seed**

Place corned beef with seasoning packet in a Dutch oven; cover with water. Add peppercorns, bay leaves, garlic, cinnamon sticks and pepper flakes; bring to a boil. Reduce heat; cover and simmer for 4 to 4-1/2 hours or until meat is tender. Drain, discarding juices; blot brisket dry. In a small bowl, combine glaze ingredients. Rub onto top of warm meat. Grill or broil for 5-10 minutes on each side until glazed. Slice meat; serve warm or chilled on buns. **Yield:** 12-16 servings.

Freezing Vegetables

Frozen vegetables will taste fresh for months to come if properly prepared. Pack blanched or scalded vegetables loosely in airtight, moisture/vapor-proof containers. Quart or pint plastic freezer bags are readily available and take up little space in your freezer. Be sure to press out as much air as possible before sealing the bags.

You can also use canning jars or plastic freezer containers to prevent "freezer burn".

Corn Salad

This sensational salad is a delight to serve because you can make it ahead and it's an easy way to put garden bounty to good use. With colorful ingredients like corn, tomato and green pepper, it's also pretty in the bowl and on your plate.

✓ Uses less fat, sugar or salt. Includes Nutritional Analysis and Diabetic Exchanges.

  2 **cups fresh *or* frozen whole kernel corn, cooked and drained**
3/4 **cup chopped tomato**
1/2 **cup chopped green pepper**
1/2 **cup chopped celery**
1/4 **cup chopped onion**
1/4 **cup prepared ranch salad dressing**

In a large salad bowl, combine vegetables; stir in dressing. Cover and refrigerate until serving. **Yield:** 8 servings. **Nutritional Analysis:** One 1/2-cup serving (prepared with fat-free dressing) equals 56 calories, 93 mg sodium, 0 cholesterol, 15 gm carbohydrate, 2 gm protein, 1 gm fat. **Diabetic Exchanges:** 1 starch.

3 cups all-purpose flour
1 cup sugar, *divided*
1-1/2 teaspoons baking powder
1/2 teaspoon salt
1/2 cup butter *or* margarine
2 eggs
1 tablespoon vanilla extract
3 to 4 tablespoons milk
8 cups thinly sliced peeled baking apples
2 tablespoons quick-cooking tapioca
1/2 teaspoon ground cinnamon
TOPPING:
1 tablespoon milk
3/4 teaspoon sugar
1/4 teaspoon ground cinnamon

In a bowl, combine flour, 1/4 cup sugar, baking powder and salt. Cut in butter until crumbly. In another bowl, lightly beat eggs and vanilla; add to crumb mixture. With a fork, gently mix in milk to moisten. Stir until dough forms a ball. Press half of the dough into the bottom of a greased 13-in. x 9-in. x 2-in. baking pan. Chill the remaining dough. Toss apples with tapioca, cinnamon and remaining sugar; place over dough in pan. On a lightly floured surface, roll chilled dough to fit top of pan. Place over apples. Brush with milk. Combine sugar and cinnamon; sprinkle on top. Bake at 350° for 45-50 minutes or until apples are tender and crust is golden. **Yield:** 12-16 servings.

Stuffed Cherry Tomatoes

Try this simple recipe for a crowd-pleasing appetizer. They may be small, but these tasty tomatoes have big garden-fresh flavor enhanced by the cool, zesty filling.

2 packages (one 8 ounces, one 3 ounces) cream cheese, softened
2 tablespoons mayonnaise
1 package (.4 ounce) ranch salad dressing mix
3 dozen cherry tomatoes
Alfalfa sprouts, optional

In a mixing bowl, blend cream cheese, mayonnaise and salad dressing mix until smooth. Cut a thin slice off the tops of tomatoes and carefully remove insides; invert on paper towel to drain. Fill with cream cheese mixture. Serve on a bed of alfalfa sprouts if desired. **Yield:** 12-16 servings.

Apple Cobbler

A treasured family recipe, this cobbler is a delicious old-fashioned dessert. It travels well and slices nicely, so it's perfect for picnics or tailgate parties. We like apples, but you can use your favorite fruit.

Guests are always fed well by this terrific cook, whose love of cooking is reflected in her old-fashioned meals.

By Ruth Andrewson, Peck, Idaho

I HAVE a large notebook filled with down-to-earth, delicious recipes I keep close at hand so I can have a "from scratch" meal ready in short order when guests drop in. I call this collection of favorite recipes my "treasure book".

Its pages reflect a love of cooking that began with my childhood on a farm and has lasted through raising a family and owning a small restaurant.

One page in particular is well-worn and contains this simple but special chicken dinner that has roots back in Michigan's Upper Peninsula, where we owned a restaurant for a number of years.

Like many of my tried-and-true dishes, I modified a basic recipe from one of the church or specialty cookbooks I collect and came up with Honey-Glazed Chicken.

Adding curry powder spiced up the quick-and-easy basting sauce that richly glazes this tasty entree. Patrons of our restaurant loved the down-home country flavor.

Spiced Carrot Strips have a delicate buttery flavor with just a hint of cinnamon. It's a pretty as well as nourishing side dish.

The sauteed Paprika Potatoes proved so successful that we served them often at our restaurant...and still do to family and friends. This recipe is especially nice because it leaves the oven free for other foods.

And for the perfect ending to this meal, I frequently prepared delectable Fruit 'n' Nut Cherry Pie. Because it's not too heavy or rich, this pie remains a much-requested recipe today.

I hope you find these delicious new jewels irresistible...and hope you add them to your own "treasure book" of family favorites!

PICTURED AT LEFT: Honey-Glazed Chicken, Spiced Carrot Strips, Paprika Potatoes and Fruit 'n' Nut Cherry Pie (recipes are on the next page).

Honey-Glazed Chicken

My family raves over this nicely browned chicken. The rich honey glaze gives each luscious piece a spicy tang. This dish is simple enough to prepare for a family dinner and delightful enough to serve to guests.

- 1/2 **cup all-purpose flour**
- 1 **teaspoon salt**
- 1/2 **teaspoon cayenne pepper**
- 1 **broiler-fryer chicken (about 3 pounds), cut up**
- 1/2 **cup butter *or* margarine, melted, *divided***
- 1/4 **cup packed brown sugar**
- 1/4 **cup honey**
- 1/4 **cup lemon juice**
- 1 **tablespoon soy sauce**
- 1-1/2 **teaspoons curry powder**

In a bowl or bag, combine flour, salt and cayenne pepper; add chicken pieces and dredge or shake to coat. Pour 4 tablespoons butter into a 13-in. x 9-in. x 2-in. baking pan; place chicken in pan, turning pieces once to coat. Bake, uncovered, at 350° for 30 minutes. Combine brown sugar, honey, lemon juice, soy sauce, curry powder and remaining butter; pour over chicken. Bake 45 minutes more or until chicken is tender, basting several times with pan drippings. **Yield:** 4-6 servings.

Paprika Potatoes

These tasty potatoes are golden and crusty on the outside and tender on the inside. I've served them with many kinds of meat. When a meal needs a comforting, homey touch, I whip up a batch. With just three ingredients, this side dish couldn't be easier to prepare.

- 4 **large potatoes, peeled, cooked and quartered**
- 3 **tablespoons butter *or* margarine**
- 1/2 **teaspoon paprika**

In a large skillet, slowly saute potatoes in butter until golden brown, about 10-15 minutes. Sprinkle with paprika. **Yield:** 4-6 servings.

Potato Pointers

Buy potatoes with clean, smooth skins and a firm texture; avoid ones with soft or moldy spots.

Potatoes will keep for several weeks if stored in a cool, well-ventilated place.

Scrub potatoes under cold running water before using. Cut away any eyes or green spots.

Spiced Carrot Strips

(Pictured on page 236)

Carrots are readily available year-round, but their beautiful harvest color is perfect in fall. These lightly sweet strips get unique flavor from cinnamon, which enhances the fresh carrot taste. Give this special yet simple side dish a try!

    5 large carrots, julienned
    2 tablespoons butter *or* margarine,
      melted
    1 tablespoon sugar
    1 teaspoon salt
  1/4 teaspoon ground cinnamon

Place carrots in a saucepan; cover with water. Cook until tender, about 8-10 minutes. Drain. Combine butter, sugar, salt and cinnamon; pour over carrots and toss to coat. **Yield:** 4-6 servings.

Fruit 'n' Nut Cherry Pie

It's a pleasure to serve this festive ruby-colored pie, which tastes as good as it looks! The filling is an irresistible combination of fruits and nuts. Topped with a bit of whipped cream, a lovely slice of this pie is a cool, refreshing end to an enjoyable meal.

    1 can (21 ounces) cherry pie filling
    1 can (20 ounces) crushed pineapple,
      undrained
  3/4 cup sugar
    1 tablespoon cornstarch
    1 teaspoon red food coloring, optional
    4 medium firm bananas, sliced
  1/2 cup chopped pecans *or* walnuts
    2 pastry shells (9 inches), baked
Whipped cream, optional

In a saucepan, combine pie filling, pineapple, sugar, cornstarch and food coloring if desired; mix well. Bring to a boil over medium heat, stirring constantly. Cook and stir for 2 minutes. Cool. Fold in bananas and nuts. Pour into pie shells. Chill for 2-3 hours. Garnish with whipped cream if desired. Store in the refrigerator. **Yield:** 12-16 servings.

Meals in Minutes

These ready-in-half-an-hour meals are a boon to busy cooks like you. Mix and match the rapid recipes for countless speedy suppers.

— 🍶 🍶 🍶 —

30-MINUTE MEALS. Clockwise from upper left: Beckon Your Clan with Burgers (p. 246), Sizzling Chicken Skillet Supper Is Speedy (p. 248), No More Fishing for Fast Foods (p. 242) and Italian-Style Supper in a Snap (p. 244).

No More Fishing For Fast Foods

DO YOU find yourself fishing for quick-to-fix dishes, especially during the hectic holiday season?

The homemade meal here, shared by Jean Ann Perkins of Newburyport, Maryland, goes from start to serving in about 30 minutes!

"I use this mouth-watering meal for my family and for guests, too," reports Jean Ann. "It's a wonderful combination of colors and flavors—and no fuss.

"With a seasoned bread-crumb coating, Baked Lemon Haddock is my husband's favorite dish. It bakes while I prepare the rest of the meal."

She continues, "Harvard Beets make a pretty accompaniment to this or any meal and have wonderful flavor. Even those who normally shy away from beets will gobble these up," assures Jean Ann.

"Almonds give Orange and Onion Salad special flair. It's a refreshing salad I serve year-round," she explains. "For dessert, Chocolate Mint Delight is especially nice for the holidays."

— ▼ ▼ ▼ —

Baked Lemon Haddock

✓ Uses less fat, sugar or salt. Includes Nutritional Analysis and Diabetic Exchanges.

   2 **pounds haddock fillets**
   1 **cup seasoned dry bread crumbs**
1/4 **cup butter *or* margarine, melted**
   2 **tablespoons dried parsley flakes**
   2 **teaspoons grated lemon peel**
1/2 **teaspoon garlic powder**

Cut fish into serving-size pieces. Place in a greased 11-in. x 7-in. x 2-in. baking dish. Combine remaining ingredients; sprinkle over fish. Bake, uncovered, at 350° for 25 minutes or until fish flakes easily with a fork. **Yield:** 6 servings. **Nutritional Analysis:** One serving (prepared with margarine) equals 266 calories, 706 mg sodium, 86 mg cholesterol, 15 gm carbohydrate, 31 gm protein, 9 gm fat. **Diabetic Exchanges:** 4 lean meat, 1 starch.

— ▼ ▼ ▼ —

Harvard Beets

   1 **can (16 ounces) sliced beets**
1/4 **cup sugar**
1-1/2 **teaspoons cornstarch**
   2 **tablespoons vinegar**
   2 **tablespoons orange juice**
   1 **tablespoon grated orange peel**

Drain beets, reserving 2 tablespoons juice; set beets and juice aside. In a saucepan, combine sugar and cornstarch. Add vinegar, orange juice and beet juice; bring to a boil. Reduce heat and simmer for 3-4 minutes or until thickened. Add beets and orange peel; heat through. **Yield:** 4-6 servings.

— ▼ ▼ ▼ —

Orange and Onion Salad

   1 **head Boston lettuce, separated into leaves**
   1 **medium red onion, thinly sliced into rings**
   1 **can (11 ounces) mandarin oranges, drained**
Sliced almonds
Bottled poppy seed dressing

Arrange lettuce leaves, onion and oranges on salad plates. Chill. Just before serving, sprinkle with almonds. Serve with poppy seed dressing. **Yield:** 4-6 servings.

— ▼ ▼ ▼ —

Chocolate Mint Delight

   1 **package (3.9 ounces) instant chocolate pudding mix**
   2 **cups cold milk**
  28 **miniature cream-filled chocolate cookies, crushed, *divided***
1/4 **cup crushed candy canes *or* peppermint candy**
Frozen chocolate-flavored whipped topping, thawed
Additional peppermint candy *or* miniature candy canes

Prepare pudding with milk according to package directions. Divide among individual dessert dishes. Reserve 2 tablespoons crushed cookies; sprinkle the remaining cookies over pudding. Top with crushed candy. Spoon whipped topping over candy. Sprinkle with reserved crushed cookies. Garnish with peppermints or miniature candy canes. **Yield:** 4-6 servings.

Italian-Style Supper In a Snap

WHEN YOU NEED a satisfying supper in a hurry, nothing compares to the ease of preparation like skillet specialties.

So it's no surprise Marcia Hostetter of Canton, New York reaches for her Quick Chicken Cacciatore recipe often when dinnertime rolls around.

"It's a colorful, zesty meal that I like to serve with a crisp lettuce and tomato salad topped with my family's favorite dressing," says Marcia. "The aroma while this saucy main dish simmers on the stovetop draws my family to the table."

Myrtle Albrecht's brood in Cameron Park, California loves the fabulous flavor of fresh-from-the-oven bread. But when time doesn't allow for Myrtle to make bread from scratch, she simply dresses up refrigerated breadsticks and serves Mini Blue Cheese Rolls.

"I've made this recipe for more than 30 years and find the rolls also make quick appetizers to hold the family until dinner," Myrtle reveals. "It's easy to keep the ingredients on hand for last-minute meals on busy weeknights."

Proving that a quick meal doesn't have to go without dessert, Jeanette Fuehring of Concordia, Missouri adds her recipe for No-Cook Coconut Pie. It's a hassle-free favorite that's impressive enough to serve family as well as company. "This cool and creamy dessert always disappears quickly around our dinner table," shares Jeanette.

— ☕ ☕ ☕ —

Quick Chicken Cacciatore

1 medium green pepper, cut into strips
1 medium onion, sliced into rings
8 ounces fresh mushrooms, sliced
1 tablespoon olive *or* vegetable oil
4 chicken breast halves, boned and skinned
1 can (15 ounces) tomato sauce
1 can (4 ounces) chopped green chilies
1/4 to 1/2 teaspoon dried basil
1/4 to 1/2 teaspoon dried oregano
1/8 to 1/4 teaspoon garlic powder
Dash cayenne pepper
Cooked spaghetti *or* rice, optional

In a large skillet, saute green pepper, onion and mushrooms in oil for 4-5 minutes or until crisp-tender. Place the chicken breasts over the vegetables. In a bowl, combine tomato sauce, chilies and sea-

sonings. Pour over the chicken; cover and simmer for 20 minutes or until chicken is tender and no longer pink. Serve over spaghetti or rice if desired. **Yield:** 4 servings.

— ☕ ☕ ☕ —

Mini Blue Cheese Rolls

1/4 cup butter *or* margarine
1/2 cup (4 ounces) blue cheese
1 tube (11 ounces) refrigerated breadsticks

In a saucepan, melt the butter and blue cheese over low heat. Unroll dough and cut each breadstick into six pieces; place in a foil-lined 11-in. x 7-in. x 2-in. baking pan. Pour cheese mixture over dough. Bake at 400° for 20 minutes or until butter is absorbed and rolls are lightly browned. Carefully lift foil out of pan; place on a serving dish. Serve hot. **Yield:** 4-6 servings.

— ☕ ☕ ☕ —

No-Cook Coconut Pie

2 packages (3.4 ounces *each*) instant vanilla pudding mix
2-3/4 cups cold milk
1 teaspoon coconut extract
1 carton (8 ounces) frozen whipped topping, thawed
1/2 cup flaked coconut
1 graham cracker crust (9 inches)
Toasted coconut

In a large mixing bowl, beat pudding mixes, milk and coconut extract on low speed until combined. Beat on high for 2 minutes. Fold in whipped topping and coconut. Pour into the crust. Sprinkle with toasted coconut. Chill until serving time. Refrigerate leftovers. **Yield:** 6-8 servings.

Toasting Coconut

Place flaked coconut in a single layer on a baking sheet with shallow sides. Bake at 325° for about 10 minutes or until golden brown, stirring occasionally.

Beckon Your Hungry Clan with Burgers!

YOU CAN COUNT ON a satisfying sandwich and refreshing salad when you have to get a hearty lunch or light supper on the table in a hurry.

Three time-conscious cooks share these rapid recipes that will fill the bill when you find yourself short on time.

"Pronto Pizza Burgers are my family's all-time favorite quick main dish," admits Karen Kruse of Gahanna, Ohio. "Just one bite and they can't resist these zesty sandwiches.

"Some pizza burgers call for cooked and crumbled ground beef," Karen continues. "But in this recipe, pizza-like ingredients—such as Parmesan cheese and tomato paste—are stirred into hamburger patties."

Salad with Vinaigrette Dressing is shared by Fayne Lutz of Taos, New Mexico. "The unique dressing really gives the lettuce and vegetables some zip. And it's a nice change of pace from bottled dressings. I also like to serve this for special dinners," Fayne adds.

Lemon Custard Cake, from Sue Gronholz of Columbus, Wisconsin, is treasured for two reasons. "This recipe from my grandma has been in the family for generations, and now I proudly pass it on to you. I'm sure you, too, will receive requests for this yummy dessert."

Sue continues, "Plus, being quick and easy, it's nice to whip up when unexpected company drops in. This old-fashioned treat is cool and creamy!"

Pronto Pizza Burgers

- 1 pound lean ground beef
- 1/3 cup grated Parmesan cheese
- 1 tablespoon chopped onion
- 1 tablespoon tomato paste
- 1 teaspoon dried oregano
- 1/2 teaspoon salt
- 1/4 teaspoon pepper
- 4 English muffins, split
- 8 tomato slices
- 8 mozzarella cheese slices

Additional oregano, optional

In a bowl, mix beef, Parmesan cheese, onion, tomato paste, oregano, salt and pepper just until combined. Toast the muffins in broiler until lightly browned. Divide meat mixture among muffins. Broil 4 in. from the heat for 8-10 minutes or until meat is cooked. Top with tomato and cheese slices. Return to broiler until cheese is melted. If desired, sprinkle with oregano. Serve immediately. **Yield:** 4 servings.

Salad with Vinaigrette Dressing

- 3/4 cup vegetable oil
- 1/4 cup white wine vinegar
- 1 teaspoon salt
- 1 teaspoon ground mustard
- 1/2 teaspoon sugar
- 1/2 teaspoon garlic powder
- 3 to 4 drops hot pepper sauce

Salad greens
Bell peppers, mushrooms, tomatoes *and/or* other vegetables of your choice

In a jar with a tight-fitting lid, combine the first seven ingredients and shake well. Toss salad greens and vegetables in a large bowl or arrange on individual salad plates. Serve with dressing. **Yield:** 1 cup dressing.

Lemon Custard Cake

- 1 prepared angel food cake (10 inches)
- 1 package (3.4 ounces) instant lemon pudding mix
- 1-1/2 cups cold milk
- 1 cup (8 ounces) sour cream
- 1 can (21 ounces) cherry *or* strawberry pie filling

Tear the angel food cake into bite-size pieces. Place in a 13-in. x 9-in. x 2-in. pan. In a mixing bowl, combine the pudding mix, milk and sour cream. Beat until thickened, about 2 minutes. Spread over cake. Spoon pie filling on top. Chill until serving time. **Yield:** 12-16 servings.

Tomato Slices for Sandwiches

When slicing tomatoes for sandwiches, cut from stem end to stem end with a serrated knife.

Sizzling Chicken Skillet Supper Is Speedy

AS any country cooks knows, fresh air builds big appetites. So after a day outdoors, fast-to-fix, nutritious meals that keep time spent in the kitchen to a minimum are treasured possessions!

Thanks to three cooks, such a meal is right at your fingertips. This colorful spread is ready in a snap.

Lemon Chicken is shared by Lori Schlecht of Wimbeldon, North Dakota. "I originally tried this recipe because I love rice and chicken," Lori reports. "I made a few changes to suit my tastes and was pleased with how it looks.

"Your family will love the combination of tender chicken and crunchy carrots and broccoli," she assures. "With my busy schedule, I appreciate this recipe's one-pot convenience." To save time at dinner, cut up the chicken, carrot and onion the night before and place the frozen broccoli in the refrigerator.

Herb Bread comes from Debbie Carlson of San Diego, California. "This bread is especially nice for a no-fuss meal," remarks Debbie. "It's my mom's recipe, so every time I make it, wonderful memories come back to me!"

Quick Fruit Salad is a beautiful, refreshing side dish or dessert from Sue Call of Beech Grove, Indiana. "With canned peaches and fresh bananas, strawberries and grapes, it's a great way to round out meals year-round!" Feel free to toss in some other fruits your family favors.

Lemon Chicken

☑ Uses less fat, sugar or salt. Includes Nutritional Analysis and Diabetic Exchanges.

- 1 pound boneless skinless chicken breasts, cut into strips
- 1 medium onion, chopped
- 1 large carrot, thinly sliced
- 1 garlic clove, minced
- 2 tablespoons butter *or* margarine
- 1 tablespoon cornstarch
- 1 can (14-1/2 ounces) chicken broth
- 2 to 3 tablespoons fresh lemon juice
- 1 teaspoon grated lemon peel
- 1/2 teaspoon salt, optional
- 1-1/2 cups uncooked instant rice
- 1 cup frozen chopped broccoli, thawed
- 1/4 cup minced fresh parsley

In a skillet, cook chicken, onion, carrot and garlic in butter until chicken is lightly browned, about 5 minutes. In a bowl, combine the cornstarch and broth; stir in lemon juice, peel, salt if desired and rice. Add to skillet and bring to a boil. Reduce heat; add broccoli and parsley. Cover and simmer 5-10 minutes or until rice is tender. **Yield:** 4 servings. **Nutritional Analysis:** One serving (prepared with margarine and low-sodium broth and without added salt) equals 346 calories, 211 mg sodium, 67 mg cholesterol, 39 gm carbohydrate, 31 gm protein, 9 gm fat. **Diabetic Exchanges:** 3 lean meat, 2 starch, 1 vegetable.

Herb Bread

- 6 tablespoons butter *or* margarine, softened
- 1 to 2 garlic cloves, minced
- 2 teaspoons dried parsley flakes
- 1/2 teaspoon dried oregano
- 1/2 teaspoon dill weed
- 1 teaspoon grated Parmesan cheese
- 1 loaf sourdough *or* French bread, sliced

In a bowl, combine the first six ingredients. Spread on one side of each bread slice; wrap loaf in foil. Bake at 350° for 20-25 minutes or until heated through. **Yield:** 6-8 servings.

Quick Fruit Salad

- 1 can (21 ounces) peach pie filling
- 3 firm bananas, sliced
- 2 cups strawberries, halved
- 1 cup seedless grapes

Combine all ingredients in a bowl. Refrigerate until serving. **Yield:** 6-8 servings.

Juicing a Lemon

A medium lemon will yield about 3 tablespoons juice. To get the most juice from a lemon, first bring the fruit to room temperature and roll it on the countertop with your palm.

Mexican Meal Features Plenty of Produce

THERE'S NOTHING LIKE sitting down to a hearty meal that spotlights fresh produce—like green peppers! You can make this mouth-watering meal no matter the season.

In her Taco-Filled Peppers, Nancy McDonald of Burns, Wyoming dresses up plain green peppers for a filling main meal.

"With the refreshing vegetables and zippy beef and beans, these stuffed peppers stand out from any others," Nancy states. "This tasty dish is so easy to make, I serve it often during summer and fall...much to my family's delight!"

Anne Yaeger of Washington, D.C. proves that from-scratch rice can be easy to prepare and very flavorful. "You'll find my Spanish Rice is so much better than any boxed variety found in grocery stores," assures Anne.

"Best of all, it can be prepared in about the same time as those so-called convenience foods using items found in your pantry."

Cool and creamy Caramel Pie comes from Ozela Haynes of Emerson, Arkansas and complements the slightly spicy peppers. Ozela explains, "I got the recipe for this sweet, fluffy dessert from my niece many years ago. Whenever this pie is served, it goes fast! You'll find yourself making this pleasing pie even when you do have time."

Taco-Filled Peppers

1 pound ground beef
1 envelope taco seasoning mix
1 can (8 ounces) kidney beans, rinsed and drained
1 cup salsa
4 medium green peppers
1 medium tomato, chopped
1/2 cup shredded cheddar cheese
1/2 cup sour cream

In a large skillet, brown the ground beef; drain. Stir in the taco seasoning, kidney beans and salsa. Bring to a boil; reduce heat and simmer for 5 minutes. Cut peppers in half lengthwise; remove and discard seeds and stems. Immerse peppers in boiling water for 3 minutes; drain. Spoon about 1/2 cup meat mixture into each pepper half. Place in an ungreased 13-in. x 9-in. x 2-in. baking dish. Cover and bake at 350° for 15-20 minutes or until the peppers are crisp-tender and filling is heated through. Top each with tomato, cheese and a dollop of sour cream. **Yield:** 4 servings.

Spanish Rice

1/4 cup butter *or* margarine
2 cups uncooked instant rice
1 can (14-1/2 ounces) diced tomatoes, undrained
1 cup boiling water
2 beef bouillon cubes
1 medium onion, chopped
1 garlic clove, minced
1 bay leaf
1 teaspoon sugar
1 teaspoon salt
1/4 teaspoon pepper

In a saucepan over medium heat, melt butter. Add rice and stir until browned. Add remaining ingredients; bring to a boil. Reduce heat; cover and simmer 10-15 minutes or until the liquid is absorbed and rice is tender. Remove bay leaf before serving. **Yield:** 4-6 servings.

Caramel Pie

4 ounces cream cheese, softened
1/2 cup sweetened condensed milk
1 carton (8 ounces) frozen whipped topping, thawed
1 graham cracker crust (9 inches)
1/2 cup caramel ice cream topping
3/4 cup coconut, toasted
1/4 cup chopped pecans, toasted

In a mixing bowl, blend cream cheese and milk; fold in the whipped topping. Spread half into pie crust. Drizzle with half of the caramel topping. Combine coconut and pecans; sprinkle half over the caramel. Repeat layers. Chill or freeze until serving. **Yield:** 6-8 servings. **Editor's Note:** This is also a convenient recipe for serving a crowd. The recipe can be doubled as well as made ahead of time and stored in the freezer.

Serve Up Fresh, Flaky Fish in a Flash

WHEN cooler days signal the start of the busy pre-holiday season, you'll give thanks for unwrapping this fast-to-fix meal featuring flaky fish!

"I rely on seafood recipes for quick meals," reports Marilyn Paradis of Woodburn, Oregon. "Sole in Herbed Butter is a much-asked-for meal in my family.

"But I don't mind making it often…it's easy to prepare and is ready in minutes," Marilyn admits.

Red Potato Medley is a dish Cathy Buetow Schroeder shares at family gatherings in Taylor, Texas. Now she's glad to share her recipe with you!

"The fresh flavors of potatoes, onion and parsley blend well in this salad, and it's so pretty on the table," Cathy says.

Is your family in the mood for pumpkin pie, but you don't have time to prepare it? Linda Clapp of Stow, Ohio guarantees they'll be delighted when you dish out Pumpkin Whip.

"Even though this dessert is quick to fix, it has a creamy pumpkin taste and golden harvest look…just like traditional pumpkin pie," assures Linda. "It's a great dessert for both everyday dinners and special-occasion suppers."

You and your family are guaranteed to fall for this fast-to-fix flavorful meal hook, line…and sinker!

Sole in Herbed Butter

✓ Uses less fat, sugar or salt. Includes Nutritional Analysis and Diabetic Exchanges.

- 4 tablespoons butter *or* margarine, softened
- 1 teaspoon dill weed
- 1/2 teaspoon onion powder
- 1/2 teaspoon garlic powder
- 1/2 teaspoon salt, optional
- 1/4 teaspoon white pepper
- 2 pounds sole fillets
- Fresh dill and lemon wedges, optional

In a bowl, mix butter, dill, onion powder, garlic powder, salt if desired and pepper. Transfer to a skillet; heat on medium until melted. Add the sole and cook for several minutes on each side or until it flakes easily with a fork. Garnish with dill and lemon if desired. **Yield:** 6 servings. **Nutritional Analysis:** One serving (prepared with reduced-fat margarine and without added salt) equals 178 calories, 209 mg sodium, 72 mg cholesterol, trace carbohydrate, 28 gm protein, 7 gm fat. **Diabetic Exchanges:** 4 lean meat, 1/2 fat.

Red Potato Medley

- 2 tablespoons butter *or* margarine
- 3 cups cubed red potatoes (about 2-1/2 pounds)
- 1-1/2 cups diagonally sliced carrots
- 3/4 cup chopped onion
- 1/4 cup minced fresh parsley
- 1 garlic clove, minced
- 1/4 teaspoon salt
- 1/4 teaspoon pepper

In a large skillet over medium heat, melt butter. Add potatoes and carrots; toss to coat. Add remaining ingredients and mix well. Reduce heat to medium-low. Cover and cook for 15-20 minutes or until vegetables are tender, stirring every 5 minutes. **Yield:** 6 servings.

Pumpkin Whip

- 1 package (3.4 ounces) instant butterscotch pudding mix
- 1-1/2 cups cold milk
- 1 cup canned pumpkin
- 1 teaspoon pumpkin pie spice
- 1-1/2 cups whipped topping
- Gingersnaps, optional

In a mixing bowl, beat pudding and milk until well blended, about 1-2 minutes. Blend in pumpkin and pie spice. Fold in whipped topping. Spoon into dessert dishes. Chill. Garnish with gingersnaps if desired. **Yield:** 6 servings.

Sole Secrets

Sole is a lean saltwater fish with fine, white, mild-flavored flesh. If your grocery store doesn't carry sole, flounder or pike can be substituted with equally good results.

Meals on a Budget

Budget-conscious cooks prove you can offer your family and friends flavorful foods without breaking the bank.

FRUGAL FARE. Clockwise from upper left: Taco Bake and Mixed Vegetable Salad (p. 258); Ambrosia Fruit, Jellied Biscuits and Hearty Egg Scramble (p. 266); Rhubarb Berry Delight and Crunchy Chicken Salad (p. 260); and Meatless Spaghetti and Tomato Parmesan Salad (p. 264).

Feed Your Family for 99¢ a Plate!

NOTHING feeds a family more economically than a hearty casserole served alongside oven-fresh bread. The two delicious dishes featured here come from two budget-minded cooks, who realize the importance of being able to feed the family a well-balanced meal without spending a fortune. Our test kitchen estimates the cost to be just 99¢ a setting.

Carol Allen of McLeansboro, Illinois shares her recipe for Favorite Corn Bread. "A great addition to any meal, this corn bread uses basic ingredients and is simple to make," reports Carol. "My family thinks the hearty squares also pair well with a steaming bowl of soup or chili."

Savory Sausage 'n' Sauerkraut comes from Robert Walker of Glen Dale, West Virginia. "Not only is it economical, it's delicious as well. Your family will love the hearty, down-home flavor," assures Robert. "I'm positive you'll serve it often."

— ▼ ▼ ▼ —

Favorite Corn Bread

  1 cup all-purpose flour
  1 cup cornmeal
1/4 cup sugar
  4 teaspoons baking powder
3/4 teaspoon salt
  1 cup milk
  2 eggs
1/4 cup shortening

In a mixing bowl, combine flour, cornmeal, sugar, baking powder and salt. Add the milk, eggs and shortening; beat for 1 minute. Pour into a greased 9-in. square baking pan. Bake at 425° for 20-25 minutes or until bread is golden brown and tests done. **Yield:** 9 servings.

— ▼ ▼ ▼ —

Sausage 'n' Sauerkraut

2 pounds fresh Polish sausage
1 can (14 ounces) sauerkraut, rinsed and drained

1 can (14-1/2 ounces) diced tomatoes, undrained
1 cup chopped celery
1 large onion, chopped
1 large green pepper, chopped
3 tablespoons brown sugar
1 bay leaf
1 teaspoon dried oregano
1/2 teaspoon salt

1/4 teaspoon pepper
Mashed potatoes, optional

Cut the sausage into 1-in. slices; saute in a Dutch oven until fully cooked and browned. Drain. Add sauerkraut, tomatoes, celery, onion, green pepper, brown sugar and seasonings; mix well. Cover and simmer for 20-25 minutes or until vegetables are tender. Discard bay leaf. Serve over mashed potatoes if desired. **Yield:** 8 servings.

Grocery Store Savings

Before shopping, plan your menus and grocery list using store flyers, coupons and items in your pantry. Stick to your list and avoid impulse items.

Buy items such as potatoes, onions and ground beef in bulk or family-size packages.

Feed Your Family for $1.28 a Plate!

YOU don't need to take your family to a Mexican restaurant to enjoy some Southwestern fare. By using economical ingredients found in your own kitchen, you can present a festive meal at home.

The two zesty dishes featured here come from two great cooks who know how to pinch a penny at dinnertime. Our test kitchen estimates the cost to be $1.28 per plate.

When Marlene Logan's family in Colorado Springs, Colorado has a taste for something with a little zip, she likely makes Taco Bake. "I keep the ingredients for this slightly spicy casserole in my refrigerator and pantry," states Marlene. "I think this hearty dish is perfect for feeding my hungry family during the week."

Mixed Vegetable Salad from Anita Gibson of Clinton, Illinois gets a head start from frozen mixed vegetables and canned kidney beans, so you can put it together in no time. This cool, refreshing side dish goes well with a variety of main courses.

Marlene and Anita guarantee your family will enjoy these palate-pleasing recipes!

— 🍴 🍴 🍴 —

Taco Bake

- 1 **pound ground beef**
- 1 **small onion, chopped**
- 3/4 **cup water**
- 1 **envelope taco seasoning**
- 1 **can (15 ounces) tomato sauce**
- 1 **package (8 ounces) shell macaroni, cooked and drained**
- 1 **can (4 ounces) chopped green chilies**
- 2 **cups (8 ounces) shredded cheddar cheese, *divided***

In a skillet, cook ground beef and onion over medium heat until meat is no longer pink; drain. Add the water, taco seasoning and tomato sauce; mix. Bring to a boil; reduce heat and simmer for 20 minutes. Stir in macaroni, chilies and 1-1/2 cups of cheese. Pour into a greased 1-1/2-qt. baking dish. Sprinkle with the remaining cheese. Bake at 350° for 30 minutes or until heated through. **Yield:** 6 servings.

— 🍴 🍴 🍴 —

Mixed Vegetable Salad

- 1 **package (10 ounces) frozen mixed vegetables**
- 1 **can (16 ounces) kidney beans, rinsed and drained**

1/2 cup chopped celery
1/2 cup chopped onion
1/2 cup chopped green pepper
3/4 cup sugar
1 tablespoon cornstarch
1/2 cup vinegar

In a saucepan, cook the mixed vegetables until crisp-tender. Drain; place in a large bowl. Add the kidney beans, celery, onion and green pepper. In the same saucepan, combine sugar and cornstarch. Stir in vinegar and bring to a boil. Cook and stir for 2 minutes or until thickened. Cool slightly. Pour over vegetables and toss. Refrigerate until serving. **Yield:** 8 servings.

Feed Your Family for $1.38 a Plate!

WOULD YOU like to host a special spring luncheon for family and friends without breaking your budget? Try this colorful, not costly, meal shared by two country cooks. The cost per serving (including the purchased breadsticks!) is approximately $1.38!

Crunchy Chicken Salad from Diane Hixon of Niceville, Florida features tender chicken and crunchy vegetables. With peanut oil, soy sauce and toasted sesame seeds, the dressing has a slight Oriental flair.

To save time when entertaining, you can cook the chicken and prepare the dressing the day before.

Rhubarb Berry Delight—from Joan Sieck of Rensselaer, New York—will be an instant success. This layered gelatin dish does take some time to prepare.

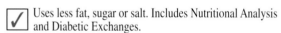

Crunchy Chicken Salad

✓ Uses less fat, sugar or salt. Includes Nutritional Analysis and Diabetic Exchanges.

  4 **cups sliced cooked chicken**
  2 **cups torn lettuce**
  1 **cup julienned carrots**
  1 **cup sliced cucumber**
2/3 **cup green onion strips (2-inch pieces)**
  1 **cup fresh bean sprouts**
DRESSING:
  2 **tablespoons peanut *or* vegetable oil**
  2 **tablespoons lemon juice**
  2 **tablespoons sesame seeds, toasted**
1-1/2 **teaspoons soy sauce**
  1/2 **teaspoon salt, optional**
  1/4 **teaspoon pepper**
  1/4 **teaspoon ground mustard**
Hot pepper sauce to taste

In a large salad bowl, toss the chicken, lettuce, carrots, cucumber, green onions and bean sprouts. Refrigerate. In a small bowl, combine dressing ingredients. Refrigerate. Just before serving, pour dressing over salad and toss gently. **Yield:** 10 servings.
Nutritional Analysis: One 1-cup serving (prepared with vegetable oil and light soy sauce and without added salt) equals 141 calories, 80 mg

sodium, 48 mg cholesterol, 5 gm carbohydrate, 19 gm protein, 6 gm fat. **Diabetic Exchanges:** 2 lean meat, 1 vegetable, 1/2 fat.

Rhubarb Berry Delight

  4 **cups diced rhubarb**
  2 **cups fresh *or* frozen strawberries**
1-1/2 **cups sugar, *divided***
  1 **package (6 ounces) raspberry gelatin**
  2 **cups boiling water**
  1 **cup milk**

      1 envelope unflavored gelatin
    1/4 cup cold water
1-1/2 teaspoons vanilla extract
      2 cups (16 ounces) sour cream

In a saucepan, cook rhubarb, strawberries and 1 cup sugar until fruit is tender. In a large bowl, dissolve raspberry gelatin in boiling water. Stir in fruit; set aside. In another pan, heat milk and remaining sugar over low until sugar is dissolved. Meanwhile, soften unflavored gelatin in cold water. Add to hot milk mixture and stir until gelatin dissolves. Remove from the heat; add vanilla. Cool to lukewarm; blend in sour cream. Set aside at room temperature.

Pour a third of the fruit mixture into a 3-qt. bowl; chill until almost set. Spoon a third of the sour cream mixture over fruit; chill until almost set. Repeat layers twice, chilling between layers if necessary. Refrigerate until firm, at least 3 hours. **Yield:** 12 servings.

Bean Sprout Basics

Rinse fresh bean sprouts, pat dry and store with a dry paper towel in a plastic bag for 3 days. Rinse again before using.

Feed Your Family for $1.50 a Plate!

AN ECONOMICAL MEAL can satisfy even the most hearty appetites. Just ask Judith Anglen. Here she shares a down-home dinner (including purchased dinner rolls) that can be put together for $1.50 a setting.

"One of our favorite meals around here is also really affordable," assures this Riverton, Wyoming cook. "I buy chicken thighs when they're on sale and freeze them for use in this meal later.

"Everyone enjoys the country-style combination of chicken, rice and mushrooms. Using chicken bouillon adds to this dish's wonderful flavor," attests Judith.

"Marinated Garden Salad is colorful, tangy and crunchy and complements the main dish nicely. With six simple ingredients, it's a salad I can toss together in minutes," Judith explains. "Then let it marinate for 1 hour to beautifully blend the flavors."

She adds, "This spread makes fabulous company fare. Friends and family are always happy to see this meal on the table."

Leave it to a country cook like Judith to prove inexpensive foods can be flavorful.

— 🍷 🍷 🍷 —

Chicken Rice Dinner

       1/2 cup all-purpose flour
         1 teaspoon salt
       1/2 teaspoon pepper
        10 chicken thighs (about 3 pounds)
         3 tablespoons vegetable oil
         1 cup uncooked long grain rice
       1/4 cup chopped onion
         2 garlic cloves, minced
         1 can (4 ounces) mushroom stems and
           pieces, undrained
         2 chicken bouillon cubes
         2 cups boiling water
Minced fresh parsley, optional

Combine flour, salt and pepper; coat chicken pieces. In a large skillet over medium heat, brown the chicken in oil. Place rice in an ungreased 13-in. x 9-in. x 2-in. baking dish. Sprinkle with onion and garlic; top with mushrooms. Dissolve bouillon in boiling water; pour over all. Place chicken pieces on top. Cover and bake at 350° for 1 hour or until chicken juices run clear and rice is tender. Sprinkle with parsley if desired. **Yield:** 5 servings.

Real Crisp Radishes

For added crispness, cover radishes with water and refrigerate for 2 hours before slicing.

Marinated Garden Salad

☑ Uses less fat, sugar or salt. Includes Nutritional Analysis and Diabetic Exchanges.

1/2 cup sliced celery
1/2 cup sliced cucumber
1/2 cup sliced carrots
1/2 cup sliced radishes
1/2 cup bottled Italian salad dressing

5 cups torn salad greens

In a large bowl, combine the celery, cucumber, carrots and radishes. Add the dressing and refrigerate for 1 hour. Just before serving, add greens and toss. **Yield:** 5 servings. **Nutritional Analysis:** One serving (prepared with fat-free dressing) equals 28 calories, 239 mg sodium, 0 cholesterol, 5 gm carbohydrate, 1 gm protein, trace fat. **Diabetic Exchanges:** 1 vegetable.

Feed Your Family for $1.65 a Plate!

DO YOU have a taste for Italian food but think you can't capture that terrific flavor at home? These recipes from two great cooks show you how easy it is to make flavorful food in your own kitchen and save money on dining out.

For just $1.65 a setting (including purchased bread-sticks), you can offer your family an Italian dinner without spending a fortune.

Meatless Spaghetti is a delicious main dish from Barbara Njaa of Nikishka, Alaska. "This chunky sauce is so good you'll think it's loaded with meat. But it actually features a whole bushel of fantastic produce," shares Barbara.

"I can start this sauce early in the afternoon and have it slowly simmer on the stove until dinnertime," Barbara explains. "It's nice to rely on no-fuss recipes like this on busy days."

Tomato Parmesan Salad—from Michelle Bently of Niceville, Florida—adds just the right amount of color and crunch to this Italian-style supper.

"The homemade oil and vinegar dressing is what makes this salad unique," reports Michelle. "Plus, it features two kinds of lettuce and garden-fresh tomatoes and onions. To save time, I make the dressing in advance and set it aside until supper."

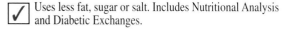

Meatless Spaghetti

✓ Uses less fat, sugar or salt. Includes Nutritional Analysis and Diabetic Exchanges.

  6 garlic cloves, minced
  1 cup chopped celery
  1 medium *or* large onion, chopped
  2 tablespoons vegetable oil
  6 small zucchini, chopped (about 2 pounds)
  1 green pepper, chopped
  1 can (6 ounces) pitted ripe olives, drained and sliced
  4 beef bouillon cubes
  1 cup hot water
  1 jar (6 ounces) sliced mushrooms, drained
  1 can (28 ounces) diced tomatoes, undrained
  2 cans (15 ounces *each*) tomato sauce
  1 can (6 ounces) tomato paste
  1 tablespoon brown sugar, optional
  2 teaspoons dried basil
  2 teaspoons dried oregano
  2 teaspoons dried parsley flakes
  1 teaspoon salt, optional
1/2 teaspoon pepper
  2 pounds spaghetti, cooked and drained

In a large saucepan or a Dutch oven, saute garlic, celery and onion in oil until tender. Add zucchini, green pepper and olives; saute for 2-3 minutes. Dissolve bouillon in water; add to vegetables. Add the next 10 ingredients and bring to a boil. Reduce

heat; cover and simmer for 1 hour, stirring occasionally. Serve over spaghetti. **Yield:** 14 servings.
Nutritional Analysis: One 1-cup serving of sauce (prepared with low-sodium bouillon and without brown sugar or salt) equals 77 calories, 366 mg sodium, 0 cholesterol, 9 gm carbohydrate, 4 gm protein, 5 gm fat. **Diabetic Exchanges:** 1-1/2 vegetable, 1/2 fat.

Tomato Parmesan Salad

1-1/3 cups vegetable *or* olive oil
1 cup red wine vinegar

2 garlic cloves, minced
Salt and pepper to taste
2 bunches romaine lettuce, torn
1 head iceberg lettuce, torn
2 small red onions, thinly sliced
2 large tomatoes, diced
1 jar (4 ounces) diced pimientos, drained
2/3 cup shredded Parmesan cheese

In a small bowl or jar with a tight-fitting lid, combine oil, vinegar, garlic, salt and pepper; set aside. In a large salad bowl, combine all remaining ingredients. Chill until ready to serve. Just before serving, whisk or shake dressing; pour over salad and toss. **Yield:** 14 servings.

Feed Your Family for $1.03 a Plate!

LOOKING for a low-budget menu that's perfect for a breakfast or brunch? Marsha Ransom of South Haven, Michigan dishes up generous helpings of this mouth-watering morning meal for just $1.03 a setting.

An egg entree is always flavorful and filling...and it won't put a crack in your bank account. Hearty Egg Scramble is extra special because it's loaded with ham and potatoes.

You can capture the flavor of fresh fruit anytime of year with Ambrosia Fruit. With its combination of canned pineapple, fresh apples and flaky coconut, it's the perfect recipe to rely on no matter the season.

Marsha adds that this breakfast wouldn't be complete without pretty and pleasing Jellied Biscuits. "They're a pleasure to serve because they look so lovely with the colorful jelly," Marsha shares.

Why not try these dishes today for a rise-and-shine morning meal your family is sure to savor?

— 🍴 🍴 🍴 —

Hearty Egg Scramble

- 1/3 cup chopped onion
- 1/4 cup chopped green pepper
- 1/4 cup butter *or* margarine
- 2 medium potatoes, peeled, cooked and cubed
- 1-1/2 cups julienned fully cooked ham
- 6 eggs
- 2 tablespoons water

Dash pepper

In a large skillet, cook onion and green pepper in butter until crisp-tender. Add potatoes and ham; cook and stir for 5 minutes. In a bowl, beat eggs, water and pepper; pour over ham mixture. Cook over low heat, stirring occasionally, until eggs are set. **Yield:** 6 servings.

Heat Advisory

For best flavor, scramble eggs over low to medium heat. Cooking over a higher temperature will make them tough and rubbery.

Ambrosia Fruit

- 1 can (20 ounces) pineapple tidbits
- 1/4 cup packed brown sugar
- 1/2 teaspoon grated orange peel
- 2 medium oranges
- 2 medium unpeeled apples, diced
- 1 tablespoon flaked coconut

Drain pineapple, reserving 1/4 cup of juice in a saucepan; set pineapple aside. Add brown sugar and orange peel to the juice; heat until sugar dissolves. Peel and section oranges into a large bowl,

reserving any juice; add the apples and pineapple. Add pineapple juice mixture and stir gently. Chill. Just before serving, sprinkle with coconut. **Yield:** 6 servings.

— 🍶 🍶 🍶 —

Jellied Biscuits

2 cups all-purpose flour
4 teaspoons baking powder
2 teaspoons sugar
1/2 teaspoon salt
1/2 teaspoon cream of tartar
1/2 cup shortening
3/4 cup milk
1/3 cup jelly

In a bowl, combine flour, baking powder, sugar, salt and cream of tartar. Cut in shortening until the mixture resembles coarse crumbs. Add milk; stir quickly with a fork just until mixed. Drop by rounded tablespoonfuls onto a greased baking sheet. Make a deep thumbprint in tops; fill each with 1 teaspoon of jelly. Bake at 450° for 10-12 minutes or until biscuits are browned. **Yield:** about 1 dozen.

Getting in the Theme of Things

The next time you're planning a get-together for a special occasion or "just because", turn to these festive menu and decorating ideas.

——— 📨 📨 📨 ———

PARTY FAVORITES. Clockwise from upper left: Picnic Celebrates Red, White and Blue (p. 276), Harvest Mood Flavors Birthday Buffet (p. 280), Romantic Valentine Dinner for Two (p. 272) and Apples Brighten Bridal Shower (p. 278).

'Card Party' Makes Great Get-Together

By Mary Anne McWhirter, Pearland, Texas

Do you procrastinate when it comes to getting your Christmas cards in the mail? Make that often-tedious task more fun for yourself and a group of friends with a Christmas card writing party!

For my "card party", I first created "shopping bag" invitations to hang on guests' doorknobs. On home-made Christmas cards I taped to small shopping bags, I detailed the date and time for supper and the evening of card writing. I suggested guests use the bag to bring their cards, stamps and pens.

As friends arrived, I surprised each of them with a wooden strawberry basket stenciled with a Christmas design and filled with candies, a pen and Christmas

notepaper. You could tuck in some Christmas stamps or other goodies of your choice.

Of course, no party's complete without food. What better way to warm up a cold winter night than with a spicy Tex-Mex menu?

I whetted guests' appetites with Tex-Mex Dip. We scooped into its colorful tasty layers with large tortilla chips.

When we sat down to supper, I pulled Beef Enchiladas from the oven. This hearty casserole has a creamy filling of cottage cheese and is topped with a zesty tomato sauce.

For a fun and fitting dessert, I made Sopaipillas—

Mexican pastry-like goodies that my family thinks are special. Dust them with confectioners' sugar or serve with honey if you wish.

Our pre-Christmas evening was filled with laughter and good conversation—plus, we actually wrote some cards! My friends assured me the card writing theme made this party memorable.

For me—a busy wife, mother of two teenage boys and school secretary—coming up with easy, economical theme "get-togethers" is relaxing and fun. In fact, I've hosted so many that I'm periodically invited to share my ideas with area women's groups.

Perhaps you'd like to give my "card party" a try…or use my south-of-the-border recipes for any other gathering you plan throughout the year.

------- 🥄 🥄 🥄 -------

Tex-Mex Dip

While writing holiday greeting cards with friends or relaxing with your family, you'll find this creamy dip adds some zip. Colorful and festive looking, it's easy to make ahead—perfect for this hectic time of year.

- 2 cans (9 ounces *each*) bean dip
- 3 avocados, peeled
- 2 tablespoons lemon juice
- 1/2 teaspoon salt
- 1/4 teaspoon pepper
- 1 cup (8 ounces) sour cream
- 1/2 cup mayonnaise
- 1 envelope taco seasoning
- 2 cups (8 ounces) shredded cheddar cheese
- 1 cup sliced ripe olives
- 4 green onions with tops, sliced
- 1 large tomato, seeded and chopped

Tortilla chips

Spread bean dip on a 12-in. serving plate. In a small bowl, mash the avocados with lemon juice, salt and pepper; spread over bean dip. Combine sour cream, mayonnaise and taco seasoning; spread over the avocado layer. Sprinkle with cheese, olives, onions and tomato. Serve with tortilla chips. **Yield:** 8-10 servings.

------- 🥄 🥄 🥄 -------

Beef Enchiladas

Warm up a cold winter night with a hearty serving of Tex-Mex food. These enchiladas have a flavorful combination of ingredients and a rich homemade sauce. This easy one-dish meal gives me more time to spend with guests.

- 1 pound ground beef
- 1 cup cottage cheese

- 1 can (4-1/4 ounces) chopped ripe olives, drained
- 2 tablespoons minced fresh parsley
- 1/2 teaspoon garlic powder
- 1/2 teaspoon salt
- 1/4 teaspoon pepper
- 8 flour tortillas (7 inches)

SAUCE:
- 1 medium onion, chopped
- 1/2 medium green pepper, chopped
- 1 tablespoon vegetable oil
- 1 can (15 ounces) tomato sauce
- 1 can (4 ounces) chopped green chilies
- 2 teaspoons chili powder
- 1 teaspoon sugar
- 1/2 teaspoon garlic powder
- 1 cup (4 ounces) shredded cheddar cheese

In a skillet, brown the ground beef until no longer pink; drain. Add the cottage cheese, olives, parsley, garlic powder, salt and pepper. Place about 1/3 cup filling on each tortilla; roll up. Place tortillas, seam side down, in an ungreased 13-in. x 9-in. x 2-in. baking dish. For sauce, saute the onion and green pepper in oil until tender. Add tomato sauce, green chilies, chili powder, sugar and garlic powder. Pour over tortillas. Cover and bake at 350° for 30 minutes. Sprinkle with cheese and return to the oven for 5 minutes or until cheese melts. **Yield:** 4 servings.

------- 🥄 🥄 🥄 -------

Sopaipillas

Light, crispy pastry puffs, sopaipillas are a sweet way to round out a spicy meal. They make a nice dessert served warm and topped with honey or sugar.

- 1 cup all-purpose flour
- 1-1/2 teaspoons baking powder
- 1/4 teaspoon salt
- 1 tablespoon shortening
- 1/3 cup warm water

Vegetable oil for deep-fat frying
Honey *or* confectioners' sugar, optional

In a bowl, combine flour, baking powder and salt. Cut in shortening until mixture resembles fine crumbs. Gradually add water, stirring with a fork. The dough will be crumbly. On a lightly floured surface, knead the dough for 3 minutes or until smooth. Cover and let rest for 10 minutes. Roll out into a 12-in. x 10-in. rectangle. Cut into 12 squares. In a deep-fat fryer, heat 2 in. of oil to 375°. Fry sopaipillas for 1-2 minutes per side. Drain on paper towels; keep hot in a warm oven. Serve with honey or dust with confectioners' sugar if desired. **Yield:** 6-8 servings.

Romantic Valentine Dinner for Two

By Marcy Cella, L'Anse, Michigan

Valentine's Day is my favorite holiday—just ask any of my family and friends! One Valentine's morn, I surprised husband Dave with an invitation to join me for a romantic dinner.

During the day, I prepared Dave's favorite lasagna. Before adding the top layer of cheeses, I cut a heart from foil and placed it in the center of the pan.

A sweet-tart raspberry vinaigrette dressed up my Sweetheart Salad, while Heart-Shaped Herbed Rolls rounded out the meal.

And no Valentine's Day would be complete without a plate of frosted heart cookies topped with sayings straight from the heart!

"Hearty" Lasagna

You can make this ahead, so you won't have to feel rushed when it's time to eat.

- 1-1/2 **pounds ground beef**
- 1 **medium onion, chopped**
- 1 **garlic clove, minced**
- 3 **tablespoons olive oil**
- 1 **can (28 ounces) Italian tomatoes with liquid, cut up**
- 1 **can (8 ounces) tomato sauce**
- 1 **can (6 ounces) tomato paste**
- 1 **teaspoon dried oregano**

    1 **teaspoon sugar**
    1 **teaspoon salt**
  1/4 **teaspoon pepper**
    2 **carrots, halved**
    2 **celery ribs, halved**
  12 **ounces lasagna noodles**
    1 **carton (15 ounces) ricotta cheese**
    2 **cups (8 ounces) shredded mozzarella**
      cheese
  1/2 **cup grated Parmesan cheese**

In a large skillet, cook beef, onion and garlic in oil until meat is browned and onion is tender; drain. Stir in tomatoes, tomato sauce, tomato paste, oregano, sugar, salt and pepper. Place carrots and celery in sauce. Simmer, uncovered, for 1-1/2 hours, stirring occasionally. Meanwhile, cook lasagna noodles according to package directions. Drain; rinse in cold water. Remove and discard carrots and celery. In a greased 13-in. x 9-in. x 2-in. baking dish, layer one-third of the noodles, one-third of the meat sauce, one-third of the ricotta, one-third of the mozzarella and one-third of the Parmesan. Repeat layers once. Top with remaining noodles and meat sauce. Cut a heart out of aluminum foil and center on top of sauce. Dollop and spread remaining ricotta around heart. Sprinkle with remaining mozzarella and Parmesan. Bake, uncovered, at 350° for 45 minutes. Remove and discard foil heart. Let stand 10-15 minutes before cutting. **Yield:** 12 servings.

— 🌶 🌶 🌶 —

Sweetheart Salad

The lightly sweet raspberry flavor of the vinaigrette really dresses up this salad.

RASPBERRY VINAIGRETTE:
  1/2 **cup white wine vinegar**
    3 **tablespoons sugar**
  1/2 **cup fresh raspberries**
    2 **tablespoons water**
    1 **tablespoon vegetable oil**
SALAD:
    1 **medium tomato**
Sweet red peppers
Assorted salad greens
Cherry tomatoes, halved
Pitted whole ripe olives

For dressing, combine vinegar and sugar in a pint glass jar. Microwave on high for 1 minute; stir. Add raspberries. Cover and let stand at room temperature for 1 hour. Refrigerate overnight. Just before serving, add water and oil; shake well. Make a "tomato rose" by taking a sharp knife and slowly peeling a continuous strip around tomato,

keeping the peel in one piece. Turn the tomato skin in on itself, forming a rose (see diagram at right). With a small heart-shaped metal cutter, cut out hearts from red peppers. Place salad greens on a serving platter; place tomato rose in the center and surround with the red pepper hearts, cherry tomatoes and olives. Serve dressing with salad. **Yield:** 3/4 cup dressing.

— 🌶 🌶 🌶 —

Heart-Shaped Herbed Rolls

Refrigerated crescent rolls give me a head start in this recipe.

  1 **tube (8 ounces) refrigerated crescent rolls**
  1 **tablespoon butter *or* margarine, softened**
  1 **teaspoon Italian seasoning**

Cut crescent roll dough apart along the perforations. Spread all eight triangles with butter and sprinkle with Italian seasoning. Make four stacks by placing two pieces of dough on top of each other, stretching as needed to match the shapes. Using a 2-1/2-in. cookie cutter, cut two heart shapes out of each stack. Place on an ungreased baking sheet. Bake at 375° for 11-13 minutes. Serve warm. **Yield:** 8 rolls.

— 🌶 🌶 🌶 —

Frosted Valentine Cookies

Demonstrate your love by making a batch of these buttery cookies.

    2 **cups butter *or* margarine, softened**
    1 **cup confectioners' sugar**
    4 **cups all-purpose flour**
    2 **cups quick-cooking oats**
    2 **teaspoons vanilla extract**
  1/2 **teaspoon almond extract**
  1/2 **teaspoon salt**
  1/2 **pound semisweet *or* milk chocolate**
      confectionery coating, melted
Confectioners' sugar icing, optional

In a mixing bowl, cream butter and sugar. Add flour, oats, extracts and salt; mix well. Roll out dough to 1/4-in. thickness. Cut with a 3-in. heart-shaped cookie cutter; place on ungreased baking sheets. Bake at 350° for 12-15 minutes. While cookies are warm, spread melted chocolate on tops. Cool. Using a pastry tube, decorate with confectioners' sugar icing if desired. **Yield:** 3-1/2 dozen.

Kid-Pleasing Barnyard Birthday Party

By Karen Kenney, Harvard, Illinois

When it came to planning a birthday party for our daughter, Katelyn, I looked no farther than our own dairy farm for a theme!

"I just want to have fun with my friends on our farm," Katelyn suggested. Thus, our "barnyard birthday" plans took shape.

Decorating the table was such fun! I used a Holstein-print tablecloth and made place mats from bandannas, folded into triangles with corners tied.

A toy barn, silo, fencing, farm animals and tractors set the stage for our rural centerpiece. I even found an old feed scoop to hold the napkins.

As the guests arrived, they were assigned to an activity group. The "Cows", "Pigs", "Chickens" and "Sheep" made their way through a hay-bale maze, timed by my husband, Kerry, then went on to search (to the tune of *Turkey in the Straw*) for hundreds of pennies hidden in straw.

Racing through a barnyard obstacle course, each group had to milk a saw-horse cow, carry an egg on a spoon and jump into bib overalls. Finally, a scavenger hunt had clues in places like a bushel of shelled corn and a basket of sheep's wool.

When outdoor activities were finished, we piled into the house for snacks with a dairy-farm flair.

The youngsters used crunchy apple slices to scoop up my creamy Dairy Delicious Dip. Its sweet goodness is enhanced by maple syrup.

Easy to eat in hand, Farmhouse Barbecue Muffins have a hearty flavor that kids love. Refrigerated buttermilk biscuits make a tender crust for the ground beef filling, which is then topped with plenty of cheddar cheese.

And, while the mention of Cow Pies might cause a country kid's nose to wrinkle, our chocolaty clusters by that name converted all doubters with one yummy bite!

As our barnyard birthday party drew to a close, Katelyn presented her friends with favors of handmade bluejean tote bags filled with Holstein bookmarkers, pig erasers, farm notepads and turkey cookies.

Her simple suggestion of an afternoon on the farm turned into a memorable event. Even if your home is in town, you might be "moo-ved" to adapt some of our barnyard food and fun ideas for a country-style good time!

— 🏆 🏆 🏆 —

Dairy Delicious Dip

Munching on fruit becomes so much more fun when there's a sweet, creamy dip to dunk your slices in. After working up an appetite playing party games, the kids enjoyed this dip. I enjoyed its ease of preparation.

> 1 package (8 ounces) cream cheese, softened
> 1/2 cup sour cream
> 1/4 cup sugar
> 1/4 cup packed brown sugar
> 1 to 2 tablespoons maple syrup

In a small mixing bowl, combine cream cheese, sour cream, sugars and syrup to taste; beat until smooth. Chill. Serve with fresh fruit. **Yield:** 2 cups.

— 🏆 🏆 🏆 —

Farmhouse Barbecue Muffins

Our daughter's friends all "plowed" through a batch of these sandwiches at her "barnyard birthday party". The tangy barbecue sauce, fluffy biscuits and cheddar cheese make them real kid-pleasers.

> 1 tube (10 ounces) refrigerated buttermilk biscuits
> 1 pound ground beef

> 1/2 cup ketchup
> 3 tablespoons brown sugar
> 1 tablespoon cider vinegar
> 1/2 teaspoon chili powder
> 1 cup (4 ounces) shredded cheddar cheese

Separate dough into 10 biscuits; flatten into 5-in. circles. Press each into the bottom and up the sides of a greased muffin cup; set aside. In a skillet, brown ground beef; drain. In a small bowl, mix ketchup, brown sugar, vinegar and chili powder; stir until smooth. Add to meat and mix well. Divide the meat mixture among biscuit-lined muffins cups, using about 1/4 cup for each. Sprinkle with cheese. Bake at 375° for 18-20 minutes or until golden brown. Cool for 5 minutes before removing from tin and serving. **Yield:** 10 servings.

— 🏆 🏆 🏆 —

Cow Pies

A barnyard birthday party just wouldn't be complete without cow pies! The kids loved 'em once they got a taste of these yummy treats packed with raisins and almonds and covered in rich milk chocolate.

> 2 cups (12 ounces) milk chocolate chips
> 1 tablespoon shortening
> 1/2 cup raisins
> 1/2 cup chopped slivered almonds

In a heavy saucepan or microwave, melt the chocolate chips and shortening over low heat, stirring until smooth. Remove from the heat; stir in raisins and almonds. Drop by tablespoonfuls onto waxed paper. Chill until ready to serve. **Yield:** 2 dozen.

Easy Entertaining

When planning your menu, include dishes that can be made ahead. This will save you time on the day of the party, allowing you to relax and double check small details without becoming frazzled.

Write down your menu for the party, including the decorations, cups, plates, napkins and utensils you'll need. Refer to your menu when putting together your grocery list so that nothing is overlooked.

Try to do most of the grocery shopping several days in advance. You can always make a quick trip to the store the day before the party for any fresh bread or produce.

Early on the day of the party, set up tables and chairs, put on tablecloths and set out plates, bowls and utensils to be used.

Picnic Celebrates Red, White and Blue

By Sue Gronholz, Columbus, Wisconsin

Inspired by the Stars and Stripes, I decided to go all out with red, white and blue for the Fourth of July picnic husband Todd and I host annually.

Among the lineup of delicious foods were my hearty All-American Barbecue Sandwiches and Grandma's Potato Salad, which has a cooked dressing well worth the little extra effort.

I really waved the flag when it came to Patriotic Gelatin Salad and Red, White and Blue Dessert!

We carried lunch to the lawn to cheer our community's Independence Day parade going by.

The next time you're entertaining on the Fourth, I hope you might try my ideas!

All-American Barbecue Sandwiches

I came up with this delicious recipe on my own. It's a big hit with family and friends.

4-1/2 **pounds ground beef**
1-1/2 **cups chopped onion**
2-1/4 **cups ketchup**
   3 **tablespoons prepared mustard**
   3 **tablespoons Worcestershire sauce**
   2 **tablespoons vinegar**
   2 **tablespoons sugar**
   1 **tablespoon salt**
   1 **tablespoon pepper**

18 hamburger buns, split

In a Dutch oven, cook beef and onion until meat is browned and onion is tender; drain. Combine ketchup, mustard, Worcestershire, vinegar, sugar, salt and pepper; stir into beef mixture. Heat through. Serve on buns. **Yield:** 18 servings.

— ☕ ☕ ☕ —

Grandma's Potato Salad

Our Fourth of July feast wouldn't be complete without this cool, old-fashioned potato salad. It's Grandma's treasured recipe.

      1 cup water
  1/2 cup butter *or* margarine
  1/4 cup vinegar
      2 eggs
  1/2 cup sugar
4-1/2 teaspoons cornstarch
  3/4 cup salad dressing *or* mayonnaise
  3/4 cup whipping cream, whipped
      6 pounds red salad potatoes, cooked,
        peeled and sliced
  1/2 cup chopped onion
  1/4 cup sliced green onions
      1 teaspoon salt
  1/2 teaspoon pepper
Leaf lettuce, optional
      3 hard-cooked eggs, sliced
Paprika

In the top of a double boiler over boiling water, heat water, butter and vinegar. In a bowl, beat eggs; add sugar and cornstarch. Add to butter mixture; cook and stir constantly until thick, about 5-7 minutes. Remove from the heat and allow to cool. Stir in the salad dressing; fold in the whipped cream. In a large bowl, toss potatoes, onion, green onions, salt and pepper. Pour the dressing over and mix gently. Chill. Serve in a lettuce-lined bowl if desired. Garnish with the hard-cooked eggs and sprinkle with paprika. **Yield:** 18 servings.

— ☕ ☕ ☕ —

Patriotic Gelatin Salad

Almost as spectacular as the fireworks, this lovely salad makes quite a "bang" at our July Fourth meal. It's exciting to serve, and our guests love the cool fruity and creamy layers.

      2 packages (3 ounces *each*) berry blue
        gelatin
      2 packages (3 ounces *each*) strawberry
        gelatin
      4 cups boiling water, *divided*

2-1/2 cups cold water, *divided*
      2 envelopes unflavored gelatin
      2 cups milk
      1 cup sugar
      2 cups (16 ounces) sour cream
      2 teaspoons vanilla extract

In four separate bowls, dissolve each package of gelatin in 1 cup boiling water. Add 1/2 cup cold water to each and stir. Pour one bowl of blue gelatin into an oiled 10-in. fluted tube pan; chill until almost set, about 30 minutes. Set other three bowls of gelatin aside at room temperature. Soften unflavored gelatin in remaining cold water; let stand 5 minutes. Heat milk in a saucepan over medium heat just below boiling. Stir in softened gelatin and sugar until sugar is dissolved. Remove from heat; stir in sour cream and vanilla until smooth. When blue gelatin in pan is almost set, carefully spoon 1-1/2 cups sour cream mixture over it. Chill until almost set, about 30 minutes. Carefully spoon one bowl of strawberry gelatin over cream layer. Chill until almost set. Carefully spoon 1-1/2 cups cream mixture over strawberry layer. Chill until almost set. Repeat, adding layers of blue gelatin, cream mixture and strawberry gelatin, chilling in between each. Chill several hours or overnight. **Yield:** 16 servings. **Editor's Note:** This salad takes time to prepare since each layer must be almost set before the next layer is added.

— ☕ ☕ ☕ —

Red, White and Blue Dessert

Serving this rich, fresh-tasting dessert is a great salute to the nation's independence! I found this recipe and made some modifications.

      2 packages (8 ounces *each*) cream cheese,
        softened
  1/2 cup sugar
  1/2 teaspoon vanilla extract
  1/2 teaspoon almond extract
      2 cups whipping cream, whipped
      2 quarts strawberries, halved, *divided*
      2 quarts blueberries, *divided*

In a large mixing bowl, beat cream cheese, sugar and extracts until fluffy. Fold in the whipped cream. Place a third of the mixture in a 4-qt. bowl. Reserve 20 strawberry halves and 1/2 cup blueberries for garnish. Layer half of the remaining strawberries and blueberries over cream mixture. Top with another third of the cream mixture and the remaining berries. Spread the remaining cream mixture on top. Use the reserved strawberries and blueberries to make a "flag" on top. **Yield:** 18 servings.

Apples Brighten Bridal Shower

By Marlys Benning, Wellsburg, Iowa

When two friends and I began planning a grocery shower for the fiancee of a neighbor, we wanted an appealing theme…so I suggested "You Are the Apple of Our Eye".

My friends bit on it immediately, and one fruitful idea led to another.

The wonderful aroma of Hot Apple Cider greeted guests. We sipped cider and chatted with Lisa, the guest of honor, before enjoying lunch featuring Chicken Salad Puffs, Cinnamon-Apple Angel Food Cake and Apple Cutout Sugar Cookies.

Although easy to make, the Chicken Salad Puffs look like you fussed over them. The apple glaze topping the cake was right in line with our theme, as were frosted cookie "apples".

Hot Apple Cider

In this recipe, brown sugar and spices add extra flavor to already delicious apple cider.

- **2/3 cup packed brown sugar**
- **1 teaspoon whole cloves**
- **1 teaspoon ground allspice**
- **3 cinnamon sticks (3 inches), broken**
- **1 gallon apple cider**

Fill the filter-lined basket of a large automatic percolator with the brown sugar, cloves, allspice and cinnamon sticks. Prepare as you would coffee according to manufacturer's directions, but substitute cider for water. **Yield:** 16-20 servings. **Editor's Note:** Do not use a drip-style coffeemaker for this recipe.

Chicken Salad Puffs

For a unique way to serve chicken salad, these puffs can't be beat! The tasty filling gets color and crunch from the olives and celery. Guests who attended our unique theme shower have since told me they are delicious and satisfying.

CREAM PUFFS:
 2 eggs
 1/2 cup water
 1/4 cup butter *or* margarine
 1/2 cup all-purpose flour
Dash salt
FILLING:
 2 cups diced cooked chicken
 3/4 cup chopped celery
 1 can (2-1/4 ounces) sliced ripe olives, drained
 1/3 cup mayonnaise *or* salad dressing
 1 tablespoon lemon juice
 1 teaspoon grated onion
 1/4 teaspoon Worcestershire sauce
 1/8 teaspoon pepper
Salt to taste

Let eggs stand at room temperature for 30 minutes. In a medium saucepan, bring water and butter to a boil. Add flour and salt all at once; stir until a smooth ball forms and does not stick to pan. Remove from the heat; let stand 5 minutes. Add eggs, one at a time, beating well after each addition. Continue to beat until dough is well blended. Drop by rounded tablespoonfuls onto a greased baking sheet, making six mounds 3 in. apart. Bake at 400° for 30-35 minutes or until golden brown and dry and firm to the touch. Transfer to a wire rack. Immediately split puffs open; remove tops and set aside. Discard soft dough from inside. Cool puffs. For filling, combine the chicken, celery and olives in a large bowl. In a small bowl, combine remaining ingredients; stir into chicken mixture. Fill puffs just before serving. **Yield:** 6 servings.

Cinnamon-Apple Angel Food Cake

This heavenly dessert is as light as a feather and melts in your mouth. The cinnamon-apple glaze is delightful, and the exquisite flavor and texture prove it's a true from-scratch dessert!

1-1/2 cups egg whites (about 12 eggs)
1-1/2 teaspoons cream of tartar
 1/4 teaspoon salt
 1 cup sugar
 1 teaspoon vanilla extract
 1/2 teaspoon almond extract

1-1/2 cups confectioners' sugar
 1 cup cake flour
GLAZE:
 1/3 cup butter *or* margarine
 2 cups confectioners' sugar
 1/2 teaspoon ground cinnamon
 3 to 4 tablespoons apple juice *or* cider

In a mixing bowl, beat egg whites, cream of tartar and salt on medium speed until soft peaks form. Add sugar, 2 tablespoons at a time, beating well after each addition; beat until smooth and glossy and stiff peaks form. Add extracts on low speed. Combine confectioners' sugar and flour; gently fold into egg mixture. Pour into an ungreased 10-in. tube pan. Bake on the lowest rack at 375° for 35-40 minutes or until top crust is golden brown and cracks feel dry. Immediately invert cake in pan to cool completely. Loosen sides of cake from pan and re-move. For glaze, melt butter in a sauce-pan. Stir in the confectioners' sugar and cinnamon. Add apple juice slowly until glaze is thin enough to drizzle. Drizzle over cake. **Yield:** 12-16 servings.

Apple Cutout Sugar Cookies

Not only are these pretty cookies fun to serve, but they bake up delicate and flaky and taste wonderful. Plus the dough is so easy to roll out and cut.

1-1/2 cups confectioners' sugar
 1 cup butter *or* margarine, softened
 1 egg
1-1/2 teaspoons vanilla extract
2-1/4 cups all-purpose flour
 1 teaspoon baking soda
 1 teaspoon cream of tartar
FROSTING:
 2 cups confectioners' sugar
 1/4 cup light corn syrup
 2 tablespoons water
Red and green food coloring

In a large mixing bowl, combine the first seven ingredients in order given and mix well. Chill dough 2-3 hours or until easy to handle. Roll out on a lightly floured surface to 1/4-in. thickness. Cut with an apple-shaped cookie cutter dipped in flour. Place on greased baking sheets. Bake at 375° for 7-8 minutes or until lightly browned. Cool on wire racks. For frosting, combine sugar, corn syrup and water in a small bowl. Transfer three-fourths of the frosting into another bowl; add red food coloring for apples. Add green food coloring to remaining frosting for stems. Frost cookies. Allow to sit overnight for frosting to harden. **Yield:** 4 dozen.

Harvest Mood Flavors Birthday Buffet

By Julianne Johnson, Grove City, Minnesota

Since our daughters, Kelsey and Whitney, both have fall birthdays, we celebrate with a theme rich with hearty flavors and colors of the season.

For the casual buffet supper, I decorate the house with plenty of pumpkins, corn shocks, Indian corn and bittersweet.

Although I vary the menu somewhat from year to year, my Wild Rice Harvest Casserole is a savory standard the family requests time and again.

Our state of Minnesota is famous for the dark-brown nutty-tasting rice that not only grows wild, but also is cultivated by farmers here.

It combines deliciously with chicken and mush-

rooms in this satisfying casserole that smacks of harvesttime. Added cashews make it company fare and give extra crunch.

Festive Fruit Salad is another dish that disappears fast. Offering a taste of fall, it mixes apples, walnuts, pears and citrus with a light colorful dressing that lets the delicate fruit flavors come through.

For dessert, Pumpkin Cake is always sure to please. While the shape and orange butter cream icing make it look like a pumpkin on the outside, inside is moist banana cake. To form the pumpkin's "stem", I use half a banana iced with green-tinted frosting.

To round out our buffet, I often add crisp apple

slices with a creamy dip, cranberry bread, and cookies cut and decorated to look like pumpkins.

Though it's best suited to fall, you don't need a birthday to enjoy this festive fare.

———🝖 🝖 🝖———

Wild Rice Harvest Casserole

Fall is the ideal time to enjoy a big helping of this hearty casserole, packed with wild rice and chicken and topped with cashews. When we serve this for our two daughters' birthday party, it gets raves!

    4 to 5 cups diced cooked chicken
    1 cup chopped celery
    2 tablespoons butter *or* margarine
    2 cans (10-3/4 ounces *each*) condensed
      cream of mushroom soup, undiluted
    2 cups chicken broth
    1 jar (4-1/2 ounces) sliced mushrooms,
      drained
    1 small onion, chopped
    1 cup uncooked wild rice, rinsed and
      drained
    1/4 teaspoon poultry seasoning
    3/4 cup cashew pieces
Chopped fresh parsley

In a skillet, brown chicken and celery in butter. In a large bowl, combine soup and broth until smooth. Add the mushrooms, onion, rice, poultry seasoning and chicken mixture. Transfer to a greased 13-in. x 9-in. x 2-in. baking dish. Cover and bake at 350° for 1 hour. Uncover and bake for 30 minutes. Stir; sprinkle with cashews. Return to the oven for 15 minutes or until the rice is tender. Garnish with parsley. **Yield:** 10-12 servings.

———🝖 🝖 🝖———

Festive Fruit Salad

As colorful as the leaves on the autumn trees, this fruit salad disappears fast down to the last spoonful. The light dressing doesn't hide the refreshing flavors of the fruit. Pecans add crunch and the rich flavor of the harvest season.

    1 can (20 ounces) pineapple chunks
    1/2 cup sugar
    3 tablespoons all-purpose flour
    1 egg, lightly beaten
    2 cans (11 ounces *each*) mandarin oranges,
      drained
    1 can (20 ounces) pears, drained and
      chopped
    3 kiwifruit, peeled and sliced
    2 large unpeeled apples, chopped
    1 cup pecan halves

Drain pineapple, reserving juice. Set pineapple aside. Pour juice into a small saucepan; add sugar and flour. Bring to a boil. Quickly stir in egg; cook until thickened. Remove from the heat; cool. Refrigerate. In a large bowl, combine pineapple, oranges, pears, kiwi, apples and pecans. Pour dressing over and blend well. Cover and chill for 1 hour. **Yield:** 12-16 servings.

———🝖 🝖 🝖———

Pumpkin Cake

A slice into this fun pumpkin-shaped dessert reveals a moist banana cake inside. A tempting nut filling joins two cakes to form the pumpkin. Decorating is easy with orange-tinted frosting. We use it as a birthday cake, but it also would be nice following a special fall meal.

    2 boxes (18-1/2 ounces *each*) banana cake
      mix
    2 tablespoons butter *or* margarine
    2 tablespoons all-purpose flour
    1/2 cup half-and-half cream
    1/2 cup sugar
    1 teaspoon vanilla extract
    1/2 teaspoon salt
    1/2 cup chopped pecans
BUTTER CREAM FROSTING:
    3/4 cup butter *or* margarine, softened
    3/4 cup shortening
    6 cups confectioners' sugar
    1 teaspoon vanilla extract
    2 to 4 tablespoons milk
Red, yellow and green food coloring
Ice cream cone *or* banana

Prepare and bake cakes in 12-cup fluted tube pans according to package directions; cool. For filling, melt butter in a saucepan. Stir in flour to form a smooth paste. Gradually add cream and sugar, stirring constantly until thick. Boil 1 minute; remove from heat. Stir in vanilla and salt. Fold in pecans; cool. Cut thin slice off bottom of each cake. Spread one cake bottom with filling; put cakes together with bottoms together. Set aside. In a mixing bowl, cream butter and shortening. Beat in sugar and vanilla. Add milk until desired consistency is reached. Combine red and yellow food coloring to make orange; tint about three-fourths of the frosting orange. Tint remaining frosting green. Place a small glass upside down in the center of the cake to support the "stem". Put a dollop of frosting on the glass and top with an ice cream cone or banana. Cut the cone or banana to the correct length; frost with green frosting. Frost cake with orange frosting. **Yield:** 12-16 servings.

Substitutions & Equivalents

Equivalent Measures

3 teaspoons	=	1 tablespoon	16 tablespoons	=	1 cup
4 tablespoons	=	1/4 cup	2 cups	=	1 pint
5-1/3 tablespoons	=	1/3 cup	4 cups	=	1 quart
8 tablespoons	=	1/2 cup	4 quarts	=	1 gallon

Food Equivalents

Grains

Macaroni	1 cup (3-1/2 ounces) uncooked	=	2-1/2 cups cooked
Noodles, Medium	3 cups (4 ounces) uncooked	=	4 cups cooked
Popcorn	1/3 to 1/2 cup unpopped	=	8 cups popped
Rice, Long Grain	1 cup uncooked	=	3 cups cooked
Rice, Quick-Cooking	1 cup uncooked	=	2 cups cooked
Spaghetti	8 ounces uncooked	=	4 cups cooked

Crumbs

Bread	1 slice	=	3/4 cup soft crumbs, 1/4 cup fine dry crumbs
Graham Crackers	7 squares	=	1/2 cup finely crushed
Buttery Round Crackers	12 crackers	=	1/2 cup finely crushed
Saltine Crackers	14 crackers	=	1/2 cup finely crushed

Fruits

Bananas	1 medium	=	1/3 cup mashed
Lemons	1 medium	=	3 tablespoons juice, 2 teaspoons grated peel
Limes	1 medium	=	2 tablespoons juice, 1-1/2 teaspoons grated peel
Oranges	1 medium	=	1/4 to 1/3 cup juice, 4 teaspoons grated peel

Vegetables

Cabbage	1 head	=	5 cups shredded	Green Pepper	1 large	=	1 cup chopped
Carrots	1 pound	=	3 cups shredded	Mushrooms	1/2 pound	=	3 cups sliced
Celery	1 rib	=	1/2 cup chopped	Onions	1 medium	=	1/2 cup chopped
Corn	1 ear fresh	=	2/3 cup kernels	Potatoes	3 medium	=	2 cups cubed

Nuts

Almonds	1 pound	=	3 cups chopped	Pecan Halves	1 pound	=	4-1/2 cups chopped
Ground Nuts	3-3/4 ounces	=	1 cup	Walnuts	1 pound	=	3-3/4 cups chopped

Easy Substitutions

When you need...		Use...
Baking Powder	1 teaspoon	1/2 teaspoon cream of tartar + 1/4 teaspoon baking soda
Buttermilk	1 cup	1 tablespoon lemon juice *or* vinegar + enough milk to measure 1 cup (let stand 5 minutes before using)
Cornstarch	1 tablespoon	2 tablespoons all-purpose flour
Honey	1 cup	1-1/4 cups sugar + 1/4 cup water
Half-and-Half Cream	1 cup	1 tablespoon melted butter + enough whole milk to measure 1 cup
Onion	1 small, chopped (1/3 cup)	1 teaspoon onion powder *or* 1 tablespoon dried minced onion
Tomato Juice	1 cup	1/2 cup tomato sauce + 1/2 cup water
Tomato Sauce	2 cups	3/4 cup tomato paste + 1 cup water
Unsweetened Chocolate	1 square (1 ounce)	3 tablespoons baking cocoa + 1 tablespoon shortening *or* oil
Whole Milk	1 cup	1/2 cup evaporated milk + 1/2 cup water

Cooking Terms

HERE'S a quick reference for some of the cooking terms used in *Taste of Home* recipes:

Baste—To moisten food with melted butter, pan drippings, marinades or other liquid to add more flavor and juiciness.

Beat—A rapid movement to combine ingredients using a fork, spoon, wire whisk or electric mixer.

Blend—To combine ingredients until *just* mixed.

Boil—To heat liquids until bubbles form that cannot be "stirred down". In the case of water, the temperature will reach 212°.

Bone—To remove all meat from the bone before cooking.

Cream—To beat ingredients together to a smooth consistency, usually in the case of butter and sugar for baking.

Dash—A small amount of seasoning, less than 1/8 teaspoon. If using a shaker, a dash would comprise a quick flip of the container.

Dredge—To coat foods with flour or other dry ingredients. Most often done with pot roasts and stew meat before browning.

Fold—To incorporate several ingredients by careful and gentle turning with a spatula. Used generally with beaten egg whites or whipped cream when mixing into the rest of the ingredients to keep the batter light.

Julienne—To cut foods into long thin strips much like matchsticks. Used most often for salads and stir-fry dishes.

Mince—To cut into very fine pieces. Used often for garlic or fresh herbs.

Parboil—To cook partially, usually used in the case of chicken, sausages and vegetables.

Partially set—Describes the consistency of gelatin after it has been chilled for a small amount of time. Mixture should resemble the consistency of egg whites.

Puree—To process foods to a smooth mixture. Can be prepared in an electric blender, food processor, food mill or sieve.

Saute—To fry quickly in a small amount of fat, stirring almost constantly. Most often done with onions, mushrooms and other chopped vegetables.

Score—To cut slits partway through the outer surface of foods. Often used with ham or flank steak.

Stir-Fry—To cook meats and/or vegetables with a constant stirring motion in a small amount of oil in a wok or skillet over high heat.

Guide to Cooking with Popular Herbs

HERB	APPETIZERS SALADS	BREADS/EGGS SAUCES/CHEESE	VEGETABLES PASTA	MEAT POULTRY	FISH SHELLFISH
BASIL	Green, Potato & Tomato Salads, Salad Dressings, Stewed Fruit	Breads, Fondue & Egg Dishes, Dips, Marinades, Sauces	Mushrooms, Tomatoes, Squash, Pasta, Bland Vegetables	Broiled, Roast Meat & Poultry Pies, Stews, Stuffing	Baked, Broiled & Poached Fish, Shellfish
BAY LEAF	Seafood Cocktail, Seafood Salad, Tomato Aspic, Stewed Fruit	Egg Dishes, Gravies, Marinades, Sauces	Dried Bean Dishes, Beets, Carrots, Onions, Potatoes, Rice, Squash	Corned Beef, Tongue Meat & Poultry Stews	Poached Fish, Shellfish, Fish Stews
CHIVES	Mixed Vegetable, Green, Potato & Tomato Salads, Salad Dressings	Egg & Cheese Dishes, Cream Cheese, Cottage Cheese, Gravies, Sauces	Hot Vegetables, Potatoes	Broiled Poultry, Poultry & Meat Pies, Stews, Casseroles	Baked Fish, Fish Casseroles, Fish Stews, Shellfish
DILL	Seafood Cocktail, Green, Potato & Tomato Salads, Salad Dressings	Breads, Egg & Cheese Dishes, Cream Cheese, Fish & Meat Sauces	Beans, Beets, Cabbage, Carrots, Cauliflower, Peas, Squash, Tomatoes	Beef, Veal Roasts, Lamb, Steaks, Chops, Stews, Roast & Creamed Poultry	Baked, Broiled, Poached & Stuffed Fish, Shellfish
GARLIC	All Salads, Salad Dressings	Fondue, Poultry Sauces, Fish & Meat Marinades	Beans, Eggplant, Potatoes, Rice, Tomatoes	Roast Meats, Meat & Poultry Pies, Hamburgers, Casseroles, Stews	Broiled Fish, Shellfish, Fish Stews, Casseroles
MARJORAM	Seafood Cocktail, Green, Poultry & Seafood Salads	Breads, Cheese Spreads, Egg & Cheese Dishes, Gravies, Sauces	Carrots, Eggplant, Peas, Onions, Potatoes, Dried Bean Dishes, Spinach	Roast Meats & Poultry, Meat & Poultry Pies, Stews & Casseroles	Baked, Broiled & Stuffed Fish, Shellfish
MUSTARD	Fresh Green Salads, Prepared Meat, Macaroni & Potato Salads, Salad Dressings	Biscuits, Egg & Cheese Dishes, Sauces	Baked Beans, Cabbage, Eggplant, Squash, Dried Beans, Mushrooms, Pasta	Chops, Steaks, Ham, Pork, Poultry, Cold Meats	Shellfish
OREGANO	Green, Poultry & Seafood Salads	Breads, Egg & Cheese Dishes, Meat, Poultry & Vegetable Sauces	Artichokes, Cabbage, Eggplant, Squash, Dried Beans, Mushrooms, Pasta	Broiled, Roast Meats, Meat & Poultry Pies, Stews, Casseroles	Baked, Broiled & Poached Fish, Shellfish
PARSLEY	Green, Potato, Seafood & Vegetable Salads	Biscuits, Breads, Egg & Cheese Dishes, Gravies, Sauces	Asparagus, Beets, Eggplant, Squash, Dried Beans, Mushrooms, Pasta	Meat Loaf, Meat & Poultry Pies, Stews & Casseroles, Stuffing	Fish Stews, Stuffed Fish
ROSEMARY	Fruit Cocktail, Fruit & Green Salads	Biscuits, Egg Dishes, Herb Butter, Cream Cheese, Marinades, Sauces	Beans, Broccoli, Peas, Cauliflower, Mushrooms, Baked Potatoes, Parsnips	Roast Meat, Poultry & Meat Pies, Stews & Casseroles, Stuffing	Stuffed Fish, Shellfish
SAGE		Breads, Fondue, Egg & Cheese Dishes, Spreads, Gravies, Sauces	Beans, Beets, Onions, Peas, Spinach, Squash, Tomatoes	Roast Meat, Poultry, Meat Loaf, Stews, Stuffing	Baked, Poached & Stuffed Fish
TARRAGON	Seafood Cocktail, Avocado Salads, Salad Dressings	Cheese Spreads, Marinades, Sauces, Egg Dishes	Asparagus, Beans, Beets, Carrots, Mushrooms, Peas, Squash, Spinach	Steaks, Poultry, Roast Meats, Casseroles & Stews	Baked, Broiled & Poached Fish, Shellfish
THYME	Seafood Cocktail, Green, Poultry, Seafood & Vegetable Salads	Biscuits, Breads, Egg & Cheese Dishes, Sauces, Spreads	Beets, Carrots, Mushrooms, Onions, Peas, Eggplant, Spinach, Potatoes	Roast Meat, Poultry & Meat Loaf, Meat & Poultry Pies, Stews & Casseroles	Baked, Broiled & Stuffed Fish, Shellfish, Fish Stews

General Recipe Index

This handy index lists every recipe by food category, major ingredient and/or cooking method, so you can easily locate recipes to suit your needs.

APPETIZERS & SNACKS
Cold Appetizers
 Cheesy Onion Roll-Ups, 12
 Fruit on a Stick, 18
 Stuffed Cherry Tomatoes, 235
 Yogurt Deviled Eggs, 31
Dips
 Broccoli Dip, 19
 Dairy Delicious Dip, 274
 Quick Guacamole, 10
 Seafood Dip, 10
 Tex-Mex Dip, 271
Hot Appetizers
 Cheesy Garlic Bread, 108
 Cheesy Herb Snacks, 16
 Crab and Spinach Quiche, 12
 Italian Stuffed Mushrooms, 19
 Mini Hamburgers, 8
 Quick Turkey Nachos, 13
 Sausage Cheese Bites, 16
 Stromboli, 10
 Tater-Dipped Veggies, 9
 Tomato Cheese Melt, 13
Snacks
 Cajun Party Mix, 16
 Candied Popcorn, 15
 Caramel Corn, 14
 Cheese Popcorn, 15
 Chewy Snack Squares, 12
 Edible "Play Dough", 10
 Nutty O's, 161
 Parmesan-Garlic Popcorn, 15
 Puffed Wheat Balls, 9
 Snack Crackers, 13
 Sweet and Spicy Popcorn, 15
 Sweet Graham Snacks, 12
Spreads
 Horseradish Cheese Spread, 10
 Onion Cheese Ball, 167
 Pimiento Cheese Spread, 12
 ✓Shrimp Spread, 17
 ✓Triple Cheese Spread, 18
 Tuna Dill Spread, 18

APPLES
 "ABC" Sandwiches, 43
 Ample Brown Betty, 167
 Apple Cobbler, 235
 Apple Crisp Pizza, 142
 ✓Applesauce Oatmeal Pancakes, 77
 Apple Tart, 139
 Apple-Topped Oatcakes, 68
 Apple Turnovers with Custard, 137

 Baked Apple Slices, 213
 Candied Sweet Potatoes, 52
 Candy Apple Pie, 138
 Caramel Apple Cake, 159
 Cinnamon-Apple Angel Food
  Cake, 279
 ✓Cranberry Apple Relish, 152
 Delicious Apple Pie, 146
 Herbed Pork and Apples, 63
 Hot Apple Cider, 278
 Lemony Apple Dumplings, 134
 Mini Apple Crisp, 176
 Missouri Peach and Applesauce
  Salad, 25
 Nutty Apple Muffins, 105
 Overnight Apple French Toast, 88
 Paradise Cran-Applesauce, 56
 Raspberry Baked Apples, 144
 Saucy Apple Cake, 111
 ✓Sugarless Applesauce, 152
 Sweet Potato Apple Salad, 25
 Sweet Potatoes with Apples, 52

APRICOTS
 Apricot Almond Bars, 112
 Apricot Almond Coffee Cake, 99
 Apricot Banana Bread, 102

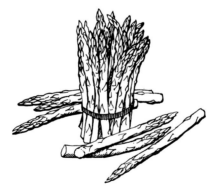

ASPARAGUS
 Asparagus Cheese Strata, 87
 Asparagus with Sesame Butter, 222
 Pasta with Asparagus, 53
 Saucy Chicken and Asparagus, 62
 Sugared Asparagus, 56

BACON
 "ABC" Sandwiches, 43
 Black-Eyed Peas with Bacon, 192
 Confetti Rice, 196
 Deluxe German Potato Salad, 22
 Hot Potato Salad for 100, 159

 Old-Fashioned Wilted Lettuce, 25
 Scrum-Delicious Burgers, 40
 Sheepherder's Breakfast, 73
 Wilted Lettuce Salad, 200

BANANAS
 Apricot Banana Bread, 102
 Banana Bread Pudding, 133
 Banana Cream Pie, 209
 Banana Nut Layer Cake, 126
 Banana Poppy Seed Dressing, 151
 Banana Spice Cookies, 124
 Banana Squares, 112
 Black-Bottom Banana Bars, 125
 Creamy Banana Pie, 132
 French Banana Pancakes, 78
 Frosted Banana Bars, 120
 Frozen Cranberry Banana Salad, 33
 Layered Banana Pudding, 147
 Pumpkin Cake, 281
 South Seas Chicken and Bananas, 87
 Tropical Salad Bar, 24

BARLEY (*see Rice & Barley*)

BARS & BROWNIES
 Apricot Almond Bars, 112
 Black-Bottom Banana Bars, 125
 Chewy Maple Bars, 118
 Frosted Banana Bars, 120
 Fudge Brownies, 116
 No-Bake Raisin Bars, 121
 Praline Brownies, 124
 Salted Nut Squares, 162
 Sugar-Free Raisin Bars, 129
 Triple Layer Cookie Bars, 117

BEANS
 Barbecued Bean Salad, 160
 Basil Buttered Beans, 182
 Big-Batch Bean Soup, 165
 Country Green Beans, 213
 Fourth of July Bean Casserole, 167
 Green Beans with Hazelnut-Lemon
  Butter, 58
 Hawaiian Baked Beans, 169

✓ Recipe includes Nutritional Analysis and Diabetic Exchanges

✓ *Recipe includes Nutritional Analysis and Diabetic Exchanges*

✓ Recipe includes Nutritional Analysis and Diabetic Exchanges

✓ Recipe includes Nutritional Analysis and Diabetic Exchanges

✓ Recipe includes Nutritional Analysis and Diabetic Exchanges

✓ *Recipe includes Nutritional Analysis and Diabetic Exchanges*

✓ Recipe includes Nutritional Analysis and Diabetic Exchanges

✓ Recipe includes Nutritional Analysis and Diabetic Exchanges

✓ Recipe includes Nutritional Analysis and Diabetic Exchanges

Alphabetical Recipe Index

This handy index lists every recipe in alphabetical order
so you can easily find your favorite recipes.

✓ Recipe includes Nutritional Analysis and Diabetic Exchanges

✓ Recipe includes Nutritional Analysis and Diabetic Exchanges

✓ Recipe includes Nutritional Analysis and Diabetic Exchanges

✓ *Recipe includes Nutritional Analysis and Diabetic Exchanges*